Creating Cool Web Sites with HTML, XHTML, and CSS

Creating Cool Web Sites with HTML, XHTML, and CSS

Dave Taylor

WILEY

Wiley Publishing, Inc.

Creating Cool Web Sites with HTML, XHTML, and CSS

Published by
Wiley Publishing, Inc.
10475 Crosspoint Boulevard
Indianapolis, IN 46256
www.wiley.com

Copyright © 2004 by Wiley Publishing, Inc., Indianapolis, Indiana
Published simultaneously in Canada

Library of Congress Control Number: 2004100892

ISBN: 0-7645-5738-6

Manufactured in the United States of America

10 9 8 7 6 5 4 3 2 1

1B/SQ/QU/QU/IN

WILEY

About the Author

Dave Taylor has been involved with the Internet since 1980, when he first logged in as an undergraduate at the University of California, San Diego. Since then, he's been a research scientist at Hewlett-Packard Laboratories in Palo Alto, California, reviews editor for *SunWorld* magazine, and founder of four companies: The Internet Mall, iTrack.com, AnswerSquad, and ClickThruStats.com. Currently, Dave is president of Intuitive Systems and is busy launching an electronic book publishing company called Intuitive Press.

Dave has designed over 50 Web sites, both commercial and nonprofit, and has published more than 1000 articles about the Internet, Unix, Macintosh, interface design, and business topics. His books include *Learning Unix for Mac OS X Panther* (O'Reilly), *Wicked Cool Shell Scripts* (No Starch Press), *Teach Yourself Unix in 24 Hours* (Sams Publishing), and *Solaris For Dummies* (Wiley Publishing).

Dave holds a master's degree in Educational Computing from Purdue University, an M.B.A. from the University of Baltimore, an undergraduate degree in Computer Science from the University of California at San Diego, and is an adjunct professor at the University of Colorado, Boulder, and the University of Phoenix Online.

You can find Dave Taylor online just about any time at http://www.intuitive.com/, or you can send him electronic mail at taylor@intuitive.com.

Credits

Senior Acquisitions Editor
Jim Minatel

Development Editors
Jodi Jensen
Brian Herrmann

Production Editor
Felicia Robinson

Technical Editing
Wiley-Dreamtech India Pvt Ltd

Copy Editor
Mary Lagu

Editorial Manager
Mary Beth Wakefield

Vice President and Executive Group Publisher
Richard Swadley

Vice President and Executive Publisher
Bob Ipsen

Vice President and Publisher
Joseph B. Wikert

Executive Editorial Director
Mary Bednarek

Project Coordinator
April Farling

Graphics and Production Specialists
Beth Brooks
Jonelle Burns
Jennifer Heleine

Quality Control Technician
Susan Moritz

Permissions Editor
Laura Moss

Media Development Specialist
Angela Denny

Book Designer
Kathie S. Schnorr

Proofreading and Indexing
Publication Services

Cover Design
Michael Trent

To Kiana, Gareth, and Ashley, my guardian angels

Preface

Who should buy this book? What's covered? How do I read this book? Why should I read this book? HTML? XHTML? CSS? Sheesh! Why not just use a Web page editor? Who am I?

Welcome!

"Wow! Another Web book! What makes this one different?"

That's a fair question. I want you to be confident that *Creating Cool Web Sites with HTML, XHTML, and CSS* will meet your needs as well as provide fun and interesting reading. So spend a minute and breeze through my preface to ensure that this is the book you seek. . . .

What This Book Is About

In a nutshell, *Creating Cool Web Sites with HTML, XHTML, and CSS* is an introduction to HTML, XHTML, and Cascading Style Sheets. HTML is the HyperText Markup Language, and it's the language that enables you to create and publish your own multimedia documents on the World Wide Web. Millions of users on the Internet and online services such as America Online, Earthlink, and the Microsoft Network are spending hours each day exploring the world of the Web from within their Web browser, be it Internet Explorer, Netscape Navigator, or any of a variety of other programs. XHTML is the modern "proper" version of HTML and is the future of the markup language. Cascading Style Sheets are also part of that future, and it's a rare modern Web site that doesn't use at least some element of CSS in its design and layout.

By using all these technologies, *you* can learn to quickly and easily create attractive documents that are on the cutting edge of interactive publishing. I went through the pain of learning HTML back in 1994, the very dawn of the Web era, precisely because I wanted to spread my ideas to a global audience. For me, learning was hit or miss because the only references I could find were confusing online documents written by programmers and computer types. For you, it will be a lot easier. By reading this book and exploring the software and samples included on the companion Web site, you can learn not only the nuts and bolts of HTML, XHTML, and CSS, but also quite a lot about how to design and create useful, attractive Web sites and spread the word about them on the Net.

Before you delve into this book, you should know the basics: what the Internet is, how to get on it, and how to use your Web browser. If you seek detailed information on these topics, you can find many interesting and useful books from Wiley Publishing at http://www.wiley.com/compbooks. After you have this basic knowledge, you'll find that *Creating Cool Web Sites with HTML, XHTML, and CSS* is a fun introduction to the art and science of creating interesting— and, if I may say so, cool—Web sites that you'll be proud of and that other users will want to visit and explore.

Why Not Just Use a Web Page Builder?

If you've already flipped through this book to see what's covered, you've seen a ton of different sample listings with lots and lots of < and > instructions. Yet the advertisements in every computer magazine are telling you that you don't need to get your hands dirty with HTML and CSS when you can use a Web page editor. So what's the scoop?

The scoop—or the problem, really—is that every Web page editor I've used is designed to create pages for a particular Web browser and has at best a limited understanding of the rich, complex, evolving HTML language. Use Microsoft Front Page 2000, for example, and your site will almost certainly look best in Internet Explorer (a Microsoft product).

It's a subtle but insidious problem. One clue to this lurking problem is that surveys of Web developers invariably demonstrate that almost all the most popular Web sites are coded by hand, not with fancy page-building systems.

A development company that I occasionally help with online design recently sent me a plea because they had encountered this inconsistency in browser presentation:

> Dave, Help! Everything looks different in the different browsers!! This is turning out to be a nightmare! How much effect do different browsers have on the appearance of the site? My customer is using AOL and from the e-mail she sent me, things are a mess. When I look at the site, it pretty much is ok. There are a few modifications to make - font, bold - but what's going on?

That's one of the greatest frustrations for all Web site designers: Not only do different versions of Web browsers support different versions of HTML and CSS, but the exact formatting that results from a given HTML tag or CSS style varies by Web browser, too. It's why the mantra of all good Web designers is "test, test, test."

In fact, if you're going to get serious about Web development, I would suggest that you consider a setup like I have: Before you officially say that you're done with a project, check all the pages with the two most recent major releases of the two biggest Web browsers on both a Mac and a Windows system. (That's a total of eight different browsers. Right now, I have the two most recent versions of Internet Explorer and Netscape loaded on both of my computers.)

Text Conventions Used in This Book

Stuff I ask you to type appears in bold, like this: **something you actually type**. I also use **bold** in some lines of HTML source code to point out the specific tag or attribute that the discussion is focusing on.

Filenames, directories, URLs, and names of machines on the Net appear in a special typeface, like this: `http://www.whitehouse.gov/WH/html/Guest_Book.html`.

HTML-formatted source code appears in that same special typeface, but on separate lines, like this:

```
<html>
<title>How to Create Cool Web Sites</title>
<img src="intro.gif" alt="How To Create Cool Web Sites" />
```

Icons Used to Help You Navigate

I use the following icons to help you find your way around the text and to point out important additional information that I want to emphasize.

 tip This icon points out some expert tricks and techniques that can help you work more efficiently.

 caution Pay attention to this icon. It alerts you to possible pitfalls and may help you avoid trouble.

 note Check out this icon for additional details that deserve special attention and may help you work better in the long term.

x-ref Jump to the chapters elsewhere in the book that this icon points you to. You're bound to run into some good information or more details about the topic at hand.

 on the web This icon points you to helpful information or samples on the companion Web site that accompanies this book (`http://www.intuitive.com/coolsites/`) or to sites elsewhere on the Net.

Who Should Read This Book?

You can use this book to learn HTML, XHTML, CSS, and the techniques needed to create cool Web sites. All you need is a simple text editor, such as Notepad (which comes with Windows) or TextEdit (which is part of the Macintosh operating system), and a Web browser. If you're already online and have a Web browser installed on your computer, you can easily explore all the examples in this book by going to this book's accompanying Web site at http://www.intuitive.com/coolsites/.

What's on the Companion Web Site?

What would a Web book be without a companion Web site? The *Creating Cool Web Sites with HTML, XHTML, and CSS* Web site can be found at http://www.intuitive.com/coolsites/. The site contains every single example in the book, pointers to every site mentioned, the extended table of contents for the book, and a sample chapter for your reading pleasure. In addition, you'll find an errata page in case any typos or glitches have come to light between when we wrapped up production and when you picked up this book. From this site, you can also access my Booktalk weblog, which offers a fun and informal Q&A environment where you can ask me questions about specific issues that might puzzle or confuse you.

Be Productive in No Time!

By the time you're halfway through this book, you'll be able to whip up the kind of pages you see every day, guaranteed. And by the time you finish this book, you'll know other ways to organize information to make creating Web versions of print material easy. You'll also learn about the nuances of XHTML and the tremendous power and capabilities that Cascading Style Sheets add to the equation, as well as why it's crazy not to include at least rudimentary CSS elements in your everyday site development work.

Want to contact the author? Send e-mail to taylor@intuitive.com or visit my home page on the Web at http://www.intuitive.com/.

If you're ready, let's go!

Acknowledgments

No writing project can be completed while the author is locked in a room, although if there's a good Net connection, we can probably negotiate something! Seriously, a number of Internet folk have proven invaluable as I've written the different editions of this book—some for their direct help and others for simply having produced some wickedly cool Web pages that inspired me when things were moving a bit slowly.

Special thanks go to my many students at The University of Phoenix Online and elsewhere who helped clarify what made sense and what didn't in the previous editions of the book. I also particularly appreciate the continued assistance of the team at Wiley Publishing, including notably Sharon Cox and Jodi Jensen, and Dreamtech for the technical edit. My friends and colleagues John Locke, Bo Leuf, Werner Klauser, Jon Shemitz, Richard Blum, and Jon Trelfa helped keep the content fresh and accurate and helped to continually remind me that there's more to learn. Special thanks also to search engine expert Dan Murray for his help on Google page ranking algorithms.

Most of the graphics presented in this book were created in GraphicConverter, a wonderful shareware application for the Macintosh, though I used Adobe Photoshop CS a few times. Screen shots were done with MW Snap on the PC and Snapz Pro X on the Macintosh. Most of the book was written on my aging Apple Macintosh G4/450 system (I have to admit, I'm a Mac guy at heart), and the Windows work was all done on a 900MHz Pentium III box running Windows XP.

Finally, warm hugs to Linda, Ashley, Gareth, Jasmine, Karma, Angel, and, of course, the newest member of my family, Kiana, for ensuring that I took sufficient breaks to avoid carpal tunnel syndrome or any of the other hazards of overly intense typing. The time off would be a lot less fun without ya!

Contents

Part II: Rockin' Page Design Strategies

Chapter 8: Tables and Frames 159

Chapter 9: Forms, User Input, and the Common Gateway Interface 195

Chapter 10: Advanced Form Design 219

Chapter 11: Activating Your Pages with JavaScript 235

Chapter 12: Advanced Cascading Style Sheets 261

Building a Wicked Cool Web Page

Part

1

So What's All This Web Jazz?

In This Chapter

Looking at linear media and hypermedia

Checking out some cool Web sites

Examining FTP

Introducing Microsoft Internet Explorer

Learning about URLs

This chapter covers the basics of the Web, showing how information pointers help you organize information and illustrating how Web browsers can simplify file transfer, searches, and other Internet services. It also introduces you to Microsoft Internet Explorer.

First, however, I define the concept *a web of information*. So before you study the basics of creating cool Web pages, take a close look at what the Web is, how it works, and what HTML is all about. I promise to be brief!

What Is the Web Anyway?

To understand the World Wide Web, consider how information is organized in print media. Print media, I think, is a good model for the Web, although others may feel that adventure games, movies, TV, or other information-publishing media provide a better comparison.

Linear media

Consider the physical and organizational characteristics of this book for a second. What is most notable? The book has discrete units of information—pages. The pages are conceptually organized into chapters. The chapters are bound together to comprise the book itself. What you have in your hands is a collection of pages organized in a format conducive to your reading them from the first page to last. However, there's no reason why you can't riffle through the pages and create your own strategy for navigating this information.

Are you still with me? The book is an example of *linear information organization*. Most books, including this one, are organized with the expectation that you'll start at the beginning and finish at the end.

Hypermedia

Imagine that instead of physically turning the page, you can simply touch a spot at the bottom of each page—a forward arrow—to flip to the next page. Touching a different spot—a back arrow—moves you to the preceding page. Furthermore, imagine that when you look at the table of contents, you can touch the description of a chapter to flip directly to the page where that chapter begins. Touch a third spot—a small picture of a dictionary—and move to another book entirely.

Such a model, based on the user being able to move around quickly with the click of a button, is called *hypermedia* or *hypertext*, terms coined by mid-twentieth-century computer visionaries, most notably Ted Nelson in his book *Computer Lib*. This more dynamic approach to information organization offers a number of benefits to the reader. One immediate boon is that the topical index becomes really helpful: Because you can touch an item of interest in the index, whether an explanatory narrative or descriptive reference material, you can use the same book as a reference work or as the linearly organized tutorial that it's intended to be. It's like the best of two worlds—the linear flow of an audio or video tape and the instant access of a DVD or music CD.

note   Another benefit of hypertext is how it presents footnotes. Footnote text no longer clutters up the bottom of the page. With hypertext, you merely touch the asterisk or footnote number in the text, and a tiny page pops up to display the footnote.

You can also touch an illustration to zoom into a larger version of that illustration or maybe even convert the illustration into an animated sequence or 3D space. Within the 3D space, you can cruise around and examine the item from a variety of vantage points.

Obviously, what I'm describing here are Web pages. An additional capability of the Web makes things much more fun and interesting: These pages of information can reside on systems throughout the world.

The pages themselves can be quite complex (and, ideally, cool and attractive) documents. Instead of writing on your Web page "Visit the White House Web site to learn more" (leaving readers stranded and unsure of how to proceed), you can provide a direct link to that site. Readers can click certain highlighted words—or a picture of the building—and immediately zoom to the White House site. Very cool, huh?

Cool spots on the Web

Figure 1-1 shows a typical Web document that you will explore later in the book. Notice, in particular, the underlined words, each of which is a link to another Web document on the Internet.

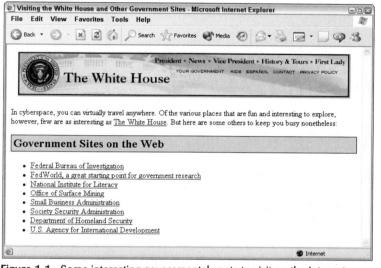

Figure 1-1: Some interesting governmental spots to visit on the Internet.

If you're on the Internet and you click the phrase National Institute for Literacy, for example, you travel (electronically) to the institute's headquarters in Washington, D.C., as shown in Figure 1-2.

What makes this electronic travel from Web site to Web site so compelling for me (and for millions of other users) is that there aren't just thousands or tens of thousands of Web documents to visit—there are millions. So many pages exist, in fact, that no one has ever visited all of them. Because so many documents are available, finding the information you're seeking is perhaps the single greatest challenge on the Internet.

Although it's certainly true that much of the information on the World Wide Web consists of rich multimedia documents written in HTML specifically for the enjoyment of Web readers, a surprising number of documents actually come from other types of information-publishing services on the Internet. These documents are presented in the most attractive formats possible within the Web browser itself.

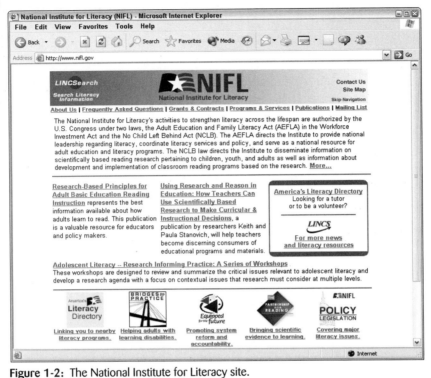

Figure 1-2: The National Institute for Literacy site.

The simplest of these alternative information services on the Internet is FTP (File Transfer Protocol). FTP is a mechanism for accessing lists of remote folders on hard disks and then directly accessing specific files within those folders. It's been around for a long time—long before the Web was ever envisioned. Traditionally, working with FTP has been a pain, and the interface has always been only a tiny step away from programming the computer directly. From a Unix host, for example, you type the following sequence of steps to connect to the Microsoft Corporation FTP archive called `ftp.microsoft.com`. (What you type is shown in boldface in the following listing; everything else is output from the system):

```
$ ftp ftp.microsoft.com
Connected to ftp.microsoft.com.
220 Microsoft FTP Service
Name (ftp.microsoft.com:taylor): anonymous
331 Anonymous access allowed, send identity (e-mail name) as password.
Password:
230-This is FTP.Microsoft.Com.
230 Anonymous user logged in.
Remote system type is Windows_NT.
ftp> dir MISC1
227 Entering Passive Mode (207,46,133,140,58,113).
125 Data connection already open; Transfer starting.
```

```
dr-xr-xr-x    1 owner      group         0 Aug  2  2002 beckyk
dr-xr-xr-x    1 owner      group         0 Aug 14  2002 BUSSYS
dr-xr-xr-x    1 owner      group         0 Aug 14  2002 DESKAPPS
dr-xr-xr-x    1 owner      group         0 Aug 14  2002 DEVELOPR
dr-xr-xr-x    1 owner      group         0 Aug  1  2002 FULLKB
dr-xr-xr-x    1 owner      group         0 Mar 28  2002 jeffreyf
-r-xr-xr-x    1 owner      group      6029 Aug  7  2002 kb.CSS
dr-xr-xr-x    1 owner      group         0 Aug  1  2002 KBSPV
dr-xr-xr-x    1 owner      group         0 Aug 14  2002 PEROPSYS
226 Transfer complete.
ftp>
```

Calling such a procedure complex would be an understatement. Of course, FTP is fast and easy to use after you learn all the magic. However, using a computer should enable you to focus on *what* you want to accomplish instead of *how* to accomplish it.

Compare the preceding example with the following procedure that shows you how to use Microsoft Internet Explorer to access the same archive directly (see Figure 1-3). Instead of typing all the information required in the preceding method, you simply choose File ⇨ Open and type **ftp://ftp.microsoft.com/MISC1** in the Open box. In this example, ftp indicates what kind of service you want, the :// part is some fancy (if mysterious) notation, and **ftp.microsoft.com/MISC1** is the name of the remote system and the directory to view. Finally, you just click on OK or press Enter.

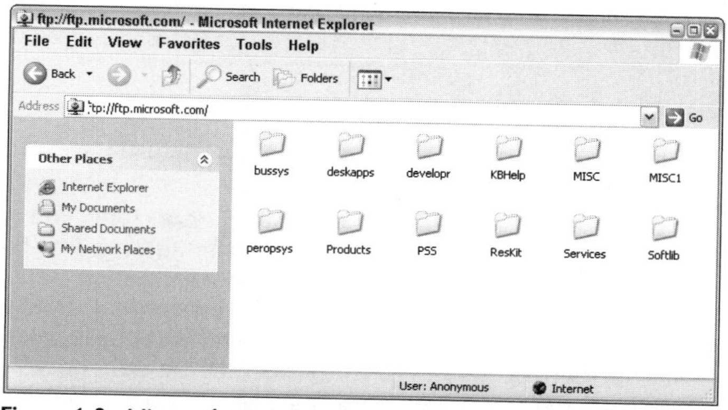

Figure 1-3: Microsoft Internet Explorer visits Microsoft's FTP archive.

The location format (ftp://ftp.microsoft.com/MISC1) is called a *Uniform Resource Locator (URL)*.

Ready to visit a listed directory or folder? Click it, and you move to that spot. Ready to grab a file? Just click the file, and Explorer automatically figures out the file type, asks what you want to call the file on your PC, and transfers it across. No fuss, no hassle.

tip Throughout this book, I use PC to refer generally to any personal computer. I'm actually writing this book on a Macintosh and double-checking things on a Windows XP system.

Easy FTP isn't a unique feature of Explorer; it's a capability of all Web browser packages, including the popular Camino open source browser on Mac OS X. Figure 1-4 shows the Microsoft FTP site in Camino.

Index of ftp://ftp.microsoft.com/MISC1/

ftp://ftp.microsoft.com/MISC1/

Back Forward Reload Stop Print View Source   Location   Sidebar

Chimera Install Page   Mozilla.Org   Entertainment

Index of ftp://ftp.microsoft.com/MISC1/

```
Up to higher level directory
beckyk/              8/2/02 12:00:00 AM
BUSSYS/             8/14/02 12:00:00 AM
DESKAPPS/           8/14/02 12:00:00 AM
DEVELOPR/           8/14/02 12:00:00 AM
FULLKB/              8/1/02 12:00:00 AM
jeffreyf/            3/28/02 12:00:00 AM
kb.CSS      6 KB     8/7/02 12:00:00 AM
KBSPV/              8/1/02 12:00:00 AM
PEROPSYS/           8/14/02 12:00:00 AM
```

Document: Done

Figure 1-4: Camino visits Microsoft's FTP archive.

Here's where the difference between the *paper* and the *words* becomes important: The type of service that you can connect with is what I call the *information transfer system,* and the actual information presented is the *content.* By analogy, the Web is the information transfer system, and *Hypertext Markup Language*—HTML—is the format used for content. Some of the HTML documents available on the Internet aren't available within the Web itself; instead, they are accessible directly via FTP. Furthermore, some documents may be right on your hard disk or on a local CD-ROM, in which case you are seeing the formatting but not the usual transport mechanism.

Introduction to Internet Explorer

Unless you were living under a rock back then, you probably noticed the hoopla surrounding the unveiling of Windows 95 in 1995. Windows 95 was much more than just an operating system; it was a whole new environment for PC users—an environment focused on making the computer easier to use and the interface more seamless and consistent. Then Microsoft released Windows 98, Windows 2000, and their latest OS, Windows XP. Each release has included a successively more sophisticated version of Internet Explorer, and each has also more tightly integrated the Web browser into the operating system itself.

Just as Netscape made constant revisions to its Navigator browser in the past, Microsoft has been on an aggressive upgrade path with major releases distributed as fast as the company can complete them. By this point, Microsoft has pulled ahead, and Netscape, now a part of Time Warner Corporation, has morphed into an open source project called Mozilla. Because of its dominant position in the marketplace, I focus primarily on Internet Explorer in this book; but where it is important, I examine pages in other browsers and talk about compatibility and cross-platform consistency of appearance.

Launching Internet Explorer

When you're ready to start browsing the Web, you need to find and launch Internet Explorer. You can most easily do so by double-clicking the *e* icon on your desktop, or launching the application from the ubiquitous Start button in Windows.

The first time you start Explorer, it tries to connect to the Microsoft home page on the World Wide Web. This could be a problem if you don't already have your Internet connection up and running. If a problem occurs, don't worry; just choose Cancel when a dialog box pops up asking for a phone number to dial or the program otherwise indicates that it's waiting for a Net connection. You end up looking at a blank page, but all the controls are there. Now, from the File menu, choose Open. That brings up the Open dialog box, as shown in Figure 1-5.

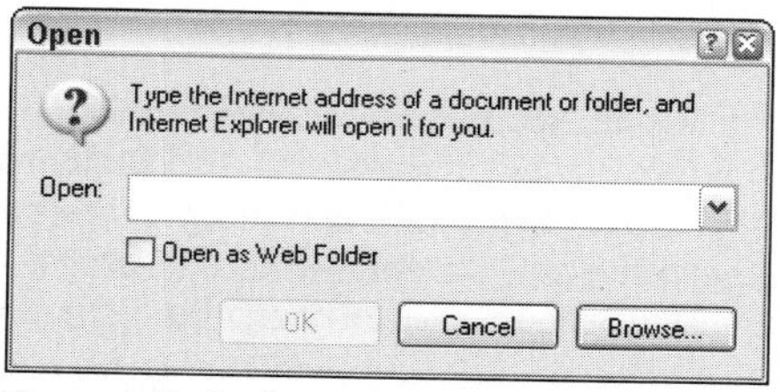

Figure 1-5: In the Open box, you can type the URL for the Creating Cool Web Sites home page (`http://www.intuitive.com/coolsites/`) and click OK.

Now you're getting somewhere! Type the URL for this book, `http://www.intuitive.com/coolsites/`, and click OK, and Internet Explorer should promptly open up the file and the associated graphics, displaying it all in one neat window. You might have different toolbars appearing on your screen, but it's easy to change back and forth by using the Preferences settings. Figure 1-6 shows how the Creating Cool Web Sites Web page should look on your screen.

Figure 1-6: The Creating Cool Web Sites home page shown in Internet Explorer.

If the Standard toolbar is displayed, you see a set of small buttons that can help you move around the Web. Starting from the left, these buttons let you move backward and forward in the set of pages you're viewing or stop the transfer of a slow page. You can also refresh the current page (that is, get a new copy of the page and rewrite the screen—this will prove a huge help as you develop your own Web pages). Finally, you can instantly zip back to your home—or default—page.

The magnifying glass enables you to pop straight to your favorite Web search engine, and the star icon enables you to open your list of favorite sites; you might have heard this called your Bookmark list. Immediately next to the star icon is a small globe and musical note button, which offers easy access to various media on the Net, including Internet radio. Next is the history button, a clock with a green arrow. (It's kind of hard to figure out the meaning of this icon. It was different in previous versions.) Use this if you forgot to bookmark a page you visited 20 minutes ago. It returns you to previous pages you've visited, in order of most recent to least recent.

The Envelope button lets you send and receive electronic mail (e-mail). Finally, use the Print button (the printer) to print the page you're viewing and the Edit button to transfer the current page into Microsoft FrontPage (if you have that program installed).

Figure 1-7 shows the Internet Explorer toolbar buttons.

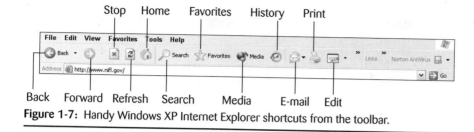

Figure 1-7: Handy Windows XP Internet Explorer shortcuts from the toolbar.

Changing the default page

Now that you have the program running, here's a useful trick before you begin your exploration of HTML and the mysteries and adventure of building cool Web pages: Change your default (home) page to the Cool Web Sites page, which should be the page currently displayed on your screen. When you have learned how to write cool Web pages, you can change the default to your own page or perhaps to a useful site on the Internet.

To change your default page, follow these steps:

1. Choose Tools ➪ Internet Options. You should see something remarkably similar to Figure 1-8.

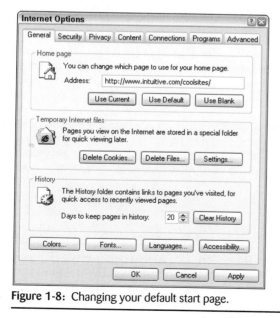

Figure 1-8: Changing your default start page.

2. Because you're currently viewing the page that you want to make your default page, simply click the Use Current button, and you're finished.

That's all there is to it. The next time you start up Internet Explorer, you'll find the cheery Creating Cool Web Sites page conveniently accessible.

Take a few minutes now to scroll around and click the Examples button to see how I've laid out the hundreds of example files so that they parallel what's discussed in this book. Remember that you can always use the back arrow on the toolbar to go back to the preceding page.

All about URLs

As our society has made the transition from products to information, we have seen the rapid acceleration of an age-old problem: identifying needed resources. Finding and obtaining resources have been important themes of world history, whether those resources be spices, fuel, raw materials, or information.

Today, computers should make searching easier. After all, aren't computers supposed to be experts at sifting through large collections of data to find what you're looking for? Well, yes and no.

First, I should differentiate between data and information. *Data* is *stuff*—an all-encompassing body including every iota of digital memory and space on hard disks and backup tapes. *Information*, on the other hand, is the data relevant to and valuable for your specific interests. If you're interested in Beat poets of the 1960s, for example, information on other topics such as municipal drainage systems or needlepoint isn't valuable at all, but rather is clutter.

Computers have tremendously expanded the proliferation of data. As a result, separating information from the massive flood of data is one of the fundamental challenges of the age of information. I can only imagine how much worse the situation will get in the next decade as more and more data flows down the wires.

When considered in this light, the Internet has a big problem. Because it has no central authority or organization, the Net's vast stores of data are not laid out in any meaningful or intuitive fashion. You are just as likely to find information on Beat poets on a machine run by a German embassy as you are to find it on a computer in a small liberal arts school in San Francisco.

URLs to the rescue

CERN (European Organisation for Nuclear Research) is a high-energy physics research facility in Switzerland that created the underlying technology of the World Wide Web. When Tim Berners-Lee and his team at CERN began to create a common mechanism for uniquely identifying information in dataspace, they realized the need for a scheme that would neatly encapsulate the various parts and that could be extended to include a wide variety of Internet services. The result was the URL.

To state the case succinctly, a *URL* is a unique descriptor that can identify any document (plain or hypertext), graphic, Usenet article, computer, or even an archive of files anywhere on the Internet or your machine. That's what makes URLs so tremendously valuable—although their format seems a bit puzzling and cryptic at first.

The name URL is something of a misnomer. Many times, jotting down URLs as you surf the Web only helps you find resources the second time, serving as a sort of memo service for your Internet travels. Resource location—finding information for the first time on the Internet and the World Wide Web—is a problem I explore later in this book, in Chapter 17. For now, think of URLs as business cards for specific resources on the network.

Reading a URL

The format for specifying a URL is consistent throughout the many services that you can reference with URLs, including Usenet news, Web documents, and FTP archives. As a general rule, a URL is composed of the following elements:

```
service    ://    hostname    /    directory-path
```

Not all these components appear in each URL, as you will see later in this chapter when you learn about the different types of URLs for different services. But the preceding example is a good general guide.

Consider the following example:

```
http://www.intuitive.com/coolsites/index.shtml
```

In this example, the service is identified as `http:`. HTTP stands for Hypertext Transfer Protocol, the method by which Web documents are transferred across the Internet. By using `http:`, you indicate to your browser—such as Explorer or Netscape Navigator—that you're connecting to a Web document. The host computer that offers the information you seek is `www.intuitive.com`. The `com` (called the *zone*) tells you that the site is a commercial site; `intuitive` is the *domain* or *host*; and `www` is the name of the Web *server*, a particular computer. Usually, as is the case here, you don't have to specify a port (ports are sort of like TV channels), because most servers use standard, default port numbers. And finally, from the server, you are asking for the file `index.shtml` from the `coolsites` directory. It is, in fact, this book's home page.

The following URL is a slightly more complex example:

```
ftp://ftp.netscape.com/pub/unsupported/windows/
```

This URL identifies a file archive for Netscape Corporation. You can see that the URL points to an archive by its service identifier (`ftp`, which stands for File Transfer Protocol, the way files are copied over the Net). The server and host in question is `ftp.netscape.com`. Notice that this URL specifies that upon connecting to the FTP server, the browser program should change to the `/pub/unsupported/windows/` directory and display the files within the it.

Here's one more example:

```
news:alt.internet.services
```

The preceding URL enables a browser to read the Usenet newsgroup `alt.internet.services`. You may notice that this URL is quite different from the other URL examples. For one thing, it doesn't specify a host. When you set up your browser program (the details differ from browser to browser), you indicate (in a preferences or configuration file) which host you can use to access Usenet. Usually, the host is the news server at your Internet service provider. As a result, no slashes are required in the URL because the browser already has that information. URLs for news resources, therefore, boil down to simply the service and newsgroup name.

You can specify a variety of Internet information-publishing services with URLs. The actual meanings of the URL components differ subtly, depending on which type of service is being specified. In the following sections, I examine URLs for each service in more detail.

FTP via URL

If you're familiar with the historical roots of the Internet and its predecessor networks (notably ARPANET), you already know that one of the earliest uses of the system was to transfer files quickly between hosts at different sites. The standard mechanism for accomplishing file transfers was and still is FTP. Although computers have acquired friendlier interfaces, FTP has remained in the Stone Age. Many users still use clunky command-line interfaces for this vital function; FTP through a Web browser, however, looks a bit friendlier.

Anonymous FTP

Millions of files are accessible throughout the Net via FTP. At a majority of hosts, you don't even need an account to download the files you seek. That's because a standard Net practice called *anonymous FTP* enables any user to log in to an FTP host using the name *anonymous*. If asked for a password, you type your e-mail address. Among other uses, you can use anonymous FTP to acquire new programs for your computer.

FTP was one of the first services addressed in the URL specification developed at CERN. An FTP URL takes the following form:

```
ftp://host/directory-path
```

The URL `ftp://ftp.microsoft.com/developr`, for example, uniquely specifies the `developr` directory of files available via FTP at the host `ftp` at Microsoft Corporation.

> **note**   In fact, the URL `ftp://ftp.microsoft.com/developr` specifies more, if only by omission. By not including a username and password (as you can see in the example in the following section), the URL suggests that the site is accessible by anonymous FTP.

Nonanonymous FTP

Although most Web-browser FTPing is done anonymously, FTP URLs can include the user-name and password for a specific account. If I had the account `coolweb` on Microsoft's machine and the password was `xyzxyz`, I could modify the URL to allow other people to connect to that account, as in the following example:

```
ftp://coolweb:xyzxyz@ftp.microsoft.com/developr
```

note You don't usually see the password included in the URL. Needless to say, it's not a good idea to explicitly include a password in a Web page URL!

Ports

Things can get even more complex when you start dealing with ports. FTP, like other programs on Internet servers, may be listening to ports other than the default port for its type of service.

Let me explain: Imagine that each computer on the Internet is like a TV station or TV set. It doesn't broadcast and receive all data across all possible frequencies; it aims specific types of data, formatted in prescribed manners, at individual frequencies or channels. On the Internet, those channels are called *ports*. If you want to watch your local ABC affiliate, for example, you may know that the station comes in on channel 7 and not on channel 4. By the same token, if you want to connect to the mail server on a specific computer, you may know that the mail server has a default port of 25. Some sites, however, opt to change these default port numbers (don't ask why, the reason is usually ugly). In such cases, you need to identify the special port within the URL.

What if a site decides to offer anonymous FTP for public use, but the site uses port 494 instead of the default FTP port? Then you have to specify that channel number in the URL, as in the following example:

```
ftp://ftp.microsoft.com:494/developr
```

The preceding URL makes a browser connect to channel 494, look for the FTP server, and then show you the contents of the `developr` directory.

If you want to use your own account and password simultaneously, put together the URL that contains all the necessary information, as follows:

```
ftp://coolweb:xyzxyz@ftp.microsoft.com:494/developr
```

Fortunately, you're unlikely to see anything so complex with an FTP URL. In fact, this is unquestionably a worst-case URL!

Using FTP URLs

The most valuable thing about FTP URLs is that if you specify a directory, most Web browsers list the files in that directory. With a click, you can either transfer the files you want or move into other directories to continue browsing. If you specify a file within the URL, the browser connects to the server and transfers the file directly to your computer.

The following URL contains all the information you need to obtain a copy of the HTML 3.0 specification document—just in case you want to read this highly complex and lengthy technical description for some reason:

```
ftp://ftp.w3.org/pub/doc/html_30.tar.Z
```

Are you curious about what else is in that directory? To find out, use the same URL, except omit the actual filename at the end, as shown in the following:

```
ftp://ftp.w3.org/pub/doc/
```

Special characters in URLs

URLs have a couple of subtle limitations, things that I had to learn by hit or miss. Fortunately, you can learn from my mistakes! Among their limitations, the most important is that a URL cannot contain spaces.

caution It's worth repeating: URLs cannot contain spaces.

This no-spaces limitation caused me much consternation and some lengthy debugging sessions when I started working with Web servers.

The other limitation is that URLs are case sensitive, even on machines that are otherwise case insensitive for filenames.

If you have a space in a filename, for example, you have to translate each space into a special character that is understood to represent a space within a URL. You can't use the underscore character (_), however, because underscores are sometimes used in filenames: if you automatically translate all spaces to underscores, then all underscores back to spaces, you'd lose the real underscore that's supposed to be part of the filename. I repeat: Don't use it.

Instead, the URL specification enables any character to be specified as—ready for this—a hexadecimal equivalent prefaced by a percent sign (%). To use *test server* in a URL, for example, replace the space with its hexadecimal equivalent (20), resulting in `test%20server`.

Instead of ranging from 0 to 9, as in the decimal (base 10) system, hexadecimal (base 16) numbers range from 0 to 15. Here are the hexadecimal numerals: 0, 1, 2, 3, 4, 5, 6, 7, 8, 9, A, B, C, D, E, F. The hexadecimal letters, A–F, represent the decimal numbers, 10–15.

To compute the decimal equivalent of a hexadecimal number, multiply each number by the base raised to the appropriate power. Hex 20, therefore, would be $2 \times 16 + 0 \times 1$, or 32 decimal. (Don't worry if this doesn't make sense; you'll probably never need to figure this out. Just remember to check Table 1-1 for the most common hex equivalents.)

Table 1-1 shows the special URL forms of some common characters that you may encounter while building URL specifications. To keep the Web browser from getting confused, use a code for the percent sign itself. Almost perverse, eh?

Table 1-1: URL Coding for Common Characters

Character	Hex Value	Equivalent URL Coding
Space	20	%20
Tab	09	%09
Percent	25	%25

E-mail via URL

URLs for e-mail are quite simple, fortunately, and require minimal explanation. You can specify any e-mail address as a URL simply by prefacing the snippet `mailto:` as the service name, as in the following example:

```
mailto:taylor@intuitive.com
```

Again, make sure that you don't use spaces in the URL. Note that you can send e-mail in a URL, but you cannot retrieve it. Why use an e-mail address as a URL? Because it's nice to have an *e-mail webmaster* link (or something similar) on your site, and `mailto:` is the URL that allows your users to e-mail the webmaster. A bit later, in the section about hypertext references, you see how this type of e-mail address URL is a powerful addition to your regular page links.

note   Almost all browsers launch a separate e-mail program to handle e-mail services.

Telnet via URL

Another service (along with the unquestionably valuable FTP) that caused Internet use to explode is Telnet. Telnet gives everyone on the Net the capability to log in to other computers on the Net, just as though they were connected to those machines directly. Not all Internet computers support Telnet, but many do.

Telnet, you will be glad to know, is easy to specify in URLs: You simply specify the service and the host to which you want to connect. For example, to log in to the Massachusetts Institute of Technology's (MIT's) media laboratory, use the following URL:

```
telnet://media.mit.edu/
```

When you use Telnet URLs, your Web browser program actually tries to launch a separate, external Telnet program to negotiate the Telnet connection, which means that nothing happens unless you've already installed and configured a separate Telnet program, such as NCSA Telnet. Netscape Navigator, Internet Explorer, Mosaic, and similar browser programs aren't designed to enable you to directly interact with the remote computer from within the browser.

Usenet news via URL

Working with Usenet news is somewhat tricky because you must find an existing server that allows you to access it. Many systems don't give you that access, even if you pay for a regular dialup account. A list of public Usenet hosts—which means hosts that attempt to provide news free of charge to all comers—is available on the Net, but in my experience only about 5 percent of them actually allow you to connect.

on the web

If you really want to read Usenet newsgroups and your ISP doesn't offer you access of some sort (almost all do), start at Google Groups at `http://groups.google.com/`.

Building a news URL is a straightforward process. Simply type `news:` followed by the exact name of the newsgroup. No slashes are needed (or allowed), and there's not yet a standard approach for specifying individual articles. Here are two examples:

```
news:news.answers
news:comp.sys.ibm-pc.announce
```

The heart of the Web: HTTP URLs

Although all the services listed so far in this chapter are valuable and interesting when used through a Web browser, the capability to connect with other Web servers via HTTP is what really makes the Web revolutionary.

The general format for HTTP references is the same as in the FTP references explained earlier. Here is a typical HTTP URL:

```
http://www.trivial.net/trivial.cgi
```

The preceding URL is for the popular Trivial.Net computer trivia game. The URL format should be quite familiar to you by this point: the service name, a colon, the double slash, the host name, a slash, and the name of a specific file with the Web standard .html filename extension to denote an HTML markup file.

note If your PC is still running Windows 3.*x*, you already know that it's unable to cope with four-letter filename suffixes. Windows simply chops off the fourth character in the extension, making it .htm instead. Throughout the Net, all files you see with the .htm suffix are exactly the same as .html files.

As it turns out, many times you don't even need to specify a filename if you'd rather not do so. The following is another example of a URL, this time for the *Boulder Daily Camera* in Boulder, Colorado:

```
http://www1.dailycamera.com/bdc/home/
```

Note that the URL contains a default directory (bdc/home). But because the URL doesn't specify a filename, the Web program is savvy enough to choose the default file—probably index.html—as configured on each server. If your system doesn't recognize index.html, try default.html or Welcome.html.

If the HTTP server is on a nonstandard port, of course, that fact would be specified in the URL, as the following example shows:

```
http://www.book.uci.edu:80/
```

The preceding URL is one way to get to the University of California at Irvine bookstore. Instead of using the default port for an HTTP server, whatever that may be, the site opted to have people explicitly specify port 80. If you want to create a URL that contains both the port and a specific filename, you can do so, as in the following example:

```
http://www.book.uci.edu:80/index.html
```

note Actually, port 80 is the default port for Web servers; I'm just explicitly showing it in these URLs to demonstrate what's going on. Try this yourself: Next time you go to a Web site, add :80 after the domain name, but before the slash.

Theoretically, you can specify an unlimited number of different URL types (although you probably don't want to know that at this point). The vast majority of the URLs that you'll see, however, are in the http, ftp, telnet, mailto, and news formats, as demonstrated in this chapter.

Summary

In this chapter, you saw how you can use information pointers to access more than just HTML documents. You learned that you can use Web browsers to transfer files via FTP and how you can change the home page on your Web browser. This chapter also familiarized you with what URLs are, how they're built, and how different types of services require different URL formats. Later in the book, you learn how to tie URLs into your own Web documents. After that, the material in this chapter will doubtless begin to crystallize and make much more sense. Chapter 2 begins the fun part of this book (indeed, the heart of the book): how to create cool Web documents!

Building Your First Web Page: HTML Basics

It's time to learn HTML! In this chapter, you go from 0 to 60 in no time flat, and by the end of it, you'll be able to create attractive Web pages. This chapter covers the basics of creating an HTML document, including head and body information, meaningful page titles, paragraph and section head marks, horizontal rules, and other miscellaneous layout information and data.

Basics of HTML Layout

What is HTML? At its most fundamental, Hypertext Markup Language (HTML) is a set of special codes that you embed in text to add formatting and linking information. HTML is based on Standard Generalized Markup Language (SGML). By convention, all HTML information begins with an open angle bracket (<) and ends with a closing angle bracket (>), for example, <html>. This tag tells an HTML interpreter (browser) that the document is written and marked up in standard HTML. An example of an HTML interpreter would be Microsoft's Internet Explorer, available for free from the Microsoft Web site; pop over to www.microsoft.com/ie/ to get your copy.

HTML, like any other markup language, has some problems. Suppose, for example, you want to show <html>—including the angle brackets—in a document. You need some way to prevent your expression from being interpreted as an HTML tag. Later in this book, you learn how to include such tricky information within your documents through *character entities*. For now, keep an eye open for this kind of problem as you read on.

 x-ref   See Chapter 5 to find out how to include text that includes special characters, such as brackets, in your Web document to ensure that the browser interprets it properly.

HTML and browsers

What happens if a program that interprets HTML, such as Internet Explorer, reads a file that doesn't contain any HTML tags? Suppose that you recently created the file not-yet.html in NotePad, but you haven't had a chance to add HTML tags. Your file looks something like this:

```
Dave's Desk
Somewhere in Cyberspace


Dear Reader,

    Thank you for connecting to my Web server, but I
regret to tell you
that things aren't up and running yet!
They will be _soon_, but they aren't today.

                Sincerely,

                Dave Taylor
```

It looks reasonable, although some of the lines seem to be shorter than you're used to seeing in a note like this. Figure 2-1 shows what the file looks like when it's opened in Explorer.

Figure 2-1 is clearly not what you want and probably would be quite puzzling to a viewer. Although placing an underscore before and after a word is a clue in some older systems that the word (soon) should be underlined, that's not part of HTML; so the underscores are left untouched, whether or not they make sense to the viewer.

The document shown in Figure 2-1 needs some HTML tags—information that Web browser programs can use to lay out and format the information. The implied formatting information contained in not-yet.html works for humans visually, but Web browsers ignore it because it's not in HTML. In other words, to you or me, seeing a tab as the first character of a sentence is a good clue that the sentence is the beginning of a new paragraph, but as you can clearly see in Figure 2-1, that just isn't the case with Web browsers.

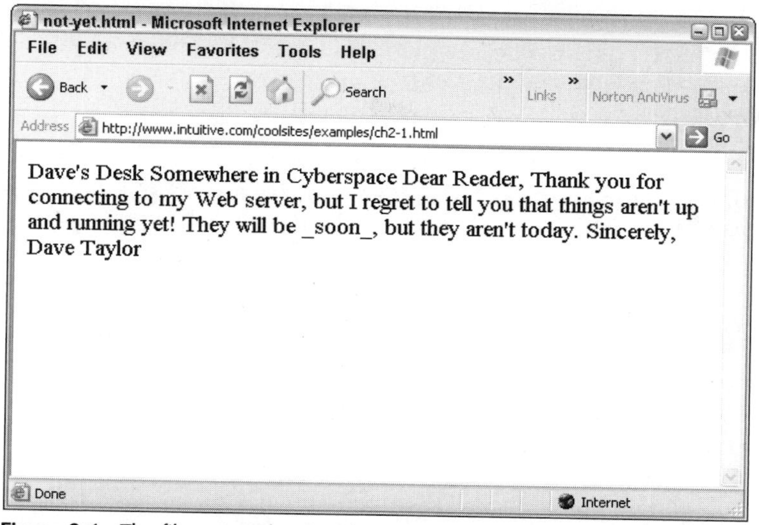

Figure 2-1: The file not-yet.html, without any HTML, shown in Internet Explorer.

Always test your HTML documents by viewing them through one or more Web browsers to ensure that everything looks the way you want it to. If you encounter a situation in which the browser is showing you all the formatting tags rather than interpreting them, a likely culprit is a file named with a .txt suffix rather than an .html suffix. Web browsers are dumb; give them a text file and they'll display it exactly as is. To fix the problem just described, you simply rename the file.

If you open it, close it

Although a small number of HTML tags are stand-alone entities, the majority are paired, with beginning and end tags. The beginning tag is called the *open* tag, and the end tag is called the *close* tag.

The most basic of all tags is the one shown earlier, <html>, which indicates that the information that follows is written in HTML. The <html> tag is a paired tag, however, so you need to add a close tag at the end of the document, which is the same as the open tag with the addition of a slash: </html>. By the same token, if you begin an italic phrase with <i> (the italics tag), you must end it with </i>. Everything between the open and close tags receives the particular attribute of that tag.

If you get confused and specify, for example, a backslash instead of a slash, as in <\html>, or some other variant, the browser program doesn't understand and simply ignores the close tag. When this happens, the attribute specified in the open tag continues past the point where you meant it to stop. In the case of the <html> tag, the problem is probably not significant because </html> appears at the end of the document. Nothing comes after it to mess up. But in many situations, a missing close tag can completely destroy a Web page, as you'll learn.

tip Develop the habit of closing any tag that you open.

What do you think would happen if you included quotation marks around a tag—suppose, for example, that you used "<html>" at the beginning of your document rather than <html>. If you guessed that only the quotes would be displayed, you're right. Let me say it one more time: Web browsers are very simple-minded in their interpretation of HTML. Any tags that vary from the specific characters in the HTML-language specification result in something other than what you were expecting, or your formatting requests are ignored completely.

Breaking at Paragraphs and Lines

The most helpful markup tags—and probably the tags that you'll use most often—specify that you want a *paragraph break* or a *line break*. Several variants of these tags exist, but you can create readable and useful Web documents by using only the tags <p></p> and <br />.

To specify that you want a paragraph break, use the <p> tag. (Many HTML tags are mnemonic: *p* for *paragraph*.) The following example adds some <p> tag pairs to the not-yet.html file shown in Figure 2-1 and also wraps the file in the <html> and </html> tags. Notice that the <p> tag is a *container*. The open tag appears before the passage to be affected, and the close tag appears at the end of the passage:

```
<html>
Dave's Desk
Somewhere in Cyberspace
<p>
Dear Reader,
</p><p>
   Thank you for connecting to my Web server, but I
regret to tell you
that things aren't up and running yet!
They will be _soon_, but they aren't today.
</p><p>

               Sincerely,
</p><p>

               Dave Taylor
</p></html>
```

Figure 2-2 shows what this HTML text looks like in a browser.

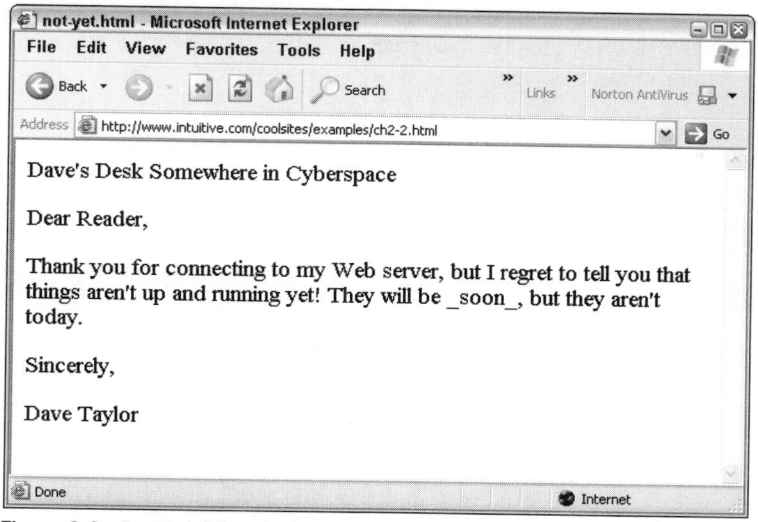

Figure 2-2: Paragraph breaks in not-yet.html.

The version of the file in Figure 2-2 is a huge improvement over Figure 2-1, but some problems still exist, not the least of which is that the first few lines don't look right. In their zeal to organize the text neatly, Web browsers, by default, fill as many words into each line as they can manage. Filling the lines works well for the main paragraph of the file, but the first few lines display more appropriately if you indicate that the browser should break the line between items.

note Paragraph tags have a somewhat checkered history in HTML. Although they were always intended to be used as containers (that is, a paired tag), for many years people recommended that they be used as stand-alone tags instead, with a <p> wherever a break was desired. As HTML has become more sophisticated, using the <p> tags as a proper container has become more important, and it's a very good habit—worth learning and sticking with—as you'll see when we talk about XHTML later in this chapter.

To break lines in HTML, use the break tag, <br />. Like any tag, the break tag can appear anywhere in the text, including at the end of the line you want to break. HTML tags are also case insensitive, meaning that <BR />, <br />, and <bR /> all mean exactly the same thing. Having said that, however, good form is to use all lowercase in your HTML tags as consistently as possible because that's required for the XHTML standard. (More about that at the end of this chapter.) Now is the time to develop good habits—while you're just figuring this stuff out—so you don't have to break bad habits later!

note Because I'm following XHTML standards in this book, all stand-alone tags have a slightly odd appearance, with a /> sequence at the end rather than the more common > by itself. You can use <br> for a break, but
 (with a space before the slash) is our goal here. As I said in the note above, learning good habits now will ensure that your pages work properly in the future as HTML and the Web evolve.

Here is the HTML file when the break tag is used:

```
<html>
Dave's Desk <br />
Somewhere in Cyberspace
<p>
Dear Reader,
</p><p>
    Thank you for connecting to my Web server, but I
regret to tell you
that things aren't up and running yet!
They will be _soon_, but they aren't today.
</p><p>


                              Sincerely,

</p><p>

                              Dave Taylor

</p></html>
```

From a stylistic perspective, you should try to have a consistent scheme for your tags, especially because, in case of a problem, you may have to go into fairly complex files and figure out what's wrong. I suggest that you place all line breaks at the end of text lines and all paragraph marks on their own lines. This book uses that style throughout.

Figure 2-3 shows the output of the not-yet.html file when <br /> is used.

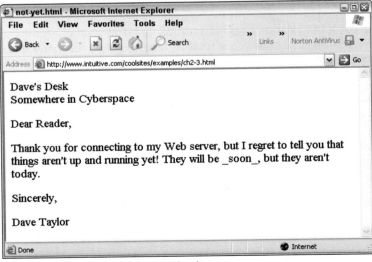

Figure 2-3: The break tag in not-yet.html.

One remaining problem with the layout is that I intended for the signature information to be shifted to the right a few inches, as in a standard business letter. In the browser, however, you can see that it stays at the left edge of the document.

To remedy this problem, you can use the preformatted information tag, `<pre>`. The `<pre>` tag is also a paired tag (a container), so it works across as many lines as needed, without any fuss, and ends with `</pre>`. The following example shows how `<pre>` preserves all character and line spacing; in this case, `<pre>` preserves the tabs I used to indent the closing and signature lines. I've changed the last few lines of the `not-yet.html` file to reflect the use of this tag:

```
<html>
Dave's Desk <br />
Somewhere in Cyberspace
<p>
Dear Reader,
</p><p>
   Thank you for connecting to my Web server, but I
regret to tell you
that things aren't up and running yet!
They will be _soon_, but they aren't today.
</p><pre>

                        Sincerely,

                        Dave Taylor

</pre>
</html>
```

By adding the `<pre>` tags, you achieve the desired formatting, but now another problem has cropped up: The text in the preformatted block (the stuff between `<pre>` and `</pre>`) appears in a different, *monospace* typeface! You can see the difference in Figure 2-4, if you look closely.

note *Typeface* refers to a particular style of letters in a variety of sizes. A font, by contrast, is a typeface in a specific size and style. Helvetica is a typeface, but 12-point Helvetica italic is a font. A *monospace* typeface is one in which every letter has exactly the same width. Ten lowercase *i* characters (iiiiiiiiii), for example, end up exactly as wide as 10 lowercase *m* characters (mmmmmmmmmm). In this book, I use a *proportional* typeface rather than monospace for this note so that you can clearly see that the ten *i* characters are considerably narrower than the ten *m* characters.

The browser changed the typeface in Figure 2-4 because the browser assumed that the preformatted text was a code listing or other technical information. That's the most common context for the `<pre>` tag. So it worked, sort of, but it's not quite what you wanted. (You can use `<pre>` to your advantage in other situations, however, as you see later in this chapter.)

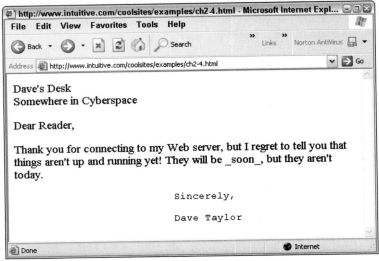

Figure 2-4: The format is correct, but the typeface is wrong.

Building Your First Web Page

Now that you've gotten a tiny taste of the world of HTML markup, take a slight time-out and go through the steps necessary to duplicate this on your own computer. I'm going to assume here that you're running Windows 98, Windows XP, or some other version of Windows, but the steps are very similar if you're on a Macintosh or Linux/Unix machine.

Launching your HTML editor

To start, I suggest you use NotePad, a terrific—albeit simple—text editor included with the Windows operating system. It's free and ready for you to start up, even if you didn't realize you had it!

tip   Mac users should use TextEdit; it's a very similar sort of plaintext editor found in your Applications folder, and Linux/Unix users can choose between vi, emacs, pico, and many other text editors, all accessible from a Terminal command line.

In just about every Windows configuration I've ever seen, NotePad is accessible by clicking the Start button on the bottom-left corner of the window, and then choosing Programs ⇨ Accessories. You should see a list of choices similar to Figure 2-5; NotePad is about half way down the list.

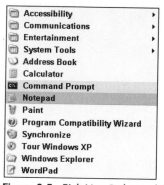

Figure 2-5: Pick NotePad out of the many accessory choices in Windows.

After NotePad launches, it shows you a blank page where you can type the HTML. As an example, type the simple page shown earlier in Figure 2-4. The result looks like Figure 2-6.

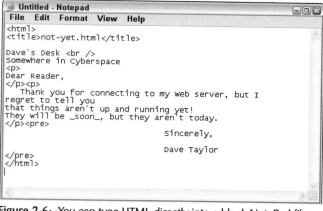

Figure 2-6: You can type HTML directly into a blank NotePad file.

Saving your file as HTML

After you type an adequate amount of material in your HTML, it's time to save the file to disk. Then you can open it in your favorite Web browser and see how it looks when the HTML is *rendered* (interpreted by the browser). Choose File ➪ Save, which pops up the Save As dialog box shown in Figure 2-7.

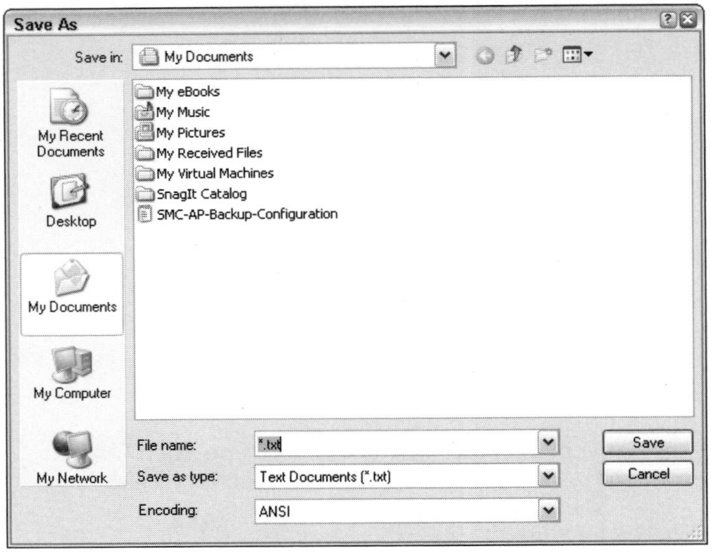

Figure 2-7: The Save As dialog box.

When you save this new HTML document, it's critical that you append either the .htm or .html filename suffix to ensure that the Web browser properly recognizes it as an HTML document. You can do this by explicitly typing .html as the suffix in the File Name box. Give this file a name, such as **firstpage.html**, and type that name directly into the File Name box.

caution If you don't specify a filename suffix, by default NotePad uses .txt. Saving the file with this extension causes problems! When you look at the page later in your Web browser, you see the HTML itself rather than having it interpreted. If that happens, and you find that you've already saved the file with a .txt or another extension, simply open the file again in NotePad, choose File ⇨ Save As, and resave the file with the .html suffix.

There's one more decision you must make before the file is ready to save: Where do you want to put it? I save this example to the desktop because it's easy to find the desktop. But you can save it someplace else on your hard drive if you want. Simply use the drop-down arrow in the Save In field of the Save As dialog box and browse to the folder where you want to store the file.

Now you're ready: You have named the file, remembered the .html suffix, made sure that it's stored in the directory you want, and clicked Save. Voilà! You've created your first Web page.

Notice that after you save this file, the title bar of the NotePad program changes to the name of the file—a helpful reminder that you've named the file.

Opening the file in Internet Explorer

Now it's time to launch a Web browser and have a look. I launch Internet Explorer because I have the icon right on my desktop. I double-click the blue *e* icon, and the Web browser opens to the Creating Cool Web Sites home page. To open a different page—the Web page you just created—choose File ⇨ Open. The Open dialog box appears, as shown in Figure 2-8.

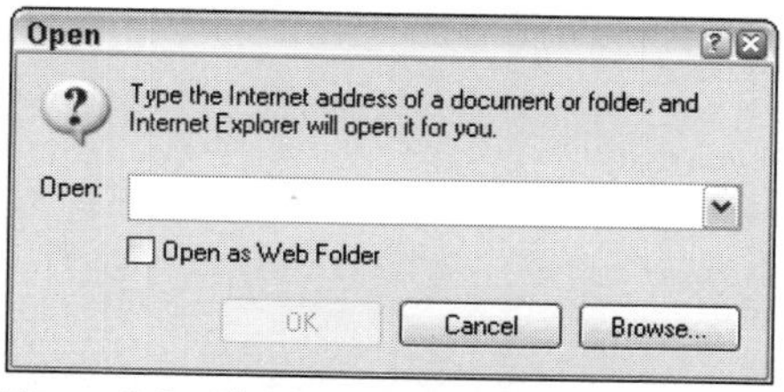

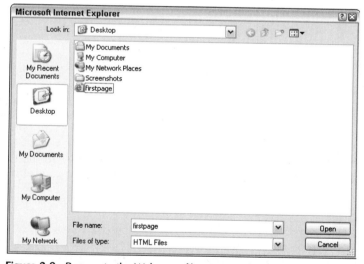

Figure 2-8: The Open dialog box, ready for you to enter a URL or browse to a file.

To open the Web page you just created, click Browse. The dialog box shown in Figure 2-9 opens.

Figure 2-9: Browse to the Web page file you saved earlier and choose the file.

When you find the file, click Open and then OK. You should be looking at your HTML page (see Figure 2-10).

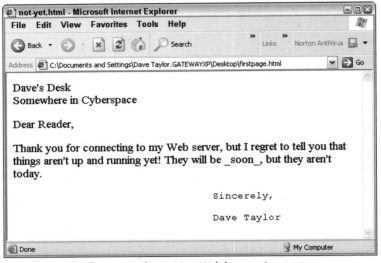

Figure 2-10: Finally, your Web page in a Web browser!

Pretty cool, eh?

Improving the HTML and viewing it in the browser

With both NotePad and the Web browser running, it's a simple matter to make changes in the editor and then preview the changes in the browser. Type any changes you want to make in NotePad, and then make sure you choose File ➪ Save to update the copy stored on your hard drive.

Then, one more step: Click the Refresh button in the Web browser (the button with the two green curving arrows pointing at each other) and you should see the results of your efforts instantly!

And now, back to your HTML. . . .

Breaking Your Document into Sections

If you take a close look at a fully specified HTML document, you'll find that it's divided into two sections: what I call the stationery section (the information that would be preprinted on the pad if the file were a physical note) and the body of the message. Think of the information you typically find at the top of a memo:

```
M E M O R A N D U M
To:
From:                                    Date:
                                         Subject:
```

These common items of information come at the beginning of a memo, usually followed by a rule (a line) and then by blank space in which you write the actual content of the memo.

Similarly, for the sake of organization, HTML files are commonly broken into two sections: the header, which contains the introductory page-formatting information, and the body. You use the paired tags <head> </head> and <body> </body> to surround each section. The following example shows how the not-yet.html file looks when you add these tags:

```
<html>
<head>
</head>
<body>
Dave's Desk <br />
Somewhere in Cyberspace
<p>
Dear Reader,
</p><p>
    Thank you for connecting to my Web server, but I
regret to tell you
that things aren't up and running yet!
They will be _soon_, but they aren't today.
</p><pre>

                          Sincerely,

                          Dave Taylor

</pre>
</body>
</html>
```

The <head> </head> and <body> </body> formatting information doesn't add anything to the display, I admit. The document also doesn't contain any introductory HTML-formatting information yet, so the head area is empty. If you were to view the preceding HTML text in a Web browser, it would look identical to Figure 2-3. Later, when you start learning some of the more complex parts of HTML, you will see why section-block notation such as <head> </head> can be helpful.

What do you think would happen if I fed the following information to a Web browser?

```
<html><head></head><body>
Dave's Desk <br />Somewhere in Cyberspace<p>Dear Reader,
</p><p>    Thank you for connecting to my Web server, but I
regret to tell you that things aren't up and running yet!
They will be _soon_, but they aren't today.</p><pre>
                          Sincerely,

                          Dave Taylor</pre></body></html>
```

If you guessed that the screen output of the preceding example would look exactly like the carefully spaced material shown earlier (see Figure 2-4), you're correct.

tip Remember that Web browsers ignore carriage returns, tabs, and multiple spaces when the document is reformatted for display. That suggests that you can save a great deal of space, and display a great deal more of your document *source* (the HTML tag information) on-screen, simply by skipping all the extra returns; but I strongly recommend against such a strategy. Why? In a nutshell, writing your Web documents with the markup tags in logical places makes the document easier to work with later. I've written and had to debug more than a thousand HTML documents, and I can assure you that the more things are jammed together, the less sense they make a few weeks later when you find you have to add information or modify the content.

Adding a Title to Your Page

One of the subtle (but quite important) things you can do to make your Web page look smart is to give it a good title with the `<title>` tag. The title usually appears in the top border (title bar) of the window displayed on the user's computer. Go back and look at the information in the header of Figure 2-4: The browser shows the name of the file, which is remarkably dull: `ch2-4.html`.

The `<title>` tag enables you to define the exact title you want in the document. It is a paired tag and appears within the `<head>` `</head>` block of information, as follows:

```
<head>
<title>This is the title</title>
</head>
```

For the document you've been developing in this chapter, `not-yet.html`, a nice title is one that reinforces the message in the file itself, as in the following example:

```
<html>
<head>
<title>This page is not yet ready for prime time</title>
</head>
```

Figure 2-11 shows how the new title text looks within Internet Explorer. Notice the change in the title bar.

x-ref The text in the `<title>` tag is also used as the link information when a user saves a Web document into a *bookmark* or *hotlist*—compiled URLs for sites you've visited and want to remember. So, a meaningful title for each page you create can be very helpful to your readers. Furthermore, titles add to the searchability of the page, as you find out in Chapter 17.

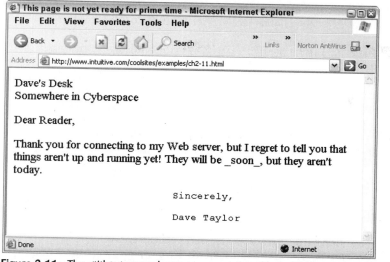

Figure 2-11: The <title> tag produces an appropriate title for the browser window.

Adding Footer Material

Just as you commonly see certain information, such as the title, used in the header of a Web document, certain other information is commonly placed at the foot of the document. On the Web, you usually find copyright information and contact data for the creator of the page at the bottom of documents.

The tag I use for this contact information is <blockquote>. It's a paired tag (<blockquote> information</blockquote>). The following example shows this tag added to the not-yet.html document:

```
<html>
<head>
<title>This page is not yet ready for prime time</title>
</head>
<body>
Dave's Desk <br />
Somewhere in Cyberspace
<p>
Dear Reader,
</p><p>
    Thank you for connecting to my Web server, but I
regret to tell you
that things aren't up and running yet!
```

Continued

```
Continued
They will be _soon_, but they aren't today.
</p><pre>
                                    Sincerely,

                        Dave Taylor

</pre>
<blockquote>
Page Design by Dave Taylor (taylor@intuitive.com)
</blockquote>
</body>
</html>
```

Do you have to use the <blockquote> tag and include this information on your page? Nope. Like various other items that appear in HTML pages, it can be used or skipped. (In Web pages I create, I tend not to include address information, but many people like to have that information at the bottom of each page.) As you can see in Figure 2-12, the address information is presented with an indent, which can look quite attractive on certain Web pages.

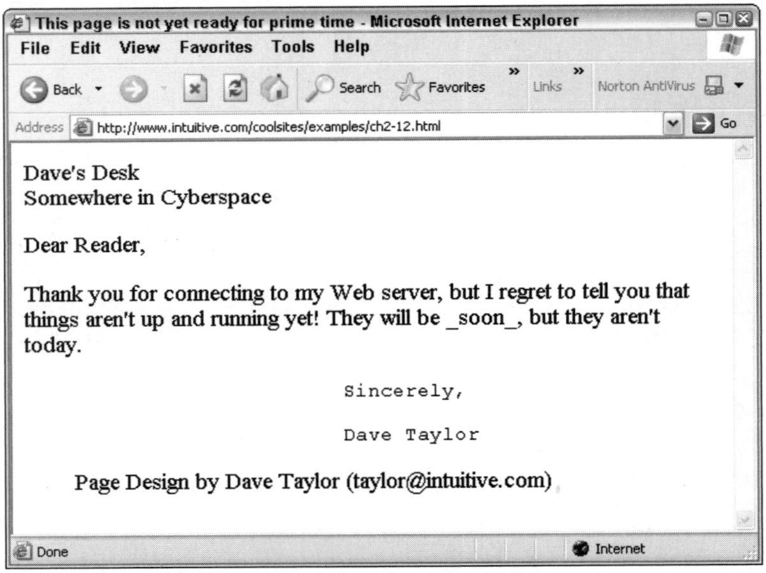

Figure 2-12: <blockquote> information added to the Web page.

Defining Section Heads

The formatting information discussed so far in this chapter enables you to create attractive text. But what if you want to organize your Web page with sections or subsections? The various levels of header-format tags enable you to handle just such a situation.

Each header-format level has an open and close tag. The highest-level header-format tag is h1; the lowest is h6. To specify a top-level header, use

```
<h1>First Header</h1>
```

Header-format tags are best illustrated in an HTML page other than not-yet.html, because that document doesn't need headers. The following code shows the beginning of a table of contents for a movie information Web site:

```
<html>
<head>
<title>The Cool Web Movie Database</title>
</head>
<body>
Welcome to the Cool Web Movie Database. So far we offer
information on the many brilliant films of David Lean:
soon, a lot more will be online.
<h1>Films with Sam Spiegel Productions</h1>
<h2>The Bridge on the River Kwai (1957)</h2>
<h2>Lawrence of Arabia (1962)</h2>
<h1>The Later Years</h1>
<h2>Doctor Zhivago (1965)</h2>
<h2>Ryan's Daughter (1970)</h2>
<blockquote>
This information maintained by Dave Taylor
</blockquote>
</body>
</html>
```

Figure 2-13 shows how the preceding HTML appears in a Web browser.

Most Web pages that you design probably won't have quite as many headers as the example in Figure 2-13.

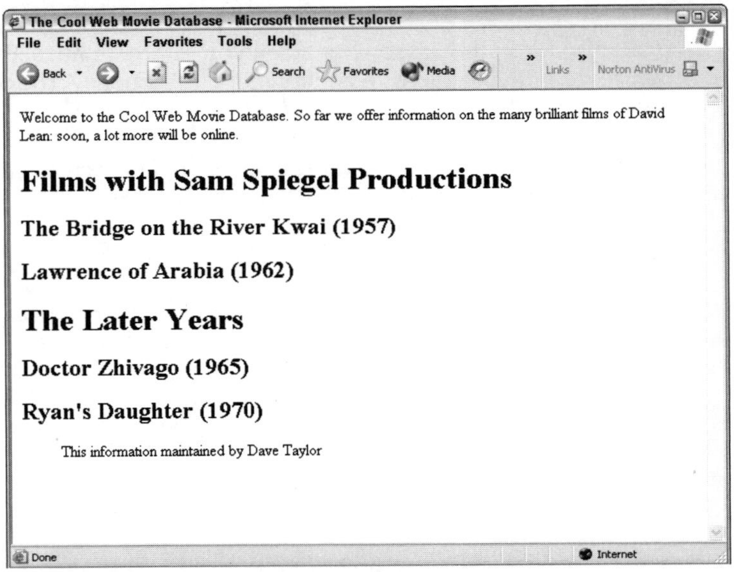

Figure 2-13: Examples of <h1> and <h2> headings.

The following example adds a little more information about some of the films to show the value of using various header sizes:

```
<html>
<head>
<title>The Cool Web Movie Database</title>
</head>
<body>
Welcome to the Cool Web Movie Database. So far we offer
information on the many brilliant films of David Lean:
soon, a lot more will be online.
<h1>Films with Sam Spiegel Productions</h1>
<h2>The Bridge on the River Kwai (1957)</h2>
Produced by Sam Spiegel, this film was the first of the
Lean blockbuster movies, and featured a young Alec
Guinness, William Holden, and a brilliant performance
from Sessue Hayakawa.<h2>Lawrence of Arabia (1962)</h2>
One of my all-time favorite movies, this epic
adventure starring Peter O'Toole established Lean as
a director who could truly envision film on a grand scale.
<h1>The Later Years</h1>
<h2>Doctor Zhivago (1965)</h2>
```

```
<h2>Ryan's Daughter (1970)</h2>
<blockquote>
This information maintained by Dave Taylor
</blockquote>
</body>
</html>
```

When the preceding example is viewed in a browser, the different headers appear in different size type, and information that is not part of the header appears in a nonbold, roman typeface (see Figure 2-14).

note One thing to remember about HTML is that users can alter the actual fonts, sizes, and layout of the final presentation based on the preferences they set in their browsers. I contend, however, that precious few people actually alter their preference settings, so if your page looks good with the default values, you should be okay. If the default values look a little weird, as may well be the case with Explorer in particular, by all means experiment with the settings. Just remember what you've changed. You'll see why as you proceed through the book.

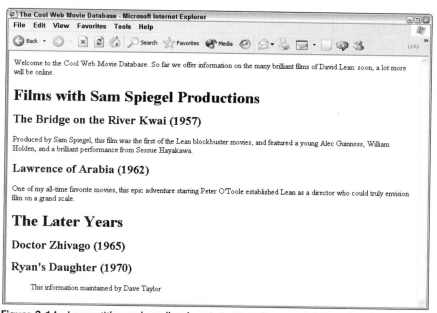

Figure 2-14: Larger titles and smaller descriptive text demonstrate the value of different header levels.

Using the Horizontal Rule

A very useful tag for organizing your document visually is the horizontal rule tag: <hr />. Dropped anywhere in a Web document, it produces a skinny line across the page. The following example shows the movie information page with the <hr /> tag added:

```
<head>
<title>The Cool Web Movie Database</title>
</head>
<body>
Welcome to the Cool Web Movie Database. So far we offer
information on the many brilliant films of David Lean:
soon, a lot more will be online.
<hr />
<h1>Films with Sam Spiegel Productions</h1>
<h2>The Bridge on the River Kwai (1957)</h2>
Produced by Sam Spiegel, this film was the first of the
Lean blockbuster movies, and featured a young Alec
Guinness, William Holden, and a brilliant performance
from Sessue Hayakawa.
<h2>Lawrence of Arabia (1962)</h2>
One of my all-time favorite movies, this epic
adventure starring Peter O'Toole established Lean as
a director who could truly envision film on a grand scale.
<hr />
<h1>The Later Years</h1>
<h2>Doctor Zhivago (1965)</h2>
<h2>Ryan's Daughter (1970)</h2>
<hr />
<blockquote>
This information maintained by Dave Taylor
</blockquote>
</body>
</html>
```

tip Remember to use the XHTML style (<hr />) to close the stand-alone rule tag, as illustrated here.

As with any other formatting or design element in a Web page, you can overuse the horizontal rule. Used judiciously, however, the <hr> tag is tremendously helpful in creating cool pages. Figure 2-15 shows the browser view of the preceding HTML code.

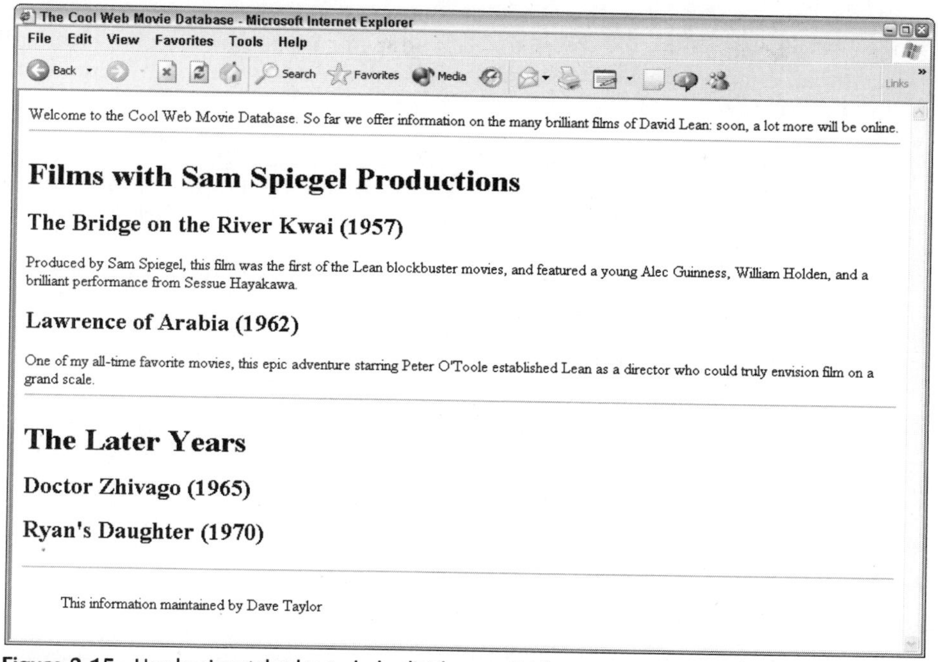

Figure 2-15: Use horizontal rules to help divide your Web pages into easy-to-read sections.

Introducing XHTML

One of the biggest recent changes in the world of HTML is the emergence of XML, the eXstensible Markup Language. Because it allows site designers to designate what things are (for example, album titles, book publication dates, and other database-field-like identifiers), rather than how to present them (that is, italics, bold, green text), XML looks vaguely like HTML; but it is a completely different beast. Fortunately, you don't have to worry about XML in this book!

One way that XML has influenced HTML is through the growth of XHTML, a variation of HTML inspired by the formal structure of XML. The best way to think about XHTML is that it's a formalized version of HTML. Gone are the sloppy mixed case tags of yesteryear and the random differences between tag usage. Instead, XHTML insists that

- All tags are paired or have a `/>` ending.
- All attributes are quoted.
- All attributes must be presented as `name=value` pairs.
- All tags and attributes must be in lowercase only.

What's an *attribute*? That's something I explore in Chapter 3, but here's a sneak preview: Just about every HTML tag allows you to change its behavior by adding specific attributes. For example, you can change the width of a horizontal rule by adding a width value to the `<hr>` tag, as in `<hr width="60%" />`.

Fortunately, after you get the hang of it, writing XHTML is no more difficult than writing regular HTML. In this book, I write XHTML exclusively. By the end of the book, you'll think that regular HTML looks slightly weird and that everything should be written in XHTML. You'll see!

note   Even though I write XHTML code exclusively throughout the rest of this book, XHTML and HTML are very similar. So don't be confused if I sometimes refer to *HTML* when I'm contrasting a particular block of code with code written for Cascading Style Sheets (CSS), which you learn about in Chapter 4.

Table 2-1: HTML Tags Covered in This Chapter

HTML Tag	Close Tag	Meaning
`<blockquote>`	`</blockquote>`	Indicates indentation block
`<body>`	`</body>`	Indicates the body of the HTML page
` `		Signifies a line break
`<head>`	`</head>`	Provides HTML-formatting information
`<hn>`	`</hn>`	Indicates the document header level ($n = 1-6$)
`<hr />`		Inserts a horizontal rule
`<html>`	`</html>`	Defines a Web-formatted file
`<p>`	`</p>`	Blocks a paragraph
`<pre>`	`</pre>`	Indicates preformatted information

Summary

A great deal of information was presented here. You learned many of the basic HTML tags, and you created your first Web page. With the basics you learned in this chapter, you should be able to reproduce formatted information (like this chapter of this book, to pick the most immediate example) in an attractive format for users on the World Wide Web. Chapter 3 continues to explore HTML by explaining how to use boldface and italic formatting, how to add other types of emphasis to text, and how to make various other changes within sentences and paragraphs.

Presenting Text Attractively

In This Chapter

Using bold and italics for navigation

Changing text with underlining, alignment, and other styles

Applying font sizes, colors, and faces

Working with styles

This chapter explores some of the nuts and bolts of text presentation and infor-mation layout. When I talk about *text styles*, I mean the specification of bold-face, italics, and other changes that you can make to text. The preceding chapter showed you, in the proverbial one fell swoop, the basics of HTML document lay-out. But, as you've probably figured out, there's much more to creating cool Web pages.

When you were given your first box of crayons, you probably went wild and tried to use all the colors for each picture you colored. Eventually, however, it dawned on you (unless you were a young Peter Max) that a subset of colors can be much more useful and attractive. The same holds true for the various formatting com-mands in HTML. It is possible to use all the commands everywhere, but a better strategy is to use them only when they are most appropriate. Many Web pages already tend to be cluttered, and using too much italic or boldface typeface makes the clutter even worse.

Nevertheless, at times you want to highlight certain words, phrases, titles, names, or other information. In this chapter, you learn how to do that using HTML. A quick warning, however: In the next chapter you learn a completely different, and more modern, approach to formatting text using something called *Cascading Style Sheets,* or CSS. Although more complex, CSS offers dramatically greater control over the presentation of text (and much more). Purists lobby for CSS-only pages, but I'm not that hard core. I use a mélange of HTML and CSS to achieve the page results I seek, and I bet you will, too.

First, a Little History

Page design and layout have been around for thousands of years—since the beginning of writing. In Egyptian hieroglyphs, for example, vertical lines separate columns of glyphs to make them easier to read. Before the year A.D. 1000, scribes all over the world were using various techniques to present information on a page, including illumination (adding gold or silver to the ink, or including other illustrations in the margins or twined around the letters), illustration, and other devices.

By the time Johann Gutenberg introduced his printing press in the fifteenth century, with its revolutionary movable type supplanting etched- or engraved-plate printing, designers and artists were codifying various approaches to page design. A glance at the Gutenberg Bible reveals that it foreshadows many aspects of modern text design, including italicized and boldface text.

on the web See `http://prodigi.bl.uk/gutenbg/` to have a peek at the Gutenberg Bible. It's an astonishing piece of history.

Why am I rambling on about the history of page layout? Well, it's important to realize that italics and boldface text have commonly accepted standard meanings. You don't have to follow the rules to the letter, but if your goal is to help people breeze through your Web material and quickly find what they're looking for, you should keep the guidelines in mind.

Helping Readers Navigate with Bold and Italic

In the examples in Chapter 2, I mention that standard computer notation for underlining doesn't always work. In Figure 2-1, I include this text as an example:

```
_soon_,
```

By placing underscore characters before and after *soon,* my hope is that a browser will read the text and italicize, underline, or otherwise present the word in a manner that emphasizes it.

One of the most important characteristics of any document layout—on the Web or in print—is the use of different fonts and various styles to help the reader navigate the material. Imagine this page without any spacing, paragraph breaks, headings, italics, or boldface words; it would look pretty boring. More important, it would be difficult to skim the page for information or to glance at it quickly to gain a sense of what's being discussed.

tip I like to remember the different text treatments by imagining that I'm reading the material to an audience. Italicized words or phrases are those that I *emphasize* in my speech. Words or phrases in boldface I imagine to be *anchors*—items that help me skim the material and find specific spots. Apply this practice to text, and you see why section headings are in bold rather than italic: Headings would be harder to find if they didn't stand out. The same reasoning applies to text size; larger words stand out from smaller adjacent text.

Now take a look at how bold and italic work in Web page design. Italic and boldface formatting require paired tags:

- The italic formatting tag is `<i>`, which is paired with `</i>`.
- The boldface formatting tag is `<b>`, and its partner is `</b>`.

Here's how a brief HTML passage looks with both bold and italics text:

```
It turns out <b>Starbucks</b>, the popular and
fast-growing coffee chain, got its name from the
coffee-loving first mate in Melville's classic
tale of pursuit and revenge, <i>Moby Dick< /i >,
although few people realize it.
```

Figure 3-1 shows how the preceding information looks in a Web browser. Notice I made a slight mistake in the coding: The name of the book, *Moby Dick*, has an open italics tag, but I incorrectly added spaces within its partner, the close italics tag. As a result, the request to end the italics passage doesn't take effect when the title of the book is complete. Also, if you view this exact same snippet in Explorer and Navigator, you find that each has a slightly different way of dealing with an error of this form. Another good reason to double-check your Web pages in multiple browsers!

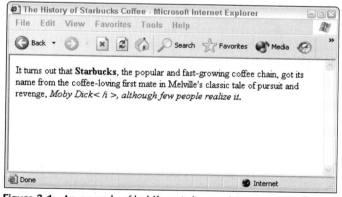

Figure 3-1: An example of boldface, italics, and a coding mistake.

caution   Always follow the opening angle bracket of an HTML formatting tag with the format code immediately; no spaces are allowed.

Underlining, Monospace, and Other Text Changes

A number of other formatting options are available within Web documents:

- The underline formatting tag is `<u>`, which is paired with `</u>`.
- The monospace tag is `<tt>`, which is paired with `</tt>`.
- Superscripts are denoted by `<sup>` and `</sup>`, subscripts by `<sub>` and `</sub>`.
- Text can be crossed out using `<strike>`, which ends with `</strike>`.

`Monospace` is so named because each letter in a monospace typeface occupies exactly the same width as every other letter, even if the letter itself is quite narrow. Monospace type typically looks like the product of a typewriter:

```
This is an example of a monospace typeface.
```

Proportional typefaces are more common in the text you see everyday. The text you are reading now is a proportional typeface. Note that it varies the width of the letters for easier reading; five occurrences of the letter *i*, for example (iiiii) aren't as long as five occurrences of the letter *m* (mmmmm).

Don't use the `<u>` and `<tt>` tags too often because of possible browser conversion problems. Some versions of Internet Explorer, for example, ignore the `<u>` format. When you create a Web document that contains links to other documents, the links are displayed in a different color—usually blue. To make links stand out more, however, and to ensure that people with grayscale or black-and-white displays can recognize links, links also appear with an underline. Therein lies the problem with the `<u>` formatting tag. If you use it on a Web page, it is difficult for visitors to tell which underlined words or phrases are links and which simply represent underlined text. Figure 3-2 demonstrates this underlining problem more clearly.

You can't tell by looking at Figure 3-2, but the word *Starbucks* is a pointer to another document on the World Wide Web, whereas the book title, *Moby Dick,* is just an underlined word. As you can see, using underlining in Web pages can be confusing, so it isn't often used.

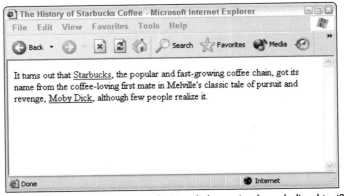

Figure 3-2: Underlines on a Web page: links or simply underlined text?

Monospace is often more useful than underlining, but it's not used extensively in Web pages either. If you want to simulate computer input or output, for example, you might display that text in monospace, as in the following:

```
Rather than typing <b><tt>DIRECTORY</tt></b> to find out
what files you have in your Unix account, you'll instead
want to type <b><tt>ls -l</tt></b>, as shown:
<pre>
$ <b>ls -l</b>
total 8
-rw-------   1 taylor           1689 Feb 11 09:51 that
-rw-------   1 taylor              0 Feb 11 09:51 the-other
-rw-------   1 taylor            563 Feb 11 09:51 this
</pre>
```

As shown in Figure 3-3, this example demonstrates that the preformatted text tag <pre> produces text in monospace typeface, but it also preserves the original line breaks and extra spacing between words.

You can combine some HTML tags to produce exactly the output you want. In Figure 3-3, the terms DIRECTORY and ls appear in bold monospace text.

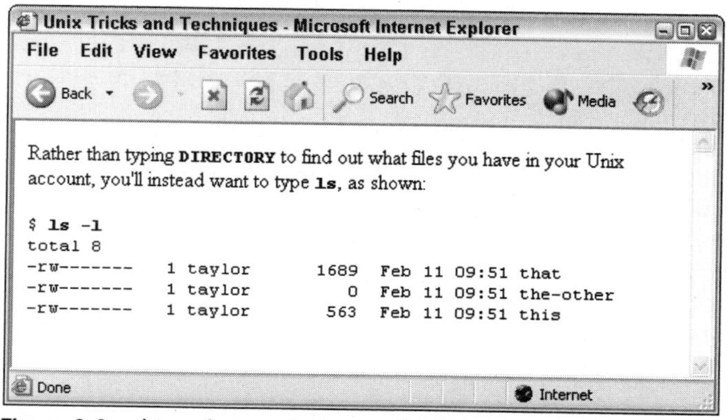

Figure 3-3: <b> and <tt> together produce bold monospace.

If you're working with mathematical formulas or otherwise have reason to use superscripts and subscripts on your Web pages, two tags offer easy formatting, as shown here:

```
If you could double the amount of water on the
planet - essentially H<sub>2</sub>O<sup>2</sup> - you'd
never have to worry about mowing the lawn again; it'd be
under the ocean!
```

The resulting format is very attractive and lends itself to slick formulas and instant math, as you can see in Figure 3-4.

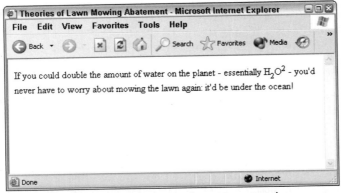

Figure 3-4: Superscript and subscript format tags at work.

Finally, sometimes you want to be able to show a change in text to someone visiting your page. In this situation, showing deleted text can be quite useful, and you can do this in most Web browsers by using the <strike> strikethrough tag. Here's how it looks as source code:

```
If you could double the amount of water on the
planet - essentially H<sub>2</sub>O<sup>2</sup> - you'd
never have to worry about <strike>mowing the lawn again:
everything would be under the ocean!</strike>buying a
dryer: everything would be permanently wet!
```

The strikethrough formatting works well in this case, as you can see in Figure 3-5, because the text is a reasonable size. But if the text were smaller, the strikethrough line itself could make the underlying text unreadable. Therefore, be sure you carefully preview any <strike> text before you unleash it on the world.

By the way, commerce sites such as Amazon.com use the <strike> tag extensively: Every time you see the retail price shown and then Amazon's discounted price, the <strike> is being used to cross out the retail price!

caution   Depending on the Web browser you're using, some HTML tags can be combined and others can't. You can learn more about this through experimentation, but common combinations work fine, such as <b><i> to get bold and italics.

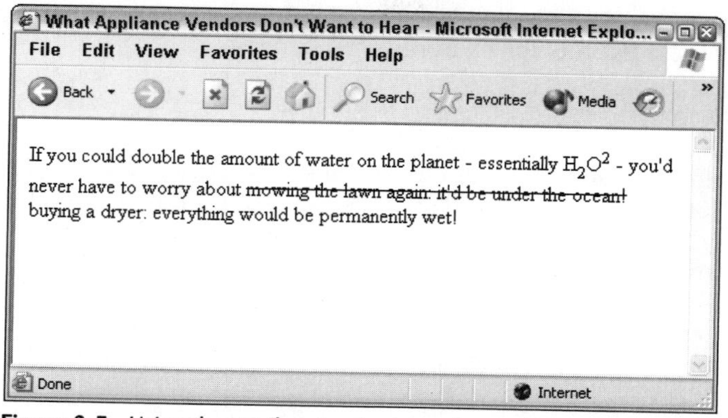

Figure 3-5: Using the <strike> tag to show changed text on-screen.

Specifying Font Sizes, Colors, and Faces

One valuable improvement to your Web pages is the capability to change font sizes, colors, and faces. Using pure HTML formatting, rather than CSS, HTML font sizes range from size 1 to size 7, with 1 being the smallest and 7 the largest. Unfortunately, this is the opposite of the numbering system for header tags, where Header 1 is the largest and Header 6 the smallest.

All font changes are variations on the `<font>` tag, and it's the first tag I've discussed so far that includes specific attributes. HTML tags that can include attributes specify them as `name="value"` pairs. The `<font>` tag is a fine example. To change the size of a passage of text, you can use this formatting:

```
<font size="7">some important text</font>
```

In this example, the words *some important text* are displayed at the largest possible size in the browser.

tip   Notice that the closing tag `</font>` doesn't need to include the attributes of the opening tag: You don't have to use `</font size="7">` to end the larger text. This is an important nuance and a great time-saver as you start to explore more complex formatting.

You can specify font sizes absolutely, as in the previous example, or you can use relative size changes. Here's the HTML to make a particular word one font size larger than the text surrounding it:

```
This is a <font size="+1">very</font> important issue to us.
```

The default font size in Web browsers is `size="3"`. Relative changes can't go below `size="1"` or above `size="7"`, so if you have a default size of 3 and add 10 to it, with a tag like `font size="+10"`, it'll be identical in function to `font size="7"` (or `font size="+4"`).

You can specify color for a range of text in a similar manner by using a different `font` attribute. To display a passage of text in blue, for example, you can use

```
<font color="BLUE">I'm blue</font>
```

You can choose from a wide variety of colors that can be specified by name, and you can have even finer resolution of color control by using RGB (red-green-blue) hexadecimal values. For basic colors, however, you can work without worrying about the RGB values and, instead, just specify them by name.

x-ref Chapter 7 provides an explanation of the red-green-blue color identification technique and includes a table of RGB hexadecimal values.

The markup language has a nice feature that enables you to specify several attributes within one HTML tag, thereby achieving multiple effects. If you want big red text, for example, you do it with this code:

```
<font size="6" color="red">Clifford</font>
```

It doesn't matter in what order you specify the `name="value"` pairs. So to the browser

```
<font color="red" size="6">
```

is identical to

```
<font size="6" color="red">
```

However, the attributes must be tucked within the `<>` pair, so `<font><size="6"><color="red">` won't work, nor will `<font size="6"><color="red">`. Both are common errors for neophyte HTML coders, however, so be alert that this doesn't creep into your own markup work.

The third possible attribute for the `font` tag is the typeface specifier `face`. This is a tricky one, however, because you need to specify the exact typeface name on the user's system, and typefaces have different names on different platforms. For example, on my Macintosh, the standard typeface is Times, but in Windows, the equivalent typeface is called Times Roman. Many typefaces are included on computers nowadays, but again, no standardization exists.

This means you must specify typefaces with the `face` attribute to the `font` tag, and you can specify a list of typefaces as the value. If you want to ensure that you get either Arial (a popular typeface on Windows) or Chicago (a popular face on the Macintosh), you specify the following:

```
<font face="Arial,Chicago">special text</font>
```

The browser, upon receiving this HTML instruction, looks for Arial. If Arial is found, the browser uses it to display *special text* on the screen. If Arial isn't available, the browser uses Chicago. If Chicago is not available, the text is displayed in the default proportional typeface.

Here is a more complex example:

```
<font size="4" color="blue" face="Helvetica Narrow,Arial
Narrow">Skinny Text</font>
```

Again, the browser displays the text in Helvetica Narrow, if available, or Arial Narrow, or the default typeface.

One final tag and you have an example that demonstrates all these modifications: To change the default size of all text on a page, you use `<font size="4">` or a similar tag at the very top of the document. However, you can use a tag intended for just this purpose called `<basefont>`. However, `<basefont>` only lets you change the size of the type, so most modern sites use the appropriate CSS styles to specify the type family, size, and other layout elements, as you learn in Chapter 4. Here is a tantalizing preview of both the CSS body style and the HTML unordered (or bullet) list:

```
<style type="text/css">
body { font-family: Arial,Helvetica,serif; font-size: 90%;
       line-height:1.5 }
</style>
<font size="7">Common Foods of the French
Quarter</font><br />
You can visit <font size="+1">New Orleans</font> and have a
great time without ever leaving
the picturesque and partyin' French Quarter area,
particularly if you partake of some of these
fabulous local foods:
<ul>
<li><font color="RED">Beignets</font> - small deep-fried
donuts in powdered sugar. Best with
a steaming fresh <font size="+1">cup of coffee</font>.</li>
<li><font color="GREEN">Seafood Gumbo</font> - a stew-like
soup that's delicious.
Typically served with a side of white rice
that's best dumped into the soup directly. Skip the
chicken gumbo some
places serve too: the seafood is definitely better!</li>
<li><font color="ORANGE" size="+2">Jambalaya</font> - the best
of all possible dinners. You'll just have
to order it so you can find out what it's about.</li>
<li><font size="2" color="BLUE">alcohol</font> - it's the
grease on the wheels of the tourist experience in the
French Quarter, but I'm not convinced it's as necessary
for a good time as the bars suggest... </li>
</ul>
Whatever you do, make sure you have <font
size="+1">F</font><font size="+2">U</font>
<font size="+3">N</font>!
```

This code creates a screen full of fun and interesting text in a variety of sizes and colors (see Figure 3-6).

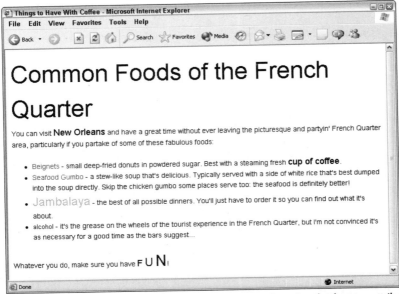

Figure 3-6: You can make your text fun and interesting by using the font tag attributes to specify a variety of colors and sizes.

tip

There's another way to change the color of text on your page, but it applies to all text on the page at once: Add the text attribute to the body tag. For example, to have all text blue, add the following line of code:

```
<body text="blue">
```

Again, however, CSS offers more graceful solutions.

Applying Logical Styles

The style directives discussed up to this point specify how you want the material displayed when the page is formatted and presented to the reader. The HTML language also supports what are called *logical* styles. Logical styles enable readers (and their software) to indicate *what* things are, rather than how they should be presented.

The most common logical styles are <em> </em> for emphasis and <strong> </strong> for stronger emphasis. Figure 3-7 shows the results of using these tags.

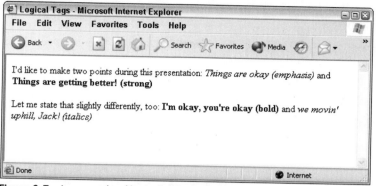

Figure 3-7: An example of logical styles in HTML.

In the example shown in Figure 3-7, the first point (shown in italics) is specified as

```
<em>Things are okay </em>
```

The second point (boldfaced) is specified as

```
<strong>Things are getting better!</strong>
```

note I have to admit that I don't particularly like the logical tags and never use them myself. I have no way of knowing if a particular browser will think `<em>` should be in bold or italics, and the two have very different meanings in layout, as discussed at the beginning of this chapter.

Many other logical tags are specified in the HTML standard but are rarely used. I list them all in Table 3-1 for your information. You may want to experiment with them to see if they meet any of your specific formatting needs; but in most browsers, they're all synonymous with the `<tt>` monospace-type tag. More important, the markup world is moving to CSS, and that's really what you should be using for these kinds of logical formatting. With CSS, you can fine-tune the results to be exactly what you want, and then some!

Table 3-1: A Variety of Logical Text Tags

HTML Tag	Close Tag	Meaning
<cite>	</cite>	Bibliographic citation
<code>	</code>	Code listing
<dfn>	</dfn>	Word definition
<kbd>	</kbd>	Keyboard text (similar to `<CODE>`)
<samp>	</samp>	Sample user input
<var>	</var>	Program or other variable

Putting It All Together

The following example is a complex HTML document viewed within a Web browser. This example also includes material covered in Chapter 2.

```
<html>
<head>
<title>Travels with Tintin</title>
<style type="text/css">
body { font-family: Arial,Helvetica; font-size: 90% }
</style>
</head><body>
<h2><font color="ORANGE">Travels with Tintin</font></h2>
<p>
Of the various reporters with whom I've travelled around
the world, including writers for <i>UPI</i>, <i>AP</i>,
and <i>Reuters</i>, the most fascinating has clearly been
<b>Tintin</b>, boy reporter from Belgium (<tt>tintin@intuitive.com</tt>).
</p><p>
Probably the most enjoyable aspect of our travels was his
dog <b>Snowy</b>, though I don't know that our hosts would
always agree!
</p><p>
<font size="6" color="blue">The First Trip: Nepal</font>
</p><p>
After winning the Pulitzer for <i>Red Rackham's Treasure</i>,
Tintin told me he wanted a vacation. Remembering some of his
earlier adventures, he decided to visit Nepal. Early one
Sunday, I was sipping my tea and reading the <i>Times</i>
when he rang me up, asking whether I'd be able to take a
break and come along...
</body>
</html>
```

Can you guess how the preceding text will look in a browser? Check Figure 3-8 to find out.

The document in Figure 3-8 is quite attractive, albeit with some poor spacing around the italicized acronyms in the first sentence. Fortunately, some of the most recent Web browsers realize that an additional space is needed after the last italicized character. It would make this document even more readable. Also notice the spacing around the h2 format compared to the two <p> tags I added later in the document when I opted to use the font size="6" tag to create my own section head.

Table 3-2 provides a summary of the many HTML character-formatting tags covered in this chapter.

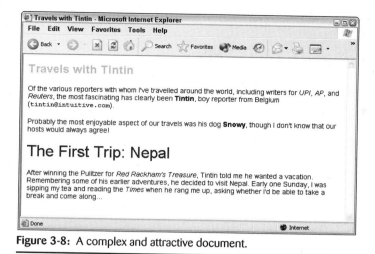

Figure 3-8: A complex and attractive document.

Table 3-2: Summary of Tags in This Chapter

HTML Tag	Close Tag	Meaning
`<b>`	`</b>`	Displays text in bold
`<i>`	`</i>`	Displays text in italic
`<u>`	`</u>`	Underlines specified text
`<tt>`	`</tt>`	Specifies monospace text
`<cite>`	`</cite>`	Specifies bibliographic citation
`<code>`	`</code>`	Specifies code listing
`<dfn>`	`</dfn>`	Specifies word definition
`<em>`	`</em>`	Indicates logical emphasis style
`<kbd>`	`</kbd>`	Specifies keyboard text (similar to `<code>`)
`<samp>`	`</samp>`	Specifies sample user input
`<strong>`	`</strong>`	Indicates logical stronger emphasis
`<var>`	`</var>`	Specifies program or other variable
`<basefont size="n">`		Specifies default font size for page. Range is 1–7, 7 being largest. Default: 3.
`<font size="n" face="a,b" color="s">`	`</font>`	Specifies attributes for enclosed text. Size of text: range is 1–7, 7 being largest. Specifies typeface to use: *a* if available, or *b*. Color of text, either as color name or RGB value.

Summary

This chapter focused on formatting characters and words using the traditional HTML tags most frequently used to build Web pages. Chapter 4 re-examines all these issues but from the perspective of Cascading Style Sheets. It explains what they are, how to use them, and why they leave these crude HTML tags in the proverbial dust.

Moving into the 21st Century with Cascading Style Sheets

In This Chapter

Examining the types of CSS

Understanding the format of CSS

Underlining, monospace, and other text changes

Working with font sizes, colors, and faces

Discovering other cool font tricks in CSS

Putting it all together

After reading the last chapter you might think that text markup is pretty straightforward—with tags such as <b>, <i>, and the like—but not very powerful. After all, when you look at Web pages from large commercial sites such as ESPN, Disney, or The Wall Street Journal, you see a variety of typefaces, type treatments, and even line-spacing variations.

So how do the Web site creators accomplish those effects? They use a new and vastly improved addition to Web page design called *style sheets*. You might be familiar with the concept of style sheets from working with document-processing applications like Microsoft Word, where choosing a particular *style* produces a complex set of changes in typeface, color, size, indentation, and much more. Style sheets give you a corresponding capability as you design Web pages

One very important characteristic of style specifications, both in applications, such as Microsoft Word, and in Web documents, is that attributes are *inherited*. Suppose that a paragraph in your document appears in 14-point Times Roman.

Then you apply a style to a single word in the paragraph that puts the selected word in blue. Besides having the blue added, that word also inherits the typeface, typeface size, and any other attributes from the *parent* style applied to the remainder of the paragraph. In Web parlance, this is known as *cascading* (style attributes cascade down until something changes them). The style sheets I'll be talking about are, therefore, logically called *Cascading Style Sheets* and succinctly referred to as CSS.

In this chapter, I begin showing you how to interweave traditional HTML tags and formatting (actually, I use XHTML, but for simplicity, every time you see HTML, imagine that you really see XHTML) with the newer, more powerful CSS capabilities. Why weave them together? Because although CSS is wonderful for many things, it frankly requires too much work when you want to make just one or two simple, straightforward changes. If I want a word in bold on my page, it's usually much simpler to specify <b> than to figure out the CSS details.

Types of CSS

Cascading Style Sheets are really a completely different approach to page styling and layout. So first, you need to look at *where* you add CSS information to your page. CSS information can be specified in three different places:

- Within the specific tags in the document body
- At the top of the document within a <style> block, or combined with named <div> or <span> containers in the document body
- In one or more separate files shared across many Web pages

These may all be combined with a well-defined inheritance (which is why they are called *cascading* style sheets). Don't worry, this will all make sense as you explore CSS.

Inline CSS

Basically, styles can be specified with the style attribute within almost any HTML markup tag. For example, you can have a bold tag that also changes the color of the text within by using the following HTML:

```
<b style="color: blue">this is bold and blue</b> and this isn't.
```

More commonly, styles are used within one of two otherwise empty tags called <div> or <span>. These two tags were introduced into HTML specifically for use with Cascading Style Sheets, so if you see them on a Web page, they're often used like this:

```
<span style="color:green">this is green</span> and this ain't.
```

The difference between the two is that <div> is used as a block container (it's basically identical to <p> and </p>) whereas <span> is used within a block (it's more analogous to <b> and </b>).

Take a look at this simple sequence of HTML with a simple style attribute, `color:`, applied:

```
<p>
This is a typical paragraph of text that contains
some words, perhaps a sentence or two, but that's
about all.
</p>
<div>
By contrast, this is a <span style="color:blue">vibrant</span>,
<span style="color:red">colorful</span>
<span style="font-family: monospace">div</span> block
that has lots of room for growth!
</div>
```

The result of having this code interpreted by Microsoft Internet Explorer is shown in Figure 4-1.

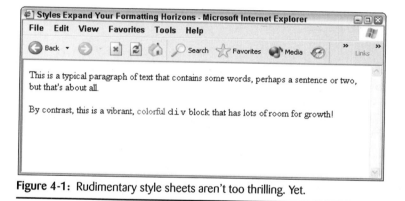

Figure 4-1: Rudimentary style sheets aren't too thrilling. Yet.

The preceding example is not going to convince you that this approach is superior to the `<font>` tag discussed in Chapter 3. But read on, and perhaps you will begin to understand the value of style sheets.

One definition, many references

The second way to work with CSS will doubtless catch your attention. To a great extent, CSS enables you to *redefine how any HTML markup is rendered*. CSS also essentially allows you to create your own tags to transform a Web page into exactly the format and layout you seek.

This is accomplished by moving the style specifications into a `<style>` block. At the top of a page, the `<style>` tag might look like this:

```
<style type="text/css">
b { color: blue }
</style>
```

This style specifies that throughout the subsequent document body, all occurrences of the bold tag `<b>` should also have a type color change to blue. Are you starting to see where this can make your life considerably easier?

More interestingly, you can specify style *classes*, which are akin to subtags. Imagine that I have a Web site that talks about my digital camera, a Nikon. I'm going to write about how it compares to other digital cameras, including those from Canon, Sony, and Kodak. To make the page consistent, each time that I mention a manufacturer I want to use the identical format. Here's how I can do that with CSS:

```
While a variety of companies manufacture digital
cameras, notably including
<span class="manuf">Kodak</span>,
<span class="manuf">Olympus</span> and
<span class="manuf">Sony</span>,
there are only two companies that offer true
digital single lens reflex (SLR) cameras:
<span class="manuf">Nikon</span> and
<span class="manuf">Canon</span>.
```

This gets interesting when you go into the `<style>` block and specify exactly how to format the manufacturer names. Because these are all specified by class, the CSS notation is to preface the classname with a dot in the style block:

```
<style type="text/css">
.manuf { font-size: 125%; color: green }
</style>
```

Figure 4-2 shows the results of using this code at the top of your page.

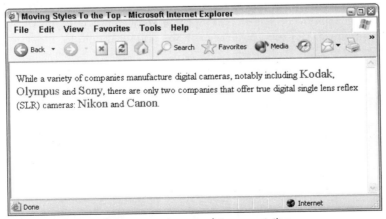

Figure 4-2: Classes let you organize your data presentation.

The more I look at Figure 4-2, the more I think, "That's not really quite what I want." Here's where the power of CSS makes things a breeze. To change the style of all the manufacturer names instantly, I simply edit the style definition in the style block. A few changes (don't worry, in a page or so I'll talk about the specific style attributes you can use) and suddenly the Web page is totally different! Here's my modified code:

```
<html>
<head>
<title>Moving Styles To the Top</title>
<style type="text/css">
.manuf { color:blue; font-weight: bold; font-style: italic }
</style>
</head><body>

While a variety of companies manufacture digital
cameras, notably including
<span class="manuf">Kodak</span>,
<span class="manuf">Olympus</span> and
<span class="manuf">Sony</span>,
there are only two companies that offer true
digital single lens reflex (SLR) cameras:
<span class="manuf">Nikon</span> and
<span class="manuf">Canon</span>.

</body>
</html>
```

Figure 4-3 shows the result of this code. Remember, the only difference between Figure 4-2 and Figure 4-3 is what's specified in the `style` block. I know that you can't see the result of the color attribute in this black-and-white screen shot, but I think you can still see that quite a difference results from such a simple change.

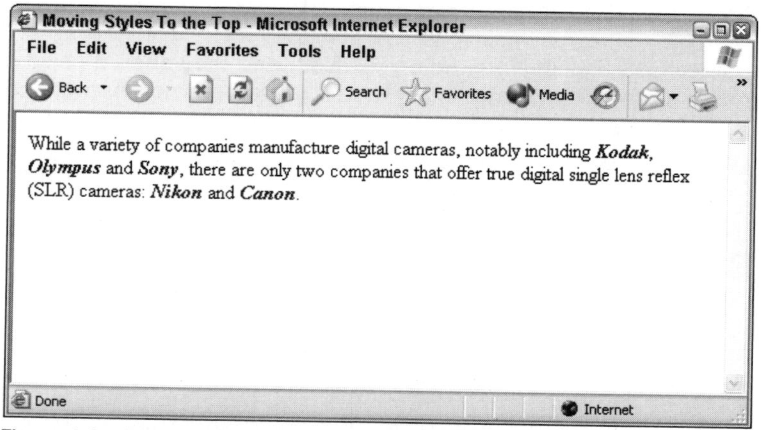

Figure 4-3: Same HTML page, different style specification.

I hope that simple example is enough to sell you on CSS as a powerful method for formatting and specifying the presentation of your Web pages!

Sharing a single style sheet

The third way that you can work with CSS is to create a completely separate document on your Web server that includes all the styles you want to use. You can then reference that document within all the Web pages on your site. You may think that having a single style definition at the top of your page makes it easy to manage the layout of that page. Imagine how handy it would be to have a site with dozens (or hundreds!) of pages of material, all using the appropriate div and span tags and classes. Add to that the capability to change the style across all occurrences of a class, on all pages, with a single edit!

To reference a separate style sheet, use the link tag:

```
<link type="text/css" href="mystyles.css" />
```

This refers to a separate style sheet called mystyles.css, stored in the same directory on the same server as the page that contains this link reference. You can also use a fully qualified URL. This is how I reference one of my CSS style sheets on my server:

```
<link type="text/css"
    href="http://www.intuitive.com/library/shared.css" />
```

The .css file should contain everything you'd otherwise put between the <style> and </style> tags. For the previous example, the entire mystyles.css might look like this:

```
.manuf { color:blue; font-weight: bold; font-style: italic }
```

As you develop your site, your shared CSS files will doubtless become longer and longer as you push more of the formatting details into style specifications and out of the HTML tags.

tip You can edit separate CSS files in NotePad or TextEdit, and they should be saved with a .css filename suffix. For example, styles.css is a common name, and you would include it in your HTML file with this <link type="text/css" href="styles.css" /> tag.

The Components of CSS

Whether it appears in a style attribute of an HTML tag, within a style block on the top of a Web page, or in a separate document, all CSS specifications have the same general format:

```
name colon value semicolon
```

Here's an example: color:blue;.

tip The very last CSS specification in a group can have the trailing semicolon omitted because there's nothing subsequent; but it's a good habit to always use a semicolon after each style specification.

CSS specifications are case-insensitive, but by convention you should use all lowercase, just as XHTML specifies all lowercase for the HTML tags.

Within a style block or separate style sheet, tags have style attributes defined within a curly-brace pair, as in the following example.

```
b { color: green; }
```

This code adds a shift to green text for any bold passages in the applicable text.

caution Within a style attribute, the content that the style changes is already implied by the usage, so no tag names and curly braces are allowed. You can't do the following, for example:

```
<b style="i { color: yellow; } color:red">this is red</b>
but <i>this should be yellow</i>, shouldn't it?
```

If you're trying to accomplish anything like this, the specification belongs in the style block instead.

Classes and IDs

I have already briefly discussed classes and how you can use them to group similarly format-ted content. But there's another type of identifier that you can use in CSS work called an `id` attribute. You use classes and `id` tags in similar ways:

```
<div class="para">
This is a standard paragraph on this page, with
<span id="emphasize8">nothing</span>
out of the ordinary.</div>
```

Within the `style` block, these two identifiers are differentiated by their first character: a dot for a class identifier, and a hash mark (#) for an `id` tag:

```
<style type="text/css">
.para { font-size: 110% }
#emphasize8 { font-weight: bold }
</style>
```

The primary difference between these two is that each unique `id` tag value is supposed to occur once and only once within a given document, whereas classes are reused as needed. In practice, almost every CSS site I've seen makes heavy use of classes and completely ignores `id` tags.

Subclasses

Another tremendously powerful trick you can use with CSS is to specify subclasses and to constrain formatting styles to a subset of your tags. For example, imagine a Web page like this:

```
<div class="special">
This is a special block and <b>bold</b> words should appear
differently than they do in regular text.</div>
<p>
And this, by contrast, is regular <b>bold</b> text,
with a little <i>italics</i> tossed in for luck
and an example of <b><i>italics within bold</i></b>.
</p>
```

To specify that only the bold tags within the class `special` should have a particular style, use the format *class class* (in the example below, notice that the `b  i` sequence changes italics within bold sequences only):

```
<style type="text/css">
.special b { color: green; font-size: 125%; }
b i { background-color: yellow; }
b,i { font-weight: bold; color: blue; }
</style>
```

Look closely to see what's specified here. Two lines contain a pair of *selectors* separated by a space; on the third line, the selectors are separated by a comma. On the two lines in which a space separates the selectors, the second selector is affected only when it falls within the first selector. In other words, bold text is green only when the <b> is used within a class="special" block, and the background color is yellow only when the <i> is used within a <b> tag. In the last of the three CSS lines, I employ a shorthand to specify that both bold tags and italic tags should be in bold with blue text. It's the same as if I had used b { ... } and i { .... }.

Put this all together and the results are as shown in Figure 4-4.

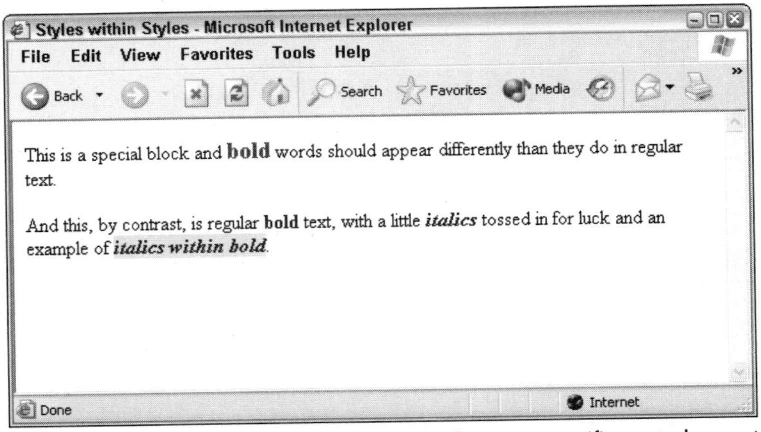

Figure 4-4: Subclasses and special selectors allow very specific control over styles.

If you're starting to think, "Hey, this stuff is pretty darn powerful," you're right! CSS is a thousand times more powerful than even the fanciest HTML formatting, and there's no question that it's the future of Web page design and layout. The price, as you can already see, is that it's more complex. There is quite a bit of difference between `<b>bold</b>` and `<span style="font-weight: bold;">bold</span>`, but stick with me and you'll get the hang of things. You may soon find that you are creating exceptional pages—and with darn little work!

Adding comments within CSS

Here's another little tip: You can add comments to your CSS in two different ways. For a single-line comment, use two slashes; anything after them is ignored through the end of the line, as in the following example:

```
b { font-weight: normal; } // disabled bold for this page
```

If you need a multiline comment, wrap it in `/*` and `*/` pairs, as shown in the following example:

```
<style type="text/css">
b { font-weight: normal; }
/* The head of layout suggested that we disable all bold text as
an experiment, so we've done so. - DaveT, Oct 11 */
</style>
```

Compatible style blocks

If you're big on backwards compatibility, consider wrapping all your style blocks as I have in the following example:

```
<style type='text/css">
<!-
b { font-weight: normal; }
// ->
</style>
```

If the Web browser understands style sheets, it ignores the comment characters, and if the browser doesn't understand CSS, it assumes that all the stuff within the `<!-` and `->` span is a comment and hides it from the final rendered page. In fact, even without CSS, you can always add comments to your HTML pages by surrounding them with `<!-` and `->`. They show up in the source code but aren't displayed in the actual Web page you see in a browser.

note

I have to admit that I typically do not use the comment sequence to hide my style blocks. CSS-compatible Web browsers first came out in 1997, so by this point, the vast majority of users should have browsers that can render CSS properly. You can make your own call, however, as there are definitely different opinions on this subject.

Text Formatting with CSS

You've looked at the skeleton of CSS long enough; it's time to dig into some specifics of CSS formats and styles! To parallel Chapter 3, I start with basic text transformations: bold, italics, colors, sizes, and typefaces.

Bold text

The most straightforward of the CSS visual text formatting styles is bold, which is specified as `font-weight`. As with all CSS tags, you can define a variety of possible values:

- `lighter`
- `normal`
- `bold`
- `bolder`

You can specify the weight of the font in increments of 100, in the range of 100–900, with 100 being the lightest and 900 being the heaviest. Normal text is weight 500, and normal bold is 700. Specifying `font-weight: 900` is the equivalent of extra-bold or, in the parlance of CSS, `bolder`.

Italics

Italics are easier to work with than bold. You simply specify a `font-style` and pick from one of the following values:

- `normal`
- `italics`
- `oblique`

note Oblique font style is similar to italics, but more slanted. On a Web page, however, it looks identical to italics.

Why have a value for `normal`? Answering this question reveals the secret magic of the *cascading* of style sheets. Imagine the following:

```
<div style="font-style: italics">
This is a paragraph where all the words should be italicized.
But what if I have a word that I don't want in italics?
</div>
```

If you want *don't* to appear in a non-italics format, the easiest way to accomplish this is to use `font-style: normal` to override the italics formatting. In fact, this does the trick:

```
<div style="font-style: italics">
This is a paragraph where all the words should be italicized.
But what if I have a word that I
<span style="font-style:normal">don't</span>
want in italics?
</div>
```

This is the same reason that the `font-weight` style has a *normal* value.

Changing Font Family, Size, and Color

As I've shown you so far in this chapter, switching between bold and italics within CSS is straightforward. Other text transformations, such as changing the font family, the font size, and the color, are also easy to do, and the following sections show you how.

Typefaces and monospace

With standard HTML markup, the `<tt>` tag produces *typewriter text*, but call it by its proper name: *monospace*. Chapter 3 talks about the difference between monospace and proportional spaced typefaces. CSS is much more accurate about this particular text transformation because it's really a typeface change . . . well, a `font-family` change, to be precise.

note   All right, I'll call the change in typeface produced by a `font-family` style what Web standards developers want me to call it, a *font*; but it's really not. A font is a specific applied instance of a typeface, style, and size. Times Roman is a typeface, for example, but Times Roman 12 point, oblique, is a font.

At its most basic, the `font-family` style enables you to specify one of a variety of different typeface families:

- `serif`
- `sans-serif`
- `monospace`
- `cursive`
- `fantasy`

The most commonly used font families on the Web are `serif` (typically Times Roman or Times) and `monospace` (typically Courier). Times Roman is the default typeface used by Web browsers, and Courier is used to show code listings and form input fields.

The `font-family` style enables you to specify a typeface by name, or even indicate a list of typefaces separated by commas, exactly as the `face` attribute of the `font` tag does in plain HTML.

Here's how you might use the `font-family` style in practice (with some additional styles thrown in for fun):

```
<style type="text/css">
b { color: blue; font-style: italic; }
i { color: green; font-family: Monotype Corsiva,cursive;
    font-style: normal; }
tt { font-family: serif; background-color: yellow; }
.mytt { color: red; font-family: monospace; font-weight: bold; }
</style>
</head><body>

<div>
This is <b>a bit of bold text</b>, with a little <i>content
displayed in italics</i>
tossed in for luck, and a <tt>monospace</tt> passage too, which
should be compared to
<span class="mytt">this tt 'emulation' passage</span>!
</div>
```

All these changes are displayed in Figure 4-5.

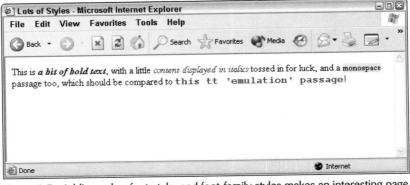

Figure 4-5: Adding color, font-style, and font-family styles makes an interesting page.

In the code shown for Figure 4-5, notice especially that you can redefine the browser's default rendering of HTML tags by redefining their style within CSS. In this case, I effectively removed the monospace typeface change from the `<tt>` tag. However, if you have sharp eyes, you can see that the resulting serif content (the word *monospace*) is slightly smaller than the surrounding text because the Times Roman typeface is naturally smaller than Courier. In addition, we've set the background to yellow too. The size change you can fix with the `font-size` style, as you will see momentarily.

Changing font size

As I've shown you in some of the earlier examples in this chapter, you use the CSS font-size style to change the size of text. This style accepts specific sizes in a variety of units (see Table 4-1) or the following specific named values:

- xx-small
- x-small
- small
- medium
- large
- x-large
- xx-large

and two relative sizes:

- smaller
- larger

Finally, you can also specify a font size by percentage: A specification of font-size: 110% means that it's 10% larger than the text would otherwise be displayed. If the 110% appears within an h1 passage, for example, it produces a larger end result than if it's in a p or div block.

Table 4-1: CSS Size Specifications

Measure	Definition	Comment
In	inches	A measurement that can prove problematic with layout, although people commonly use it. To understand why, try to figure out what 1in becomes if you're simultaneously looking at a page on a computer monitor and projecting it on a screen through an LCD projector.
cm	centimeter	The same problem as with inches; of course, a different measurement.
mm	millimeter	Same problem as with inches.
pt	points	A traditional typographic unit. There are 72 points to an inch. You see these measurements a lot because that's the mystery value whenever you talk about a typeface as 18 point (which you describe in CSS as 18pt). For display use, this measure poses the same problem as the preceding measurements.

Continued

Table 4-1: *Continued*

Measure	Definition	Comment
pc	Pica	Another traditional typographic unit of measure: 1 pica = 12 points = 1/6 inch, or 6 picas = 1 inch. Presents the same problem as the other physical-unit measurements.
em	em-width	This measure is relative to the size of the current typeface in use; it's the width of the letter *m* in the specific typeface.
px	Pixel	The size of a specific dot of information on-screen, this measure works great for screen displays, but you must redefine it for printers to avoid startling and unexpected results. Consider that a typical screen is 72–75 dpi, so each pixel is 1/72nd of an inch. On a typical modern printer, however, output renders at 300–600 dpi, so each pixel is 1/300th of an inch or smaller. Most browsers sidestep this by multiplying out the difference, so 10px is actually 40px for printing.

These give you a lot of different ways you can specify the type size. I would say that at least 99% of the time, I just use percentage specifications and ignore all these other possibilities. To jump back to my attempt to emulate the `<tt>` tag earlier, here's a better definition:

```
.mytt { color: red; font-family: monospace; font-weight: bold;
    font-size: 90%; }
```

Well, this isn't a complete emulation, of course, because I've specified the content should be red and in bold too, but the monospace type is now displayed at 90% of the size of the regular text on the page. Better yet, it's true regardless of what size type I'm working in:

```
<h2>This is <span class="mytt">my big tt</span> and</h2>
This is smaller <span class="mytt">my tt</span> text.
```

The color of text

Surprisingly, you don't change the color of text with a style called font-color. Given that every other style modification is done with font-*something*, it took me a while to remember that color is changed by simply using the attribute `color:`. Throughout this chapter, I have shown many examples of color specifications, but they've all been specific by color name. In fact, there are a bunch of ways you can specify a color within CSS, some of which are explained in more detail in Chapter 7 and all of which are listed in Table 4-2.

Table 4.2: Color Specification Options in CSS

Specifier	Example	Comment
#RRGGBB	#009900	This notation is the color specification that you've been using for a long time if you're an HTML coder. It's a two-hexadecimal–digit red, green, and blue value, where 00 is the least of a color and FF is the most. It offers more than 16 million possible colors and is explored in detail in Chapter 7.
#RGB	#090	A useful variant on the regular #RRGGBB scheme, this specification duplicates each of the values to create a six-digit color. The #090 value, therefore, is identical to #009900. It offers more than 4,000 different possible colors, although if you stick with the so-called Internet safe color palette (explained in Chapter 7) you need only 216 colors (the values of #0, #3, #6, #9, #C and #F for each of red, green and blue).
rgb(r%,g%,b%)	rgb(0%,100%,50%)	An unusual notation, in which you specify integer color values for each red, green, and blue component. It offers exactly one million possible colors.
rgb(rr,gg,bb)	rgb(128,0,128)	Similar to the previous notation, this specification enables you to use integer color values, but the value can range from 0–255. If you do the decimal to hexadecimal math, you find that the two-digit hex notation #RRGGBB offers exactly the same number of choices, just in a different way. It offers more than 16 million possible colors.
colorname	Blue	The CSS standard defines 16 colors by name, and they're the 16 colors of the original Windows VGA palette: aqua, black, blue, fuchsia, gray, green, lime, maroon, navy, olive, purple, red, silver, teal, white, and yellow. Some browsers can recognize more color names, but the specification includes only these 16.

Additional Neato Text Tricks in CSS

Before I wrap up the discussion of text transformations in CSS, take a peek at a number of additional styles that are available to change how the text on your Web page appears—transformations that aren't possible in regular HTML.

Small capitals

One of the most interesting styles accessible in CSS is the capability to specify a font-variant that has every letter capitalized, with the letters that were already capitalized slightly larger than the lowercase letters capitalized by the variant. Here's a typical usage:

```
<style type="text/css">
.smallcap { font-variant: small-caps; }
</style>
</head><body>

<h1>This is a Level One Header</h1>
<h1 class="smallcap">This is also a Level One Header</h1>
```

The CSS specification defines a number of possible font variants, but so far Web browser developers seem to have implemented only small-caps. The other possible value, to shut off small-caps, is normal.

Stretching or squishing letter spacing

Another interesting variation in font layout is the letter-spacing style, which enables you to expand or compress type by a specified per-letter value—even if it causes letters to overlap! Adjusting this space between letters is known as *kerning* in typographical circles. Here's an example:

```
<h1 style="letter-spacing: -2px;">And Another Level One Header</h1>
```

Figure 4-6 shows small-caps and letter-spacing all on the same page.

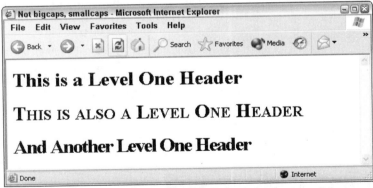

Figure 4-6: Small caps and letter spacing offer interesting type variations.

You can use any of the units specified in Table 4-1 in the letter-spacing style. In this example, I'm indicating that each letter should have two pixels *less* space for width than normal, effectively compressing the text just a bit.

Stretching or squishing words

If you don't want to have the spacing between letters adjusted, but you still want some control over the overall width of a text passage, word-spacing might be just what you need. Consider the following example:

```
.wide { word-spacing: 15px; font-weight: bold; }
.narrow { word-spacing: -3px; font-weight: bold; }
```

Be careful with these values, especially if you're trying to compress the text! A little change can quickly produce unreadable text, and just a bit more can cause words to overlap.

Changing line height

The height between the lines of text in a paragraph is known as *leading*. You probably remember having to write double-spaced papers in school. Double-spaced, in CSS terms, is line-height: 2. Unusual in a CSS style, line-height doesn't need a unit (unless you want to refer to percentages, inches, pixels, points, and so on) and accepts fractional values, too. So to get a line-height half way between single-spaced and double-spaced, use line-height: 1.5, as shown:

```
.doublespaced { line-height: 1.5; }
```

Putting it all together, here's an example of line-height and word-spacing:

```
<style type="text/css">
.wide { word-spacing: 15px; font-weight: bold; }
.narrow { word-spacing: -3px; font-weight: bold; }
.doublespaced { line-height: 1.5; }
</style>
</head><body>

<div class="doublespaced">
This is a paragraph of text that's double-spaced. This means
that the <i>leading</i>, or interline spacing, is different
from standard text layout on a Web page. Within this
paragraph, I can also have
<span class="wide">some words that are widely spaced due to
the word-spacing value</span> and, of course,
<span class="narrow">some words that are narrowly spaced,</span>
too.
</div>
<p>
By comparison, this paragraph doesn't have any special line-height
specified, so it's "single spaced." Notice the difference in the
space between lines of text.
</p>
```

The effects of both word and line spacing are shown in Figure 4-7.

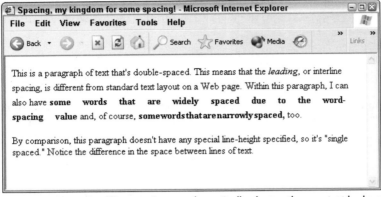

Figure 4-7: Word and line spacing can dramatically change the way text looks on a page.

Not all possible settings are good, of course. A line height that's too small results in the lines of text becoming illegible as they're overlapped. The single addition of line-height: 1.25, however, can significantly improve the appearance of a page, and you can increase line height for the entire document by changing the style of the body tag. Adding the following code to the top <style> block changes all the text on the page:

```
body { line-height: 1.25 }
```

Cool, eh? I tweak the body container again and again as I proceed. It's *very* useful!

Text alignment

HTML includes some attributes for the <p> tag that let you specify if you want the text to be left, center, or right aligned, or justified, where both the left and right margins are aligned. These attributes are replaced in CSS with the text-align style, which has the following possible values:

- left
- right
- center
- justify

Vertical text alignment

Here's one feature that you don't see in HTML except in the exceptionally awkward form of <sup> and <sub> for superscripts and subscripts, respectively. Instead, use vertical-align and pick one of the values shown in Table 4-3.

Table 4.3: CSS Vertical Alignment Values

Value	Explanation
top	Specifies that top of element aligns with top of highest element in line
middle	Specifies that middle of element aligns with middle of line
bottom	Specifies that bottom of element aligns with bottom of lowest element in line
text-top	Specifies that top of element aligns with top of highest text element in line
text-bottom	Specifies that bottom of element aligns with bottom of lowest text element in line
super	Indicates superscript
sub	Indicates subscript

A nice demonstration of this capability is a technique for having trademark (^{tm}) character sequences displayed attractively on a page:

```
.tm { vertical-align: top; font-size: 33%; font-weight: bold; }
```

In use, this might appear as

```
Though just about lost to common parlance, it remains the case that
Xerox<span class="tm">tm</span> is a trademark of Xerox Corporation.
```

Text decorations

One HTML text decoration that, surprisingly, made it to CSS is underlining. As discussed in Chapter 3, underlining text on a Web page is somewhat problematic because it can become quite difficult to differentiate links from underlined text. But the CSS text-decoration style enables more than just underlining. It provides the following four values:

- underline
- overline
- line-through
- blink

With the exception of overline, these all have HTML equivalents: <u> for underline, <strike> for line-through, and <blink> for blink. In CSS, however, it's much easier to apply a number of them simultaneously, like this:

```
h1 { text-decoration: overline underline; }
```

By using the underlining styles, you can rather dramatically change the appearance of headers throughout a document.

Changing text case

This is the last new CSS style for this chapter, I promise. I know that this chapter must seem like quite a monster with all this thrown at you at once! That's why it's incredibly important that you *try things on your computer as you read about them*. If you just sip your latté while you go through this book, your retention is likely to be minimal. But if you're trying each and every style and example on your computer, you'll have lots of "a ha!" moments, and you should start to see the tremendous value of CSS for even the most rudimentary pages.

on the web Don't forget, all the code listings are available on the book Web site at
`http://www.intuitive.com/coolsites/`.

The final style to learn in this chapter, `text-transform`, deals with the capitalization of text and has the values specified in Table 4-4.

Table 4-4: Text Transformation Values

Value	Meaning
`capitalize`	Displays the first letter of each word as caps and all others as lowercase
`uppercase`	Displays all letters as uppercase
`lowercase`	Displays all letters as lowercase
`none`	Displays characters as specified

To have a paragraph of text transformed into all uppercase, for example, use `text-transform: uppercase;`, and to instantly ensure that all header level ones are in proper case, use:

```
h1 { text-transform: capitalize; }
```

Putting it all together

Let's pull the example from the end of the last chapter and see how using CSS can help jazz up the presentation. Here's what I've produced with just a little CSS tweaking (notice that I always include a font-family default value, too):

```
<style type="text/css">
body { font-family: Arial,Helvetica,sans-serif; font-size:90%;
    line-height: 1.25; }
h1  { text-transform: capitalize; text-decoration: overline
    underline; color: blue; letter-spacing: 0.05em; text-align: center; }
i   { font-variant: small-caps; font-weight: bold; }
.email { color: #909; font-family: monospace; font-size: 90% }
.tm { vertical-align: top; font-size: 40%; font-weight: bold; }
</style>
</head><body>
```

```
<h1>Travels with Tintin</h1>
<p>
Of the various reporters with whom I've travelled around
the world, including writers for <i>UPI</i>, <i>AP</i>,
and <i>Reuters</i>, the most fascinating has clearly been
<b>Tintin</b>, boy reporter from Belgium (
<span class="email">tintin@intuitive.com</span>).
</p><div style="text-align:right">
Probably the most enjoyable aspect of our travels was his
dog <b>Snowy</b>, though I don't know that our hosts would
always agree!
</div>
<h1>The First Trip: Nepal</h1>
<p>
After winning the Pulitzer for <i>Red Rackham's Treasure</i>
<span class="tm">tm</span>,
Tintin told me he wanted a vacation. Remembering some of his
earlier adventures, he decided to visit Nepal. Early one
Sunday, I was sipping my tea and reading the <i>Times</i>
when he rang me up, asking whether I'd be able to take a
break and come along...
</p>
```

Check out the attractive result in Figure 4-8. Make sure you compare this figure to Figure 3-8 from the previous chapter to see how much more capability you've gained by moving to CSS.

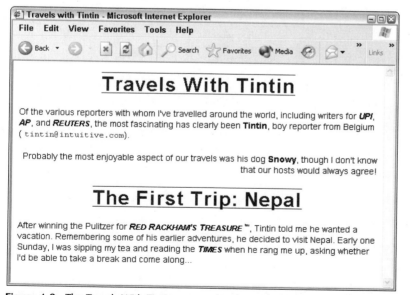

Figure 4-8: The Travels With Tintin screen shot from Chapter 3 has been enhanced with the CSS styles presented throughout this chapter.

tip One CSS shortcut that I haven't mentioned here is the `font:` style itself. Many of the individual font-related styles can be combined into a single `font:` style, saving you a lot of work. For example, the following two code lines are functionally equivalent:

```
h1 { font-weight: bold; font-size: 22pt;
```

```
    line-height: 30pt; font-family: Courier, monospace; }
h1 { font: bold 22pt/30pt Courier, monospace }
```

Well worth learning to save you typing!

Table 4-5: HTML Tags That Support CSS Covered in This Chapter

Tag	Closing Tag	Description
`<span`	`</span>`	Specifies a nonbreaking CSS container; used within sentences or headers to change individual words
`style=`		Provides specific CSS styles to apply to the `span`
`class=`		Identifies which CSS class should be applied to the `span`
`id=`		Identifies which CSS ID should be applied to the `span`
`<div`	`</div>`	Specifies a CSS container that acts identically to the `<p>` tag; forces a line break before and after
`style=`		Specifies CSS styles to apply to the `div`
`class=`		Identifies which CSS class should be applied to the `div`
`id=`		Identifies which CSS ID should be applied to the `div`
`<link`		References external CSS style sheet by name
`type=`		Specifies a type of external link; for CSS it should be `text/css`
`href=`		Indicates the URL of the style sheet; by convention, separate CSS style sheets are named with a `.css` filename suffix
`<style`	`</style>`	Specifies a block for CSS style definitions on Web page; should appear within the `<head></head>` block of the page
`type=`		Specifies the type of style sheet being used; for CSS always use `text/css`

Table 4-6: CSS Styles Covered in This Chapter

Style	Exemplary Usage	Description
font-weight	font-weight: bold	Specifies how much or how little to embolden a text passage
font-style	font-style: italic	Specifies whether to italicize, oblique, or leave the text passage non-italicized
font-family	font-family: serif	Specifies which typeface to use for the text passage, as a comma-separated list, or which font-family to use from a small predefined list
font-size	font-size: 80%	Specifies the type size of the text passage in one of a wide variety of different units and values
color	color: green	Specifies the text color in the text passage; can be color names or color values specified in a variety of ways
font-variant	font-variant: small-caps	Transforms the text passage based on the specified variation; only small-caps and none are defined
letter-spacing	letter-spacing: -3px	Changes the interletter spacing (also known as the *kerning*) to make it larger or smaller than the default
word-spacing	word-spacing: 15px	Increases or decreases the spacing between words in the text passage
line-height	line-height: 1.25	Changes the spacing between lines of text (also known as the *leading*); a variety of values are accepted, including fractional values such as 1.5 (for one and a half times normal spacing), 2 (for double spacing), and so on
text-align	text-align:center	Specifies alignment for a block of text
vertical-align	vertical-align: sub	Specifies vertical alignment of a text passage relative to other text on the line
text-decoration	text-decoration: underline	Specifies one or more of a variety of simple text decorations
text-transform	text-transform: capitalize	Specifies one of a number of text transformations involving upper- and lower-case letters
font	font: 22pt monospace	Indicates shorthand CSS notation that allows the specification of a number of different font characteristics

Summary

This chapter introduced you to the marvels of Cascading Style Sheets, showing you how a few simple changes to your HTML, such as bold, italics, underlining, text alignment, and text decorations and transformations, can result in dramatically improved Web page layout and text presentation. In the next chapter, you continue your exploration of both HTML and CSS by looking at lists and special characters.

Lists and Special Characters

chapter 5

In this chapter, I introduce you to various types of lists for Web pages, including ordered (numbered) and unordered (bulleted) lists. You learn how to change the appearance of lists using both HTML attributes and CSS styles to make them exactly what you want. I also explain how to add special and non-English characters and comments to your Web documents. You have probably noticed lots of lists on the Web. After you read this chapter, you will know how to use the different list styles to your advantage as you create your own Web pages.

Definition Lists

One of the most common elements of multipage documents is a set of definitions, references, or cross-indexes. Glossaries are classic examples; words are listed alphabetically, followed by prose definitions. In HTML, the entire glossary section is contained by a *definition list*, which is contained within a pair of *definition list tags*: `<dl>` and `</dl>`. Within the pair of listings, a definition has two parts:

- Definition term (`<dt>` and `</dt>`)
- Definition description (`<d>` and `</dd>`)

Here's how you can use a definition list in HTML to define some genetics terms:

```
<html>
<head>
<title>Miscellaneous Genetic Terms</title>
<body>
<h1>A Quick Glossary of Genetic Terms</h1>
<i>Adapted from Dawkins, The Extended Phenotype</i>
<dl>
<dt>allometry</dt>
<dd>A disproportionate relationship between size of a body
part and size of the whole body.</dd>
<dt>anaphase</dt>
<dd>Phase of the cell division during which the paired
chromosomes move apart.</dd>
<dt>antigens</dt>
<dd>Foreign bodies, usually protein molecules, which provoke the
formation of antibodies.</dd>
<dt>autosome</dt>
<dd>A chromosome that is not one of the sex chromosomes.</dd>
<dt>codon</dt>
<dd>A triplet of units (nucleotides) in the genetic code, specifying
the synthesis of a single unit (amino acid) in a protein chain.</dd>
<dt>genome</dt>
<dd>The entire collection of genes possessed by one organism.</dd>
</dl>
</body>
</html>
```

Figure 5-1 shows the result of the preceding HTML code in a Web browser. Notice the automatic indentation and formatting.

If you're writing a book about herbal remedies, for example, you may want to have a cross-reference of herbs for specific problems. Perhaps you want the ailment in bold and certain key herbs in italics for emphasis. The following example shows how you might want such a listing to look:

Blood Pressure

   Balm, Black Haw, *Garlic*, Hawthorn.

Bronchitis

   Angelica, *Aniseed*, *Caraway*, Grindelia.

Burns

   Aloe, Chickweed, *Elder*.

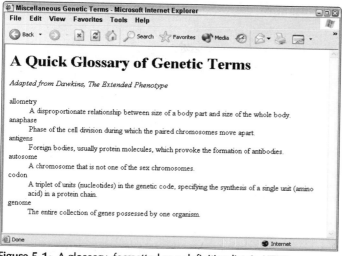

Figure 5-1: A glossary, formatted as a definition list, in HTML.

Obtaining this format within an HTML document requires the following tag placements:

```
<dl>
<dt><b>Blood Pressure</b></dt>
<dd>Balm, Black Haw, <i>Garlic</i>, Hawthorn.</dd>
<dt><b>Bronchitis</b></dt>
<dd>Angelica, <i>Aniseed, Caraway</i>, Grindelia.</dd>
<dt><b>Burns</b></dt>
<dd>Aloe, Chickweed, <i>Elder</i>.</dd>
</dt>
```

Figure 5-2 shows the result, which is, if I do say so myself, quite attractive and similar to the original design.

x-ref By now, I hope that you can read the preceding HTML snippet and understand all the paired formatting tags. If not, you might want to skip back to Chapters 3 and 4 and study it a bit more to refresh your memory on text-style formatting.

There's a smarter way to accomplish some of the formatting in this last definition list: Use a CSS style modification that makes all <dt> tags appear in bold text. It looks like the following in the <style> block:

```
dd { font-weight: bold; }
```

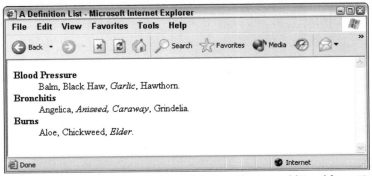

Figure 5-2: A definition list of medicinal herbs with some additional formatting.

With this style modification in place, you can simplify the previous HTML and also make it more manageable:

```
<style type="text/css">
dt { font-weight: bold; }
</style>
<body>
<dl>
<dt>Blood Pressure</dt>
<dd>Balm, Black Haw, <i>Garlic</i>, Hawthorn.</dd>
<dt>Bronchitis</dt>
<dd>Angelica, <i>Aniseed, Caraway</i>, Grindelia.</dd>
<dt>Burns</dt>
<dd>Aloe, Chickweed, <i>Elder</i>.</dd>
</dl>
```

The results are completely identical to Figure 5-2. By using CSS, however, you can further modify the presentation, including presenting the terms in a slightly larger font (font-size: 125%) or even a different color (color:green).

Good list, bad list

The basic concept of a list is exhibited in the definition-list format: a pair of tags within which other tags have special meanings. Tags such as <dt> and <dd> are *context-sensitive tags*: They have meaning only if they appear within the <dl> </dl> pair.

What happens if you use <dt> and <dd> without wrapping them in a <dl> </dl> pair? Sometimes, the result is identical to Figure 5-2: The default meanings of the dt and dd tags are consistent in the Web browser, whether they appear within a list or not. In other browsers, they are ignored. Later in this chapter, you learn about a different context-sensitive tag that definitely does the wrong thing if you don't ensure that it's wrapped within its list-definition tags.

To avoid lucky defaults that aren't consistent across all browsers, always check your HTML formatting in multiple Web browsers before concluding that the formatting is correct. This can trip up even experienced Web page designers: My friend Linda has been developing some new pages for an existing Web site and she asked me to have a peek. I responded that it looked great, but was surprised she had left the default gray background (I show you how to change the page background color in Chapter 7). She was surprised by that; she'd forgotten that her particular Web browser used white, not gray, as the default background page color!

Unordered (Bulleted) Lists

Definition lists are handy, but the type of list that you see much more often on the World Wide Web is a bulleted list, also called an *unordered* list. Unordered lists start with <ul> and close with </ul>, and <li> denotes each list item.

The format is similar to that of the definition list, as the following example shows:

```
Common Herbal remedies include:
<ul>
<li>Blood Pressure -- Balm, Black Haw, <i>Garlic</i>, Hawthorn. </li>
<li>Bronchitis -- Angelica, <i>Aniseed, Caraway</i>, Grindelia. </li>
<li>Burns -- Aloe, Chickweed, <i>Elder</i>. </li>
</ul>
```

Although many people are lazy regarding use of the closing </li> tag, it is required if you want your pages to be XHTML compliant, as discussed in Chapter 2. It's also a good habit to form.

The result as viewed from a browser is attractive, as you can see in Figure 5-3.

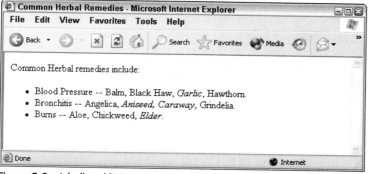

Figure 5-3: A bulleted list.

A combination of the two list types (unordered and definition) is often useful. The definition list looks very professional with the addition of a few style tweaks, and the bullets next to each item in the unordered list look slick, too. The solution is to nest lists within one another, as follows:

```
<style type="text/css">
dt { font-weight: bold; margin-top: 10px; margin-left: 1em; }
li { font-size: 80%; }
</style>
<body>
Common herbal remedies include:
<dl>
<dt>Blood Pressure</dt>
<dd><ul>
   <li>Balm</li>
   <li>Black Haw </li>
   <li><i>Garlic</i></li>
   <li>Hawthorn</li>
</ul></dd>
<dt>Bronchitis</dt>
<dd><ul>
   <li>Angelica</li>
   <li><i>Aniseed</li>
   <li>Caraway</i></li>
   <li>Grindelia</li>
</ul></dd>
<dt>Burns</dt>
<dd><ul>
   <li>Aloe</li>
   <li>Chickweed</li>
   <li><i>Elder</i></li>
</ul></dd>
</dl>
```

Figure 5-4 shows the nice result of the preceding code.

note Notice that I used some indentation on the HTML source code in the previous listing to make it clearer which lists were subordinate to which and to make the source more readable. That manual indentation is ignored when the page is rendered and displayed in the browser, but it's a convenient organizational tool and also helps find possible errors in the code.

Notice (in the listing that follows) that I use some fairly sophisticated CSS styles to achieve the desired screen display.

```
dt { font-weight: bold; margin-top: 10px; margin-left: 1em; }
li { font-size: 80%; }
```

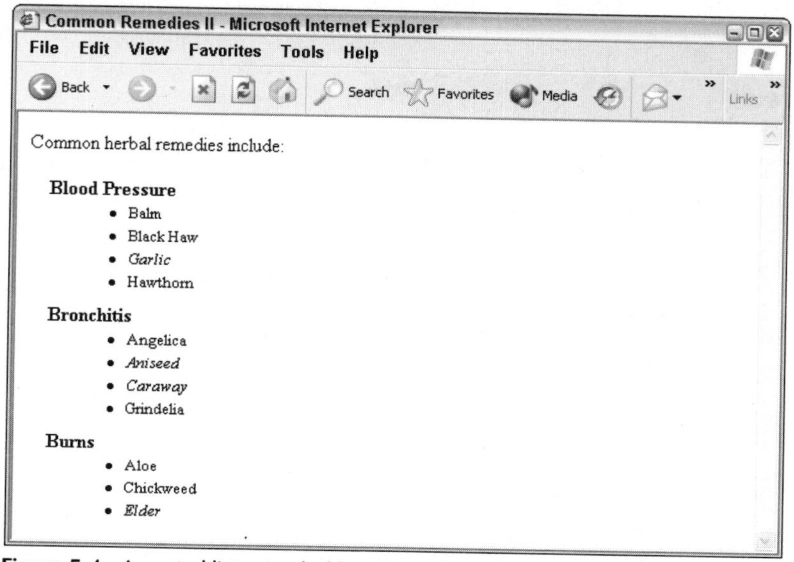

Figure 5-4: A nested list using bold, indenting, and varied font sizes.

The first statement redefines all definition terms to be in bold, with a 10-pixel space above and one em-width to the left. (I discuss margin styles in Chapter 13.) The second statement reduces all list item entries to 80% of the standard typeface size on the page. The results are attractive, and it's a nice demonstration of how HTML and CSS can work together to make this kind of result not only possible, but easy too!

Ordered (Numbered) Lists

What if you want to create a list, but with numbers instead of bullet points? The adage "simpler is better" suggests the formatting in the following example:

```
<html>
<head>
<title>Enchilada Recipe, v1</title>
</head><body>
<h2>Enchilada Sauce</h2>
    1. Heat a large saucepan and saute the following ingredients until soft:
    <ul>
    <li>Two tablespoons virgin olive oil </li>
    <li>Large onion, chopped </li>
    </ul>
    2. Add a quart of water.<br />
    3. Sprinkle in a quarter-cup of flour.<br />
```

Continued

```
Continued
    4. Jazz it up by adding:
    <ul>
    <li>Two tablespoons chili powder </li>
    <li>Two teaspoons cumin </li>
    <li>One teaspoon garlic powder </li>
    </ul>
    5. Finally, add a teaspoon of salt, if desired.
    <br /><br />
    Whisk as sauce thickens; then simmer for 20 minutes.
    </body>
    </html>
```

The result is reasonably nice, as shown in Figure 5-5.

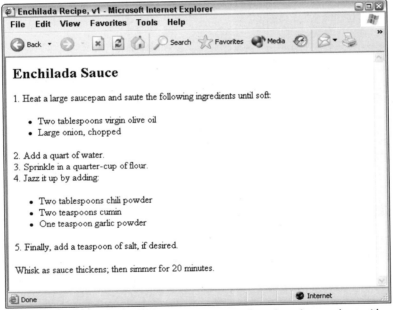

Figure 5-5: An example showing manually inserted numbered steps along with unordered lists.

Before you carry this book into the kitchen, however, I need to tell you that I got confused while I typed this recipe. The water should be added at the end, not in Step 2.

Now what? You certainly don't want to renumber all the items in the numbered list. The situation calls for the cousin of the unordered list: the ordered list <ol>. The list ends with the close tag </ol>. Each item in the list has a list item tag <li>.

Now you can see what I was talking about earlier with context-sensitive tags: You specify the list items for an ordered list using exactly the same HTML tag as you do for an unordered, bulleted list: `<li>`. Without specifying which type of list you want, how does the browser know what you mean? The meaning of the `<li>` tag depends on what kind of list it lies within.

Following is how the recipe itself looks with my gaffe corrected and the HTML rewritten to take advantage of the ordered list style:

```
<ol>
<li>Heat a large saucepan, and saute the following ingredients until soft:
<ul>
<li>Two tablespoons virgin olive oil </li>
<li>Large onion, chopped </li>
</ul>
<li>Sprinkle in a quarter-cup of flour. </li>
<li>Jazz it up by adding:
<ul>
<li>Two tablespoons chili powder </li>
<li>Two teaspoons cumin </li>
<li>One teaspoon garlic powder </li>
</ul> </li>
<li>Add a quart of water. </li>
<li>Finally, add a teaspoon of salt, if desired. </li>
</ol>
Whisk as sauce thickens; then simmer for 20 minutes.
```

The output (see Figure 5-6) not only produces a better enchilada sauce, but it is considerably more attractive because Web browsers automatically indent lists of this nature. As a result, the nested-list items are indented twice: once because they're part of the numbered list, and a second time because they're the list-within-the-list.

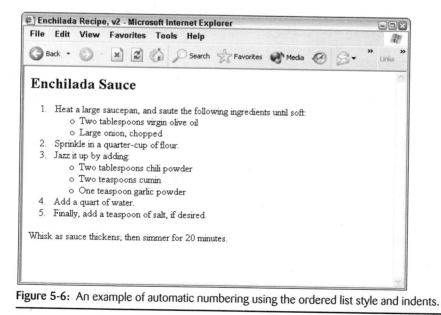

Figure 5-6: An example of automatic numbering using the ordered list style and indents.

note   A final note on lists: There are a number of additional HTML tags from the early days of Web design that are supposed to offer further list-formatting capabilities, most notably `<dir>` and `<menu>`. Unfortunately, these styles were never widely implemented and are explicitly phased out in the HTML 4.0 specification.

List Formats

You've already learned how to modify HTML in a variety of ways, from using simple formatting tags such as `<b>` and `<i>`, to more sophisticated changes using CSS styles. Some changes, however, aren't so simple.

Standard ordered-list HTML tags specify that you have an ordered list and display the list items with incremental numeric values—1, 2, 3, and so on. If you want to create a multilevel outline or other multilevel list, or if you want to have an alternative numbering system, the capability to specify different notations for the different levels is quite useful. You might want A to Z for the highest level, numbers for the second level, and a to z for the lowest level. That format is, of course, the typical outline format taught in English class, and an example of it looks like the following:

A. Introduction

   1. Title

      a. Author

      b. Institution

      c. Working title (20 words or fewer)

   2. Justification for research

      a. What? Why?

   3. Findings

   4. Conclusions

B. Body of Paper

   1. Previous research

   2. Research methods used

   3. Results and findings

C. Conclusion

   1. Implications

   2. Directions for future research

D. References

If you want to reproduce the preceding example on a Web page, you could accomplish it by using three levels of numbered-list items, many bullet points, or no indentation at all. None of these options is what you want, and that's where the enhanced ordered-list extensions come in handy.

Ordered lists have two extensions: `type`, which specifies the numeric counter style to use; and `start`, which begins the count at the value you specify, rather than at one.

You can use any of five different types of counting values:

- `<type="A">` is uppercase alphabetic (A, B, C, D).
- `<type="a">` is lowercase alphabetic (a, b, c, d).
- `<type="I">` is uppercase Roman numerals (I, II, III, IV).
- `<type="i">` is lowercase Roman numerals (i, ii, iii, iv).
- `<type="1">` (the default) is Arabic numerals (1, 2, 3, 4).

To have an ordered list count with Roman numerals, in uppercase, and start with item 4, you would use `<ol type="I" start="4">`. The default for a list is `<ol type="1" start="1">`. (Because it's the default, you don't have to include it. But if you *do* include it, nothing will break. It's up to you.)

Here's how you produce the previous outline as a Web page:

```
<ol type="A">
<li>Introduction
   <ol>
     <li>Title
     <ol type="a">
       <li>Author</li>
       <li>Institution </li>
       <li>Working title (20 words or fewer) </li>
     </ol> </li>
     <li>Justification for research
     <ol type="a">
       <li>What? Why? </li>
     </ol> </li>
```

Continued

```
Continued
      <li>Findings </li>
      <li>Conclusions </li>
    </ol> </li>
<li>Body of Paper
  <ol>
      <li>Previous research </li>
      <li>Research methods used </li>
      <li>Results and findings </li>
  </ol> </li>
<li>Conclusion
  <ol>
      <li>Implications </li>
      <li>Directions for future research </li>
  </ol> </li>
<li>References </li>
</ol>
```

This outline displays correctly in a Web browser, as you can see in Figure 5-7.

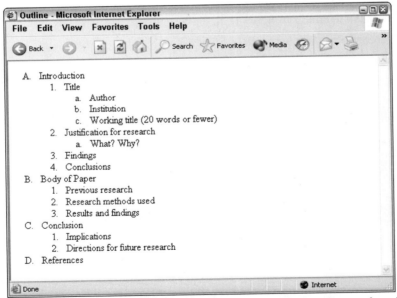

Figure 5-7: An outline using special <ol> attributes to display varied types of numbers and letters.

Bullet shapes

If you're experimenting with list styles as you read along—and I hope you are—you may have found that different levels of unordered lists produce differently shaped bullets. In fact, Web browsers support three types of bullets—a solid disc, a circle, and a square—and you can choose which bullet to use for your unordered list by specifying a `type` attribute. For example, if you want a list in which every item is bulleted with a square, `<ul type="square">` does the trick.

The following example shows how you can use these various bullet types in a Web document. Notice, also, that within the `<li>` tag, you can change the bullet shape for that specific list item by specifying `type="shape"`. You can also change the start count for an ordered list by specifying `start="value"`. In the following example, the ordered list ends before the `<div>` text. I used `<li value=3>` to restart it at 3.

```
<h3>Geometric Ramblings</h3>
<ol type="i">
<li>Facets of a Square:
<ul type="square">
<li>four sides of equal length </li>
</ul> </li>
<li>Interesting Facts about Circles:
<ul type="disc">
<li>maximum enclosed area, shortest line </li>
</ul> </li>
</ol>
<div style="text-align:center; background-color:yellow;">
Weird, unrelated information.
</div>
<ol type="i">
<li value="3"> and much, much more! </li>
</ol>
```

Figure 5-8 shows the preceding HTML text in a Web browser. Notice that the numbered list seems to flow without any interruption, something that would be impossible to accomplish without adding a subsequent `value` attribute to the ordered list.

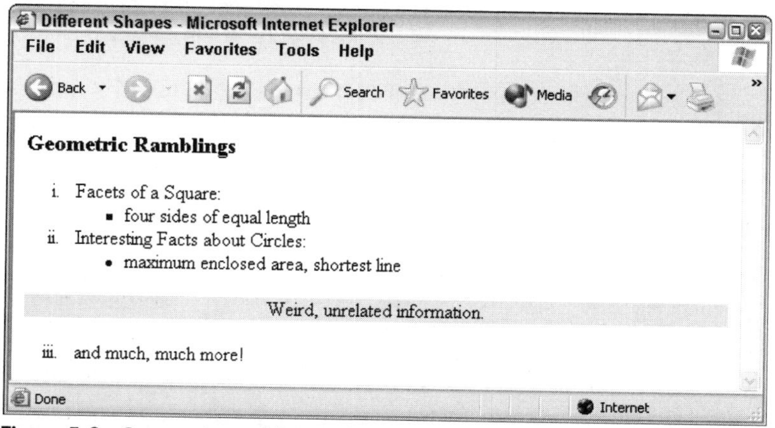

Figure 5-8: Geometric ramblings—showing off various ways you can fine-tune the presentation of list elements.

CSS control over lists

You can employ the strategies just discussed in the preceding section to fine-tune the list styles in CSS. This means that you can apply them *en masse* across all lists on a page in a style block! For example, to have all bullets on all bulleted lists, regardless of indentation level, be solid discs, use this code:

```
ul { list-style-type: disc; }
```

The entire range of possible values for `list-style-type` are as follows:

- disc
- circle
- square

Much more exciting, however, is that with CSS you can *define your own bullet!* Way cool!! Here's the solution:

```
ul { list-style-image: url(diamond.gif) }
```

This specifies that the graphic file `diamond.gif` (it can be a fully-qualified URL starting with `http://` and pointing to any server on the Web, if needed) should replace the standard bullet element.

tip   Although CSS supports relative URLs as shown here, many CSS experts recommend that you fully qualify every reference, that is, make sure it always starts with the `http://` sequence.

You can also control the exact position of the bullet within the list, all with CSS (I told you, CSS is remarkably powerful!) by using the attribute `list-style-position`. It has two possible values: `inside` or `outside`. The following code demonstrates how they differ:

```
<ul style="list-style-image: url(diamond.gif);line-height:1.5;">
<li>
"Good-night, Mister Sherlock Holmes."</li>
<li style="list-style-position: inside;">
There were several people on the pavement at the time,
but the greeting appeared to come from a slim youth
in an ulster who had hurried by.</li>
<li style="list-style-position: outside;">
"I've heard that voice before," said Holmes, staring
down the dimly lit street. "Now, I wonder who the
deuce that could have been."</li>
</ul>
```

Figure 5-9 shows the result. What a nice capability!

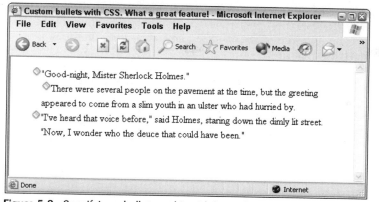

Figure 5-9: Specifying a bullet graphic with list-style-image.

Counting the CSS way

In addition to supporting the five basic ordered list numbering schemes shown earlier in this chapter, the CSS style list-style-type, when used in an ordered list, has a completely overwhelming number of possibilities, as shown in Table 5-1.

Table 5-1: The Many, Many Possible Values of list-style-type

Name	Explanation	Implemented?
decimal	The default: 1, 2, 3, . . .	☺
decimal-leading-zero	The same as decimal, but with leading zeroes: 01, 02, . . .	☹
lower-roman	Lowercase roman numerals: i, ii, iii, iv, v, vi, . . .	☺
upper-roman	Uppercase roman numerals: I, II, III, IV, V, VI, . . .	☺
lower-greek	Counts using Greek letters: alpha, beta, gamma, delta, . . .	☹
lower-alpha	Lowercase alphabetic: a, b, c, d, e, . . .	☺
lower-latin	Lowercase alphabetic – identical to lower-alpha	☹
upper-alpha	Uppercase alphabetic: A, B, C, D, E, . . .	☺
upper-latin	Uppercase alphabetic–identical to upper-alpha	☹
hebrew	Counts using Hebrew numbering	☹
armenian	Counts using Armenian numbering	☹
georgian	Counts using Georgian numbering	☹
cjk-ideographic	Counts using ideographic numbers	☹
hiragana	Counts using Japanese *hiragana* system	☹
katakana	Counts using Japanese *katakana* system	☹
hiragana-iroha	Counts using Japanese *hiragana-iroha* system	☹
katakana-iroha	Counts using Japanese *katakana-iroha* system	☹

Based on the many possibilities, you can apparently have lots of fun with different counting options, but unfortunately, only a few of these values are implemented, as the table indicates. If you're expert with the HTML `type` attribute of the `<ol>` tag, you recognize all the implemented values; they're exactly the same as the implemented values for the `list-style-type` tag.

note

So why are so many elements in the CSS standard not implemented? Two reasons: First, even though CSS has been around for a long time, these different numbering systems are still on the cutting edge; second, most of the standards I've encountered contain elements that are never implemented. HTML 4.01 also has unimplemented elements; for example, some of the elements added to aid site navigation by disabled people are consistently ignored by browser developers.

List-style shortcuts

Just as you can use the `font:` attribute as a convenient shortcut for specifying a variety of font- and typeface-related style attributes, you can also use the `list-style` attribute to make fine-tuning the presentation of your lists a breeze.

I can best demonstrate this shorthand by showing you the following snippet:

```
ul { list-style: disc outside url(diamond.gif); }
```

This example is functionally identical to the following example:

```
ul { list-style: disc; list-style-position: outside;
     list-style-image: url(diamond.gif); }
```

Character Entities in HTML Documents

If you're an alert reader, you may have noticed a typographical error in the recipe shown earlier. The recipe instructed the cook to *saute* the ingredients, yet the word should have an accent (*sauté*). Languages contain a variety of special characters that you may need to use, called *diacriticals*, particularly if you plan to present material in a language other than English. Not surprisingly, you can include special characters in HTML code by using special tags called *entities* or *entity references*.

Unlike the tags you've learned about so far, special character entities aren't neatly tucked into paired angle brackets (< >); instead, they always begin with an ampersand (&) and end with a semicolon (;). Most entities are somewhat mnemonic, as Table 5-2 shows.

Table 5-2: Special Characters in HTML

Character	HTML Code	Meaning
&	&amp;	ampersand
<	&lt;	less than
>	&gt;	greater than
©	&copy;	copyright symbol
á	&aacute;	lowercase a with acute accent
à	&agrave;	lowercase a with grave accent
â	&acirc;	lowercase a with circumflex
ä	&auml;	lowercase a with umlaut
å	&aring;	lowercase a with ring
ç	&ccedil;	lowercase c with cedilla
ñ	&ntilde;	lowercase n with tilde
ø	&oslash;	lowercase o with slash
β	&szlig;	lowercase ess-zed symbol

caution Not all Web browsers can display all these characters, particularly on Windows systems. Check them on a few browsers before you use them in your own Web page layout.

To create an uppercase version of one of the characters in Table 5-2, make the first letter of the formatting tag uppercase. Ø, for example, produces an uppercase O with a slash through it, as in the word CØPENHAGEN (which you type as CØPENHAGEN). To produce a different vowel with a diacritical mark, change the first letter of that tag. The word *desvàn*, for example, is correctly specified in an HTML document as desvàn.

The following example contains some foreign language snippets so that you can see how these formatting tags work:

```
<style type="text/css">
dt { font-weight: bold; font-size: 110%; margin: 5px }
</style>
<body>
The following demonstrate the various uses of
character entities in working with non-English
languages on Web pages.
<dl>
<dt>Gibt es ein Caf&eacute; in der N&auml;he? </dt>
```

Continued

```
Continued
<dd>Is there a caf&eacute; nearby?</dd>
<P>
<dt>Je voudrais un d&icirc;ner. </dt>
<dd>I want to eat dinner.</dd>
<P>
<dt>Y una mesa por ma&ntilde;ana, por favor.</dt>
<dd>And a table for tomorrow, please.</dd>
<P>
<dt>Oh! C'&egrave; una specialit&agrave; locale?</dt>
<dd>Oh! Is there a local speciality?</dd>
</dl>
```

I don't actually speak German, French, Spanish, or Italian particularly well, but I guarantee the preceding set of questions will confuse just about any waiter in Europe! Figure 5-10 shows the result of the preceding formatting.

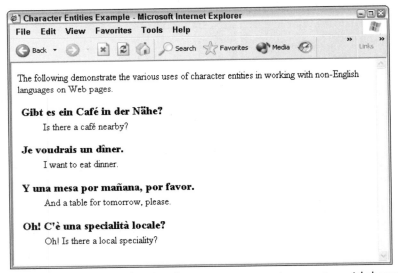

Figure 5-10: Examples of entity references you can use to present special characters on your Web pages.

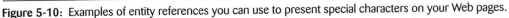

Some problems occur with the international characters supported in the basic HTML code, not the least of these being that some elements are missing. This situation is improving; you no longer have to do without the upside-down question mark (¿), for example, if you want to write in Spanish. Use ¿ to get this character in your documents. If you want to denote currency, you can code the pound sterling (£) and the cent sign (¢) as £ and ¢, respectively. If you need to acknowledge copyrights, most Web browsers display the copyright symbol (©) and the registered trademark symbol (®) with © and ®.

Nonbreaking Spaces

A special character entity that people frequently use in Web page design is one that isn't even a character and doesn't even show up on the screen: the nonbreaking space. Included as , it lets you force multiple spaces between items and ensures that items on either side of the space are always adjacent regardless of how the window may be sized.

Here's a typical scenario: You're working with a Web page on which you want to have a word set off by a number of spaces on each side. Your first attempt might be something like the following:

```
words before          important          words after.
```

But that won't work: The browser ignores the extra spaces. A better way to specify the spacing you want is like this:

```
words before     important     words
after.
```

This accomplishes exactly what you want to present.

on the web I've made a copy of the entire entity reference list included in the HTML 4.0 specification. You can view it at http://www.intuitive.com/coolsites/entities.html.

Comments within HTML Code

If you've spent any time working with complex markup languages, such as HTML, you know that the capability to include tracking information and other comments can help you organize and remember your coding approach when you return to the pages later.

Fortunately, HTML supports a specific (if peculiar) notational format for comments within your documents. Any text surrounded by the elements <!– and –> is considered to be a comment and is ignored by Web browsers, as shown in the following example:

```
<html>
<!- Last modified: 2 January 2004 ->
<title>Enchilada Sauce</title>
<!- inspired by an old recipe I heard in Mexico,
but I must admit that it's going to be very
different. Even the flour is subtly different
in Juarez and elsewhere from that found in the States. ->
<H1>Enchilada Sauce</H1>
```

When I modify the Enchilada Sauce recipe by adding the comments shown above and feed the text to a Web browser, the browser does not display the comments, as you see in Figure 5-11 (which looks just like Figure 5-6).

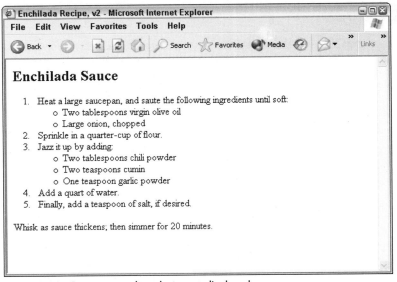

Enchilada Sauce

1. Heat a large saucepan, and saute the following ingredients until soft:
    o Two tablespoons virgin olive oil
    o Large onion, chopped
2. Sprinkle in a quarter-cup of flour.
3. Jazz it up by adding:
    o Two tablespoons chili powder
    o Two teaspoons cumin
    o One teaspoon garlic powder
4. Add a quart of water.
5. Finally, add a teaspoon of salt, if desired.

Whisk as sauce thickens; then simmer for 20 minutes.

Figure 5-11: Comments galore, but none displayed.

note You don't have to use comments, but if you're starting to build a complex Web space that offers many documents, just time stamping each file could prove to be invaluable. Me? I sometimes put jokes in my Web pages as comments, just to see if people ever view the source!

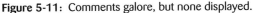

Table 5-3: HTML Tags Covered in This Chapter

HTML Tag	Close tag	Meaning
`<dd>`	`</dd>`	Indicates a definition description
`<dl>`	`</dl>`	Indicates a definition list
`<dt>`	`</dt>`	Indicates a definition term
`<li>`	`</li>`	Indicates a list item
`<ol>`	`</ol>`	Indicates an ordered (numbered) list
`type="type"`		Indicates the type of numbering (possible values are a, a, i, i, 1)
`start="x"`		Specifies the starting number of an ordered list
`<ul>`	`</ul>`	Indicates an unordered (bulleted) list
`type="shape"`		Specifies the shape of bullet to use (possible values are circle, square, disc)
`<!—`	`—>`	Indicates a comment within HTML

Table 5-4: CSS Styles in This Chapter

CSS Style	Description
list-style-type	For an unordered list, this specifies the type of bullet to use. For an ordered list, it specifies the type of numbering system to use.
list-style-image	Enables you to specify the URL of a graphic to use as an alternative bullet image. Use url(*url*) as the value.
list-style	A shortcut for specifying more than one list style characteristic.
list-style-position	Specifies the location of the bullet relative to the list content. Values are inside or outside.

Summary

Each chapter, so far, expands the depth and sophistication of your HTML skills. In this chapter, you learned about the various types of lists and how you can combine them—and many CSS styles and formatting tags—to produce attractive results. In particular, you learned about how CSS gives you a remarkable level of control over the nuances of list formatting, including using your own custom bullets, changing the type of numbering, and much more. The next chapter is lots of fun. I show you the missing link—quite literally.

Putting the *Web* in World Wide Web: Adding Pointers and Links

chapter 6

In This Chapter

Linking to other Web pages

Creating references to non-Web information

Examining relative URLs

Deciding how to organize your Web site

Defining internal document references

This chapter covers actual HTML pointers to other Web and Internet resources, shows you how to include pointers to graphics and illustrations, and builds on the URL explanation found in Chapter 1.

At this point, you should feel comfortable with your HTML composition skills. You certainly know all the key facets of HTML, with three notable exceptions: adding links to other documents, adding internal links, and adding nontext information to your pages. This chapter shows you how to add links; Chapter 7 covers graphics.

Much of the information in this chapter builds on the extensive discussion of *Uniform Resource Locators* (URLs) in Chapter 1. You may want to skim that chapter again to refresh your memory before you proceed.

Pointing to Other Web Pages

The basic HTML formatting tag for external references is the anchor tag, `<a>`, and its ending partner is `</a>`. This tag must contain attributes. Without any attributes, the `<a>` tag has no meaning and doesn't affect the formatting of information. The following, for example, would result in the display of the text without formatting:

```
You can now visit <a>the White House</a> online!
```

To make this link *live*, that is, to make it clickable in a Web browser, you need to specify the *hypertext reference* attribute: `href="value"`. The value can be empty if you don't know the actual information, but you must specify the attribute to make the link appear active to the viewer. You can rewrite the sentence as follows to make it a Web link:

```
You can now visit <a href="">the White House</a> online!
```

A Web browser would display the preceding line of HTML code with the portion between the `<a>` references (the anchor tags) appearing in blue —the default color—with an underline or highlighted in some other fashion. The information that should be contained between the quotation marks is the URL for the Web page to which you want to link. The URL for the White House Web site, for example, is `http://www.whitehouse.gov/`.

caution

One classic problem that appears in HTML code is the use of curly (*smart*, or *fancy*) quotation marks. Web servers just don't know what they mean. Double-check to ensure that the quotes in your HTML documents are all straight: "like this" rather than "like this." The same applies to apostrophes and single quotes: make sure that all the ones in your HTML documents are straight (') instead of curly ('). A rudimentary program such as NotePad or TextEdit uses straight quotes by default. Using either of these makes building Web pages easier than using a more sophisticated word processing program such as Microsoft Word.

The following is the sentence with the correct, live hypertext link to the White House:

```
You can now visit <a href="http://www.whitehouse.gov/">the
White House</a> online!
```

The following is a more comprehensive example, which combines various facets of HTML to build an interesting and attractive Web page.

```
<html>
<head>
 <title>Visiting the White House and Other Government Sites</title>
</head>
<body link="#0000FF" vlink="#0000FF">
<center>
<!— the following includes a graphic on the page. It'll be
    explained in Chapter 7 —>
<img src="whitehouse.jpg" height="92" width="669" alt="whitehouse" />
</center>
<p>
In cyberspace, you can virtually travel anywhere.  Of the various places
that are fun and interesting to explore, however, few are as
```

```
interesting as <a href="http://www.whitehouse.gov/">The White House</a>.
But here are some others
to keep you busy:
</p>
<h2 style="background-color:#ccc;padding:4px;width:100%;border: 1px
solid black;">
Government Sites on the Web</h2>
<ul>
<li><a href="http://www.fbi.gov/">Federal Bureau of Investigation</a></li>
<li><a href="http://www.fedworld.gov/">FedWorld</a>, a great starting
point for
government research</li>
<li><a href="http://www.nifl.gov/">National Institute for Literacy</a></li>
<li><a href="http://www.osmre.gov/osm.htm">Office of Surface Mining</a></li>
<li><a href="http://www.sba.gov/">Small Business Administration</a></li>
<li><a href="http://www.ssa.gov/">Social Security Administration</a></li>
<li><a href="http://www.dhs.gov/">Department of Homeland Security</a></li>
<li><a href="http://www.usaid.gov/">U.S. Agency for International
Development</a></li>
</ul>
</body>
</html>
```

Figure 6-1 shows that the preceding HTML code is quite attractive when viewed in a browser. The ugliness of the URLs is neatly hidden; readers can simply click the name of an agency to connect directly to it.

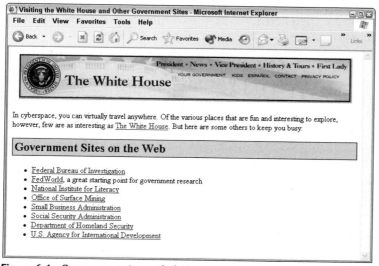

Figure 6-1: Government sites with their accompanying URL links.

Notice in the preceding HTML code that the link for the Office of Surface Mining is a complex URL with a specified starting page, not just a domain name URL. Also notice that the words *The White House* in the prose at the beginning of the Web page are highlighted and underlined, comprising a real Web link.

note Understanding this section of the chapter is a terrific step forward in learning HTML. After you grasp how to build anchors, you can build Web tables of contents—the starting points for exploration on the Internet—with the best of them.

But how do you point to information that isn't found within another Web document but is located somewhere else on the Internet—outside the relative comfort and ease of the World Wide Web? The next section shows you how.

Referencing Non-Web Information

To point to material that isn't a Web document, but instead is located elsewhere on the Internet, you simply use the appropriate URL, as specified in Chapter 1. If you learn, for example, that the Library of Congress has an FTP site, you build a URL for it like this:

```
ftp://ftp.loc.gov/
```

You can then drop the URL into your HTML code as a value in an href attribute, as follows:

```
<a href="ftp://ftp.loc.gov/">The Library of Congress</a>
```

The following example shows how the unordered list of government Web sites I discussed in the preceding section looks with the addition of a few FTP sites and an e-mail link:

```
<ul>
<li><a href="http://www.fbi.gov/">Federal Bureau of Investigation</a></li>
<li><a href="http://www.fedworld.gov/">FedWorld</a>, a great starting
point for government research</li>
<li><a href="http://www.nifl.gov/">National Institute for Literacy</a></li>
<li><a href="http://www.osmre.gov/osm.htm">Office of Surface Mining</a></li>
<li><a href="ftp://ftp.loc.gov/">Library of Congress</a></li>
<li><a href="http://www.sba.gov/">Small Business Administration</a></li>
<li><a href="http://www.ssa.gov/">Social Security Administration</a></li>
<li><a href="mailto:webmaster@doc.gov">Department of Commerce</a></li>
<li><a href="ftp://ftp.noaa.gov/">National Oceanic and Atmospheric
Administration</a></li>
<li><a href="http://www.dhs.gov/">Department of Homeland Security</a></li>
<li><a href="http://www.usaid.gov/">U.S. Agency for International
Development</a></li>
</ul>
```

In my Web browser, the preceding looks almost identical to the earlier version, except that it has three new items listed (see Figure 6-2). This example underscores one of the real strengths of the HTML language: All anchors (hypertext pointers), regardless of the kind of information they point to, look the same on a Web page. No funny little mail icons appear next to the `mailto` link, no FTP icons appear next to FTP archives, and so on. The pages contain uniform sets of pointers to other spots on the Internet that contain interesting, valuable, or fun resources.

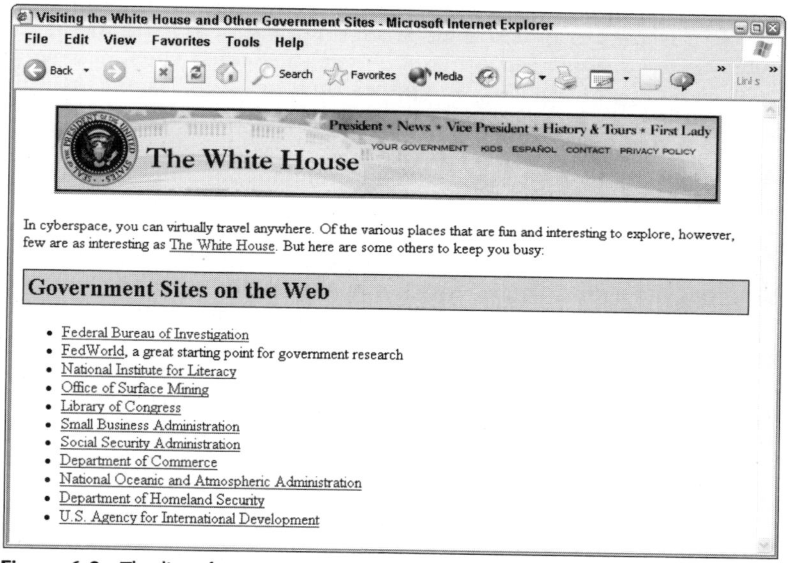

Figure 6-2: The list of government Web sites, expanded to include several that don't reference other Web pages.

Of all the links demonstrated in the HTML code for this Web document, I think that the most notable is the `mailto:` link used for the Department of Commerce. You create an e-mail hypertext reference simply by prepending "`mailto:`" to a valid e-mail address. Sometimes, a friendly `mailto:` link is presented like this:

```
Please <A HREF="mailto:taylor@intuitive.com">Click here</A>
to send updates.
```

But the preferred method is to integrate the link smoothly and transparently into the prose, like this:

```
Please <a href="mailto:taylor@intuitive.com">send
updates</a> if anything has changed.
```

Try to avoid using *Click here* and similar labels for hypertext tags; cool Web pages come from creative, meaningful, and unobtrusive integration of links into the text. On the other hand, setting expectations for what happens when users click a link is important, too. A different design for this particular Web page might include such hypertext labels as *The FTP archives of . . .* or *Send email to . . .* to set expectations. I explore this important usability factor in Chapter 14.

Referencing Internal Documents with Relative URLs

The capability to link to external information sources and sites on the Internet is a huge boon to Web designers; but if you stopped at that and never learned any more, you'd be missing half the picture. The one piece yet to learn is how to reference other documents on your own server. This is where you advance from creating cool Web pages to creating cool Web sites!

Many home pages offer a simple format similar to the examples shown in this chapter—a heading or two, a few simple paragraphs of text, perhaps a graphic or two, and then some links to corresponding sites on the Web. More complex and sophisticated sites, however, may have a number of different Web pages available. The pages on these multipage sites include the appropriate links so that readers can easily jump among them.

You can choose an easy way or a hard way to reference internal documents—documents on the server where your Web site resides. The hard way builds on the earlier examples: You figure out the full, or *absolute,* URL of each page and use those URLs as the hypertext reference tags. Each of these begins with `http://`. The easy way to reference another document on your server (the computer that holds your Web pages) is to specify the document name only, or path and name, without any of the URL preface information. This method is referred to as using *relative* URLs.

For example, if you have a starting page called `home.html` and a second page called `resume.html`, and both are stored in the same folder or directory on the server, you can create the following link:

```
You're welcome to <a href="resume.html">read my
resume</a>.
```

note Purists, of course, would use the HTML code `r&eacute;sum&eacute;` instead of `resume` to ensure that résumé has the proper accent marks.

Relative URLs work by having the browser preface the hostname and path of the *current* page to each reference. So if your Web page is at `http://www.college.edu/joe/home.html` and uses the relative URL reference `<a href="research.html">`, the actual reference built by the browser when it requests the page is `http://www.college.edu/joe/research.html`.

note It's critical to remember that if your Web server name changes, say from `http://www.college.edu` to `http://lab.college.edu`, you have to update pages employing absolute URLs but not the pages employing relative URLs. These automatically point to the correct subsequent links. This functionality is a compelling reason to use relative URLs whenever possible.

You can change the default prefix for links on your page by using the `<base href="`*new-base-url*`" />` tag. For example, `<base href="http://alt-server.college.edu/joe/" />` causes all relative URLs to be resolved to the `alt-server.college.edu` server rather than the `www.college.edu` server. More interestingly, you can use the `target` attribute of the `base` tag to point links to other windows, a subject explored in greater depth in Chapter 8, when I discuss frames and frame-based designs. For now, experiment by adding the following line to your HTML page—this forces all links to open up in new windows—and watch how all the links change their behaviors:

```
<base target="_blank" />
```

Organizing a Web Site

After you move beyond one or two Web pages and a half-dozen graphics, it quickly becomes clear that good organization makes site maintenance and management easier. To this end, a hierarchical directory approach can prove to be a big advantage.

Imagine you are building a Web site for a local delicatessen. In addition to the home page, you also want to have a variety of information available online about the sandwiches and soups the deli offers. Planning for future growth, you might opt to organize the information as shown in Figure 6-3.

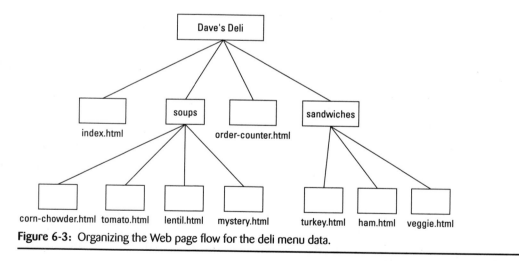

Figure 6-3: Organizing the Web page flow for the deli menu data.

When you want to translate the illustration in Figure 6-3 into an HTML layout that works with the subdirectories, you might create a first draft of the home page that looks like this:

```
<html>
<head>
  <title>Dave's Online Deli</title>
</head>
<body>
<h2>Welcome to the Virtual World of Dave's Online Deli!</h2>
Sandwich Choices:
<ul>
  <li>
    <a href="sandwiches/turkey.html">Turkey on a croissant.</a>
  </li>
  <li>
    <a href="sandwiches/ham.html">Ham and Cheese</a>
  </li>
  <li>
    <a href="sandwiches/veggie.html">Veggie Delight</a>
  </li>
</ul>
Soups of the Day:
<ul>
  <li>
    <a href="soups/tomato.html">Tomato</a>
  </li>
  <li>
    <a href="soups/tomato.html">Tomato and Rice</a>
  </li>
  <li>
    <a href="soups/lentil.html">Lentil</a>
  </li>
  <li>
    <a href="soups/corn-chowder.html">Corn Chowder</a>
  </li>
  <li>
    <a href="soups/mystery.html">Mystery Soup</a>
  </li>
</ul>
<I>Please order at <a href="order-counter.html">the counter</a>...</I>
</body>
</html>
```

The new virtual deli home page (which Web folks call the *root*, or the first page that visitors see when reaching a site) is now formatted as shown in Figure 6-4.

You can't see it, but the HTML code contains an inadvertent error. To understand the problem—a relatively common one in complex documents like this—consider what happens if someone wants more information about the tomato and rice soup instead of the tomato soup. Both soup choices point to the same second page: soups/tomato.html, but this only makes sense to the user if that page has information on both soups. Odds are, it's just for the tomato soup, which could leave fans of tomato and rice (one of my favorites) a bit baffled.

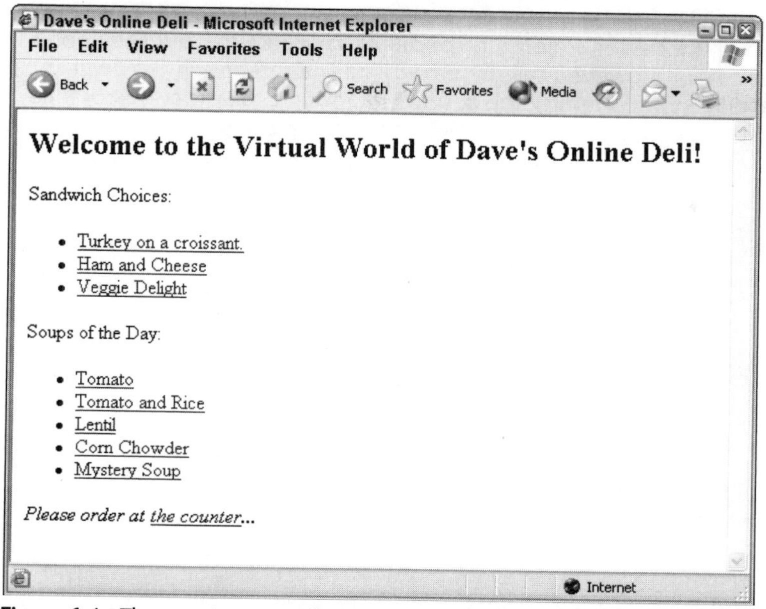

Figure 6-4: The opening page of Dave's Online Deli, with the links to other pages available.

If a Web user pops into the virtual deli and wants to find out more about the lentil soup, for example, he or she might click the hypertext link `Lentil`. The user would then see the page `soups/lentil.html`, offering information about the soup and perhaps even including a picture. But how could you add a link on that page back to the deli home page? Consider the following listing, paying close attention to the last few lines:

```
<center><img src="soupbowl.gif" alt="[bowl of soup]" /></center>
<h2>Lentil Soup</h2>
<div style="margin-bottom:12px;">
It will come as no surprise to regular patrons of the Virtual Deli
that our lentil soup has quickly become one of the most popular
items. With its combination of six different lentil beans, some
succulent organic vegetables, and our carefully filtered fresh spring
water, a hot bowl of our lentil soup on a cold day is unquestionably
one of life's pleasures.
<br /><br />
We'd love to tell you the recipe too, but why not come in and try it
for yourself.
</div>
<b>We Also Recommend: <a href="../sandwiches/veggie.html">a veggie
sandwich to accompany.</a></b>
<hr />
<a href="../deli.html">Back to the main menu.</a>
<hr />
```

When visitors to the virtual deli arrive at the page created by the preceding HTML, they have moved down a level in the server's hierarchical directory structure, but they don't know that. The URLs in the document, however, tell the story. The main menu is `../deli.html`. The recommended sandwich to accompany the soup is in another directory—hence its `../sandwiches/` folder specification. See Figure 6-5 to see what the page looks like in a browser.

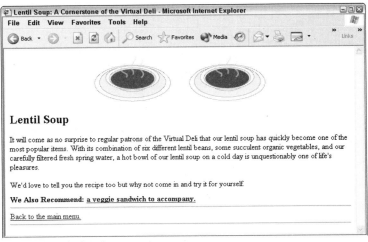

Figure 6-5: The lentil soup page.

note In the previous listings, you can see the use of relative filename addresses. For example, `../deli.html` pops up one level in the file system to find the `deli.html` page. This makes for easy HTML coding. But beware that problems can easily arise if you move any of the pages around without updating the rest of the files.

Having shorter URLs is a compelling reason to use relative URLs in your Web page design, but you have an even better reason: Your Web site (the collection of pages and graphics) is much more portable from system to system with relative addressing.

Suppose that you're building a Web site with your America Online account, and your home page address is `http://members.aol.com/d1taylor/`. Each absolute reference, therefore, has that address as the first portion, so a graphic like *landscape.jpg* in the photos directory ends up with the URL `http://members.aol.com/d1taylor/photos/landscape.jpg`.

What if you end up registering your own domain a few weeks later and want to have all the references to the `members.aol.com` domain vanish? With absolute URLs, you're stuck with editing every single reference in every HTML file—a mondo drag. If you use relative URLs, on the other hand, the photo would be referenced as `photos/landscape.jpg`. You simply move the entire set of files and graphics to the new folder, and everything works without a single modification!

Defining Web Document Jump Targets

Until now, the HTML pages shown in this book have been short, with the information confined to the visible browser-window area. Such an approach to Web document design results in pages that are easy to navigate but potentially very tedious to view, particularly if the visitor has a slower Internet connection.

If I want to put this chapter up on the Web, I could make each section a different page, but even then, some of the sections would be so long that readers would be forced to scroll down to find the information. The hassle of navigation eclipses the value of splitting your information into separate pages. A better design is one in which the entire chapter is a single document, but the topic headers are actually links to the appropriate spots further down the page. Clicking a table of contents entry moves you to that section of the document instantly.

note   One constant challenge for Web page designers is figuring out when a document works best as a single HTML file and when it works best as a set of files. My rule of thumb is to break pages at logical jump points and to minimize load time for readers. This chapter could be a single HTML document, but the book itself would clearly be a set of separate documents.

The targets of internal Web document jumps are known as *named anchors*. The HTML tag for an anchor point is an alternate attribute of the `<a>` tag: `<a name="value">`. The value can be any sequence of characters, numbers, or simple punctuation. (Dash, underscore, and dot are safe. With others it might or might not work). I recommend that you stick with a strategy of mnemonic anchor names that start with a letter, such as `section1` or `references`. Some browser software insists that all characters in the anchor be in lowercase, so you may want to experiment before you build a complex document, or stick with lowercase to avoid any potential problems.

The following shows how a set of tags might look within a document on Web design guidelines. The anchors are built from the rule name and specific rule number, which can then be referenced as links in the rest of the document. Notice that there are no spaces in anchor names:

```
<a name="guidelines"></a>
<h2>WEB DESIGN GUIDELINES</h2>
<dl>
<dt><a name="rule1">Rule #1:</a></dt>
<dd>
Understand the intended users and uses of your Web site; then focus
the design and layout around their needs and interests.</dd>
<dt><a name="rule2">Rule #2:</a></dt>
<dd>
Be sparing with graphical elements.</dd>
<dt><a name="rule3">Rule #3:</a></dt>
<dd>
```

Continued

```
Continued
Pages should load within no more than thirty seconds, including all
graphical elements.</dd>
<dt><a name="rule4">Rule #4:</a></dt>
<dd>
Minimize color palettes.</B></dd>
<dt><a name="rule5">Rule #5:</a></dt>
<dd>
Design horizontally-oriented graphical elements where possible.  </dd>
</dl>
```

Viewed in a Web browser (see Figure 6-6), the preceding document looks like an attractive list of design rules. Because anchors are destinations on the current page rather than links to go elsewhere, any text between the `<a name>` and `</a>` is not highlighted in any way when displayed. However, because the definition of the destination point is a regular anchor tag—albeit with different attributes than an `href`—it must be closed like any other paired tag, so you need to ensure that you have a corresponding `</a>` for each named anchor. Because the text isn't highlighted, most people place the `</a>` immediately after the spot is defined, as in `<a name="rule4"></a>`.

What I've done in this example is not only add links to each of the design guidelines but also add a link to the very top of the document (called *guidelines*), which could then easily be used as a shortcut to the top of the page from anywhere in the document.

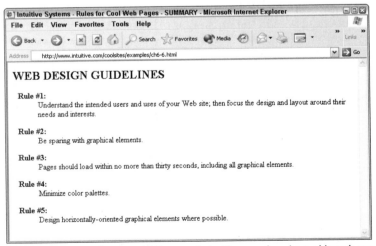

Figure 6-6: Some design guidelines coded with named anchors although you can't tell that from this output.

Adding Jump Links to Your Web Pages

The partner of an anchor in HTML documents is the formatting tag, which defines the *jump*, or active link, within the document. The formatting tag is a variation of the `<a>` tag, which you already know. The necessary attribute turns out to be another `href` hypertext reference, this time with the URL replaced by the anchor name and prefaced by a number sign (#).

For example, if the anchor you want to connect to is specified as `<a name="guidelines">`, as in the preceding example, you specify the jump as `<a href="#guidelines">go to the top of the guidelines</a>`.

tip

One of my goals in creating cool Web sites is to avoid phrases like the following:

```
<a href="#guidelines">Click here</a> to see the
guidelines.
```

Instead, try to integrate the references more smoothly into the text, as follows:

```
<a href="#guidelines">Design Guidelines</a>.
```

One common way to utilize the named anchors is to create a succinct summary line at the top of the document. Recall that the style `font-size: 80%` creates smaller type, so you can see immediately what's going here:

```
<div style="font-size:80%;text-align:center;">
<a href="#rule1">rule 1</a> |
<a href="#rule2">rule 2</a> |
<a href="#rule3">rule 3</a> |
<a href="#rule4">rule 4</a> |
<a href="#rule5">rule 5</a>
</div>
```

This extends the page I showed you previously to offer users a very simple way to jump to a specific guideline without having to scroll, as Figure 6-7 shows.

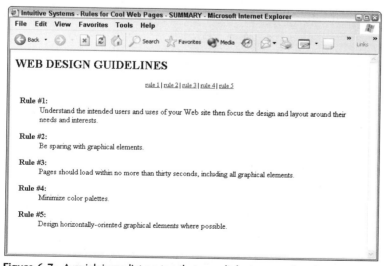

Figure 6-7: A quick jump list on top that uses links to named anchors.

For another way to use internal references, consider the following HTML that might replace the overly succinct introduction in the previous example. Notice how the links are much more informative and integrate more smoothly into the presentation:

```
<div>
While the number of web pages that are available online increases every
day, the quality of these pages seems to be declining, with more and more
people (and programs, to be fair) violating basic design guidelines.
There are a variety of reasons involved, but one that's common is a
simple lack of experience with layout.
<br /><br />
Some design rules might seem obscure, like <a href="#rule4">minimizing
the color palette size</a>, which is clearly specific to the World Wide
Web, but others,such as being <a href="#rule2">sparing with graphical
elements</a> and<a href="#rule1">focusing on the intended user of the
page</a>, are basic rules of <i>any</i> design.
<br /><br />
The most important idea is that
<span style="color:green;font-weight:bold;">
good web pages start with good content</span>
rather than with good form, layout or design. The design
should spring from the content and the information therein.
</div>
```

In a browser, the Web design guidelines shown in the preceding HTML are quite pleasing to the eye and easy to navigate. All the links and anchor information are appropriately hidden from view or sufficiently subtle that the reader can focus on the surrounding text (see Figure 6-8).

Figure 6-8: Design commentary with reference links.

One thing to keep in mind when you specify your anchor points is that the exact spot of the reference becomes the top of the displayed document. A sequence such as the following shows the possible danger resulting from this:

```
<h2>Bananas</h2>
<a name="bananas"></a>The banana
is one of the most exotic, yet most easily purchased,
fruits in the world.
```

The HTML source seems reasonable, but the resulting behavior is not what you seek. Users who jump to the `bananas` tag see `The banana is . . .` as the first line of their window; with the `<h2>` header one line off screen.

A much better strategy is to flip the two items, as follows:

```
<a name="bananas"></a>
<h2>Bananas</h2>
The banana is one of the most exotic, yet most easily
purchased, fruits in the world.
```

Can you see the difference? In the former case, the `<h2>` is just barely off the screen, whereas in the latter, the positioning of the anchor tag ensures that the header stays with the prose.

tip Always test your Web documents before unleashing them on the world. I can't overemphasize this. Subtle problems, such as where anchor tags are placed, cause classic mistakes found on otherwise spiffy Web sites.

Jumping into organized lists

Anchors and jump points are commonly used to help readers navigate large lists of alphabetically sorted information. Consider the following simple phone book layout:

```
<html>
<title>Jazz Institute Internal Phone Book</title>
<body>
<h1>Jazz Institute Internal Phone Book</h1>
Section Shortcut: <a href="#a-c">[A-C]</a>
<a href="#d-h">[D-H]</a> <a href="#i-l">[I-L]</a>
<a href="#m-n">[M-N]</a> <a href="#o-s">[O-S]</a>
<a href="#t-z">[T-Z]</a>
<br />
<a name="a-c"></a>
<h2>A-C</h2>
Benson, George (x5531) <br />
Coleman, Ornette (x5143) <br />
Coltrane, John (x5544)
```

Continued

```
Continued
<a name="d-h"></a>
<h2>D-H</h2>
Dorsey, Tom (x9412) <br />
Ellington, Duke (x3133) <br />
Getz, Stan (x1222) <br />
<a name="i-l"></a>
<h2>I-L</h2>
Jackson, Milt (x0434) <br />
Laffite, Guy (x5358) <br />
<a name="m-n"></a>
<h2>M-N</h2>
Monk, Thelonious (x3333) <br />
Noone, Jimmy (x5123) <br />
<a name="o-s"></a>
<h2>O-S</h2>
Parker, Charlie (x4141) <br />
Peterson, Oscar (x8983) <br />
Reinhardt, Django (x5351) <br />
<a name="t-z"></a>
<h2>T-Z</h2>
Taylor, Billy (x3311) <br />
Tyner, McCoy (x4131) <br />
Waller, Fats (x1321) <br />
</body>
</html>
```

Although the HTML in the preceding example is complex, Figure 6-9 shows that the result not only looks attractive but is also quite a useful way to present the information.

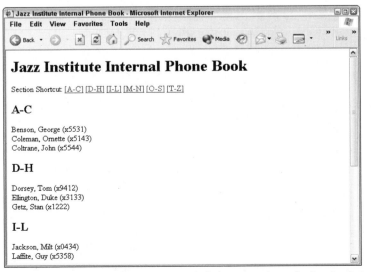

Figure 6-9: Anchors and jump points can help you navigate the Jazz Institute phone book.

You can start to get a feeling of how complex HTML text can become if you imagine that each entry in the phone list actually is a link to that person's home page or other material somewhere else on the Web. Every line of information displayed in the browser could easily be the result of four or more lines of HTML.

Linking to jump targets in external documents

Now that you're familiar with the concept of jumping around within a single document, you can also add the #anchor notation to the end of any Web URL to make that link move directly to the specific anchor point in the document.

Suppose, for example, that the Web design guidelines page resides on a system called www.intuitive.com, and that its full URL is http://www.intuitive.com/coolsites/ design.html. (It is, actually. Try it!)

A visit to the page reveals that a variety of anchor tags are embedded in the HTML, including the #highlights reference at the beginning of the document, enabling you to jump directly to the executive summary. You could link directly to that spot from another Web page with this URL:

```
http://www.intuitive.com/coolsites/design.html#highlights
```

caution

Pointing to external anchors can be useful for linking to large Web documents that contain a great deal of information that might otherwise confuse your reader. Be careful: If anyone but you maintains the anchors, the names may change, the documents may be reorganized, or other changes may suddenly invalidate your links without your knowledge. There's always a chance that a whole document might vanish from the Web, of course; but the chance that a link within a document might change is considerably higher.

Changing Link Colors

One more topic before I conclude this chapter: Using standard HTML, you can change a link's default color by specifying a few special <body> tag attributes, shown in Table 6-1.

Table 6-1: Link Color <body> Tag Attributes

Attribute	Possible Values	Function
text	Color name or hex rgb value	Specifies color of text on the page
link	Color name or hex rgb value	Specifies color of hypertext references
vlink	Color name or hex rgb value	Specifies color of links you've visited
alink	Color name or hex rgb value	Specifies color of link while mouse button is down

These attributes are almost always used together. For example, if I want to have green text and red hypertext references, I use the following:

```
<body text="green" link="red">
```

x-ref   In Chapter 7, you learn about the bgcolor and background attributes that let you further specify color schemes on your page. CSS also enables you to change colors, as discussed in Chapter 4. Look especially for the color style.

Table 6-2: HTML Tags Covered in This Chapter

HTML Tag	Close Tag	Meaning
`<a>`	`</a>`	Specifies the anchor tag
`href="url"`		Indicates a pointer to hypertext reference
`href="#name"`		References an internal anchor name
`name="name"`		Specifies an Internal anchor definition

Summary

In this chapter, you learned how to include links on your Web pages to other sites on the World Wide Web and throughout the Internet by using the anchor tag. You also learned how to organize a set of Web documents in manageable folders, how to link to other documents on your own server with minimal fuss by using relative URLs, and the HTML way of changing text and link colors. The next chapter introduces you to an exciting topic: graphics.

From Dull to Cool by Adding Graphics

By this point, you've learned enough HTML to create complex webs of information with sophisticated text formatting, but that isn't all there is to Web design; graphics are what make a Web page truly cool. The capability to place large and small images—and even to make them hypertext references—is a crucial element of good Web page design, not to mention that it's great fun to have Web pages with pictures, audio, and video clips! This chapter shows you how to jazz up your Web pages with multimedia elements and includes discussion of how to create and edit graphic images, audio, and even video clips.

In this chapter, I diverge slightly from the platform-independent approach that I've taken so far and delve into some platform-specifics to help you create graphics and images for Windows PCs and Macintoshes. The examples in this chapter utilize programs that are available for both platforms.

Image Formats

Before delving into the HTML tag itself, I want to spend some time talking about acceptable graphics formats. Hundreds of different formats exist, but Web browser software generally understands only three:

- **GIF:** CompuServe's Graphics Interchange Format
- **JPEG:** Joint Photographic Expert Group format
- **PNG:** Progressive Network Graphics format

If your Web page contains graphics in another format—for example, TIFF, BMP, PCX, or PICT—Web users might be able to display those graphics, but only in a separate application, which their Web browsers may or may not automatically launch.

The most common graphic formats on the Web, however, are GIF and JPEG, so I focus on those first. The trade-off between GIF and JPEG formats is in the subtleties. GIF images can only use a maximum of 256 colors, whereas JPEG supports millions of unique colors in a graphic. (Whether they show up correctly depends on the particular display system you have in your computer. If you have an old clunker monitor and ancient display card, you won't see millions of colors even if the graphics contain that many colors in their palette). Both graphic formats attempt to compress images to shrink down the file size, but because they compress in different ways, some images are considerably smaller in one format than in the other.

note The PNG format is a hybrid that represents the best of both JPEG and GIF format capabilities. Although it's widely supported in contemporary browsers, older browsers can't display PNG format graphics, and more unusual Web browsers (such as PDAs, and cell phones) are unlikely to include the capability to display them. As with many facets of Web design, you should consider your target audience when considering the set of technologies to include in your implementation.

The main reason that the GIF image format is so attractive to Web designers isn't that it has a small color palette but that you can trim down the palette to the bare minimum number of colors you need for a particular graphic, thereby shrinking the image's file size dramatically.

Graphic images are built out of *pixels*: individual dots of information in the graphic. In a GIF image, each pixel can have one of up to 256 different colors. But what if the image uses only two colors instead of 256, as you might find in a two-color company logo? In that case, you can chop the size of the GIF image down quite a bit: Each pixel requires one bit of information (8 bits in a byte), versus 8 bits of information for the full 256-color option. In other words, you've just chopped your file down to one-eighth its original size.

With any good graphics editor, you can easily trim your color palette to minimize your file sizes; officially, GIF supports 1-bit (2 color), 2-bit (4 color), 4-bit (64 color), and 8-bit (256 color) formats. I should point out that with 1-bit, it's any two of the 256 colors you can work with, so a blueprint that's white on light blue is still only a 1-bit-per-pixel image.

Although GIF supports up to 256 colors, not all these colors are the same on both the Mac and PC. This can be a nightmare. A picture that looks great on your PC can look awful on a Mac, and vice versa. To avoid this pitfall, you might want to explore the so-called Internet-Safe Color Palette, a subset of 216 colors that are identical on both computers.

You can see all 216 safe colors on the same Web page by looking online at http://www.intuitive.com/coolsites/colors.html.

Other useful characteristics of GIF images are the capability to designate any one color as a transparent color—I examine that more closely later in the section "Transparent Colors"—and to create interlaced graphics. If you visit a Web page and watch the images load line by line, going from out of focus into the final, crisp rendition, you're seeing an interlaced image. Although interlacing adds about five to ten percent to the size of the file, if your images are large, interlacing is a nice way to let the user quickly get a rough idea of what he or she is downloading.

The majority of images on the Web employ GIF format, particularly buttons and banners, because of their smaller file size. The JPEG format is used to most closely duplicate the exact colors of an original image. For example, a friend of mine has a Web site where he highlights some of his many excellent nature photographs. For photographic reproduction, it's imperative that he use the JPEG format for all his images. Otherwise, the nuances of color would be lost.

For your Web pages, however, your images will mostly be in the GIF format. Fortunately, a variety of freeware and shareware programs—all available on the Web—can translate common graphics formats into GIF format. For the Mac, I recommend GraphicConverter; for Windows systems, you can use Paint Shop Pro. If you have the latest version of your graphics editor or image-manipulation program, it probably has the capability to save directly into GIF format, too. Check with the vendor or your local computer store to make sure. A great starting point for finding graphics software packages on the Web is Yahoo! Specifically, go to http://www.yahoo.com/Computers/Software/Graphics/ and have a look at what is offered there.

If you want to find the specific shareware packages previously mentioned, here are their official Web addresses:

- GraphicConverter: http://www.lemkesoft.de/
- Paint Shop Pro: http://www.jasc.com/psp.html

Including Images in Web Pages

Including images in a Web document is easy—you use the <img> (image) format tag. Just like the <a> anchor tag, the <img> tag has a single critical attribute, src="graphicname", and like the <hr> horizontal rule, it requires no paired close tag. To include the graphic banner.gif, use this HTML:

```
<img src="banner.gif" />
```

When you have a graphics file, the `<img>` tag is used to place that file in the text. Suppose that I have a file called `black-box.gif` that I want to use as the opening graphic in my Web page. The following example shows how this file might appear in an HTML document:

```
<html>
<head>
<title>The Black Box</title>
</head><body>
<img src="black-box.gff" alt="black box logo" />
<h1>Welcome to the Black Box</h1>
People are always trying to figure
out how things work. From "How Things Work" to "Why Things
Work", it's an obsession. But why? Why not just think of
everything in life as a simple
<i>Black Box?</i>.
<br /><br />
Ready to change your perspective? <a href="blackbox2.html">yes</a>
</body>
</html>
```

The `<img>` formatting tag has quite a variety of attributes, as this chapter illustrates. The two attributes that must appear in the `<img>` tag are a specification of the image source file itself, in the format `src="filename"`, and a tag indicating the alternative text to display if the image cannot be loaded, the `alt="text"` tag. Figure 7-1 shows how the preceding HTML appears when viewed in a browser.

Figure 7-1: The Black Box page with graphics specified, but not loaded.

The small box at the top of Figure 7-1 with a small *x* inside is not the graphic I wanted to include; rather, it's an indication from Internet Explorer that an inline graphic was specified with the `<img>` tag, but not loaded. In this case, the graphic was not loaded because I mistyped the name of the graphics file, specifying `black-box.gff` rather than `black-box.gif`. (Did you notice?) Instead, the text of the `alt` attribute is shown, but it's definitely not what I want!

To correct the problem, simply fix the spelling. Figure 7-2 shows what the resulting Web page looks like with all the information properly loaded (more attractive than with the unloaded graphic, eh?).

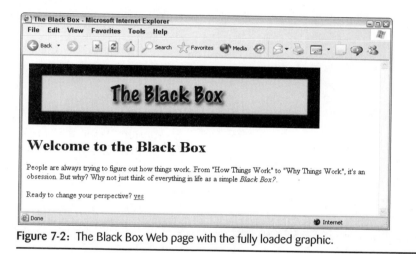

Figure 7-2: The Black Box Web page with the fully loaded graphic.

You may have a fast Internet connection, but remember that many people are trapped with slow dial-up connections at 28,800 baud or—horrors!—slower. Earthlink, America Online, and MSN users can access Web pages, but performance can be quite slow. Bigger graphics have more data to transfer to the user and, therefore, take longer to receive. Also keep in mind that, to speed up access, many users simply modify their Web browser preferences to skip loading the graphics unless they're required to understand a page.

A general guideline in gauging how long a graphic takes to download is to figure that each 1K of graphics size translates to one second of download time for dial-up users. So, when you create graphics, it's a good idea to look at the file sizes and ask yourself whether the specific graphic is worth the wait. Sometimes it is, but often it isn't and just creates a frustrating situation for the user.

A popular use of graphics is a button that you can create by wrapping the `<img>` tag with an `<a>` anchor. If I have two button graphics—`yes.jpg` and `no.jpg`—here's how I can spiff up the Black Box page:

```
<html>
<head>
<title>The Black Box, Take III</title>
</head><body>
<img src="black-box.gif" alt="black box logo" />
<h1>Welcome to the Black Box</h1>
People are always trying to figure
out how things work. From "How Things Work" to "Why Things
Work", it's an obsession. But why? Why not just think of
everything in life as a simple
<i>Black Box?</i>.
<br /><br />
Ready to change your perspective? <a href="blackbox2.html">
<img src="yes.jpg" alt="yes" /></a>
<a href="not-ready.html"><img src="no.jpg" alt="no" /></a>
</body>
</html>
```

The graphics included in this page (yes.jpg and no.jpg) are separate files in the same directory as the Web page. Figure 7-3 shows the new Web page with all graphics included.

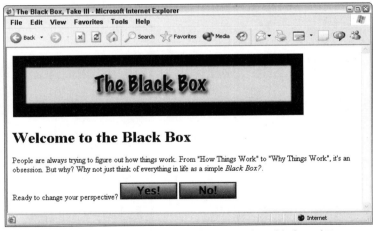

Figure 7-3: The improved Black Box page displays the added graphics.

---

tip

A critical question you might ask is the following: Where do the graphics files live? The answer to this question is that they are almost always on the same server, in the same directory, as the HTML files. If you upload your HTML file to a Web server, for example, you also need to upload the graphics used in those files. As you get more comfortable with Web site development, you might want to adopt the habit of automatically creating a Graphics folder to corral the graphics files in a single spot.

A page in which graphics are a vital part of the design, however, can look peculiar to some Web users because a small percentage of people on the Web still either cannot or opt not to download graphics when viewing Web pages. This creates a design dilemma: Should pages be designed to omit the graphics, to include them as critical, or just to add them as an afterthought?

Some Web pundits tell you to just go wild with the graphics because "within a few months" everyone will have a fast, powerful computer and a high-speed connection. I don't agree with that advice. Pundits make this claim year after year, yet a majority of Web users still don't have high-speed connections. Because the various graphic formats, already compressed, still produce large files, you should ensure that people who omit the images still see a meaningful page.

The argument over whether or not to go wild with graphics breaks down like this. Some designers insist that you should be able to design for a specific browser and platform. Those sites say stuff like *Enhanced for Internet Explorer 5.0 and Windows 2000.* I think their design is unintentionally user-unfriendly: Why immediately tell users they've got the wrong tools to visit your site? Another group believes that specific browsers shouldn't be required, but that no-graphics viewers are irrelevant to their online experience. They eschew `alt` attributes (as you see shortly) or any text alternatives for the graphical buttons and pictures. For some sites that's cool, but for many, it's just a sign of poor implementation. Finally, some think that every graphic should have a text alternate and that the pages should work wonderfully for all users. That's the safest bet, but if you want to advertise your T-shirt designs online, clearly, text descriptions aren't very useful! Which road you take definitely depends on the goal of your site and your vision of your target audience.

note Notice in the previous example that the graphical buttons had a small rectangular border. If you look at the example on your own computer, you see it's a blue border. The browser adds the border for the same reason that hypertext links are blue and underlined, to let the user know the graphic is clickable. Don't like it? You can eliminate the blue border around a graphic image that's serving as a hyperlink by adding another attribute to the `<img>` tag: `border="0"`. If the preceding example contains `<img src="yes.jpg" alt="yes" border="0" />`, the blue border vanishes.

Text Alternatives for Text-Based Web Browsers

Although the most popular browsers—Netscape and Internet Explorer—offer support for a variety of graphic formats, an important Web browser called Lynx is designed for text-only display. Lynx is found most commonly on Unix systems where users have dial-up accounts. Even at a very slow connect speed, Lynx enables many users to navigate the Web and have fun.

Graphics can't be shown in Lynx, so an additional attribute is allowed in the `<img>` format tag for just that situation. The magic sequence is `alt="alternative-text"`. Whatever replaces `alternative-text` is displayed if the user can't view graphics or chooses to skip loading graphics to speed up surfing the Web (which roughly five to ten percent of Web users still do, according to most estimates I've seen).

To understand why the alt= element is necessary, see Figure 7-4. For this example, I removed the alt tag included in the HTML and renamed the button graphics to be more like what is used in a typical Web site design.

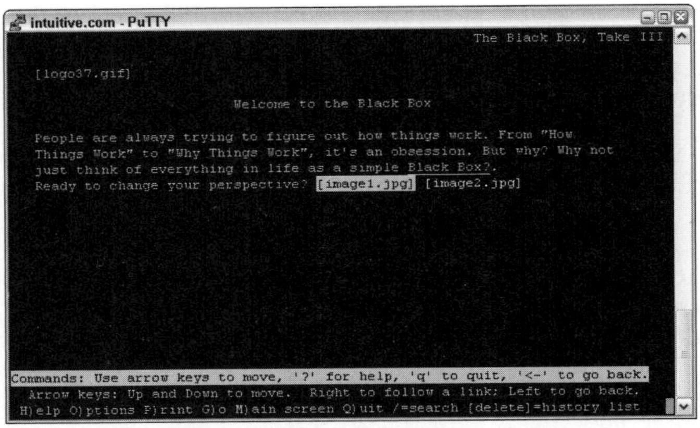

Figure 7-4: The Black Box looks much different in Lynx's text-only display.

The user faces a problem, obviously: How do you answer the question posed? That's another great reason why you should always include some meaningful information in the alt attribute.

Modern Web browsers show this alt text immediately upon loading a page and then gradually replace each placeholder with the actual graphic. Carefully planned alt text can enhance the user's experience and even be fun. For example, the text alternative for my photograph on one page I designed is *Weird picture of some random guy* rather than simply *My photo*.

> **tip**
> You don't have to place brackets, parentheses, or anything else around the text in the alt= section of the <img> tag; but in my experience, brackets or parentheses help users figure out what's on the page (and they make the text look better as well). Experimentation is the key for learning how to make this work best for your own page design.

Image Alignment Options

Go to the first section of this chapter and refer to Figure 7-3. Look carefully at the relative alignment of the text Ready to change your perspective? with the YES and NO icons. The text is aligned with the bottom of the icons, which looks good.

But what if you want a different alignment? Or what if you use various alignments for multiple graphics? You can specify a third attribute in the <img> formatting tag, align, which gives you precise control over alignment.

Standard alignment

The three standard alignments are `align="top"`, `align="middle"`, and `align="bottom"`. By default, adjacent material is aligned with the bottom of the image, as you can see in Figure 7-3. The following HTML snippet demonstrates these three alignment options:

```
<h1>More about Winter Birds</h1>
<img src="feeder.jpg" align="top" border="0" alt="feeder" />
(align="top")
There are many birds that can visit your feeder
even in the middle of the coldest period, with
snow many inches thick on the trees. Three common
birds that we see here in Colorado during the winter
months are Winter Wrens, Barrow's Goldeneyes, and Yellow-Bellied
Sapsuckers.
<br clear="all" /><hr />
<img src="feeder.jpg" align="middle" border="0" alt="feeder" />
(align="middle")
There are many birds that can visit your feeder
even in the middle of the coldest period, with
snow many inches thick on the trees. Three common
birds that we see here in Colorado during the winter
months are Winter Wrens, Barrow's Goldeneyes, and Yellow-Bellied
Sapsuckers.
<br clear="all" /><hr />
<img src="feeder.jpg" align="bottom" border="0" alt="feeder" />
(align="bottom")
There are many birds that can visit your feeder
even in the middle of the coldest period, with
snow many inches thick on the trees. Three common
birds that we see here in Colorado during the winter
months are Winter Wrens, Barrow's Goldeneyes, and Yellow-Bellied
Sapsuckers.
```

Figure 7-5 shows this example in a Web browser. It demonstrates the options for a graphic surrounded by text. Notice that the text doesn't gracefully wrap; instead, the alignment attributes affect only the first line of text subsequent to the image. All additional text moves down below the graphic.

note A simple rule of thumb for images is the following: If you don't want any material to appear to the right of the graphic, add a `<br />` tag to the end of the HTML sequence that specifies the graphic.

The three basic image alignment options refer to the alignment of information that appears subsequent to the image itself. An additional set of image-alignment options refers to the alignment of the image relative to the window, rather than the adjacent material relative to the graphic. I discuss these additional options in the following section.

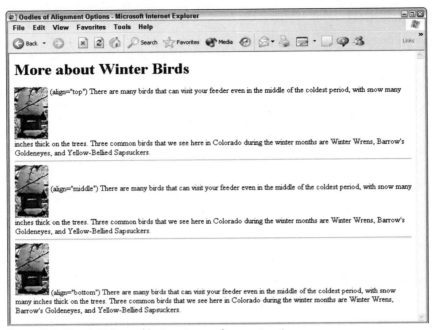

Figure 7-5: Top, middle, and bottom image alignment options.

More sophisticated alignment

The three basic image-alignment options just discussed offer considerable control of graphic positioning, but they don't enable you to wrap text around a graphic, either left or right, on the screen. To remedy this, some additional image alignment options offer much more control. But beware, they also make formatting more confusing because of the difference between alignment of the image and alignment of the adjacent material.

These options are better demonstrated than discussed. The following example improves significantly on Figure 7-5 by using both the alignment options, align="left" and align="right":

```
<h1>More about Winter Birds</h1>
<img src="feeder.jpg" align="left" border="0" alt="feeder" />
(align="left")
There are many birds that can visit your feeder
even in the middle of the coldest period, with
snow many inches thick on the trees. Three common
birds that we see here in Colorado during the winter
months are Winter Wrens, Barrow's Goldeneyes, and Yellow-Bellied
Sapsuckers.
<br clear="all" /><hr />
```

```
<img src="feeder.jpg" align="right" border="0" alt="feeder" />
(align="right")
There are many birds that can visit your feeder
even in the middle of the coldest period, with
snow many inches thick on the trees. Three common
birds that we see here in Colorado during the winter
months are Winter Wrens, Barrow's Goldeneyes, and Yellow-Bellied
Sapsuckers.
<br clear="all" /><hr />
```

Figure 7-6 shows how the preceding text is formatted using `align=left` and `align=right`— quite a step up from the primitive placement options shown earlier.

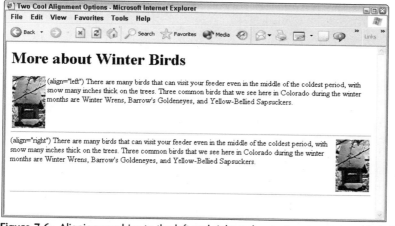

Figure 7-6: Aligning graphics to the left and right makes text more presentable in Explorer.

Not only can you specify alignment within the now complex `<img>` formatting tag, you can also specify the graphic's `width` and `height` before it loads. By specifying these attributes, the document can be rendered on the screen faster, even before your browser receives the graphic.

> **tip** Specify `height` and `width` to have your Web pages load faster!

Values are specified in pixels, as follows:

```
<img src="feeder.jpg" width="67" height="108" />
```

The preceding example reserves a 67 × 108-pixel box on the screen for the graphic, which enables the page to be displayed, including all text, even before your browser receives the graphic from the Web server. This functionality enables you to begin reading the text portion of the Web page immediately. Be careful with these attributes, however, because if you have a 100 × 200 graphic and specify height="200" and width="350", Navigator and Explorer both stretch the image to fit the 200 × 350 space, making it look pretty weird and distorted.

Another attribute that I mention earlier in this chapter is border, which you can use to great effect: The border attribute enables you to specify the exact width of the border around a linked image. The following code shows an example of the border attribute:

```
<body style='text-align: center'>
<!- Tic-Tac-Toe ->
<h2><b>Tic-Tac-Toe</b></h2>
<p>
It's X's Turn... (<span style='color:blue'>This color</span>
indicates a recommended move).</p>
<div>
<a href="topleft"><img src="Graphics/boxx.gif" border="0"
 alt="x" /></a>
<a href="topcntr"><img src="Graphics/box.gif" border="0"
 alt=" " /></a>
<a href="topright"><img src="Graphics/box.gif" border="0"
 alt=" " /></a>
<br />
<a href="left"><img src="Graphics/boxo.gif" border="0"
 alt="o" /></a>
<a href="center"><img src="Graphics/boxo.gif" border="0"
 alt="o" /></a>
<a href="right"><img src="Graphics/box.gif" border="2"
 alt=" " /></a>
<br />
<a href="btmleft"><img src="Graphics/boxx.gif" border="0"
 alt="x" /></a>
<a href="btmcenter"><img src="Graphics/box.gif" border="0"
 alt=" " /></a>
<a href="btmright"><img src="Graphics/box.gif" border="0"
 alt=" " /></a>
</div>
</body>
```

Figure 7-7 displays the resulting graphic. Notice that the border specification enables you to indicate the recommended next move by simply placing a blue (or gray, for the figures in this book) border around the box. Earlier in this chapter, I used this same attribute to turn off the blue border on the YES and NO buttons.

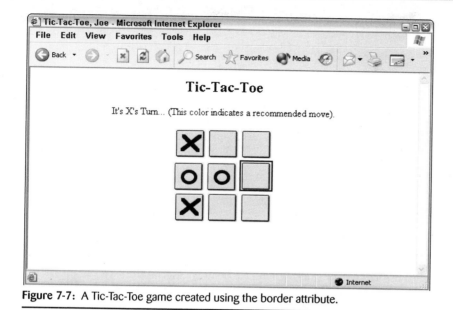

Figure 7-7: A Tic-Tac-Toe game created using the border attribute.

Two more useful image alignment and presentation attributes are `vspace` and `hspace`, which control the vertical and horizontal space around each graphic, respectively. Consider an example of a left-aligned graphic. When displayed, the text starts immediately adjacent to the edge of the graphic. By using `hspace`, I can fix this potential problem by specifying a particular number of pixels as a horizontal spacing between the graphic and the adjacent text, as the following HTML shows:

```
<h1>More about Winter Birds</h1>
<img src="feeder.jpg" align="left" border="0"
 alt="feeder" hspace="40" />
There are many birds that can visit your feeder
even in the middle of the coldest period, with
snow many inches thick on the trees. Three common
birds that we see here in Colorado during the winter
months are Winter Wrens, Barrow's Goldeneyes, and Yellow-Bellied
Sapsuckers.
<br clear="all" /><hr />
<img src="feeder.jpg" align="left" border="0"
 alt="feeder" hspace="4" />
There are many birds that can visit your feeder
even in the middle of the coldest period, with
snow many inches thick on the trees. Three common
birds that we see here in Colorado during the winter
months are Winter Wrens, Barrow's Goldeneyes, and Yellow-Bellied
Sapsuckers.
<br clear="all" /><hr />
```

Figure 7-8 demonstrates the result of this source code.

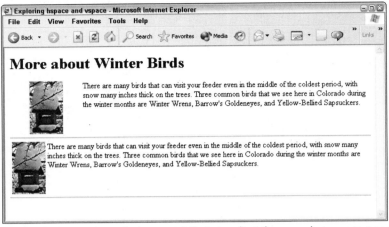

Figure 7-8: You can use the hspace attribute to adjust the space between text and an image.

A subtle thing to note in Figure 7-8 is that hspace adds the specified number of blank pixels on both sides of the graphic. vspace does the same thing with vertical space. If you specify 10 pixels of empty space above a graphic, you end up with 10 pixels of space below it, too. An alternative—if you really want space only on one side of the image, not both—is to add the empty space as part of the graphic itself, or to use a margin setting within the style attribute of the <img> tag.

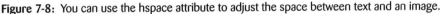

x-ref   Check out Chapter 12 to find out more about setting margins using CSS.

At this point, you're learning to have some real control over the display of your document and can begin to design some cool Web pages. But I must mention one more attribute before you go wild with the various options for the <img> tag.

If you experiment, you might find that when you're wrapping text around a large graphic, it's difficult to move any material below the graphic. The <br /> and <p> tags simply move to the next line in the wrapped area. That effect is not always what you want. To break the line and move back to the margin, past the graphics, you add a special attribute to the useful <br /> tag: clear. For example, use <br clear="left" /> to move down as needed to get to the left margin, <br clear="right" /> to move down to a clear right margin, or <br clear="all" /> to move down until both margins are clear of the image. Most commonly, you see <br clear="all" />.

Tossing all the additions into the mix, here's a Macintosh icon tutorial that uses the tags and attributes that I've just discussed:

```
<html>
<head>
<title>Intro to Macintosh Icons</title>
</head>
<body style='line-height: 1.25'>

<h2 style='text-align:center'>Intro to Macintosh Icons</h2>

<p>
<b>Generic File Icon</b><br />
<img src="mac-icons/file.gif" align="left" hspace="18" alt="file" />
This is a generic file, that is, one that doesn't have
any application ownership information stored in the Mac
file system or its own resource fork. Opening
these files typically results in the
<b>TeachText</b> or <b>SimpleText</b> application being used.
</p>
<br clear="all" />

<p>
<b>Generic Folder Icon</b><br />
<img src="mac-icons/folder.gif" alt="folder" align="left"
 hspace="15" />
This is a standard folder icon on the Macintosh. Folders
can contain just about anything, including files,
applications and other folders. Opening a folder results
in the contents of that folder being displayed in a
separate window on the Macintosh.
</p>
<br clear="all" />

<p>
<b>System Folder Icon</b><br />
<img src="mac-icons/system.gif" align="left" hspace="15"
 vspace="11" alt="system" />
A special folder at the top-most level of the boot disk
on the Macintosh is the <I>System Folder</I>. It
contains all the files, applications, and information
needed to run and maintain the Macintosh operating
system itself. The "X"
inside the folder icon indicates that this
particular <i>System Folder</i> is <i>live</i> and that
the information inside was used to actually start up
the current Macintosh.
</p>

<p>
<b>Applications Folder</b><br />
```

Continued

```
Continued
<img src="mac-icons/applications.gif" align="left"
 hspace="15" vspace="8" alt="app folder" />
All of the major applications in Mac OS X live in a shared
folder called the Applications Folder. It's easily
recognized by the 'A' on the folder icon itself and is
the first place to look when you seek any of the many
Macintosh applications included with the operating system.
</p>
</body>
</html>
```

Figure 7-9 shows the result of this code.

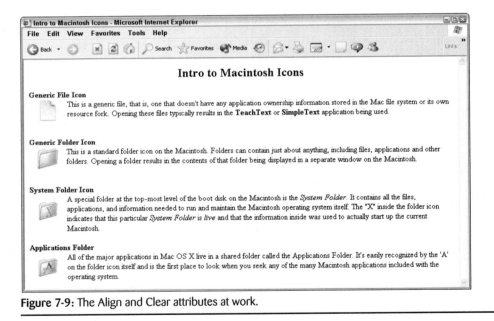

Figure 7-9: The Align and Clear attributes at work.

Background Colors and Graphics

One aspect of Web page design that I really enjoy fiddling with, an area that can dramatically change the character of your Web site, is selecting a background color for the page. Not only can you change the background color, you can also load any graphic as the background to the entire page: a graphic that's either subtle (such as a marbled texture) or way over the top (such as a picture of your cat).

To add a background color or background graphic, you add an attribute to the `<body>` tag. The `<body>` tag should already be an integral part of your existing Web pages. After you start modifying the `<body>` tag, it is absolutely crucial that you place it in the correct spot on your pages. Remember, all Web pages should start with an `<html>` tag, followed by `<head>` and `<title>` tags. A `</head>` tag ends the header section, and immediately following, you should insert the `<body>` tag. If you have the `<body>` tag in the wrong place—particularly if you place it subsequent to any specification of information to appear on the Web page itself (such as an `<h1>` tag)—your browser ignores any background changes.

You specify background colors with `bgcolor="colorname"` or `bgcolor="#rgb-value"`, and you specify a background graphic with `background="filename"`. But rather than live in the past with the HTML approach, let's look at how to use CSS. CSS enables you to change the background color by modifying the attributes of the `<body>` tag with this attribute:

```
<style type="text/css">
body { background-color: blue; }
</style>
```

If you don't want a CSS block, you can instead specify background color as a `style` attribute to the `<body>` tag itself. You can add background graphics by using the `background-image` attribute:

```
body { background-image: url(diamond.gif) }
```

In addition, you can specify the background image's position on the page with `background-position`. (One value equals the horizontal and vertical origin point of the image; two values equal the horizontal and then the vertical point of the image.) You can also specify whether the background image should repeat (old-timers call this *tile*) with `background-repeat`, which has four possible values:

- repeat
- repeat-x
- repeat-y
- no-repeat

Working with background graphics is fairly straightforward, but the specification for a color, unfortunately, isn't quite so simple. If you want to have complete control, you specify your colors as a trio of red-green-blue numeric values, two letters for each, in hexadecimal.

"Hexa-what?" I can hear you asking.

Hexadecimal is a numbering system that's base-16 rather than our regular numbering scheme of base-10 (*decimal*, as it's called). The number 10, for example, is $1 \times 10 + 0$, but in hexadecimal, it has the base-10 equivalent of $1 \times 16 + 0$, or 16.

note Hexadecimal numbers range from 0 to 9 and also use A, B, C, D, E, and F to represent larger numbers. Instead of base 10, our regular numbering system, hex uses a base-16 numbering system. So in hex, A = 10 decimal, B = 11 decimal, C = 12 decimal, D = 13 decimal, E = 14 decimal, and F = 15 decimal. 1B hex is $1 \times 16 + 11 = 27$ decimal. FF, therefore, is $F \times 16 + F$, or $15 \times 16 + 15 = 255$ decimal.

Don't worry too much if this doesn't make much sense to you. It's just important to know some typical color values as shown in Table 7-1.

Table 7-1: Common Colors as Hex RGB Values

Hex Color Value	CSS Hex Shortcut	Common Color Name
00 00 00	000	Black
FF FF FF	FFF	White
FF 00 00	F00	Red
00 FF 00	0F0	Green
00 00 FF	00F	Blue
FF FF 00	FF0	Yellow
FF 00 FF	F0F	Purple
00 FF FF	0FF	Aqua

You should experiment with different colors to see how they look on your system. If you're working with basic colors, however, you can use their names (thankfully). Table 7-2 shows some of the most common colors.

Table 7-2: Popular Colors Available by Name

Aqua	Black	Blue	Fuchsia
Gray	Green	Lime	Maroon
Navy	Olive	Purple	Red
Silver	Teal	White	Yellow

caution

If you specify a color that your system can't display, the browser tries to produce a similar color by *dithering*, or creating a textured background with elements of each of the two closest colors. Sounds nice, but it isn't; you end up with a pebbly background that can make your text completely unreadable. The trick is to use the so-called Internet-safe color choices if you're specifying color with a hex value. The good news is that it's pretty easy: Just remember that you're fine if you choose each of the three basic colors (red, green, blue) from 00 33 66 99 CC FF. For example, CCCCCC (or just CCC) is a light gray, and CCCCFF (or CCF) is an attractive light blue. Go to http://www.intuitive.com/coolsites/colors.html to see a full list.

Take a look at a page that specifies a yellow background for the page and a light blue background (color #99F) for two of the <div> tags on the page:

```
<body style="background-color: yellow">
<p>
One of the nice things about background colors is that you
```

```
can produce interesting and unusual effects
with relatively little work.
</p>
<div style="background-color: #99f">
Want to have something look exactly like a piece of paper?
Use background-color:#FFF or its
equivalent background-color:white
</div>
<div style='background-image: url(diamond.gif);
    font-size:200%;font-weight:bold;'>
Is green your favorite color? Try either
background-color:green or background-color:#0F0
</div>
<div style="background:#99f">
Another solid-background-color box, this has a nice light blue.
</div>
```

Viewing this in your browser, as shown in Figure 7-10, results in a bright, cheery, and attractive yellow background and two light blue text boxes. Another interesting example in Figure 7-10 is that of a background graphic—diamond.gif—that appears behind the second <div> block. Even with text twice the normal size, notice that the background graphic makes the text difficult to read!

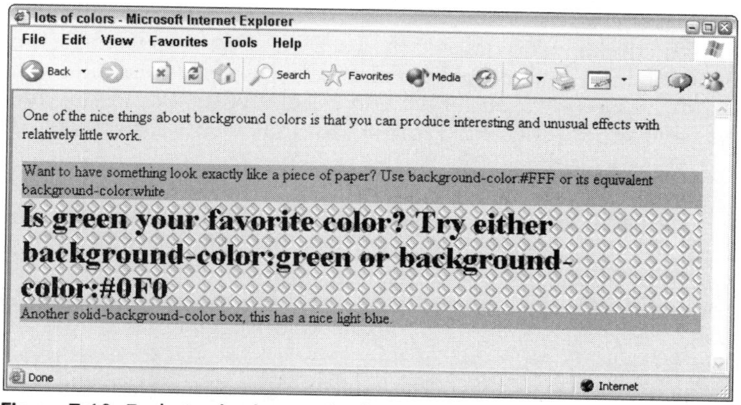

Figure 7-10: Exploring background colors and graphics.

As Figure 7-10 demonstrates, graphical backgrounds are also easy to work with, albeit a bit more dangerous. Even the simplest graphic can potentially obscure the text on a particular page.

The moral of this story: By all means, use these fun options, but be sensitive to the potential readability problems your viewers might face because of their own hardware or browser preferences or because these options have been used inappropriately.

Where Can You Find Images?

Considering that all graphics are specified with the same basic HTML tag, it's remarkable how much variation exists among different sites on the Web. Web designers create varied appearances for their pages through the types of graphics they use and their unique combination of graphics, text, and background images.

Where do these graphics come from? Here are the most common sources:

- Personally created
- Clip art or other canned image libraries
- Scanned or digital photographs
- Images grabbed off the Web

Creating your own

If you're artistically inclined or want to use straightforward graphics, buttons, or icons, the easiest way to produce graphics for your Web pages is to create them yourself. A wide variety of graphics applications are available for Windows and Mac users, at prices ranging from free to fifty dollars to thousands of dollars for real top-notch stuff.

To give you an example, I created the opening graphic for the Black Box (shown in Figure 7-2) from scratch in about 15 minutes. I used the powerful Adobe Photoshop application, a rather expensive commercial package available for both Mac and PC platforms. Photoshop has the capability to save directly to GIF format (and JPEG format, for that matter), so it was easy to produce.

Having said that, I will warn you that Photoshop is not for the faint of heart! It's a highly sophisticated program that takes quite a bit of training before you can be really productive. If you're looking for something that enables you to be productive in one afternoon, Photoshop is not the best choice. On the other hand, when you do master it, you'll join the ranks of some of the best digital artists on the Web.

If you'd prefer something simpler, GraphicConverter for the Mac and Paint Shop Pro for the PC are both quite useful programs that offer you the capability to create graphics and save them in either GIF or JPEG format. Earlier in this chapter, I indicated the official Web sites for each of these programs. Here they are again for your convenience:

- GraphicConverter: http://www.lemkesoft.de/
- Paint Shop Pro: http://www.jasc.com/psp.html

The number of graphics programs is staggering, and regardless of how fast or capable your machine, some unquestionably terrific software solutions are available. Some of the best packages are shareware—such as the two listed—but numerous commercial packages are available as well. Here are some of the more popular commercial graphics packages for each platform:

- **Windows:** Among the many applications for developing graphics in Microsoft Windows are Adobe Illustrator, Adobe Photoshop, Macromedia Fireworks, Aldus FreeHand, MetaCreations Painter, Dabbler, Canvas, Ray Dream Designer, SmartSketch, CorelDRAW!, MacroModel, AutoSketch, Kai's Power Tools, 3D Sketch, and Elastic Reality.

- **Macintosh:** Because it remains the premier platform for graphics, most graphics applications are available for the Mac. In addition to the big three—Adobe Photoshop, Macromedia Fireworks, and Adobe Illustrator—Macintosh graphics programs such as Drawing Table, Color It, Collage, KPT Bryce, Paint Alchemy, TextureScape, Painter, Kai's Power Tools, and Alias Sketch.

- **Unix:** Fewer graphics programs are available for Unix systems, but the programs that are available are quite powerful. Look for Adobe Photoshop, FusionArt, GINOGRAPH, Adobe Illustrator, Image Alchemy, Magic Inkwell, and Visual Reality, depending on your flavor of Unix.

note One request: If you do opt to use a shareware program, please remember to pay for it and register it with the shareware author. That's the only way users can continue relying on the generosity of these programmers who write such excellent software and then make it available to users directly.

Clip art or canned image libraries?

One result of the explosion of interest in Web page design is the wide variety of CD-ROM and floppy-based clip art and image libraries now available. From hundreds of thousands of drawings on multi-CD-ROM libraries (I have one image library that sprawls across thirteen different CD-ROMs!) to hand-rendered three-dimensional images on floppy—or available for a fee directly on the Web—lots of license-free image sources are available. At the same time, most of the CD-ROMs I've seen that are supposedly for Web designers are pretty mediocre—tossed-together collections of clip art that would look okay on your page if you could just figure out where it is on the disk and how to save it as a GIF or JPEG.

If you opt to explore the clip art route, I strongly recommend you be a skeptical consumer and make sure that both the product's interface and ease of finding specific images meet your needs. I have a CD-ROM of clip art for Web pages, for example, that's packaged in a very cool-looking box and includes some undeniably spiffo images, but finding the exact one I want and saving it as a Web-ready graphic is surprisingly difficult.

Of the clip-art Web sites, one that I find particularly interesting is Art Today. It has a variety of different membership options. Free membership includes access to tens of thousands of Web graphics, including tons of animated GIFs, bullets, backgrounds, buttons, themed images, rules, dividers, and icons.

To access the graphics, visit http://www.arttoday.com/.

Scanned or digital photographs

Another way to produce graphics for your Web site is to use a scanner and work with existing art. If you're a photography buff, you probably have hundreds of original photographs, or even digital photographs already on your computer, from which you can glean cool additions for your site.

A few years ago, I was traveling in Paris and took what turned out to be a great photograph of the beautiful Sacré Coeur. A few minutes of work with a scanner made the photo instant artwork to include in my Web page, as shown in Figure 7-11.

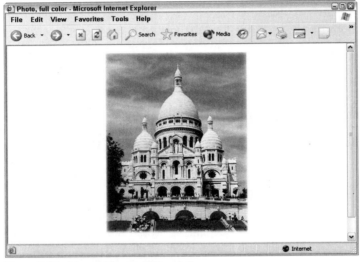

Figure 7-11: Scanned image of Sacré Coeur.

Scanners offer further options for producing fun and interesting graphics. I also scanned the image shown in Figure 7-11 as black-and-white line art, producing the interesting abstract graphic in Figure 7-12.

If I were designing a Web site that I expected to attract users with slow connections, I could use small black-and-white representations of art to save download time. Each small *thumbnail* image serves as a button that produces the full color image when clicked. The HTML for a thumbnail image looks like the following:

```
<a href="big-image.gif"><img src="little-image.gif"
border="0" alt="little image" /></a>
```

tip Thumbnail versions of large graphic images are common (and appreciated by just about everyone), so if you create a page that contains many pictures, think about minimizing the data transfer with smaller versions that refer to larger images.

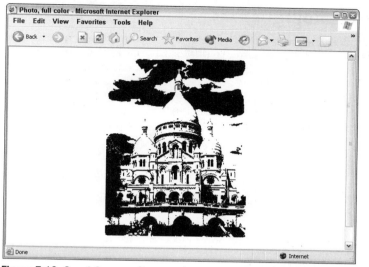

Figure 7-12: Sacré Coeur as line art, after scanning and some manipulation.

Another difference between the images in Figures 7-11 and 7-12 is file size. Figure 7-11 is a JPEG image to ensure that all the colors in the original photograph are viewable in the Web artwork. It's 48K in size. Figure 7-12, however, is a 1-bit GIF image, and even though it's exactly the same image-size as the JPEG color photo, the file is only 6K, less than one-eighth the size of the color image.

on the web Check out a pretty neat scanning Web site online at `http://www.scantips.com/`.

Another way to work with scanners is to scan scrawls, doodles, or pictures you create with pencils, pens, color markers, paint, pastels, or what have you, and then incorporate those objects into your Web page. Or get even more creative: Scan in aluminum foil, crumpled tissues, your cat (note that this would be a *cat scan*), wood, a piece of clothing, or just about anything else.

caution Copyright laws are serious business, and I strongly discourage you from scanning images from any published work that is not in the public domain. The cover of *Sports Illustrated* might be terrific this week, but if you scan it and display it on your Web page, you're asking for some very serious legal trouble.

If you work with scanners, you already know about some of the best software tools available. I always use Photoshop when I'm working with color or gray-scale scans.

tip One important scanner trick if your output is for the Web: Scan the images at between 75 dpi (dots per inch) and 100 dpi. The additional information you get from, say, a 2400 dpi scan is wasted, slows down the editing process, and produces ridiculously large graphics files anyway.

Working with digital photographs

One of the easiest ways to add images to your Web site is use of your digital camera. Whether it's a picture of how messy your desk has become to photos of your kids doing cute things, if you have a digital camera and can transfer the images from your camera to your computer, you've overcome 90% of the challenges involved. The last step required before you can use these images on your pages (and in your e-mail, for that matter) is to resize them for the intended application and make sure you've saved them in a Web-compatible graphics format (probably JPEGs, because that format is most suited for photographs).

When I include photographs on a Web page, I always reduce the size of the image to no more than about 500 pixels wide and, certainly, no more than 400 pixels high, so they don't take too long for the viewer to download. You can easily resize images using Paint Shop Pro, Graphic Converter, Photoshop Elements, or any of dozens of other applications. In Paint Shop Pro, for example, here's how I accomplish this:

1. Download and install the trial version of Paint Shop Pro (PSP) from http://www.jasc.com/

2. Choose File ⇨ Open in PSP to find the image you want.

3. Choose Image ⇨ Resize to resize the image, as shown in Figure 7-13.

Figure 7-13: Resizing a photograph in Paint Shop Pro 8.

This image is 1504 × 1000 pixels, so I'm going to reduce it to 33% of its current size, which produces an image that's much more manageable at 496 × 330 pixels. If the image seems very small all of a sudden, make sure you're viewing it at its full size. Choose View ⇨ Zoom ⇨ Zoom to 100%.

4. If you're so inclined, sharpen up the shrunken image with Adjust ⇨ Sharpness ⇨ Unsharp Mask. The default settings work fine, in my experience, and the image should be visibly improved.

5. Choose File ⇨ Save to save the image with a new image name, in this case, gilligan.jpg.

That's it! Now you have a new photograph ready to include on your Web page. You can include it like this:

```
<img src="Graphics/gilligan.jpg" border="5"
   alt="Did Gilligan escape the island, finally?" />
```

The preceding text produces the page shown in Figure 7-14.

Figure 7-14: Photograph from digital camera included on a Web Page.

tip

Note the useful trick of forcing a nonzero border with this image as a way to get the black border around the photograph. With a linked image, the border color would be the link or visited link color; without being linked, it's just black. With CSS, you can also specify a specific style of border with the border style, as I discuss in Chapter 12.

Grabbing images off the Net

Another way to get images that doesn't involve being artistic or using a camera or scanner is to find interesting, attractive graphics online. Think of Net graphics as being virtual clip art (you can use real clip art, too), but don't forget that many of the images may be copyrighted. Just because MCI has a Web site (at http://www.mci.com/) doesn't mean that you can pop over and borrow its logo without permission!

The good news is that there are a number of different sites that are archives of publicly available graphics, clip art, background graphics, and more. Here are a few of the best.

Art today

I already talked about it earlier in this chapter, but I want to remind you that it's one of the best places I know online to grab high-quality graphical elements and much more. Visit the site at http://www.arttoday.com/.

The shock zone

Chris Stephens offers a terrific set of icons that loads quickly and can add pizzazz to your Web site. His site also includes a range of animated graphics and much more. Connect to http://www.TheShockZone.com/, and you can see much more than the small selection shown in Figure 7-15.

Figure 7-15: Some of the images available at The Shock Zone.

But wait! There's more . . .

After a while, the different graphic repositories start to look alike. Call me a curmudgeon, but you have only so many different ways to create a 50 × 50 pixel bullet graphic, right? Well, if the previous two repositories don't have what you want, here are a few more good ones:

* Graphics Station: `http://www.geocities.com/SiliconValley/6603/`
* Webular Wasteland: `http://www.aceent.com/w2/`
* The Icon Bazaar: `http://www.iconbazaar.com/`

Of course, you can just travel the Net, and when you see something you like, grab it with a screen-capture program or download it directly. Different Web browsers offer different tools to accomplish just this task. With Explorer, for example, right-click a graphic, and suddenly there's a pop-up menu with the option of saving that graphic to disk. If you take this route, however, be doubly sensitive to possible copyright infringement. It is quite easy to create a site using existing graphics and only later discover the legal complications.

Another thing to be aware of is the following: If you're creating a Web site for someone else, don't be surprised if part of your agreement letter specifies that you certify that all images used on the site legally belong to the site owner. I've seen contracts that even included a clause stating that if there were any questions about the legality of material on the site, the problem was mine and that I'd have to pay any and all damages for any legal action that might ensue.

Transparent Colors

One cool thing you can do with PNG and GIF images is replace the background around the edges of the image with a *transparent* color—one that enables the background color or image to bleed through. Transparent colors (available only with PNG- or GIF-format images today) almost instantly make pages look cooler. Of course, this book is printed without any colors, but you've been pretending pretty well up to now, haven't you?

Figure 7-16 shows two versions of the same type of icon. The background of the top graphic is set to transparent; the background of the bottom graphic isn't. Some difference, eh?

To select a distinctive transparent color, choose File ➪ Export ➪ GIF Optimizer (yellow, in this case) during the Paint Shop Pro image save process, as shown in Figure 7-17.

All the major graphics and type-manipulation packages support transparent GIFs. If yours doesn't—check the documentation to make sure—it's time to upgrade.

tip For a comprehensive list of utilities and all sorts of goodies, zip over to Yahoo! (`http://www.yahoo.com/`) and look in `Computers/World WideWeb/Programming`.

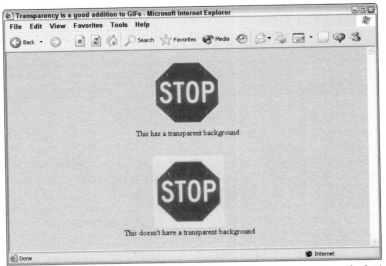

Figure 7-16: Transparent graphics can add a cool element to your icons by letting the page's background bleed through the edges of the image.

Figure 7-17: Creating a transparent graphic in Paint Shop Pro.

Animated GIF Images

Another cool element you can add to your Web pages is animated GIFs, which are based on the very simple *flip-book* premise: A sequence of graphic images with subtle changes between them can be cycled in such a way that the images appear to be animated. That's how film works, too. If you've ever looked at an individual cel of a motion picture reel, you know that it's a still image. Watch the still images at a sufficiently fast speed, and you have the illusion of motion and life.

Animated GIF images are available through a variety of sources, particularly the clip-image archive packages and Web sites listed next, but you can also create your own with some share-ware animation packages. For the Macintosh, I recommend GIFBuilder, and for Windows, I suggest you explore GIF Construction Set. Here are their homes on the Web:

- GIFBuilder: `http://www.versiontracker.com/dyn/moreinfo/macosx/10438`
- GIF Construction Set: `http://www.mindworkshop.com/alchemy/gifcon.html`

Image-Mapped Graphics

As you explore the Web on your own, you might encounter sites that eschew mundane bul-leted lists of links in favor of sexy, all-encompassing graphics that lead you off in different directions. When you click a particular spot on the graphic, the system knows where you clicked and links you to an appropriate Web page. You can perform this impressive trick by using *image maps*, graphics that associate specific regions with different URLs.

The modern, cool way to create image maps is to use *client-side* image maps, meaning that you include image-mapping information as part of the HTML document itself.

A simple example consists of these parts: the graphic image, the HTML document that includes the image, and the additional lines of HTML that turn the image into a client-side image map. For example, I have a photograph of a toy truck that would make an interesting image map, and the free Mac-based Taco HTML image map editor, found at `http://www` `.tacosw.com/`, can help me build one. The process for a PC with software such as Coffee Cup is almost identical.

tip
If you use a Mac, you can get Taco HTML and build your own image maps. Go to `http://www.tacosw.com/`. If you're on a PC, another very good image map editor is Coffee Cup Image Mapper, which is shareware, but still quite inexpensive. Go to `http://www.coffeecup.com/` to learn more.

Building an image map

After you install Taco HTML editor, launch it, and follow these steps:

1. Choose Insert ⇨ Image Map. The dialog box shown in Figure 7-18 appears.

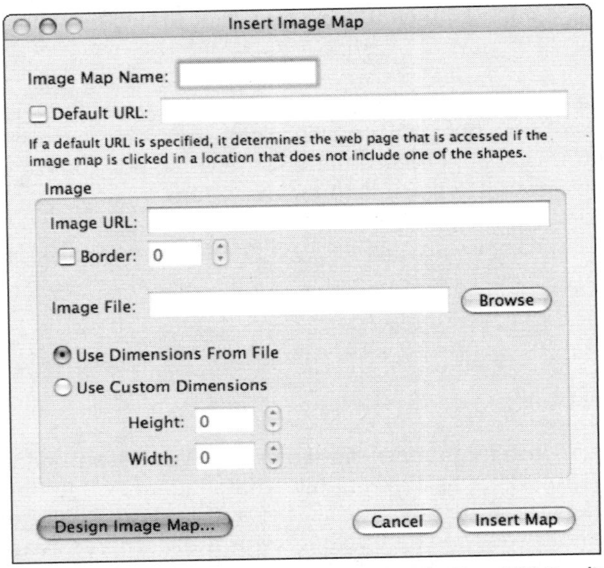

Figure 7-18: Inserting an image map using the Taco HTML editor.

2. Click Browse to select an image. For this example, I chose the image `big-truck.jpg`.

3. Choose a name for your image (such as `truck`) and enter it into the Image Map Name box at the top of the dialog box.

4. Click Design Image Map, which produces the window shown in Figure 7-19.

5. You can add geometric shapes by clicking New Circle, New Rectangle, or New Polygon, encompassing the spot where you want to associate a URL, and then entering a destination URL and Alternate Text in the table at the top. Draw a circle around something, type in a URL, and the area of the graphic within the circle is then associated with the target URL. After loading this image, I've mapped the tires to pirelli.com, and the truck's hat is mapped to mcnopoly.com, a construction supply company.

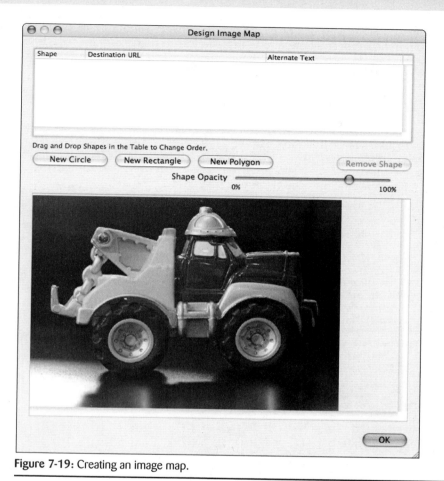

Figure 7-19: Creating an image map.

6. Click OK when you're finished building the image map; then click Insert Map on the main image map dialog box. Taco automatically updates the source code view to include the HTML image map code, which looks like this:

```
<img src="big-truck.jpg" usemap="#truck" width="497" height="352">
<map name="truck">
<area shape="rect" coords="238,10,336,67"
href="http://www.mcnopoly.com/tool.asp?catid=Hard+Hats" alt="Buy a
Hard Hat">
<area shape="circle" coords="162,239,58"
href="http://www.pirelli.com/" alt="Tires by Pirelli">
<area shape="circle" coords="368,235,59"
href="http://www.pirelli.com/" alt="Tires by Pirelli">
</map>
```

This isn't exactly XHTML, but it's pretty close. To convert Taco's HTML output to XHTML, simply add an `alt` tag for the image, and replace the `>` ending of the `<img>` and `<area>` tags with the XHTML form of `/>`. Make those changes, and the final image map is ready to include on one or more of your pages:

```
<img src="big-truck.jpg" usemap="#truck" width="497" height="352"
alt="big truck" />
<map name="truck">
<area shape="rect" coords="238,10,336,67"
href="http://www.mcnopoly.com/tool.asp?catid=Hard+Hats" alt="Buy a
Hard Hat" />
<area shape="circle" coords="162,239,58"
href="http://www.pirelli.com/" alt="Tires by Pirelli" />
<area shape="circle" coords="368,235,59"
href="http://www.pirelli.com/" alt="Tires by Pirelli" />
</map>
```

Figure 7-20 shows the final image map. Notice the location of the pointing finger cursor and the indicated target URL in the status line of the window.

Figure 7-20: A completed image map offers region-to-URL mapping.

Seeing the complexity of even this simple image map, you can understand why specific tools that help you create the map information are wonderful ways to save Web page developers lots of time. Even better, you can obtain lots of image-map assistance for free on the Internet, whether you're on a Macintosh, a Unix workstation, or a PC running Windows. You unquestionably want to have one of these programs. Without image-mapping software, you might go crazy trying to get things right, but after you figure out the application, building image maps is a lot of fun!

Audio, Video, and Other Media

Graphics definitely add pizzazz to a Web site, but there are more media that you can use to develop your cool Web pages, including audio and video. Some significant limitations plague these add-on media, however, not the least of which is that they're large and take quite a while to download.

Audio fragments are probably the most fun—it's great to hear voices or music coming from your computer, and they're quite easy to add to your own pages. The audio recordings are usually in what's called a `micro-law` (you'll see this written as mu-law) format, and can be included as a button or hot spot just like any other URL. Here's an example:

```
You're invited to listen to <a href="audio.au">a sample of
my latest album</a>
```

Users who click the phrase `a sample of my latest album` download an audio file (typically 75K or larger); then an audio player program launches to actually play the audio clip.

Two other common audio formats are used on the Web today. WAV files started their life on Windows machines but can be played on Macs and Unix systems, too, with the latest browsers. MIDI files are another way to squeeze a lot of audio into a remarkably small file because they're actually written in a musical instrument language rather than simply being compressed recordings.

Another way to add audio is to use either the `embed` or `bgsound` HTML extensions. In fact, the latest and most modern way to add audio is to use the `object` tag, but it doesn't always work with audio media, depending on how old your visitors' browsers are. For all these, use Google to learn more about how to incorporate them into your site. Try a search like "+embed +html +audio", for example.

In the meantime, if you're dying to explore some online audio files, I strongly encourage you to check out the dynamite MIDIfarm site. It has an incredible archive of over 15,000 different audio files in MIDI format, including the themes to "Mission Impossible," "Star Wars," "The Jetsons," "Batman," "the Avengers," and just about any other song or music you can imagine! It's online at `http://www.midifarm.com/`.

My only caution is the usual one about copyright and legal restrictions. If you're going to use these MIDI files on a commercial site, make sure you have permission from the original music copyright holder.

tip Be careful when you're adding audio to your site; these files can grow incredibly large. A ten-second audio clip can grow to over 150K, which represents quite a long download period for people accessing the Web via slow dial-up connections.

Modern PCs and Macintosh machines have a variety of built-in audio capabilities, including the capability to record audio directly from an attached microphone. Save the file that's produced and ensure it has a WAV or AU filename suffix. My personal favorite for recording and editing audio is a great shareware program called Wham. You can learn more about this, and many other audio tools, by visiting the audio tools on the Web area on Yahoo!

Movies all night

Movies are found in two primary formats: QuickTime and MPEG (Motion Picture Experts Group).

note If you think audio files can expand rapidly to take up lots of space, you haven't seen anything until you try video on the Web!

The format for including an MPEG sequence is simple:

```
The latest <a href="video.mpg">Music Video</a> is finally
here!
```

Web browsers see the filename suffix MPG and know to download the file specified and launch a video player program.

The other popular movie format is Apple's QuickTime, which has players available for Mac and Windows machines. QuickTime movies use the MOV filename extension.

note You can learn a lot more about working with MPEG and other video formats and sneak a peek at some public domain video and animation archive sites by popping over to Yahoo! Do so, and check out http://dir.yahoo.com/ Computers_and_Internet/Multimedia/.

Streaming audio and video

Another popular technology is *streaming media*. The concept is quite logical. Instead of forcing you to wait for the entire audio or video sequence to download, you get enough to ensure that you're downloading a few seconds ahead and then you begin playing the audio or video sequence.

The biggest proponent of this technology is Real Corporation, which you can visit online at http://www.real.com/.

A bunch of different sites use the Real audio technology, including National Public Radio (http://www.npr.org) and C-SPAN (http://www.c-span.org). You can also listen to 2FM live from Ireland at http://www.2fm.ie/, and check out some obscure music groups from Artist Underground Music at http://www.aumusic.com/.

Real also has a streaming video technology, ingeniously called RealVideo. It's quite popular, and a number of different sites help you learn more about it. Start with Polygram Records (http://www.polygram.com/), peek in at United Airlines Zurich (http://www.united-airlines.ch/), and wrap up your exploration of streaming video with Comedy Central, online at http://www.comedycentral.com/.

I think the streaming technologies are cool, but the biggest problem is that they assume transfers on the Net happen at a steady speed, and that's rarely true. So instead, you get a few seconds of audio and then it stops, or a very low quality audio signal, and the videos either jump or are used as fancy slide-shows rather than a simulated live video feed. If you have a slow Net connection, the situation is even more frustrating; I have very fast connections and still tend to avoid these most of the time.

Despite my misgivings, streaming media continues to improve. In fact, streaming audio and video technologies are growing into a viable alternative media delivery system. If you're building a Web site that requires media, supporting streaming players is the way to go. For today, the server software still costs a fair bit and isn't something I can explain to you in a paragraph or two. Stay tuned (so to speak). There'll be more from this corner of the Web soon.

Table 7-3: HTML Tags Covered in This Chapter

HTML Tag	Meaning
<img	Specifies the image inclusion tag
src="url"	Indicates the source to the graphic file
alt="text"	Specifies the alternative text to display
align="alignment"	Indicates the image alignment on page; alignment of material surrounding the image. Possible values: top, middle, bottom, left, right
height="x"	Indicates the height of graphic (in pixels)
width="x"	Indicates the width of graphic (in pixels)
border="x"	Indicates the size of the border around graphic
hspace="x"	Indicates additional horizontal space around graphic (in pixels)
vspace="x"	Indicates additional vertical space around graphic (in pixels)
<br	Specifies a line break
clear="opt"	Forces a break to specified margin (possible values are left, right, all)

Table 7-4: CSS Styles Covered in This Chapter

CSS Style	Definition
background color	Enables you to define the CSS container's background color. Use it with the body tag to change the background of the entire page. Values are most commonly specified as #rrggbb, #rgb, or color names.
background image	Specifies the background image's URL (use the form url(*value*) as the argument) for the CSS container.
background repeat	Determines whether or not to repeat (or tile) the background graphic. Values are repeat, repeat x, repeat y, or no repeat.
background position	Specifies where to place the background image within the CSS container.

Summary

I could say a lot more about the fun and frustration of working with graphics and other media in Web pages, and I will over the next few chapters. One thing's for sure: However people accomplish the task, you see a million slick graphics, icons, buttons, separator bars, and other gizmos all over the Web. Keep a skeptical eye on your own work, though, to make sure that your neat doodads don't overtake the theme and message—the content—of your site. Good Web sites are built around content, not appearance.

In my view at least, cool Web pages are those that intelligently incorporate their graphics into the overall design and that don't fall apart or become unusable (or otherwise frustrating) when users don't or can't load everything. In Chapter 8, you learn about two very important design options, tables and frames, which offer much finer control over your page layout.

Rockin' Page Design Strategies

Part

II

Tables and Frames

In This Chapter

Organizing table information

Examining some tricks with tables

Exploring frames: pages within pages

Working with iframes

I f you've been diligently reading each chapter of this book so far, I have good news! You've reached the point where many Web-page design consultants, as recently as two or three years ago, considered themselves experts. From this point on, we look at a wide variety of different advanced formatting features starting in this chapter with two essentials for modern site design: tables and frames.

Most interestingly, at this point in the book I have primarily covered the specifics of HTML 1, HTML 1.1, and HTML 2.0, although I've delved a tiny bit into some features that showed up in HTML 3.2, along with providing a decent sampling of Cascading Style Sheets information. Can you keep all these numbers straight? I can't. Remember, the sequence was 1, 1.1, 2.0, 3.2, and now 4.0. For some cryptic reason, there was never a 3.0 release of the HTML standard. Along the way, the two formatting capabilities covered in this chapter—tables and frames—brought about some of the most dramatic improvements in Web site design. As you read this chapter and see the examples, you should begin to see why.

Organizing Information in Tables

Tables are an important addition to HTML that originated in the development labs at Netscape Communications Corporation. Unlike the tables in your favorite word processor, however, HTML tables can be quite compelling. You may even find yourself naturally boxing up groups of icons, taking a list of bullet items, and making a table out of them, or who knows what else! If you want to have material adjacent on a page, perhaps multiple columns of text, tables are unquestionably your best bet.

At their most fundamental, tables are composed of data cells and organized into rows, the collection of which is called a *table*. In HTML, table data cells are denoted by <td> and </td>. These cells are collected neatly into rows with <tr> and </tr>, and the table itself starts with <table> and ends, logically enough, with </table>.

Basic table formatting

Although tables offer a lot of cool capabilities, they also have a downside: Tables can be pretty hard to build when you're just getting started. You have to specify the parameters for the table, the parameters for each row, and then ensure that each cell element is surrounded by <td> </td>—table data—tags. Here's a simple example of table formatting:

```
<h3>Common Cable TV Channels</h3>

<table border="1">
<tr>
 <td>MTV</td>
 <td>EPSN</td>
 <td>CNN Headline News</td>
 <td>WTBS Atlanta</td>
</tr>
</table>
```

This formats all data on the same line (that is, in the same row, denoted by <tr> and </tr>), as shown in Figure 8-1.

Figure 8-1: The simplest table possible—all data in a single row.

If you want to include all the information shown in the preceding example but to present each item in a separate row, the table instantly gets more complex, as the following code shows:

```
<h3>Common Cable TV Channels</h3>
<table border="1">
<tr>
 <td>MTV</td>
</tr><tr>
 <td>EPSN</td>
</tr><tr>
 <td>CNN Headline News</td>
</tr><tr>
 <td>WTBS Atlanta</td>
</tr>
</table>
```

Figure 8-2 shows this expanded format.

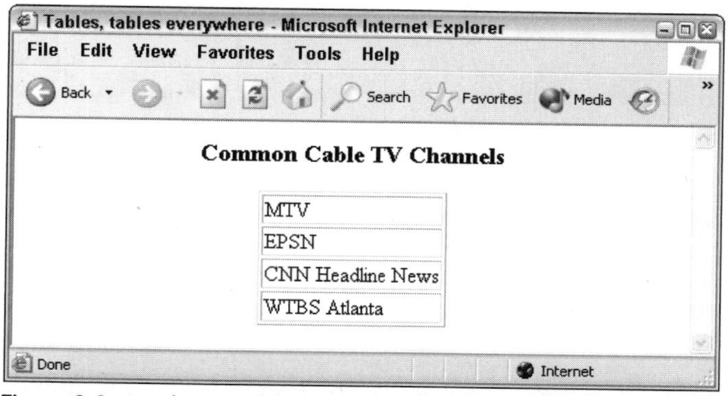

Figure 8-2: Another simple table, but with each element on its own line.

Needless to say, this stuff can get tricky because you can include graphics, text, and just about anything else (including other tables) within any element of a table. Each data cell can have a specific alignment specified with `align=` as part of the tag; and the `<table>` tag itself has a plethora of options, including all those shown in Table 8-1.

Table 8-1: Attributes for the <table> Tag

Tag	Meaning
`border="n"`	Width of enclosed area surrounding table; if `border="0"`, this also eliminates the grid lines within the table itself
`cellspacing="n"`	Spacing between individual cells
`cellpadding="n"`	Space between border and contents of cell
`width="n"`	Desired width; overrides automatic width calculations (value or percentage)

It's useful to consider how to stretch out the table so that things aren't so jammed together. Two basic attributes enable you to space things out: width and cellpadding.

The width attribute enables you to specify the exact width of the table, regardless of contents, on the screen. You can specify it either as a specific number of pixels or as a percentage of the overall width of the current viewer window. I always use the latter form, which requires a slight modification to the code used for the preceding table:

```
<h3>Common Cable TV Channels</h3>
<table border="1" width="75%">
<tr><td>MTV</td></tr>
<tr><td>EPSN</td></tr>
<tr><td>CNN Headline News</td></tr>
<tr><td>WTBS Atlanta</td></tr>
</table>
```

Notice here that I've also shrunk the HTML a bit. As you'll recall from the discussion in earlier chapters, your entire Web page can be on one long line, if you like; so certainly in a case like this, you can put the row and data specs on the same line. As you can see in Figure 8-3, the output is considerably more open than the previous table.

The other way to open up the design of your table is to specify a cellpadding factor. Two attributes initially seem similar, but they serve important but different functions in the layout of the table. cellpadding indicates the amount of space—in pixels—between the inner edge of the table cell border and the material within, whereas cellspacing refers to the width of the grid lines between the data cells.

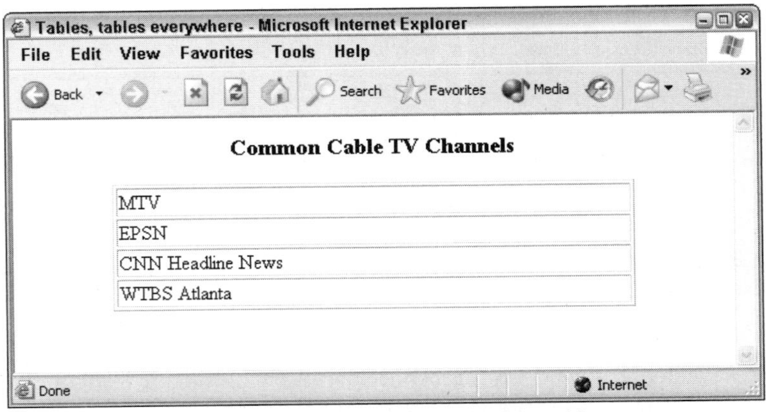

Figure 8-3: Adding some width improves the look of the table.

Here's an example of two tables, one using the cellpadding parameter and the other using cellspacing:

```
<h3>Common Cable TV Channels</h3>
<table border="1" cellpadding="10">
<tr><td>MTV</td>
   <td>EPSN</td>
   <td>CNN Headline News</td>
   <td>WTBS Atlanta</td>
</tr>
</table>
<div style='font-size:75%'>cellpadding=10</div>
<hr />

<table border="1" cellspacing="10">
<tr><td>MTV</td>
   <td>EPSN</td>
   <td>CNN Headline News</td>
   <td>WTBS Atlanta</td>
</tr>
</table>
<div style='font-size:75%'>cellspacing=10</div>
```

Consider the differences between the two examples shown in Figure 8-4. By slightly increasing the cellpadding, you increase the size of the individual data cells and improve the look of your table. Increasing cellspacing, on the other hand, makes the table look like a steamroller ran over the grid and flattened it.

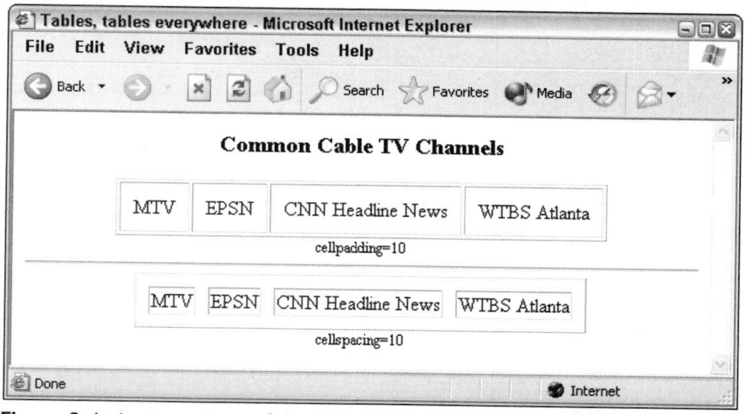

Figure 8-4: A comparison of the cellpadding and cellspacing parameters.

Within a table, not only can you specify the rows with tr and individual data elements with td but you can also specify column headings with th (which replaces the td tag in the row). The th tag is mostly identical to td, with two important changes: Text in the th tag appears in bold and is horizontally centered in the cell.

You can also specify the horizontal alignment of data cells within their space by using the `align` option. The options are `align="left"` (the default), `align="center"`, and `align="right"`, as demonstrated in the following HTML snippet. You can use `valign` to specify the vertical alignment: `valign="top"`, for example, ensures that all cells on a row have their information at the top rather than the default of vertically centered. The `valign` options are `top`, `middle`, `bottom`, and `baseline`. In the following code, I added the `<th>` tag to provide each column with a column head. I have also adjusted the cell alignment and the size of the table border:

```
<table border="5" width="75%">
<tr>
<th>Show</th><th>Airs on</th>
</tr>
<tr align="center">
<td>Sherlock Holmes</td><td>Monday</td>
</tr>
<tr align="left">
<td>Lovejoy</td><td align="right">Monday</td>
</tr>
</table>
```

In Figure 8-5, see how the `<th>` tag changes the layout of the information on the page, and you can see what happens when a larger `border` is specified. I also added some different alignment options. Alignment is inherited in a table, so if you want to have all data cells in a row share an alignment, you can put the align attribute in the `tr` tag. If you only want the alignment to affect an individual table cell, use the `align` attribute in the `td` tag instead.

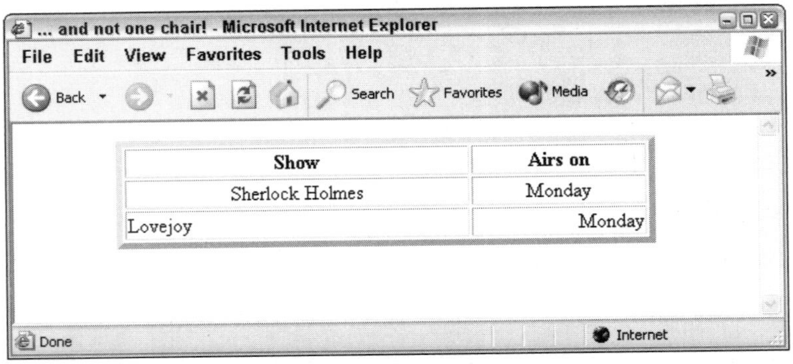

Figure 8-5: Using the <th> tag to add table headers.

Rows and columns can span more than one table unit if needed, so you can add a nice header over both columns of the previous table by specifying `colspan="2"` in a new data cell:

```
<table border="5" width="75%">
<tr>
<td colspan="2" align="center">
<span style='font-size:125%;'>
```

```
Arts &amp; Entertainment Network</span>
</td>
</tr><tr>
<th>Show</th><th>Airs on</th>
</tr>
<tr align="center">
<td>Sherlock Holmes</td><td>Monday</td>
</tr>
<tr align="center">
<td>Lovejoy</td><td>Monday</td>
</tr>
</table>
```

This simple change offers considerable control over the layout of the individual cells within the table, as shown in Figure 8-6. Notice that I've fixed the weird alignments, so everything is all lined up nicely, and I've used a CSS element, font-size, to increase the size of the type.

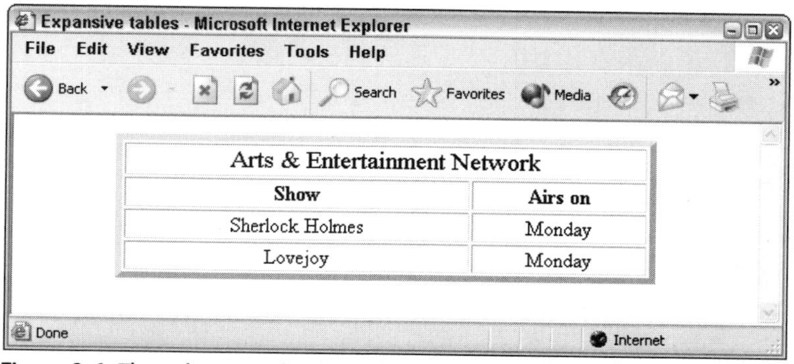

Figure 8-6: The colspan attribute enables you to add headers that span more than one column.

Advanced table formatting

A number of additional table formatting options help you learn how to really exploit this powerful set of features embodied in the table tag set. One of the most important enables you to control the colors involved with the table: the color of the cell background.

Colors within a specific data cell show up within the td tag in a way that won't surprise you:

```
<td bgcolor="yellow">text in a yellow cell</td>
```

This code makes the single cell yellow with default black text. You can accomplish the same thing by using CSS, of course. You either define a class with a background color that's then associated with a table, table row, or table data cell; or you simply redefine the colors associated with a table element. The following code shows how CSS classes can be intermingled in a table:

```
<head>
<title>Colorful tables</title>
<style type="text/css">
.title { background-color: #006; color: white; }
th { background-color: yellow; }
</style>
</head>
<body style='text-align:center'>

<table border="5" width="75%">
<tr class="title">
<td colspan="2" align="center">
<span style='font-size:125%;'>
Arts &amp; Entertainment Network</span>
</td>
</tr><tr>
<th>Show</th><th>Airs on</th>
</tr>
<tr align="center">
<td>Sherlock Holmes</td><td>Monday</td>
</tr>
<tr align="center">
<td>Lovejoy</td><td bgcolor="#99ff99">Monday</td>
</tr>
</table>
</body>
```

The result of this formatting is quite attractive, as shown in Figure 8-7, and it's even more attractive when you can see it in color!

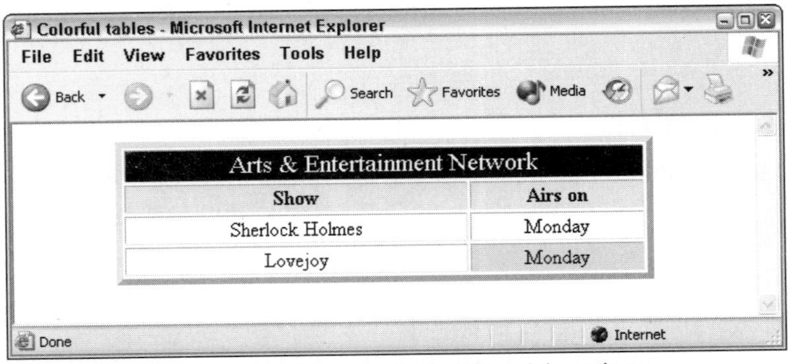

Figure 8-7: Table cells colored by using both CSS and the <td> tag.

In this code, the `style` block creates a class called `title` that has a dark blue background and white text, and then it redefines the table head (`th`) tag to have a yellow background. Then, in the table itself, the `title` class is applied to the first row by adding `class="title"` to the `tr` tag. Finally, the light green background in the bottom-right data cell is done with an old-fashioned `bgcolor` attribute, which works just as well.

One thing that might not be obvious is that you can really exploit the inheritance characteristics of table elements with colors. Want to have all the data cells share a background color? Then either redefine the table tag itself within CSS, add a `style='background-color: #xxx'` attribute to the table tag, or use a `bgcolor` attribute, also within the table tag itself.

The `colspan` attribute is pretty easy to understand, I think; but the real challenge is trying to figure out how to use its sibling attribute, `rowspan`, which lets you have a data cell across multiple rows of the table.

The next example demonstrates `rowspan`; in this case, I include a graphic image in the multi-row data cell. The graphic, `what2watch.gif`, is some text that's been rotated 90 degrees counterclockwise. Here's the source code:

```
<table border="5" cellspacing="0" width="75%">
<tr class="title">
  <td rowspan="3" align="center">
    <img src="Graphics/what2watch.gif" alt="what to watch" />
  </td>
  <th>Show</th><th>Airs on</th>
</tr>
<tr align="center">
  <td>Sherlock Holmes</td><td>Monday</td>
</tr>
<tr align="center">
  <td>Lovejoy</td><td>Monday</td>
</tr>
</table>
```

The result is a very sophisticated table, as shown in Figure 8-8. Pay attention in the figure to the result of setting `cellspacing` to zero. It's not what you think (that is, the contents of cells don't end up actually abutting each other), but it is attractive! A common graphics trick is also shown in this example. The background of the graphic has been carefully chosen to ensure that it can be duplicated as a color specification in the HTML. So however large or small the table becomes, the graphic seems to shrink or stretch to fit. It doesn't really; it's just that the background of the table data cell is identical.

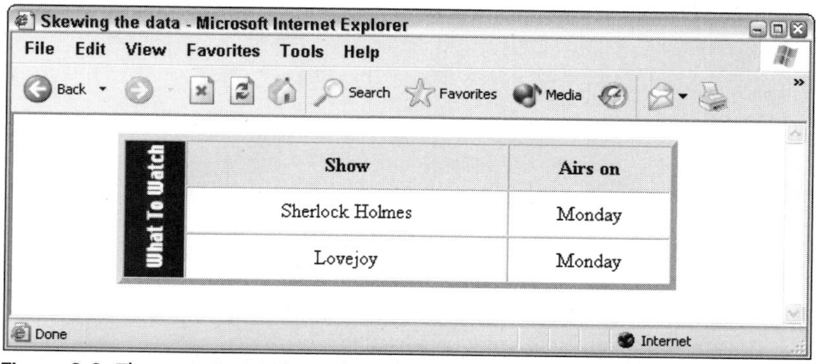

Figure 8-8: The rowspan attribute demonstrated.

Table attributes that aren't 100 percent portable

Although all the table attributes shown so far work across the major Web browsers, Microsoft has expanded the definition of tables a bit further than even the HTML 4 specification details.

The most recent HTML specification details how to set background colors for specific cells using `bgcolor`, and CSS enables you to specify the colors of a table cell as a regular CSS container. But Internet Explorer adds its own additional attributes. The `background` tag allows background graphics in table cells, and the `bordercolor` tag gives you detailed control over the border color. If the latter is not exact enough, Internet Explorer also offers the capability to set the two colors used in the border with `bordercolorlight` and `bordercolordark`. Further, Internet Explorer is the only Web browser that enables you to specify background graphics within individual data cells by using `background=graphic-file` rather than `bgcolor` solid colors, although CSS also allows background graphics.

 x-ref See Chapter 7 for more about adding graphics to your Web pages, including background graphics with CSS.

All these new attributes are demonstrated in the following example:

```
<table bordercolor="blue" border="5" cellspacing="0"
 cellpadding="20" width="75%">
<tr>
 <td background="Graphics/tiedye-background.gif"
  align="center">
  <span style='font-size: 175%;font-weight:bold;color:white;
   background-color:black;'>
  What a Long, Strange Trip It's Been</span>
  </td>
</tr>
</table>
<hr />
<table bordercolorlight="yellow" bordercolordark="red"
 border="10" cellspacing="0" cellpadding="8" width="50%">
<tr>
 <td align="center">
  Classic Rock from guys in BMWs.
  </td>
</tr>
</table>
```

Figure 8-9 shows the result of this code. Looks good, doesn't it?

Figure 8-9: Table-edge colors specified for a different appearance: This capability is only available in Internet Explorer.

on the web This example looks good here, but to really see this rainbow of colors at its best, you'll want to view the file on your own computer! Just go to http://www.intuitive.com/coolsites/, and then go to the Examples area to see it in full color.

Modifying edges and grid lines

Two table attributes are new in the HTML 4 specification. Both offer even finer granularity of control over the borders around the table and between the individual data cells. The two attributes are frame and rules, and their values are defined as shown in Tables 8-2 and 8-3.

Table 8-2: Values for the <table frame= Attribute>

Value	Result
void	Removes all outside table borders
above	Displays a border on the top side of the table frame
below	Displays a border on the bottom side of the table frame
hsides	Displays a border on the top and bottom sides of the table frame
lhs	Displays a border on the left-hand side of the table frame
rhs	Displays a border on the right-hand side of the table frame
vsides	Displays a border on the left and right sides of the table frame
box	Displays a border on all sides of the table frame
border	Displays a border on all sides of the table frame

Table 8-3: Values for the <table rules= Attribute>

Value	Result
none	Removes all interior table borders
groups	Displays horizontal borders between all table groups. Groups are specified by thead, tbody, tfoot, and colgroup elements.
rows	Displays horizontal borders between all table rows
cols	Displays vertical borders between all table columns
all	Displays a border on all rows and columns

The frame and rule attributes combine to give you a remarkable amount of control over the borders and edges in a Web table, but they're pretty complex. I offer you one example and encourage you to tweak the source yourself to see how these attributes work in different combinations:

```
<table border="10" frame="vsides" cellspacing="0"
  rules="rows" width="50%">
<tr align="center">
  <td> January </td>
  <td> $25,404,384.08 </td>
</tr>
<tr align="center">
  <td> February </td>
  <td> $28,498,294.38 </td>
</tr>
<tr align="center">
  <td> March </td>
  <td> $31,978,193.55 </td>
</tr>
<tr align="center">
  <td> April </td>
  <td> $18,559,205.00 </td>
</tr>
</table>
```

Read through this code example closely (and remember that all the important work is being done in the table tag) and compare it to Figure 8-10 to see if this makes sense to you. Try opening the same example in Netscape or an older version of Internet Explorer—which doesn't yet support these HTML 4.0 additions—and consider how different the table looks.

tip

Try taking out the cellspacing="0" in the previous example, and notice the rule lines are broken with a very small invisible grid line or 3D bar (depends on which browser you're using). Specify that there should be no spacing, and the problem goes away. This nuance of layout spacing is also true when you work with background colors in your data cells.

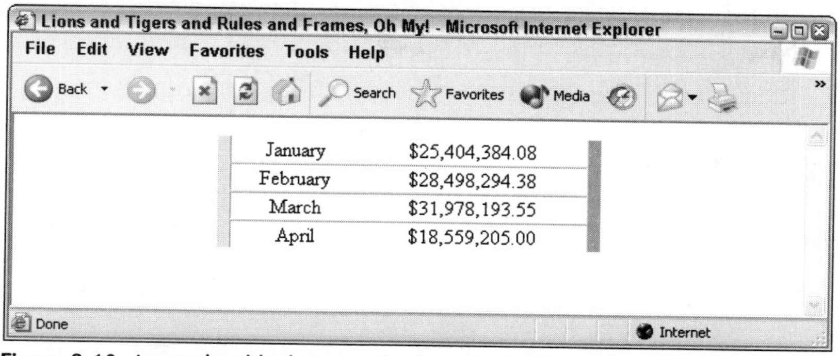

Figure 8-10: A sample table that uses the frame and rules attributes.

Tricks with Table Layouts

Before we leave tables and move on, I'd like to show you two more examples of how you can use tables to dramatically change the appearance of material on your Web page.

Tables within tables

The first trick is a table within a table. This is a real-life example: It's the signup form from the local bus pass program—EcoPass—site that I manage at http://www.ourecopass.org/. Here's the source:

```
<html>
<head>
<title>Contact the EcoPass Coordinators</title>
<style type="text/css">
<!-
.text    { font-size: 95% }
body     { width:80%; margin-left:10%; background-color:white; }
// -->
</style>
</head>
<body>
<h2 style='text-align:center;background-color:#99c'>
Contact The Norwood/Quince EcoPass Team</h2>

We welcome email, whether you're interested in talking about
the EcoPass system, you're a member of the NQ EcoPass
community, or you'd like to learn more about it. If you'd
rather not contact us, you can <a href="index.html">go to
our home page</a> or learn about our
```

Continued

Continued

```
<a href="lists.html">mailing lists</a>.

<br /><br />

<div style='text-align:center'>
<table cellpadding="7" cellspacing="0" border="0">
<tr><td valign="top" bgcolor="#cccccc">

<form method="POST" action="mailform.cgi">
<table border="0" cellpadding="2">
<tr>
<td align="right" class="text">
Your name:</td>
<td><input name="name" size="35" /></td>
</tr><tr>
<td align="right" class="text">
Your email:</td>
<td><input name="email" size="35" /></td>
</tr><tr>
<td align="right" class="text">
Your phone:</td>
<td><input name="phone" size="35" /></td>
</tr><tr>
<td align="right" class="text">
Street address:</td>
<td><input name="address" size="50" /></td>
</tr><tr>
<td colspan="2" class="text">
Your Message (write as much as you'd like!):<br />
<textarea rows=5 cols=70 name="note"
 style="margin-left: 2em;margin-top:3px"></textarea>
<br /><div style='text-align:center'>
<input type="submit" value="send it in"
 style="font-size: 80%;" />
</div>
</td>
</tr>
</table>

</td></tr>
</table>

</form> <!- it's out of order, but forms have layout peculiarities ->

</div>
<div style='padding:3px;font-size:80%;
text-align:center;background-color:#99c'>
```

```
<a href="http://www.intuitive.com/">Web site by Dave Taylor</a>
</div>
</body>
</html>
```

You haven't yet seen one big part of this listing: forms. The `input` tags and the `form` and `/form` tags are all part of the HTML necessary for a Web page to send data back to the server for processing. Figure 8-11 shows the result of this code. A lot is going on within layout, I know, but grab the source code and make some changes to see how it's all assembled. For example, change `border="0"` in the inner table to `border="1"` and watch how suddenly all the elements of the table are obvious and visible.

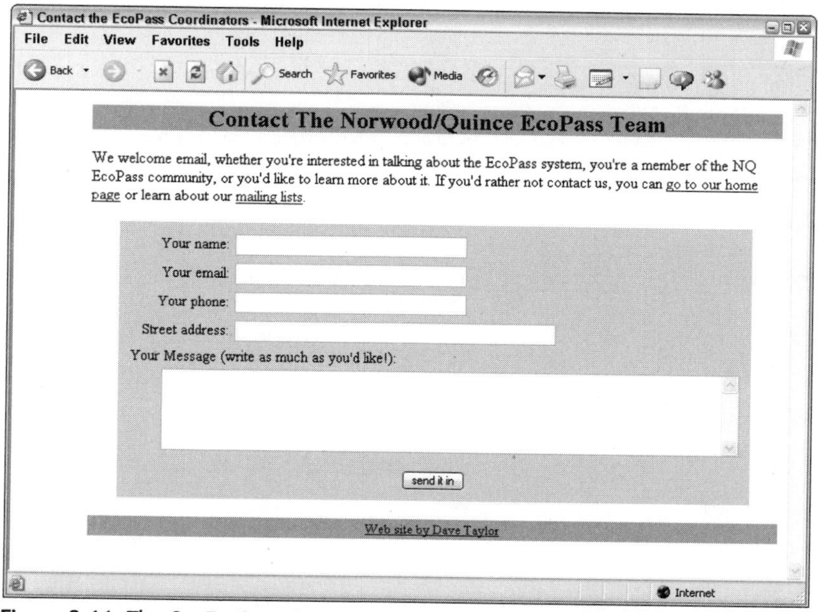

Figure 8-11: The OurEcoPass Contact Us page, showing a table within a table.

---

x-ref   I discuss forms in detail in Chapter 9.

Also notice in this example how you can gracefully intersperse CSS and HTML to offer great flexibility and an attractive appearance, almost effortlessly.

tip   When I'm working with table layouts, I always leave the border on until I'm just about done with everything. Then I switch it off and test the layout on a few different browsers.

The second table trick I want to demonstrate is using a table as a tool for developing the layout of an entire page rather than an element within the page. For this, I call on another example: a home page template for a small business site, built using tables.

```
<html>
<head>
  <title>Tables as a Page Layout Tool</title>
  <style type="text/css">
  .name { color: white; font-weight: bold; font-size: 110%;
        margin-top: 10px; }
  body  { color: #336; font-family: sans-serif; }
  td    { font-size: 90%; }
  </style>
</head>
<body>
<table border="0" width="640" cellspacing="9">
<tr>
<td width="115" align="center" valign="top" bgcolor="#666666">
<div class="name">
Small Business International, Inc.
</div>
<br />
<table border="1" cellpadding="14" cellspacing="0"
 bgcolor="#DDDDDD">
<tr><td align="center">
  <a href="mission.html">Mission</a>
</td></tr>
<tr><td align="center">
  <a href="approach.html">Approach</a>
</td></tr>
<tr><td align="center">
  <a href="staff.html">Staff</a>
</td></tr>
<tr><td align="center">
  <a href="links.html">Links</a>
</td></tr>
<tr><td align="center">
  <a href="index.html">Home</a>
</td></tr>
</table></td><td width="525">
<div style="text-align:center;">
<img src="Graphics/sbi-logo.gif" alt="logo" />
</div><div>
Small Business International, Inc. ("SBI") is a strategy
consulting and new venture development firm serving the
global retail industry. The firm was founded in 1974 to
assist US-based retail enterprises in realizing their
international growth objectives and to capitalize on
```

```
emerging retail trends through the creation and financing
of promising new ventures.
</div>
<div style="text-align:center;">
<img src="Graphics/sbi-image1.gif" vspace="3"
 alt="sbi-map" /><br />
<div style="font-size: 75%">A strategic focus: Japan.</div>
</div>

</td></tr>
</table>

</body>
</html>
```

By now, every line of this example should make sense to you. Everything being used here has been explained earlier in the book, with the exception of margin settings in the CSS. A quick glance at Figure 8-12, and you can immediately see that this is how people create multiple column designs, like that used on the Microsoft home page (`http://www.microsoft.com/`), for example.

x-ref I cover margin settings and other advanced aspects of CSS in Chapter 12.

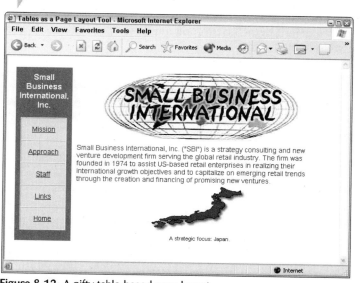

Figure 8-12: A nifty table-based page layout.

The hidden problem with this design, however, is that it's explicitly designed for a standard VGA monitor resolution: 640 pixels wide. You can see that in the `table width` specification:

```
<table border="0" width="640" cellspacing="9">
```

If the user has a screen that's considerably wider (800, 1024, or more pixels), a lot of unused blank space remains on the right side of the screen, and you can't do much about it.

One experiment that might give you good results is using relative widths at the top of the table, like this:

```
<table border="0" width="80%" cellspacing="9">
```

You can then specify the exact size of the column you are working with, like this:

```
<td width="150">
```

With this method, you let the browser calculate the width of any other columns of data you might specify. This works reasonably well, but there's a hidden *gotcha* if you have a screen that's too small. It's a problem that is present on the Small Business International page, too, if displayed on too narrow a screen. When you specify relative widths on a narrow screen, the browser sometimes calculates the width of a column to be narrower than the items within. The table of possible areas to explore on the SBI page can end up being resized and, as a result, its edge might actually overlap the main column of data, a very unacceptable result.

To avoid the potential problem of overlapping columns, you can create a blank graphic that is the specific width of the widest element in the column plus a dozen pixels or so. You then include that as a hidden spacer element.

 tip   If your table looks bizarre when you view it and you're using a mix of specific pixel widths and percentage widths, try switching exclusively to pixel widths or percentage widths. It's not always a problem, but I've definitely seen some weird table layouts suddenly fix themselves when I change from mixed specifications to a single type.

Grouping table elements for faster rendering

You have a lot of ways to slice and dice tables to produce just the layout you want in HTML. As you push the envelope further, however, sometimes you find that it takes a while for tables to render in a Web browser. Just as the `img` tag provides you with the capability to specify the height and width to speed up rendering graphical elements, there is an analogous capability called `colgroup`—column groups for tables. You won't see them used too often on the Web, but it's worth a brief peek to see how they work!

With these additional HTML tags, you can now specify the number and exact size of each row of a table with a combination of the `colgroup` and `col` tags within a `table` tag. There is a `cols` attribute to the `table` tag, but if you want to start including hints about your table size in your page, `colgroup` is a much better, more flexible strategy.

Why bother indicating the number of columns? Because if you have ever worked with complex tables, you already know that the browser can't start rendering the first line of the table until it has received every snippet of information. To understand why you should indicate the number of columns, consider what happens when the following table is displayed onscreen:

```
<table border="1" cellspacing="3">
<tr><td>The</td><td>Rain</td><td>in</td><td>Spain</td>
</tr><tr>
<td>Falls</td><td>Mainly</td><td>On</td><td>The</td>
<td>Plain</td>
</tr><tr>
<td>and where is that plain?</td><td>in Spain! In
Spain!</td>
</tr>
</table>
```

Figure 8-13 shows the result: Pay close attention to the spacing of cells and the number of cells in the first row of the table.

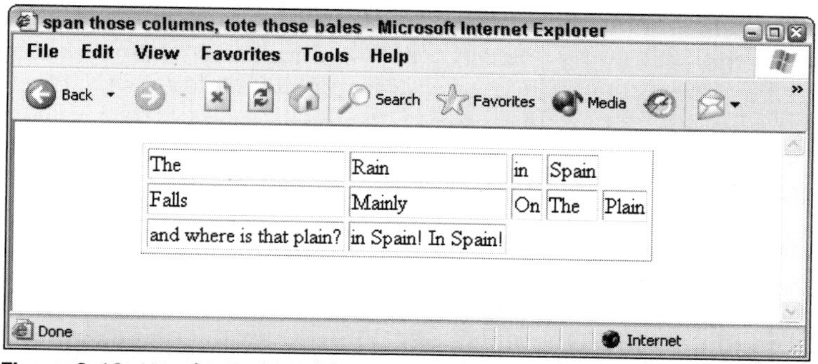

Figure 8-13: How big is this table? It can be hard to compute when the layout is sufficiently complex.

If the table is as small as the previous example, a delay of a fraction of a second in rendering the page isn't a big deal; but when you get into large tables—and I've created tables with over 1,000 data cells—the delay in transmitting information and rendering the table can be substantial.

Grouping tables to speed up display

The solution is to use the `colgroup` and `cols` tags to give the browser an idea of what's coming next. Here's how you can rewrite the code for the preceding table to use these new tags:

```
<table border="1" cellspacing="3">

<colgroup align="center" />
  <col width="2*" />
```

Continued

```
Continued
  <col width="4*" />
<colgroup />
  <col />
  <col width="15%"><col width="150" />

<tr><td>The</td><td>Rain</td><td>in</td><td>Spain</td>
</tr><tr>
<td>Falls</td><td>Mainly</td><td>On</td><td>The</td>
<td>Plain</td>
</tr><tr>
<td>and where is that plain?</td><td>in Spain! In
Spain!</td>
</tr>
</table>
```

This may look a bit confusing, but the sizing parameters are similar to how you specify frame sizes when you use the `frameset` tag, which I explain shortly in the section "Pages within Pages: Frames." In a nutshell, you can specify sizes by percentage of the width of the window (`width="15%"`), the specific number of pixels (`width="150"`), having the browser compute the smallest possible width for the cells in the column (`<col>` without any width specified), or by specifying how much of the remaining unallocated space should be allocated to the different columns. Notice that the 2* and 4* for the first `colgroup` specify ratios of space allocated: Whatever space is allocated for the first column, twice as much should be given to the second. This could also be accomplished with * and 2*.

In the previous example, 2* appears once, 4* appears once, and `<col>` appears once without a width specification, which is identical to `<col width="*">` or `<col width="1*">`. Add these specs up (2+4+1) and you get 7 portions that encompass the entire width of the browser window. Subtract the space for the 15 percent width and 150-pixel-width columns, and the remaining space on the window is allocated for the remainder of the table, broken into ⅔, ⁴⁄₇, and ⅐. When the entire width of the screen is 1000 pixels, 15 percent is 150 pixels, and the width consumed by the last two columns is 300 pixels (15 percent + 150). The remainder is 700 pixels, which is divided up into seven equal portions and then allocated. The result: Column 1 is 200 pixels wide, Column 2 is 400 pixels wide, Column 3 is 100 pixels wide, and the last two you already know. I know, I know, this makes your head swim!

A glance at Figure 8-14 demonstrates how this all works, and it also shows how `colgroup` lets you apply formatting to a set of columns simultaneously with the `align="center"` attribute.

Notice one thing here: Internet Explorer 6.0, which I used for these screenshots, doesn't understand the asterisk width notation for `col`, so although it applied the percentage and absolute pixel widths, and even caught the `align="center"` in the `colgroup` tag, the first and second columns ended up the same width (even though the second should be twice as wide as the first).

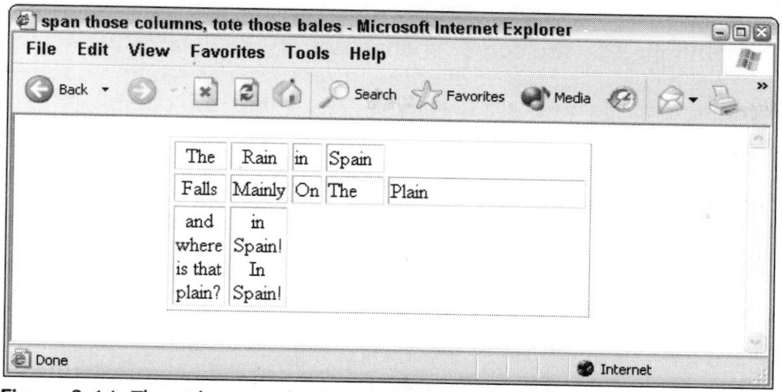

Figure 8-14: The colspan and col tags define table attributes.

Therefore, not only is `col` useful for specifying the number of columns, it's also quite useful for specifying the width of a given column. Even better, you can also specify other attributes for a given column, as demonstrated in the following example and shown in Figure 8-15:

```
<table border="1" width="90%">
<colgroup />
<col align="right" />
<col align="char" char=":" />
<thead>
<tr><th>What I'm Doing</th><th>Time Of Day</th></tr>
</thead>
<tbody>
<tr><td>Waking Up</td><td>8:30 am</td></tr>
<tr><td>Driving to Work</td><td>9:00 am</td></tr>
<tr><td>Eating Lunch</td><td>12:00 noon</td></tr>
<tr><td>Driving Home</td><td>6:00 pm</td></tr>
</tbody>
</table>
```

To help organize complex tables, `<thead>` and `<tbody>` have been added: They're not mandatory, and it's too soon to tell if people will actually start using them. More than anything, they're just a layout convenience to help clarify what elements are serving what purposes in the actual table HTML.

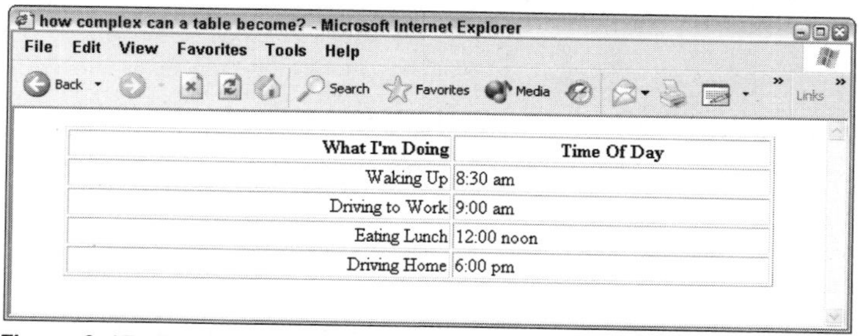

Figure 8-15: Organizing a table with thead and tbody doesn't affect appearance.

The other interesting thing about this example is that I'm specifying that I want to have the second column of information aligned by the colon (:) character in the data cell contents. The attribute align="char" specifies a character alignment, and char is where you specify which character to use for alignment. If you don't specify a char value, the default is '.', which aligns numeric values along the decimal point.

tip   Alas, character alignment isn't supported in Internet Explorer 6.0, so Figure 8-15 doesn't show the times aligned along the colons. It'll just magically work one day, I expect.

Another possible align option (and, like the align="char" option, it can appear anywhere you can specify an alignment) that you might well have been waiting for since the first release of HTML has arrived: justified text. The align="justify" attribute should eliminate the ragged right margin of text, while keeping the left margin also aligned.

This attribute can also be used with the p or div tag, as discussed earlier in the book. Consider this HTML sequence:

```
<p align="justify">
While the rain slowly poured down the
rooftops in Spain, the same storm was dumping water in
Paris too, pooling at the edge of the buildings and
seeping slowly into the Seine. Tintin, our hero, was
undaunted. He held his
chin high and walked quietly along the Rue Sienna, looking
for his beloved dog.
</p>

<table border="1" cellpadding="5">
<col align="justify" /><tr><td>
Just when he was beginning
to give up hope, a small "yip" from a dark alleyway caused
Tintin to spin about and yell out "Snowy?  Come on, boy!"
Within moments, there was a happy reunion in the rain
between the boy reporter and his faithful - but ever-
curious - pet.
</td></tr>
</table>
```

Now look at how it all formats in Figure 8-16. As you can see, justification is implemented within the p tag in this version of Internet Explorer, but justification within the data cell is ignored.

tip   Dying for that visual justified effect? Just wrap the table data cell in <p align="justify"> and you achieve the results desired.

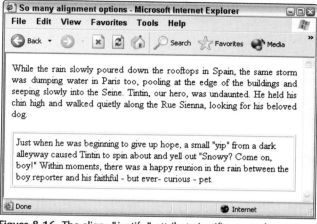

Figure 8-16: The align="justify" attribute justifies text when it is used within the <p> tag but not when used within a table data cell.

Pages within Pages: Frames

Okay, I think you're ready. Take a deep breath. It's time for us to explore something that makes tables look easy: frames. Frames answer the question: What if each data cell in your table was its own Web page?

When Netscape first introduced frames, prior to the release of HTML 3.2, lots of people didn't like them. Enough sites, however, started to develop around a frame design, splitting a single Web page into separate panes, that they gradually became popular in spite of complaints.

Meanwhile, many sites that had introduced frame versions of their home pages had to also offer a no-frame version for people who didn't like frames; and today the first frame site I ever saw, the Netscape home page, is now a frames-free site. If you want to be an HTML expert, you should definitely know how to work with frames; but you'll undoubtedly find that when you become an expert in CSS, designing with tables with their myriad uses is the better way to go.

The basics of frames

Unlike many of the tags you've seen so far, frames are an all-or-nothing proposition. Individual frames are specified with the `frame` tag, which is itself wrapped in a `frameset` specifier that indicates the amount of space to allocate to each pane of information. Here's a very basic frame page that breaks the screen into two sections; the top pane is 75 pixels high, and the second pane consumes the remainder of the screen:

```
<html>
<title>A Simple Frames-based Design</title>
<frameset rows="75,*">
    <frame src="frames/top.html" />
    <frame src="frames/bottom.html" />
</frameset>
</html>
```

Figure 8-17 shows what happens in the browser: You have the single page split into two rows as specified in the `frameset` tag. The first row (pane) is 75 pixels high with a white background, and the second row, with its black background, consumes the remaining space (specified by *).

You can't see here that three Web pages are actually involved in getting this to format correctly: the *root* page shown above and two additional pages, `top.html` and `bottom.html`. The first file, `top.html`, contains this code:

```
<body bgcolor="white">
<h2 style="text-align:center;">This
is the top pane on the page!</h2>
</body>
```

The second file, `bottom.html`, looks like this:

```
<body style="background:black; color:white;">
<div style="margin-top: 10%;text-align:center;">
<h2>this is the bottom section of the page!</h2>
</div>
</body>
```

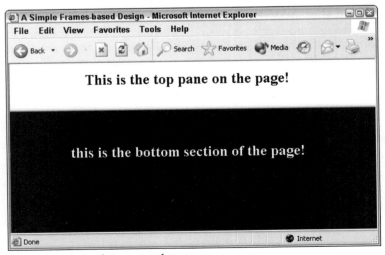

Figure 8-17: A simple two-pane frame page.

That's the basic concept of frame documents: Instead of a single page defining all the information displayed to the visitor, the information is split into multiple pages, each given its own small piece of the window.

Specifying frame panes and sizes

Now that you're an expert with tables, it will come as no surprise that you have lots of options for frames, too, only a few of which are vitally important to understand.

The most important tag to learn about is `frameset`. The `frameset` tag creates a *frameset*: a set of frames into which the Web page is split. In addition to being able to specify `rows` to split the Web page into horizontal panes, you can alternatively use `cols` to specify vertical panes. You can use three different values for these attributes:

- A simple number to specify the desired size in screen pixels
- An asterisk to specify the remaining space on the page
- A percentage of page width by using the `n%` notation

If you think you got all that, here's a test for you: What does `<frameset cols="30%,19,*">` mean?

The sequence `cols="30%,19,*"` is interpreted as the first column being allocated 30 percent of the width of the window, the next column being allocated a slim 19 pixels, and the third column getting the remainder of the space on the window.

You can create complex multipane Web pages, where each pane has autonomous behavior, by combining these attributes in creative ways:

```html
<html>
<title>Lots of frames</title>
<frameset cols="80%,*">
   <frameset rows="30%,70%">
     <frame src="frames/top.html" />
     <frame src="frames/bottom.html" />
   </frameset>
   <frameset rows="33%,33%,*">
     <frame src="frames/advert1.html" />
     <frame src="frames/advert2.html" />
     <frame src="frames/advert3.html" />
   </frameset>
</frameset>
</html>
```

In this case, what I've done is specify two columns of information. One column is 80 percent of the width of the screen; the latter gets the remaining width. That's specified with the following line:

```html
<frameset cols="80%,*">
```

The first pane here is the second frameset: two rows, the first (`top.html`) 30 percent of the available height, and the second (`bottom.html`) the remaining 70 percent:

```
<frameset rows="30%,70%">
    <frame src="frames/top.html" />
    <frame src="frames/bottom.html" />
</frameset>
```

The second column of information (the * width in the first frameset specification) contains three advertisements evenly spaced, each 33 percent of the vertical space:

```
<frameset rows="33%,33%,*">
    <frame src="frames/advert1.html" />
    <frame src="frames/advert2.html" />
    <frame src="frames/advert3.html" />
</frameset>
```

The result of this code is shown in Figure 8-18.

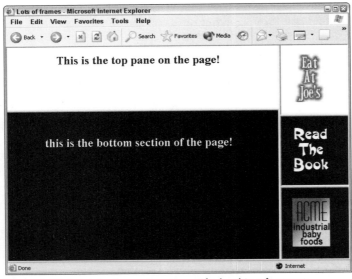

Figure 8-18: Lots of pain, er, panes, specified within a frameset.

You can specify a couple of different attributes for frames, the most important of which is the `name=` attribute. Each specific frame can be given a unique name (similar to `<a name=>`) that can then be used as a way to control which window is affected by specific actions. What's the point of this? Imagine that your site includes a table of contents in a small pane that is always present. Any user who clicks one of the links on the table of contents actually causes the information in the main pane to change—not the information in the table of contents pane.

That's the idea behind the `name=` attribute. A partner attribute also appears in the anchor tag for any hypertext reference (`a href`). The following provides an example of this at work. First, a simple frames page:

```
<html>
<frameset cols="20%,*">
   <frame src="frames/toc.html" />
   <frame src="frames/default.html" name="main" />
</frameset>
</html>
```

Notice in this example that the second `frame` tag now has a name associated with it: `main`.

Here are the contents of the `default.html` page:

```
<html>
<body style="text-align:center;">
<img src="animal-image.gif" alt="butterfly" />
</body>
</html>
```

And here's the all-important `toc.html` page with the `target="main"` attribute, where `"main"` is the name of the specific target pane as specified in the `frame` tag itself:

```
<html>
<body style="background-color:yellow">
<div style="text-align:center; font-size:120%; font-weight:bold;">
<h2>Pick An Animal</h2>
<div style='line-height:2.0;'>
<a href="dog.html" target="main">DOG</a>
<br />
<a href="cat.html" target="main">CAT</a>
<br />
<a href="bird.html" target="main">BIRD</a>
<br />
<a href="default.html" target="main">(HOME)</a>
</div>
</div>
</body>
</html>
```

Figure 8-19 shows how it looks, but you'll definitely want to try this out.

Check out the example files for this chapter on this book's companion Web site at `http://www.intuitive.com/coolsites/` to learn how these attributes work. In particular, experiment with excluding the target attribute. Watch what happens when you click a link and what happens when you use the Back button on your browser.

Figure 8-19: Navigational panes offer flexibility in layout and presentation.

The `frame` tag itself also has two attributes worth highlighting. The first enables you to specify the width of a frame border: `frameborder` (makes sense, eh?), with an attribute in pixels. The second, `scrolling`, enables you to force or prohibit a scroll bar, even if the pane is too small for the information within it. Possible values are `yes`, `no`, and `auto`; the latter adds a scrollbar if needed, but hides it otherwise. Here is a small sample of the `scrolling` attribute:

```
<html>
<title>Animals Tour</title>
<frameset cols="20%,*">
  <frame src="frames/toc.html" scrolling="yes" />
  <frame src="frames/default.html" name="main" />
</frameset>
</html>
```

Compare the results in Figure 8-20 with Figure 8-19.

By default, visitors can drag around the frame borders to resize elements of the page design. If you'd rather that didn't occur, add the `noresize` attribute, which, when written as xhtml, is the odd looking `noresize="noresize"`.

When working with frames, remember and compensate for the visitors who might not be able to see your frames-based design. The most recent versions of the major Web browsers, Navigator and Explorer, support frames quite well, but if you have visitors with older software, their browsers probably won't support the entire frames tag set.

Hypertext Reference Target Values

It should be clear that you can *aim* events at a specific pane of a frames-based design by using the `name="name"` attribute to specify the name of the pane within the `frame`-tag. Then, on the navigational pages, use `target="name"` as part of the `href` to have the events affect the specified pane rather than the one that you're working within. It turns out, however, that you can specify other values within the `target` attribute, values that let you gain a bit more control over what's going on. Table 8-4 summarizes the four key targets with which you should experiment.

Table 8-4: Values of the target Attribute for Greater Frame Control

Name	Meaning
_blank	Loads the document in a new, unnamed window.
_self	Loads the document into the current window (the default).
_parent	Loads the document into the parent window (only relevant when you have more than one window on the screen).
_top	Loads the document into the very topmost window, thus canceling all other frames that might be in the window.

When you see a Web site that has a frames-based design and a button that says "no frames," the code underneath is doubtless similar to

```
<a href="noframes.html" target="_top">no frames</a>
```

As a fifth possible value, you can use the `target` attribute to point to a named window that doesn't exist, and thereby create a new window with that name.

Judicious use of the special `target` values can considerably improve your frames-based design and offer, for example, a navigational window that sticks even while the user wanders around other areas of the site.

If you don't want to type the `target` value for each of your links, and they're all pointing to the same place, a shortcut in HTML saves you oodles of typing:

```
<base target="value">
```

If specific links are supposed to aim elsewhere, you are still free to override things with a `target` attribute within an individual `a href` tag. That's where you'd use the `target="self"` attribute.

Remembering that any HTML tags that aren't understood are ignored, what do you think would be the result of having a nonframes browser receive something like the source code shown just before Figure 8-20? If you guessed that it'd be a blank page, you're right on the mark!

As a result, the standard way that people circumvent this problem is to have a section in their frames root page that's wrapped with the `noframes` option. If the browser understands frames, it ignores what's in that section; if the browser doesn't understand frames, the material in the `noframes` area is all that it's going to display.

Figure 8-20: Navigational panes with an added scroll bar.

Here's how I might modify the previous listing to include some `noframes` information:

```
<html>
<frameset cols="20%,*">
  <frame src="frames/toc.html" scrolling="yes" />
  <frame src="frames/default.html" name="main" />
</frameset>
<noframes>
<body style="text-align:center;">
<h2>Sorry, but our site is designed for a frames-compliant
browser</h2>
To visit us you'll need to upgrade your Web software.
</body>
</noframes>
</html>
```

Displaying the preceding source with your regular Web browser, if it's at least Internet Explorer 3.0 or Netscape Navigator 2.0, shows you the multiple-frame design as expected. Otherwise, you see the page that would be rendered as if you'd been sent the following HTML sequence:

```
<html>
<body style="text-align:center;">
<h2>Sorry, but our site is designed for a frames-compliant
browser</h2>
To visit us you'll need to upgrade your Web software.
</body>
</html>
```

More fun with frames

Before leaving frames behind, I want to spend a little time looking at some of the cool attributes you can use to fine-tune the appearance of frames in a frameset. First and foremost, you can get rid of the annoying grid line between frame elements by tweaking either the `border` attribute or (depending on the browser) the `frameborder` attribute. Whichever one you use, it goes in the `frameset` tag:

```
<frameset cols="20%,*" border="0">
  <frame src="frames/toc.html" />
  <frame src="frames/default.html" name="main" />
</frameset>
```

But that's pretty similar to the other examples so far. Before you look at how that changes things, however, I want to switch to a different example so that you can see a different, interesting characteristic of frames design: how it spaces out page content. To do this, I use the same basic frameset layout, but I point to a different page, a page that has a simple graphic and lots of text:

```
<html>
<title>The Gettysburg Address</title>
<frameset cols="50%,*" border="5">
  <frame src="frames/gettysburg1.html" marginheight="0"  marginwidth="0"
/>
  <frame src="frames/gettysburg2.html" marginheight="30" marginwidth="30"
/>
</frameset>
</html>
```

The page being displayed to demonstrate the `marginheight` and `marginwidth` attributes is a copy of Abraham Lincoln's Gettysburg Address. The only difference between `gettysburg1.html` and `gettysburg2.html` is the background color, by the way. The results are shown in Figure 8-21, and pay particular attention to the results of specifying a `border` width of five pixels and the dramatic differences in margin changes.

Of course, it's worth mentioning that the `margin` CSS style also offers significant flexibility to change margins if used to modify the `<body>` tag. But sometimes you don't have control over the material that's in your frames-based design. The margin style is explored in depth later, in Chapter 12.

 note   Read the entire Gettysburg Address at http://www.intuitive.com/library/ Gettysburg.shtml. It's time well spent.

Creating a multipane frame site isn't too difficult. What's tricky is to do a really good job of it: to produce a site that makes sense and actually helps people find what they want when they explore your site.

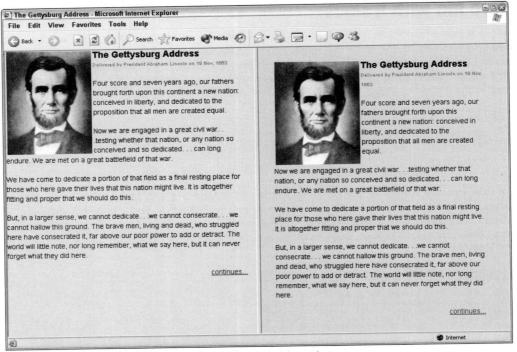

Figure 8-21: The same Web Page with different frame margin settings.

on the web

Be sure to take a few minutes to explore the examples included on this book's companion Web site at `http://www.intuitive.com/coolsites/`. Many of them are presented in a frames-based design.

Inline Frames

One of the coolest things that Microsoft introduced into the HTML language with its popular Internet Explorer browser is the concept of *inline frames*—frame windows completely enclosed by their surrounding window. They are now an official part of the HTML 4 specification and can be used for more sites than in the past.

An inline frame is specified with the `iframe` tag in a manner quite similar to how you specify the `frame` tag, as shown in the following simple example:

```
<iframe src="inset-info.html" height="40%" width="50%"></iframe>
```

In this case, I'm specifying that I want an inline frame window that's 40 percent of the height and 50 percent of the width of the current page and that the HTML within should be the page `inset-info.html`. To use this in a more complex example, I pick up the Gettysburg Address file again:

```html
<html>
<head><title>The Gettysburg Address</title></head>
<body style="text-align:center;">
<div style="margin:25;text-align:left;">
The Gettysburg Address, as delivered by President Abraham
Lincoln to the soldiers and general assembly at the
Gettysburg battlefield during the American Civil War,
November 19, 1863.
</div>
<p align="center">
<iframe src="frames/gettysburg1.html" height="70%" width="75%">
  <table border="1" cellpadding="20"><tr>
  <td align="center">You can't see the information here,
  which should be in a separate inline frame.
  <p>
  <a href="frames/gettysburg1.html">read the Gettysburg Address</A>
  </td></tr></table>
</iframe>
</p>
More information about Lincoln can be found at
<a href="http://www.netins.net/showcase/creative/lincoln.html">
Lincoln Online</A>
</body>
</html>
```

The results in Internet Explorer, as shown in Figure 8-22, are quite attractive. Older browsers that don't understand the `iframe` tag ignore both parts of the `<iframe>` `</iframe>` pair and, instead, interpret the HTML between the two tags. In this case, it says "You can't see the information here. . . ."

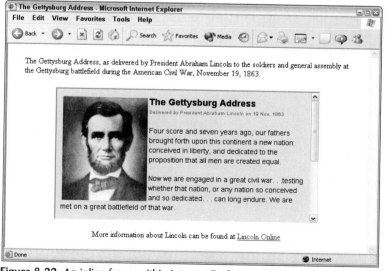

Figure 8-22: An inline frame within Internet Explorer.

A number of options to the iframe tag (that mirror frame capabilities) are worth exploring, particularly frameborder, which can have a value of 0 or 1, depending on whether you'd like a border. The marginwidth and marginheight attributes offer finer control over the spacing between the margin of the inline frame and the contents, and scrolling can be yes, no, or auto, exactly what the frame tag lets you specify.

note   The iframe tag is popularly used on Web sites for those license agreements you generally see prior to downloading software.

You have one final mechanism to explore as you further exploit inline frames on your site: You can name the inline frame with the name attribute, and you can point references to the inline frame with target, just as you would for a regular frames layout.

Table 8-5 summarizes the many HTML tags presented in this chapter.

Table 8-5: Summary of Tags in This Chapter		
HTML Tag	**Close Tag**	**Meaning**
<table	</table>	Creates a Web-based table.
border="x"		Places border around table (pixels or percentage).
cellpadding="x"		Adds additional space within table cells (in pixels).
cellspacing="x"		Adds additional space between table cells (in pixels).
width="x"		Forces table width (in pixels or percentage).
frame="val"		Fine-tunes the frames within the table (see Table 8-2).
rules="val"		Fine-tunes the rules of the table (see Table 8-3).
bordercolor="color"		Specifies color of table border (RGB or color name).
bordercolorlight="color"		Produces the lighter of the two colors specified (RGB or color name).
bordercolordark="color"		Produces the darker of the two colors specified (RGB or color name).
<tr	</tr>	Indicates a table row.
bgcolor="color"		Specifies the background color for the entire row (RGB or color name).
align="align"		Specifies alignment of cells in this row (left, center, right).
<td	</td>	Indicates table data cell.

HTML Tag	Close Tag	Meaning
`bgcolor="color"`		Indicates background color for data cell (RGB or color name).
`colspan="x"`		Indicates number of columns for this data cell to span.
`rowspan="x"`		Indicates number of rows for this data cell to span.
`align="align"`		Specifies alignment of material within the data cell. Possible values: left, center, right.
`valign="align"`		Specifies vertical alignment of material within the data cell. Possible values: top, middle, bottom.
`background="url"`		Specifies the background picture for the cell.
`<frameset`	`</frameset>`	Defines a frame-based page layout.
`cols="x"`		Indicates number and relative sizes of column frames.
`rows="x"`		Indicates number and relative sizes of column rows.
`<frame`		Defines a specific frame.
`src="url"`		Indicates source URL for the frame.
`name="name"`		Indicates name of the pane (used with target=name as a part of the <a> anchor tag).
`scrolling="scrl"`		Sets scroll bar options. Possible values: on, off, auto.
`frameborder="x"`		Indicates size of border around the frame.
`<noframes>`	`</noframes>`	Indicates section of page displayed for users who can't see a frames-based design.

Summary

This chapter gave you a whirlwind tour of the remarkable formatting capabilities offered by the table and frame tag sets. From the basics of the `table`, `tr`, and `td` tags, you learned about the many different attributes of these tags and how they can work together to produce quite sophisticated and interesting layouts. In addition, the exploration of frames offered a new way of looking at site design, particularly in terms of navigational control. I introduce some tricky formatting tag sets, so make sure you've had a chance to digest these before you proceed. Chapter 10 introduces a bunch of advanced design features, including changing backgrounds, Explorer-only marquees, and lots more!

Forms, User Input, and the Common Gateway Interface

In This Chapter

Introducing HTML forms

Extending your forms with fancy formatting

Executing searches from your page

Examining hidden variables

Understanding the CGI backend

This chapter provides an introduction to forms. In some ways, forms on Web pages are just like the ubiquitous paper forms with dozens of fill-in boxes standard in any bureaucratic organization, but they can also include some interesting and helpful capabilities of their own.

I'm going to be honest with you right up front. I've broken this topic into two separate sections. I want to highlight that tasks such as working with forms, requesting information from the user, and sending it to a designated program are separate from the more challenging programming work needed on the server—receiving the data. The communication path between the browser and server is called the *common gateway interface* (CGI) and that's something I have space to address only briefly later in this chapter. But you can find out more by turning to a variety of books that cover just this one topic.

For now, let's explore the wide range of form tags and attributes and how to use them to spice up your site with easy access to search engines, login sections, and more.

An Introduction to HTML Forms

Forms enable you to build Web pages that let users actually enter information and send it back to the server. The forms can range from a single text box for entering a search string—common to all the search engines on the Web—to a complex multipart worksheet that offers powerful submission capabilities.

All forms are the same on the Web, but information can be transmitted from the Web browser software back to the server on the other end in two ways. If you submit information from a form and the URL that it produces includes the information you entered (like `search.cgi?p=aardvark`), the form is called a `method=get` or `get` form. The alternative is that you submit the information and the URL of the next page looks perfectly normal, with no cryptic stuff stuck on the end. If that's the case, you have submitted a `method=post` or `post` form.

I explore the differences between these two forms later in the chapter; for now, it's helpful to be aware that information on forms can be sent in two basic ways. You can start by looking at the design and specification of forms themselves.

HTML forms are surrounded by the `form` tag, which is specified as `<form action="url" method="method">` and `</form>`. The `url` points to the remote file or application used for digesting the information, and the `method` is specified as either `get` or `post`.

Inside the `form` tag, your Web page can contain any standard HTML formatting information, graphics, links to other pages, and any combination of the new tags specific to forms. For the most part, all input fields within a form are specified with the `input` tag and different attributes thereof. The other two possibilities are `select`, for a drop-down list, and `textarea`, for a multiline text input box.

The various new tags let you define the many different elements of your form, as shown in Table 9-1. The most important of the three tags is `input` because it's used for so many different types of form elements.

Table 9-1: The form Tags and Their Attributes

Tag	Close Tag	Meaning
`<input`		Specifies text or other data-input field
`type="opt"`		Specifies the type of `input` entry field
`name="name"`		Specifies the symbolic name of a field value
`value="value"`		Specifies the default content of the text field
`checked="opt"`		Indicates the button or box checked by default
`size="x"`		Indicates the number of characters in the displayed text box
`maxlength="x"`		Indicates the maximum number of characters accepted
`<select`	`</select>`	Specifies a drop-down or multiline menu

Tag	Close Tag	Meaning
`name="name"`		Specifies the symbolic name of a field value
`size="x"`		Determines whether it's a pop up (`size=1`, the default) or a multiline scrolling region
`multiple="multiple"`		Enables users to select more than one value
`<option`	`</option>`	Indicates individual values within the `select` range
`value="x"`		Returns the value of the specified menu item
`selected="selected"`		Denotes the default value in the list
`<textarea`	`</textarea>`	Specifies a multiline text-entry field
`name="x"`		Specifies the symbolic name of a field value
`rows="x"`		Indicates the number of rows (lines) in the `textarea` space
`cols="x"`		Indicates the number of columns in the `textarea` space
`wrap="x"`		Specifies the type of word wrap within the `textarea` (`virtual` is typical, which shows words wrapping but sends them as a single long line when submitted)

The sheer number of different attributes within the `input` tag can be confusing, but you can understand the overloaded tag if you know that the original design for forms had all possible input specified as variants to `input`. It didn't quite work out, however, because two types of information, drop-down lists and text area boxes, ended up spilling out as their own tags: `select` and `textarea`.

Current Web browsers support nine different `input` types, each of which produces a different type of output. Here are the user input types:

- `text`: The default, with `size` used to specify the default size of the box that is created and `maxlength` used to indicate the maximum number of characters the user is allowed to enter.

- `password`: A text field with the user input displayed as asterisks or bullets for security. Again, `size` specifies the displayed input-box size and `maxlength` can be used to specify the maximum number of characters allowed.

- `checkbox`: Offers a single (ungrouped) check box; the `checked` attribute enables you to specify whether the box should be checked by default. The `value` attribute can be used to specify the text associated with the check box.

- `hidden`: Enables you to send information to the program processing the user input without the user actually seeing it on the display. This type is particularly useful if the page with the HTML form is automatically generated by a CGI script.

- `file`: Provides a way for users to actually submit files to the server. Users can either type the filename or click the Browse button to select the file from the PC.

- `radio`: Displays a toggle button; different radio buttons with the same `name=` value are grouped automatically so that only one button in the group can be selected at a time.

The most important `input` types, as you'll see, are the following:

- `submit`: Produces a push button in the form that, when clicked, submits the entire form to the remote server.
- `image`: Identical to `submit`, but instead of specifying a button, it enables you to specify a graphical image you can click for submission.
- `reset`: Enables users to clear the contents of all fields in the form.

The `<select>` tag is a drop-down list of choices, with a `</select>` partner tag and `<option>` tags denoting each of the items in the list. The default `<option>` can be denoted with `selected="selected"`. You must specify a `name` that uniquely identifies the overall selection within the `select` tag itself. In fact, all form tags must have a `name` specified, and all names must be unique within the individual form. You'll see why when we consider how information is sent to the server in the next section.

Here's a simple `select` example that uses `selected` for the `option` attribute:

```
<select name="soup">
<option selected="selected">(none)</option>
<option>chicken noodle</option>
<option>seafood gumbo</option>
<option>tomato and rice</option>
</select>
```

You can also specify a `size` with the `select` tag, indicating how many items should be displayed at once, and `multiple`, indicating that it's okay for users to select more than one option. If a default value exists, add `selected` to the `option` tag (as in `option selected`) to indicate that value. You can see that in the simple preceding example, the default menu choice is `(none)`.

The `textarea` tag enables you to produce a multiline input box. Like `select`, `textarea` requires a unique name, specified with `name=`. The `textarea` tag enables you to specify the size of the text input box with `rows` and `cols` attributes, specifying the number of lines in the box and the width of the lines, respectively. The `<textarea>` tag has a closing tag, `</textarea>`, as the following example shows:

```
<textarea name="comment" rows="4" cols="60"></textarea>
```

This code produces a text input box that is 60 characters wide, 4 lines tall, and has the name *comment*.

Asking for feedback on your site

Have you always wanted to have some mechanism for letting the visitors who come to your site send you e-mail if they have comments? Of course, you could use `a href="mailto:your@ address"`, but that's rather dull and easily harvested by spammers. Instead, it would be much more fun to have a Web page that prompts users for some simple information and then auto-matically sends what they specify. Figure 9-1 shows a form that prompts for the user's name and e-mail address and then offers a text box in which the user can enter comments.

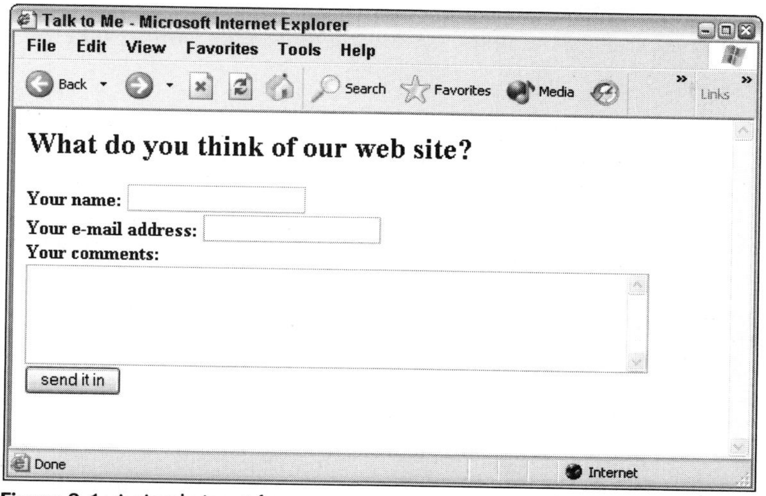

Figure 9-1: A simple input form.

The source code for this form shows that the form's tags aren't too difficult to use:

```
<h2>What do you think of our web site?</h2>

<form action="http://www.intuitive.com/coolsites/cgi/query.cgi"
 method="get">
<b>Your name:</b>
<input type="text" name="yourname"><br />
<b>Your e-mail address:</b>
<input type="text" name="e-mail"><br />
<b>Your comments:</b><br />
<textarea name="feedback" rows="5" cols="60"></textarea><br />
<input type="submit" value="send it in">
</form>
```

Perhaps the most complex line of this form is the very first, the `form` tag. It specifies two things: the `method` by which the information from the form is to be sent to the server program, and the `action`, the actual URL of the program that receives the information from the form (when the user clicks the Submit button).

Other than that, the name and e-mail address are both one-line text boxes, so `input type="text"` is the needed specifier, with each box being assigned a unique name by the designer—in this case, `yourname` and `e-mail`. The multiline input box is specified with `textarea`, the name of the box is specified with `name="feedback"`, and I want it to be 60 characters wide by 5 lines tall, which is specified with `rows="5"` and `cols="60"`.

The Submit button (`type="submit"`) is crucial to any form: It's the button that, when clicked, causes the Web browser to package up and transmit the information to the program specified in the `action` attribute of the `form` tag. All forms must have a Submit button; if you want to have your own graphic instead of the default text button, you can use `input type="image"` and specify the URL of the graphic with an `src="url"` additional attribute. Because I've opted for a simple text button, I instead specify the text to be displayed on the button with the `value` attribute.

Adding drop-down lists and radio buttons

The next generation of this form includes more complex form elements, most notably a family of radio buttons and a drop-down list using the `select` tag. Figure 9-2 shows how the form looks on the screen.

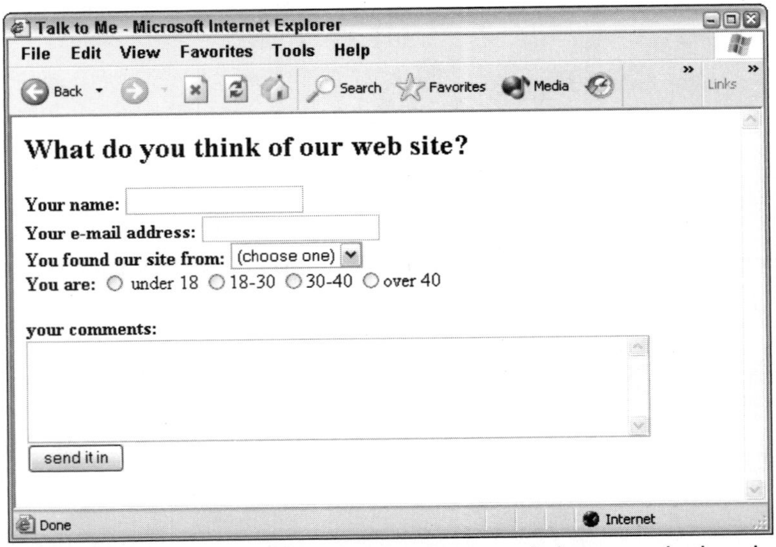

Figure 9-2: A more complex form that incorporates radio buttons and a drop-down list.

Notice that the drop-down list shows you only a single value: Clicking the displayed value brings up all the possible choices; then moving the cursor enables the visitor to select the specific value that's best.

Here's what I've added to the form HTML you've already seen:

```
<b>You found our site from:</b>
<select name="foundus">
<option selected="selected">(choose one)</option>
<option>Yahoo</option>
<option>Google</option>
```

```
<option>MSN</option>
<option>other...</option>
</select><br />

<b>You are:</b>
<input type="radio" name="age" value="kid" /> under 18
<input type="radio" name="age" value="genx" />18-30
<input type="radio" name="age" value="30something" />30-40
<input type="radio" name="age" value="old" />over 40

<br /><br />
```

Only two new areas are added. The `select` tag builds the drop-down list, with each menu value specified as an `option`, and the set of four radio buttons is specified with `input type="radio"`. The first drop-down list item is the default, which is indicated with the addition of the `selected="selected"` attribute:

```
<option selected="selected">(choose one)</option>
```

Pay careful attention to the radio button set. Notice that all buttons in the set share the same `name` value. That's how they become a *family* of radio buttons, ensuring that only one of them can be selected out of the set. If they had different names, you could select both the Under 18 and Over 40 categories, for example.

> **tip** To tie radio buttons together, even if they're in different areas of the page, just ensure that they have exactly the same `name` attribute.

A secret concerning radio buttons: The actual value they send back to the server, if checked, is specified with the `value` attribute. The actual text displayed next to a radio button is irrelevant to the program on the server: The only thing it knows about what's selected is that the specified family (by `name`) had a radio button selected with the specified `value`. If you choose 18–30, the value that would be sent back to the server would be `age=genx`.

You recall that I said each input type in a form requires a name? Now you can see the reason for that: Each form element is packaged up and sent back to the server as a `name=value` pair. The drop-down list, for example, might be `foundus="MSN"`, and the username, when typed, might be sent back to the server as `yourname="Kiana"`. If you neglected to name an input, that element is sometimes not even displayed in the browser because the specified information can't be sent back to the server.

Tweaking the select element

To have more than one menu item displayed at a time with a select box, simply change the `select` tag by adding the attribute `size`. With this attribute, I can specify how many choices should be visible at the same time. For example, `size="4"` produces a scrolling list of options, with four visible at a time.

If you want to let the visitor to your site have the possibility of choosing multiple values from the selection box, you can add a second attribute: `multiple`. A list such as the following would display a three-line–high select box with ten different values in it:

```
<h2>Pick your favorite color:</h2>
<select size="3" multiple="multiple" name="favorites">
<option>black</option>
<option>blue</option>
<option>brown</option>
<option>gold</option>
<option>green</option>
<option>orange</option>
<option>red</option>
<option>white</option>
<option>yellow</option>
<option>a color not otherwise specified</option>
</select><br />
<div style='font-size:75%;color:#666;'>Use control+click
to make multiple selections</div>
```

Figure 9-3 shows just this form element on a page with two colors selected: the first by clicking, the second by holding down the Ctrl key and clicking.

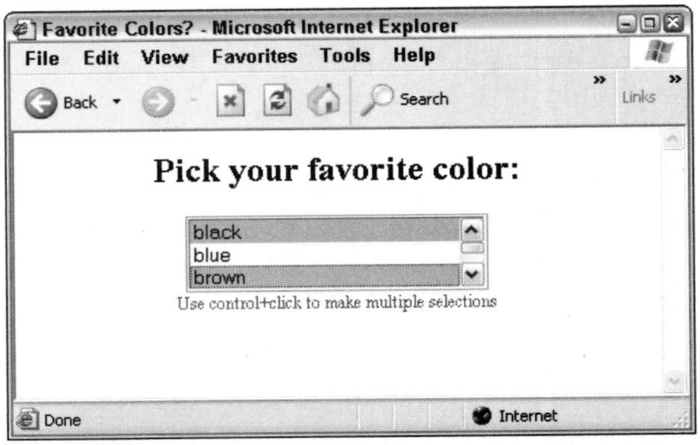

Figure 9-3: Multiple select options in a small scrolling window.

You could select any number of these colors as your favorites or, if you didn't select any, because no default is specified, the default value for `favorites` would be none.

The other unusual tag you can include in a form is `textarea`, which enables you to create large boxes in which users can type their information. It has several options, starting with the mandatory `name` attribute that denotes the symbolic name of the field. You can specify rows and cols to indicate the size of the resulting text field with units in characters. The wrap attribute specifies that the text the user enters wraps automatically when the user reaches the right margin. The <textarea> tag is a paired tag, partnered by </textarea>. Any text between the two tags is displayed as the default information in the text box.

You saw this demonstrated with the e-mail feedback form earlier, but now I create a more complex form to show you how things can work together. As it turns out, I am building a form for a Web site I'm working on, so I'll step through this form design to show how to utilize a textarea field, as well as a number of other elements:

```
<h2>Contact The School</h2>
<form method="get"
 action="http://www.intuitive.com/coolsites/cgi/query.cgi">
Name: <input type="text" name="fullname" />
<br />
Address: <input type="text" name="address" size="60" />
<br />
Phone: <input type="text" name="phone" />
<br />
Email: <input type="text" name="email" />
<br />
Your child is in
<select name="child1">
 <option selected>(please choose one)</option>
 <option>pre-kindergarten</option><option>Kindergarten</option>
 <option>First</option><option>Second</option><option>Third</option>
 <option>Fourth</option><option>Fifth</option><option>Sixth</option>
 <option>Seventh</option><option>Eighth</option><option>Ninth
 </option><option>Tenth</option><option>Eleventh</option>
 <option>Twelfth</option><option>(not applicable)</option>
</select>
<br />
<input type="checkbox" name="sendInfo"> Please send
me an information packet on the school.<br />
<input type="checkbox" name="thisYear"> I'm
interested in learning about enrollment opportunities
for this school year.
<br />
<input type="submit" value="Submit Query" />
</form>
```

Figure 9-4 shows the preceding form in a Web browser.

This is a rudimentary form, but you can do quite a bit to jazz it up. You'll learn how to do just that in the next section.

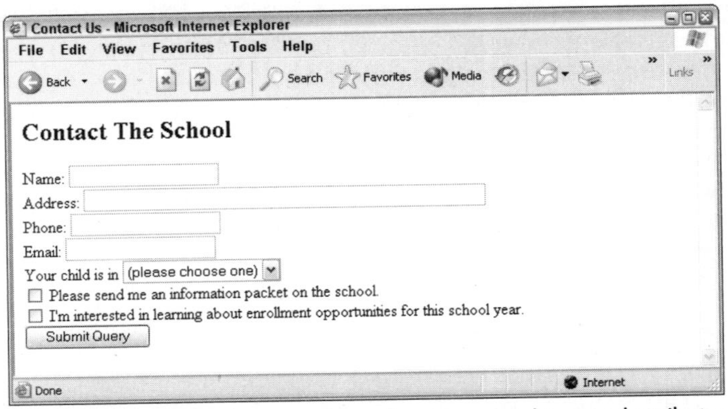

Figure 9-4: The school contact form showing several tags and attributes in action.

Fancy Form Formatting

The forms shown so far are reasonably attractive, but when you start combining form elements with other formatting tags that you've already learned, you can produce really beautiful pages requesting user input. In this section, I show you a couple of examples.

Probably the most common strategy for creating attractive forms is to drop the various fields into a table. This enables you to line up all the prompts and input boxes quite easily. To spruce up the school contact form, I do that as appropriate and also add a div block in order to add a CSS border.

Remember, the goal of any good form is to encourage people to fill out the information properly. Usability is an important part of form design.

> **x-ref** Chapter 12 talks about CSS border options in great detail, and Chapter 15 gives you more information about usability issues.

```
<html> <head>
<title>Contact Us</title>
</head><body>

<h2>Contact The School</h2>
<form method="get"
  action="http://www.intuitive.com/coolsites/cgi/query.cgi">

<p>
Please fill out the form as completely as possible so we can
```

```
best answer your query. If you'd like our catalog and other
information about the school, don't forget to check the "send
information" option.
</p>


<center>
<table border="0">
<tr>
<td>Name:</td><td><input type="text" name="fullname" /></td>
</tr><tr>
<td>Address:</td>
<td><input type="text" name="address" size="60" /></td>
</tr><tr>
<td>Phone:</td><td><input type="text" name="phone" /></td>
</tr><tr>
<td>Email:</td><td><input type="text" name="email" /></td>
</tr><tr>
<td colspan="2">
This school year, your child is in:
<select name="child1">
 <option selected>(please choose one)</option>
 <option>pre-kindergarten</option><option>Kindergarten</option>
 <option>First</option><option>Second</option><option>Third</option>
 <option>Fourth</option><option>Fifth</option><option>Sixth</option>
 <option>Seventh</option><option>Eighth</option><option>Ninth
 </option><option>Tenth</option><option>Eleventh</option>
 <option>Twelfth</option><option>(not applicable)</option>
</select>
<div style="border: 3px groove #ccc;padding:3px;margin-top: 5px;">
<input type="checkbox" name="sendInfo"> Please send
me an information packet on the school.<br />
<input type="checkbox" name="thisYear"> I'm
interested in learning about enrollment opportunities
for this school year.
</div>
</td>
</tr><tr><td colspan="2" align="center">
<input type="submit" value="submit request" />
</td></tr>
</table>
</center>
</form>
</body>
</html>
```

This is a pretty long example, but if you compare it to Figure 9-5, you see that it's a great improvement over the earlier form.

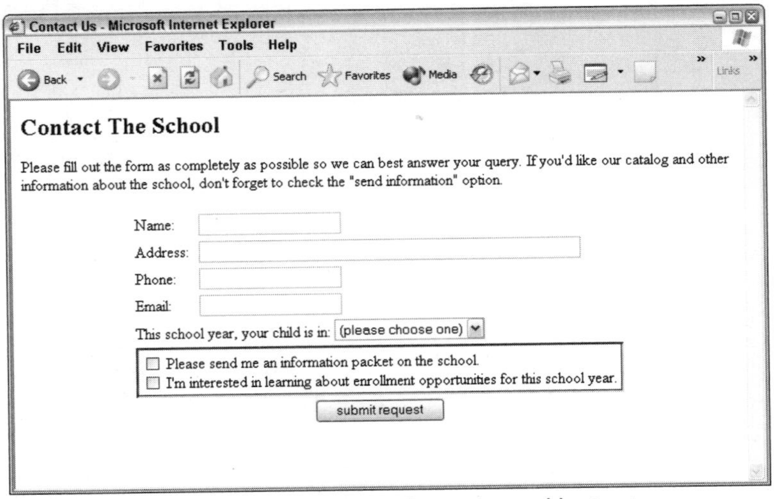

Figure 9-5: The improved school contact form using a table structure.

Easy Searching from Your Page

Now that you're becoming an absolute forms development genius, take a look at how you can exploit forms on other sites to actually duplicate their input on your own page. For example, perhaps you'd like to have a Google search box on your own page to let people who visit your site easily flip over to Google to find something.

Popping over to the Google home page, you can perform a View Source and see, in the veritable thicket of HTML, a rather convoluted sequence of lines that defines Google's simple search form. By trimming it down to just the entries needed for the search itself, you end up with the following snippet:

```
<form action="http://www.google.com/search" name=f>
  <input type=hidden name=hl value=en>
  <input type=hidden name=ie value="ISO-8859-1">
  <input maxLength=256 size=55 name=q value=""><br>
  <input type=submit value="Google Search" name=btnG>
  <input type=submit value="I'm Feeling Lucky" name=btnI>
</form>
```

This is the code for the actual search box shown on the top of the Google home page. Because I've pulled the code out, however, it's easy for me to include this sequence of commands on my own Web page, as you can see in Figure 9-6.

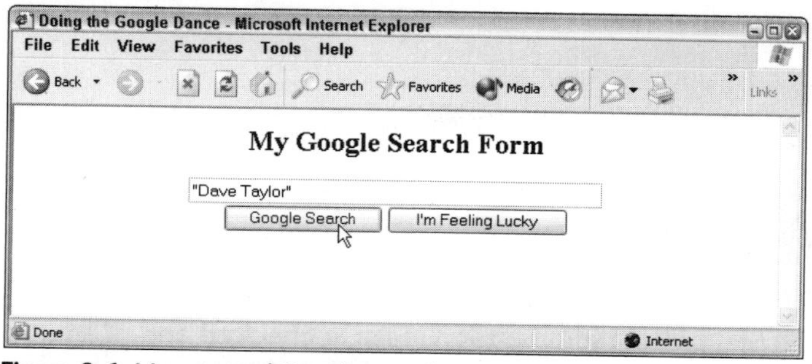

Figure 9-6: My personal Google search.

Of course, it would be nice to rewrite it as proper xhtml, so here's the very same code, properly written:

```
<form action="http://www.google.com/search" name="f">
  <input type="hidden" name="hl" value="en" />
  <input type="hidden" name="ie" value="ISO-8859-1" />
  <input maxlength="256" size="55" name="q" value="" /><br />
  <input type="submit" value="Google Search" name="btnG" />
  <input type="submit" value="I'm Feeling Lucky" name="btnI" />
</form>
```

If you're willing to delve into JavaScript for a few lines of code, you can make a couple of modifications to this search form that can turn it into a far cooler addition to your site! First, eliminate the I'm Feeling Lucky button and replace it with two radio buttons: my site only or all the web. In addition, the Submit button is shrunk down a bit with some savvy CSS, and the onclick event (which is triggered when someone clicks the submit button) is tied to a JavaScript function:

```
<form action="http://www.google.com/search" name="searchbox"
 method="get">
  <input type="hidden" name="hl" value="en" />
  <input type="hidden" name="ie" value="ISO-8859-1" />
  <input maxlength="256" size="55" name="q" value="" /><br />
  <input type="radio" name="scope" value="me" checked /> my
  site only, or
  <input type="radio" name="scope" value="all" /> all
  the web<br /><br />
  <input type="submit" value="search!" name="btnG"
    style="font-size:75%;" onclick="tweakValue();" />
</form>
```

The next step is to write the JavaScript tweakValue function, which tests the value of the radio button and appends the special Google search constraint +site:*domain* to limit the search results to pages from the domain specified only:

```
<script language="JavaScript">
function tweakValue()
{
  if (document.searchbox.scope[0].checked)
    document.searchbox.q.value += " +site:intuitive.com";
}
</script>
```

Without too much foreshadowing of Chapter 11, where JavaScript is explored in depth, this function tests to see whether the first of the radio button values is checked and, if so, it appends the specified search constraint to the search pattern before handing it off to Google.

> **tip**   This JavaScript script block is properly placed in the head section of the page, not the body.

The form itself is quite simple when viewed in a browser, as shown in Figure 9-7.

Figure 9-7: My personal Google search box.

Another Look at Hidden Variables

Now that you've learned quite a bit about forms, you can peek at how the popular online game *Etymologic* works.

> **tip**   Try the game for yourself at http://www.Etymologic.com/

The game itself is quite simple: You're asked a question and upon answering it you're asked another, until you have tried to answer 10 different questions. At that point, the game figures out how many you answered correctly and gives you a final score.

To make it work properly, however, the game program needs to know how many questions have been asked, what specific questions have been asked, and the exact question being asked at any point in the game sequence.

Here's how the HTML looks—well, the part that's relevant to the form—when I'm halfway through a game:

```
<form action="http://www.etymologic.com/etymologic.cgi"
  method="post">
<input type="hidden" name="total_questions" value="184" />
<input type="hidden" name="current_question" value="48" />
<input type="hidden" name="asked" value="7" />
<input type="hidden" name="right" value="5" />
<input type="hidden" name="ingame" value="10" />
<input type="hidden" name="already_asked"
  value="95 30 79 53 60 165 114 48" />
<input type="hidden" name="phrase" value="ole" />
<div style="font-family: arial,tekton,helvetica" />
Where does the Spanish bullfight expression <b>Ole!</b>
originate?
</div>
<br />
<table border="0">
<tr><td valign="top">
  <input type="radio" name="answer" value="t" /></td>
<td style="font-family: arial,tekton,helvetica">
 From the arabic "Allah" (God!)
<input type="hidden" name="correct"
 value="from the Arabic 'allah' (God!)" />
</td>
</tr><tr>
<td valign="top">
  <input type="radio" name="answer" value="f" /></td>
<td style="font-family: arial,tekton,helvetica">
 From the Spanish "Hola!" (Hello!)
</td>
</tr><tr>
<td valign="top">
  <input type="radio" name="answer" value="f" /></td>
<td style="font-family: arial,tekton,helvetica">
 From the Spanish "Hoja!" (Blade!)</td>
</tr>
</table>

<input type="submit"
 value="please indicate your answer then click here" />
</form>
```

Notice that almost all the variables are `type="hidden"`: There's a lot going on behind the scenes on this Web site!

Also, if you look closely at the values for the radio buttons, you see that you can View Source and cheat: If `value="f"`, then it's the wrong answer. If `value="t"`, it's correct.

How CGI Scripts Work

To understand how the common gateway interface works, take a brief step back to the most basic of Web concepts. All Web browsers talk with Web servers using a language (well, protocol, to be exact) called HTTP, the Hypertext Transfer Protocol. At its simplest, HTTP defines the interaction between the browser and server, which can be boiled down to "I want" from the browser and "here is" or "don't have" from the server.

Forget all the fancy stuff from the last eight chapters. The simple *I want/here is* dialog is what the Web and, indeed, the Internet are really all about. Your Mac or PC is asking a server somewhere on the Net for a particular file, picture, resource, or what-have-you, and the Net is responding either "Here it is!" or "I don't have it!" In fact, when you have an HTML document that includes graphics, each graphic is requested from the server through its own dialog of a similar nature. That's why you see the source to some pages before you get all the graphics, because the back and forth looks like this:

```
PC: I want "test.html"
Server: here is "test.html"
PC: oh, now I want "opening.gif"
Server: here is "opening.gif"
PC: and I want "photo.jpeg"
Server: here is "photo.jpeg"
PC: and I want "logo.gif"
Server: here is "logo.gif"
and finally I want "lastpict.gif"
I don't have "lastpict.gif" Error 404: file not found
```

Although this may seem tedious—and it is—it's also a great design because it's so easily extended into other areas. In particular, what happens if instead of the "I want" request, the browser asked, "Please run the following program and send me the output"?

That capability is what programming for Web servers is built around, and the environment on the server within which you communicate with your programs is the Common Gateway Interface. Working within the CGI environment, in the programming language of your choice, you can replace any Web page or graphic with a program that performs calculations, looks up information in a database, checks the weather, reads a remote sensor, or whatever you'd like. The program then returns the results of that action to the user as Web data.

On many servers you can recognize a CGI script by the `.cgi` filename suffix that occurs within the URL of the referenced page, but any file or graphic can actually be a program, the output of which is sent to the user. The best news is that the use of CGI scripts can be invisible to the Web visitor. Visitors just wander through your site and see page after page. If some of the pages are the result of running scripts, the visitors may never know.

The world's simplest CGI example

Let's dive right in and have a look at a CGI script that might replace a static Web page with something more dynamic: `hello.cgi`, written as a Perl programming language script:

```
#!/usr/bin/perl
print "Content-type: text/html\n\n";
print "<html><body>\n";
print "<h1>Hi Mystery Web Visitor</h1>\n";
print "</body></html>\n";
exit 0;
```

The `print` command outputs whatever you specify to standard output, which, in this case, because it's being run as a CGI script, is sent through the Web server to the remote Web browser. The `\n` sequences are translated in carriage returns, so the `\n\n` at the end of the first `print` statement produces a blank line after the `Content-type: text/html` sequence.

As you can see, the program `hello.cgi` is required to return an actual HTML document. This is done so that everything remains transparent to the user: The user requests a Web document, and it comes back all neatly formatted and ready to be displayed by the browser.

note The first responsibility of any CGI program is to return a valid HTML document to the browser. Any additional capabilities must be built on top of that basic requirement, and if you forget, you'll get various scary error messages when you try to test things yourself.

Notice that the first output line of any CGI script, as shown in this example, must identify the particular type of information being sent back to the browser. In this case, it's HTML text, and the formal description for that is `Content-type: text/html`. That line must be followed in the output by a blank line (which you get by having two `\n` sequences) and then, finally, the actual HTML code can appear. This first section is called the *preamble*, and I like to think of it as the envelope within which the Web page is sent.

Functionally, this program output is identical to a *static* Web page that contains:

```
<html><body>
<h1>Hi Mystery Web Visitor</h1>
</body></html>
```

So why go through the bother? Because these scripts can output virtually anything your heart desires. Let's look at a more sophisticated example. This one uses the Perl `localtime` function to return the current date and time on the server:

```perl
#!/usr/bin/perl

print "Content-type: text/html\n\n";
print "<html><head><title>LocalTime</title>\n";
print "</head><body style='text-align:center'>\n";
print "<h2>Oh Mystery Web Visitor, the time is... </h2>\n";

# first, get the values from the localtime function
($sec,$min,$hr,$mday,$mon,$year,$wday) = localtime(time);

# now let's make them pretty, suitable for display
$today    = (Sun,Mon,Tues,Wed,Thurs,Fri,Sat)[$wday];
$thismon = (Jan,Feb,March,April,May,June,July,
            Aug,Sep,Oct,Nov,Dec)[$mon];
$year    += 1900;

print "$today, $thismon $mday, $year at precisely $hr:$min:$sec\n";

print "</body></html>\n";
exit 0;
```

Figure 9-8 shows how that script would look to a user visiting my Web site and requesting `http://www.intuitive.com/coolsites/cgi/localtime.cgi`—try it yourself, too!

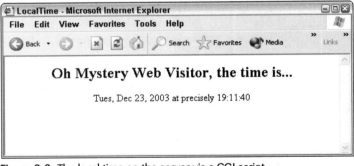

Figure 9-8: The local time on the server via a CGI script.

You can do a lot with programs that output content based on the environment at the moment the page is requested. For example, the `localtime` function returns the current date as a series of individual values, so it takes remarkably little work to get the hour of the day and have a CGI program that produces different output during daylight and nighttime hours.

Although this little script is useful, CGI offers a considerably richer environment for developing sophisticated sites. It's an environment in which you can make decisions about what kind of HTML to output based on the browser that's in use, where the user is located, and much more. And we haven't even talked about receiving information from the user yet!

Sending information via the environment

Every HTTP transaction (the *I want/here is* pair) actually includes a collection of environmental characteristics that is sent along and is accessible by the CGI program. I like to think of it as a briefcase chock full of information about the user. What might surprise you is that all the information is sent on *every interaction between the browser and server,* even if it's just a request for a graphic or static Web page.

To see all the environment variables, I've created another CGI script that uses a slick Perl looping mechanism to show the environment given to the script at runtime:

```perl
#!/usr/bin/perl

print "Content-type: text/html\n\n";
print "<html><head><title>Your CGI Environment</title>\n";
print "<style type='text/css'>td { font-size: 80% }</style>\n";
print "</head><body>\n";
print "<table border='0' cellspacing='4' width='100%'>\n";

print "<tr><td align='right' valign='top'>$a</td><td>$b</td></tr>\n"
   while ($a,$b) = each %ENV;

print "</table>\n";
print "</body></html>\n";

exit 0;
```

The results for Internet Explorer are as shown in Figure 9-9.

Notice particularly the variable HTTP_USER_AGENT. This identifies the specific browser in use. In this case, you can also see a bit of a trick that Microsoft's Internet Explorer performs: It identifies itself as Mozilla (a code name for Netscape) 4.0, but then correctly identifies itself in the parentheses as Internet Explorer 6.0.

note   If I request the very same Web CGI script from a different Web browser, the output is very different. This suggests, correctly, that CGI scripts can ascertain what kind of browser you're running, among other things.

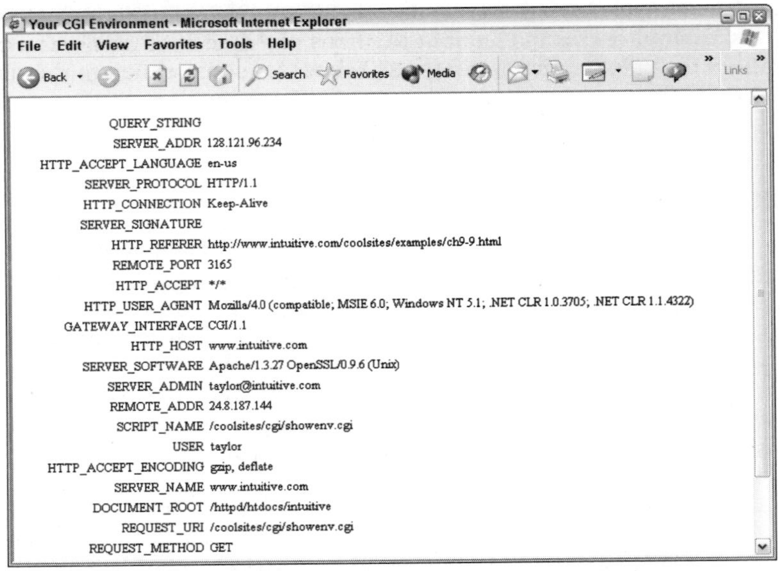

Figure 9-9: My CGI environment for writing scripts in Internet Explorer.

Sending and reading data

Another variable in the environment is very important for interactive pages: QUERY_STRING. The Google search form explored earlier in this chapter is a great example of just this type of interaction.

As I touched on earlier, you have two ways to transfer information from the browser to the server, based on the setting of the method parameter in the form tag. You'll recall the two possible values: get and post. If the form specifies a method=get, then the information entered by the user, in name=value pairs, is available to the CGI program as the environment variable value query_string.

Go to Yahoo! and enter a word or phrase for it to seek. When you get the search results, you see a page of matches as you'd expect. Most important, however, you also see a slightly weird URL. If I search for *disney world,* the URL shown in the Address box of the browser is http://search.yahoo.com/bin/search?p=disney+world.

This URL is consistent with what I explained about URLs way back in the beginning of the book, but there's a new twist. The ? indicates information to be sent to the remote system, and the p=disney+world is the value sent to the server from the client. For the CGI program on the server specified in the action attribute of the form tag, the QUERY_STRING variable contains the exact information specified after the question mark.

You can do some neat things now that you know about this QUERY_STRING URL format. Perhaps you're working on a Web site that's all about the films of Alfred Hitchcock. You can add a link to your Web page that automatically searches Yahoo! for sites related to the director. You don't require the user to enter anything:

```
<a href="http://search.yahoo.com/search?p=alfred+hitchcock">
Information on Alfred Hitchcock</a>
```

You can see that spaces were transformed into + signs so that they are transmitted safely to the CGI script. A variety of other characters are also specially encoded so that they can be transmitted safely too, as detailed in Table 9-2.

Table 9-2: Common Character Encoding

Code	Real Meaning	Code	Real Meaning	Code	Real Meaning
%21	!	%26	&	%2F	/
%22	"	%27	'	%3A	:
%23	#	%28	(	%3D	=
%24	$	%29	)	%3F	?
%25	%	%2B	+	%5C	\

Because you know that special characters are *wrapped up* for transmission by converting them into escape sequences, it shouldn't surprise you that the first step a script must take after receiving data from the remote server is to decode the given information. Fortunately, Perl is ideal for this sort of task, and this translation can be easily accomplished by first translating all the plus (+) signs into spaces and all percent (%) sign hexadecimal sequences into their equivalent character values.

Receiving information from forms

The CGI behind forms is more complex because the very environment you work with when processing the form depends heavily on the operating system used on the server. Scripting a gateway (hence, the Common Gateway Interface, or CGI, moniker for these scripts) can be quite different on a Unix system than it is on a Windows machine or a Macintosh.

The biggest difference involves what programming languages and tools are available. On a Unix system, it's quite simple to create a shell script, Perl script, or even a C or C++ program or two to process and act on input. Windows machines rely on either a DOS command template or what's known informally as a *jacket* script. Fortunately, the Perl-interpreted programming language is also available on PCs and Macs, and that's what I recommend you use for CGI programming—as I have throughout this chapter—although a number of Windows-based CGI scripts are written in C and Visual Basic.

note The Perl home page is at http://www.perl.com, and there's a terrific Perl FAQ at ftp://ftp.cis.ufl.edu/pub/perl/faq/FAQ. You can also get a free Perl interpreter for Windows at http://www.ActiveState.com/ or for the Mac at http://www.macperl.com/.

Learning more about CGI programming

Don't be worried if this CGI stuff seems complex. It is. The good news is that many of the larger Web-page hosting companies offer a set of useful CGI scripts that you can use without having to do any custom programming. Ask your ISP before you spend hours trying to write your own scripts.

In case it isn't obvious, I really enjoy working with CGI programs (indeed, the CGI program that powers the Etymologic.com Web site you've already seen is over 1,200 lines of C code) and find it to be one of the most enjoyable areas of the Web to explore. If you're intrigued by this, too, please consider getting a book on CGI programming and—after you're finished with this book, of course—go through it to learn how to make your sites maximally interactive. It's fun!

caution Security is a critical issue when building your own CGI programs. One smart trick is to set the *taint* flag on your Perl CGI scripts, letting the Perl interpreter help ensure that things stay safe. There's an excellent FAQ online at http://gunther.web66.com/FAQS/taintmode.html.

Table 9-3: HTML Tags Covered in This Chapter

HTML Tag	Close Tag	Meaning
`<form`	`</form>`	Indicates an interactive HTML form
`action="url"`		Indicates a CGI program on a server that receives data
`method="method"`		Indicates how data is transmitted to server (`get` or `post`)
`<input`		Indicates text or other data-input field
`type="opt"`		Indicates the type of `<input>` entry field: Possible values, `text`, `password`, `checkbox`, `hidden`, `file`, `radio`, `submit`, `reset`, `image`
`name="name"`		Specifies the symbolic name of a field value
`value="value"`		Indicates default content of text field
`checked="opt"`		Indicates a button or box checked by default
`size="x"`		Specifies the number of characters in a text field
`maxlength="x"`		Specifies the maximum number of characters accepted
`<select`	`</select>`	Indicates grouped check boxes
`name="name"`		Specifies the symbolic name of a field value

HTML Tag	Close Tag	Meaning
`size="x"`		Indicates the number of items to show at once (`default = 1`)
`multiple= "multiple"`		Allows multiple items to be selected
`<option`	`</option>`	Indicates a specific choice within a `<select>` range
`value="value"`		Determines the resultant value of this menu choice
`<textarea`	`</textarea>`	Specifies a multiline text-entry field
`name="name"`		Specifies the symbolic name of a field value
`rows="x"`		Specifies the number of rows in a `textarea` box
`cols="x"`		Specifies the number of columns (characters) on a line within the box

Summary

In this chapter, you learned quite a bit about how forms work on Web pages, including how to duplicate Yahoo! or Google search forms on your own site. Even better, you saw a way that you can utilize Google to offer searches that look through only the content on your site. In addition, nuances of form layout were introduced, and different ways to work with the `textarea` tag, and you explored drop-down lists.

Advanced Form Design

In This Chapter

Examining the button input type

Labeling to organize user focus

Learning to divide forms into fieldsets

Facilitating input with the Tab key

Examining accesskey attributes

Using disabled and read-only elements

Because forms are such an integral part of complex site design and because, if you design them well, they can really help your users have a good experience on your site, this chapter presents additional ways to create complex and attractive forms. Just about everything covered in this chapter is HTML 4.0 or more recent, so if you have an older browser, don't be surprised if some of these features don't work properly.

It's one of the basic challenges for Web site designers: If you're going to use all the most recent HTML tags and capabilities, you must also have a backup plan if some of them do not work properly. What happens when someone with a PDA Web browser visits your new site and can't see frames-based design? What happens when your form is designed to exploit `fieldset` tags, but your third-world visitor doesn't have a computer that can run a modern Web browser? The key is to *know your target audience*, and then plan for *graceful degradation*.

If you're building a Web site for your company's internal use—an Intranet in the jargon—and by corporate decree everyone must run Internet Explorer 6.0, you can safely design for that browser. If you're building a Web site that's an informational source for Kenyan safari venues, however, or a site about hitchhiking through the Middle East, the chances of your having visitors with slower connections and older software go up significantly. It is well worth testing with those configurations before you say that you're done with your design.

Graceful degradation just means that if you build a site for the most modern browser systems, you also test to ensure that your site is (at least) functional with older, less capable browsers. Try not to penalize users for having out-of-date software. Think of it as an effort to give users with more modern browsers a better experience, while still using basic HTML as the baseline for your site's functionality.

With this in mind, the following sections look at tags so modern—so new—that you'll have a hard time finding Web sites that use them even today (although they should be)!

The button Input Type

In Chapter 9, you learned about the overloaded `input` tag and its many possible `type` values, including the following:

- `text`
- `checkbox`
- `radio`
- `password`
- `submit`
- `reset`

Another value that I didn't talk about in that chapter is `type="button"`. The `button` type is intended to be a general-purpose button on a Web page, perhaps not even associated with a specific script, often used for JavaScript scripts tied to the `onclick` event.

x-ref JavaScript is explored in Chapter 11.

Look at this pretty interesting example:

```
<input type="button" value="Open window"
  onclick='miniWindow=window.open("","mini",
    "resizable=no,width=300,height=250")'>
 
<a href="pop-up.html" target="mini">Learn About Starbucks</A>
 
<input type="button" value="Close window"
  onclick="miniWindow.close()">
```

Figure 10-1 shows what appears when this snippet is first loaded into the browser: two buttons and a small hypertext reference between them.

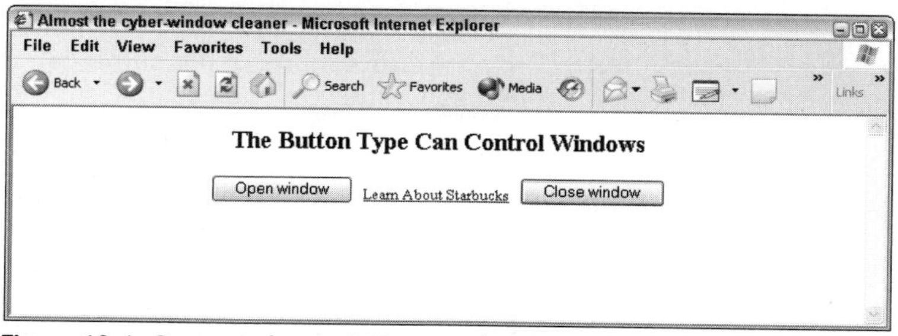

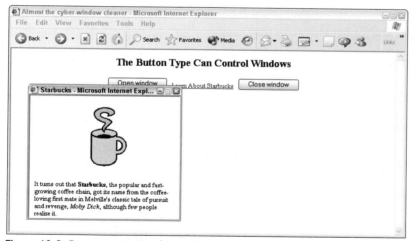

Figure 10-1: Open window and Close window buttons and a Learn About Starbucks hypertext reference appear.

Click the button labeled Open Window and a new window pops up on the screen, 300 pixels by 250 pixels, called *mini*. The window object is defined in the JavaScript environment with the name *miniWindow*. That's all defined in the `onclick` event on the second line. Click on the hypertext reference `Learn about Starbucks`, and the contents of the file `pop-up.html` are loaded into the new navigational window (that's what the `target="mini"` does). Figure 10-2 shows how this looks on the screen.

Figure 10-2: Pop-up navigational controls implemented with JavaScript and an empty HTML form.

Click the second button, Close Window, and the separate window closes, vanishing entirely from the screen. This is done with a request for the browser to run the `close()` function for the `miniWindow` object.

These input buttons need not be part of a form, even though the `input` tag is defined to have meaning only within the context of the `<form> </form>` pair. Internet Explorer is flexible, but Netscape is picky; it wants to see `form` tags even if they don't specify any attributes. In other words, if you list the preceding code, but you don't have `<form>` before it and `</form>` after it, it won't work in some browsers. Internet Explorer doesn't care, and the preceding code snippet, typed exactly as written, works fine.

note A button tag (that is, `<button onclick=...>`) offers many of the same capabilities as `input type="button"`, but it's much less widely supported.

Although this example might seem like a simple use of an input button, this feature can, in fact, be quite a powerful mechanism for helping people explore a very complex Web site. It can, for example, pop up a window that contains a cycling sequence of advertisements or even function as part of a game.

Rather than consider ads that appear when a page loads, consider *interstitials*, or advertisements that pop up and play for ten or fifteen seconds when you request to move to another page. After the ad is finished, the small window vanishes and the next page is displayed. Instead of having the window opener tied to a button event, it's tied to the loading of the window by using `onLoad` within the body tag (see Chapter 11 for more details on JavaScript and event-handling code).

The following code demonstrates one more neat button trick that I use with pop-up windows:

```
<input type="button" value="CloseMe" onclick="window.close()">
```

If a user clicks the CloseMe button, the window vanishes. Imagine having a new window pop up for user feedback; if a user cancels the message, the `window.close()` JavaScript snippet closes the window and enables the user to focus on the main Web page.

Using Labels to Organize User Focus

Although Web-based form tags are quite flexible, some definitely needed improvement. Up until now, the text adjacent to an input element on a Web page was dead, useless text. A small improvement causes this text to actually be associated with the element itself so that it matches the behavior of Windows or Mac dialog boxes. In a typical application dialog box, if you click the description adjacent to a radio button, you have effectively also clicked on the button itself. The way to accomplish this in a Web form is to use the `label` attribute. To see how things have changed with the advent of the new `label` element, note that clicking Taxi in the following example causes the box to be checked:

```
☑ Call for a Taxi
```

This association of text with a specific form element is exactly what the new `label` element accomplishes.

You can work with labels in your HTML form in two ways. You can aim labels at specific form elements by using the `id` attribute within a form element, or you can wrap a form element within a `<label> </label>` pair.

Here's an example of how aiming a label might look:

```
<form method="post" action="someURL">
    <input type="checkbox" name="taxi" id="cab">
    <label for="cab">Call for a Taxi</label>
    <br />
    <input type="submit" value="submit">
</form>
```

On a modern HTML 4.0-compliant browser, this code lets you click anywhere in the phrase `Call for a Taxi` to check or uncheck the associated check box. Of course, you can still click the check box itself to change the value.

note This functionality is exactly what graceful degradation is all about. If your browser doesn't support the `label` tag, you never realize what you're missing, and it won't adversely impact your visit.

The following `label` example is slightly more complex because it pours the check boxes into a table:

```
<form method="post" action="someURL">
<div style='margin-left: 3em;margin-right:3em;'>
The following is a demonstration of the <b>label</b> tag and
how it can be used to increase your form usability.
Click on the words adjacent to the checkbox to see what
happens!
<div style='margin-left: 3em;margin-right:3em;'>
   <table border="0" cellpadding="3">
   <tr>
   <td align="right">
       <label for="willcall">I'll call tomorrow</label>
   </td>
   <td>
       <input type="checkbox" name="call" id="willcall">
   </td>
   </tr><tr>
   <td align="right">
       <label for="willup">I'd like to upgrade
       my membership</label>
   </td><td>
       <input type="checkbox" name="upgrade" id="willup">
   </td></tr>
   </table>
</div></div>
</form>
```

In this example, as you can see in Figure 10-3, two check boxes are presented with the associated text, `I'll call tomorrow` and `I'd like to upgrade my membership`. The figure also shows the latter box checked, but notice where the cursor is located.

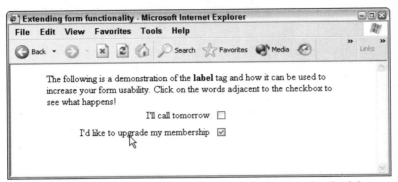

Figure 10-3: By including the label tag, clicking the text next to the check box causes the box to be checked.

The second way to use the `label` tag as a wrapper is shown in the following code:

```
<form method="post" action="someurl">
 <label>
    <input type="radio" name="gender" value="male">
    male
 </label>
 <label>
    <input type="radio" name="gender" value="female">
    female
 </label>
</form>
```

note As of this writing, wrapper-style labels don't work properly in any of the Web browsers I tested.

Dividing Forms into Fieldsets

The combination of the `fieldset` and `legend` elements enables you to create a document that is not only more attractive and more logically presented but also more accessible for people with disabilities. The tags' intent is to allow grouping of thematically related controls within a form.

First, here's a fancy but straightforward form that is actually organized into multiple logical areas without any fieldsets:

```
<html>
<head>
<title>Advanced Forms</title>
<style type='text/css'>
.title { background: #9cc; font-size:150%;
         font-weight: bold; }
.head  { background: #9cc; font-size: 125% }
.submit { font-size: 75%; background: #9cc; }
</style>
</head><body>
<form method="get" action="someURL">
<table cellpadding="2" width="100%">
 <tr>
  <td class="title" align="center" colspan="2">
    Software Defect Report
  </td>
 </tr><tr>
  <td class="head" align="center" colspan="2">
    User Profile Information
  </td>
 </tr><tr>
  <td>Name:</td>
  <td>
    <input type="text" name="name" size="50" />
  </td>
 </tr><tr>
  <td>Company:</td>
  <td>
    <input type="text" name="company" size="50" />
  </td>
</tr><tr>
  <td class="head" align="center" colspan="2">
    What seems to be the problem?
  </td>
 </tr><tr>
  <td colspan="2" align="center">
    <textarea name="problem" rows="4" cols="60"></textarea>
  </td>
 </tr>
</table>
<center>
  <input type="submit" value=" submit report " class="submit" />
</center>
</form>
</body>
</html>
```

As shown in Figure 10-4, the layout is attractive, but quite complex.

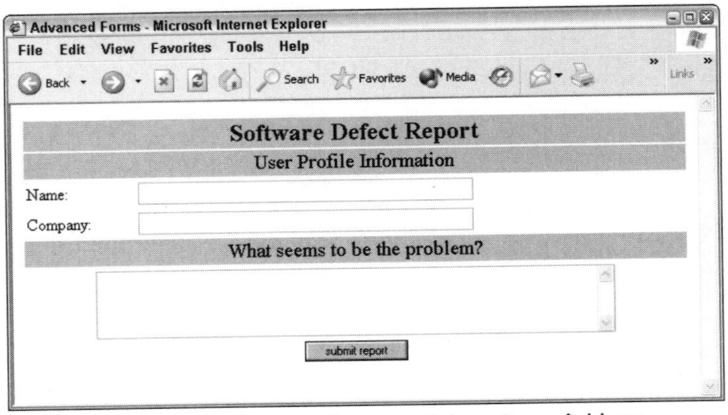

Figure 10-4: An attractive forms layout that doesn't use fieldsets.

tip   Did you notice that I used CSS to change the appearance of the Submit button on the page? It's easy to do and can really help fine-tune the page.

The fieldset and legend tags become important here. The fieldset tag is a paired tag that enables you to organize your form into logical sections, and legend enables you to assign a caption to a specific fieldset area. The form shown in Figure 10-4 could be rewritten as follows using the fieldset and legend tags:

```
<style type='text/css'>
.title { background: #9cc; font-size:150%; margin-bottom: 10px;
        font-weight: bold; text-align:center; }
.submit { font-size: 75%; background: #9cc; }
</style>
</head><body>

<form method="get" action="someURL">
<div class="title">Software Defect Report</div>

<fieldset>
 <legend style="font-size:80%; color:#666">User Profile</legend>
 <table cellpadding="2" width="100%">
 <tr>
  <td>Name:</td>
  <td>
    <input type="text" name="name" size="50" />
  </td>
 </tr><tr>
  <td>Company:</td>
  <td>
    <input type="text" name="company" size="50" />
  </td>
```

```
   </tr>
   </table>
 </fieldset>
<!— separation between sections —> <br />
<fieldset>
  <legend style="font-size:80%; color:#666">Problem
  Description</legend>
  <table cellpadding="2" width="100%">
  <tr>
   <td colspan="2">
    Please describe the problem in as much detail as possible:
      <textarea name="problem" rows="4" cols="60"></textarea>
   </td>
  </tr>
  </table>
 </fieldset>
<!— separation before the submit button —> <br />
<center>
  <input type="submit" value=" submit report " class="submit" />
</center>
</form>
```

The fieldset tags are easy to add—they add a nice touch to the design, as you can see in Figure 10-5—but I did have to break the monolithic table into a set of smaller tables so each could be encircled by the lines associated with the fieldset legend.

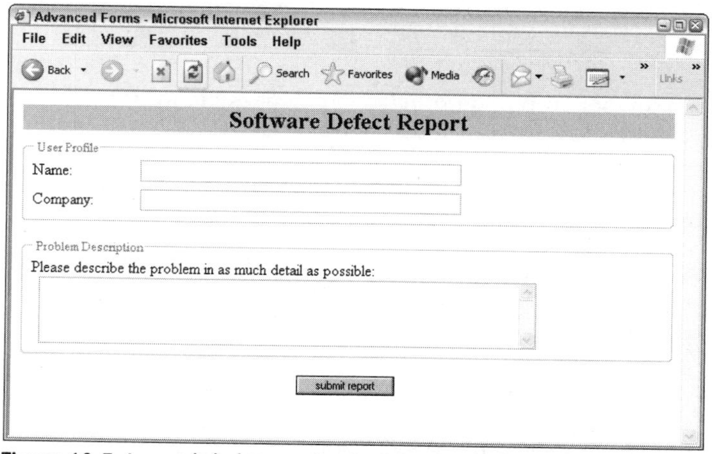

Figure 10-5: Legends help organize the requested information.

The fieldset tag has no options or attributes. The legend tag has four possible values for the align attribute: top, bottom, left, and right. The default location is top, and the others are ignored, as far as I can tell.

Tab Key Control on Input

If you've filled out any forms online, you already know that it can be a pain to move the mouse to each input field, click to move the cursor, and then type in the specific value. Fortunately, you can use the Tab key on regular Web input forms to step from the top-left to the bottom-right.

That's where the nifty `tabindex` attribute comes into play. HTML 4.0 added the capability to define the exact tabbing sequence on your form. If you want to move people down the entries on the left side, then the right side, you can do so by specifying the appropriate ascending `tabindex` values.

Table 10-1 shows which HTML tags can have a `tabindex` specified.

Table 10-1: tabindex-Enabled HTML Tags

Tag Name	Meaning
a	Anchor tag
area	Client-side image map
object	Object inclusion (see Chapter 11)
input	Text, radio button, check box input field
select	Pop-up or multiple selection menu
textarea	Multiline text input box
button	Analogous to `input type="button"`

The `tabindex` can help you make your Web page much more accessible to people who want to stick with a keyboard rather than fiddle with a mouse or trackball.

Here's an example of a form that uses the `tabindex` attributes to ensure that users can step through the entries with the Tab key in the order the designer wants:

```
<html>
<head><title>A veritable tab lovefest!</title>
</head><body style="text-align:center;">
<a href="index.html" tabindex="10">
  <img src="whitehouse.jpg" border="0" alt="logo" /></a>
<form method="post" action="">
<table border="0" cellpadding="10" width="90%">
<tr><td>
```

```
<fieldset><legend>About You</legend>
<table><tr><td>
 Your Name:</td><td><input type="text" name="name" tabindex="2" />
</td></tr><tr><td>
 Address:</td><td><input type="text" name="addr" tabindex="4" />
</td></tr><tr><td>
 Telephone:</td><td><input type="text" name="phone" tabindex="3" />
</td></tr><tr><td>
 E-Mail:</td><td><input type="text" name="email" tabindex="1" />
</td></tr><tr><td>
 You are:</td><td><select name="city" tabindex="5" />
  <option>Republican</option><option>Democrat</option>
 </select>
</td></tr></table>
</fieldset>
<!-- split between the two columns --> </td><td>
<fieldset><legend>Your Views</legend>
Your opinion of the President<br />
of the United States of America:
<blockquote>
<input type="radio" name="opinion" value="great" tabindex="6" />
 He's doing great!<br />
<input type="radio" ame="opinion" value="super" tabindex="8" />
 He's doing super!<br />
<input type="radio" name="opinion" value="wonderful" tabindex="7" />
 He's doing wonderful!
</blockquote>
</fieldset>
</td></tr>
</table>
<input type="submit" value="Send your message to the President"
tabindex="9" />
</form>
```

If you follow the numbering, you see that the first entry in the tab sequence is the e-mail address, jumping to the name, back to the telephone number, then to the address, and so on as you dance around on the page tab by tab. Then the visitor can tab to the select pop-up menu and step through the three possible radio button values. Finally, the submit button itself is in the tabindex sequence, and the anchor wrapping around the graphic, which returns to the site's home page, is the last (10th) entry in the tabindex.

Figure 10-6 shows you what the form looks like, but you should try using the Tab key to step through the tabindex values yourself.

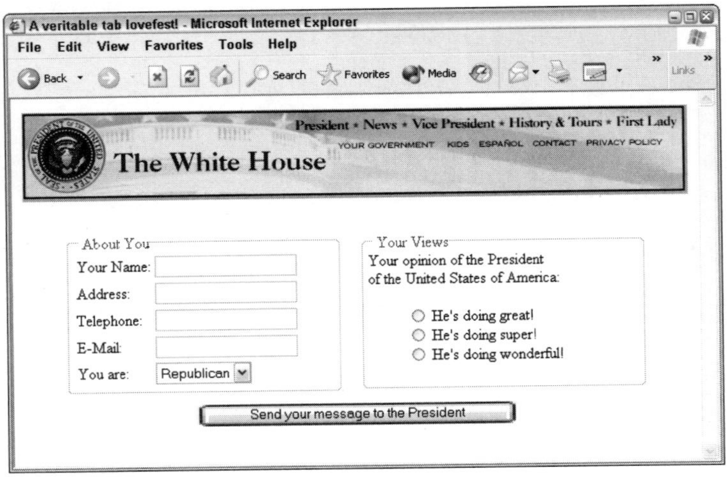

Figure 10-6: Trying the tabindex-enabled form.

note   Notice how the `fieldset` and `legend` tags help create an attractive layout.

The accesskey Attribute

You can use an additional attribute to offer even easier navigation of your Web pages via keyboard: You can assign keyboard shortcuts to let people quickly get to a specific spot on a form or a specific anchor. This is done with the `accesskey="key"` sequence, although don't be fooled—on a PC, you must use Alt + the key specified, and on the Macintosh you use the Command key.

tip   On the Mac, you might be more familiar with calling the Command key the Apple or Cloverleaf key. It's usually on both sides of your spacebar.

Here's a succinct example of how the `accesskey` attribute might be used:

```
<a href="http://www.yahoo.com/" accesskey="y">Yahoo</a>
```

Of course, if you're going to have a keyboard shortcut, it might be valuable to show the user what key to use. The Windows system has a nice standard for this: The letter in question is underlined. You can do this with the otherwise marginally useful U underline tag, as shown here:

```
<a href="http://www.yahoo.com/" accesskey="y"><u>Y</u>ahoo</a>
```

As this becomes widely implemented in Web browsers, it will undoubtedly prove to be a great addition to your page implementation toolkit.

Disabled and Read-Only Elements

The `tabindex` and `accesskey` attributes can be quite valuable in Web site design. By contrast, I am not at all sure why two more attributes, `disabled` and `readonly`, have been added.

The `disabled` attribute enables you to display form elements that cannot be changed by the user and are intended to be displayed in a *grayed out* or in some other fashion that makes the disabled status obvious. The `readonly` attribute is very similar but shouldn't be visually different from the other fields, just unchangeable.

Here's how you might use these two in your own form:

```
<form method="post" action="#">
<table border="0" cellpadding="3">
<tr>
 <td align="right">Name:</td>
 <td><input type="text" name="yourname" /></td>
</tr><tr>
 <td align="right">Login:</td>
 <td><input type="text" name="login" /></td>
</tr><tr>
 <td align="right">Host:</td>
 <td><input type="text" name="host" value="hostname.com"
   readonly="readonly" /></td>
</tr><tr>
 <td align="right">Date:</td>
 <td><input type="text" value="3 August, 2004"
   disabled="disabled" /></td>
</tr>
</table>
</form>
```

In this example, I've already filled in the value of *host* for the visitor. (This is probably based on the user's `remote_host` CGI environment variable. See Chapter 9 for more details on how you can get this value dynamically.) I've also filled in the current date, but it's a disabled field because I'm not letting the user change the date.

> **note**   To ensure XHTML compliance, the attributes are in the odd form of `disabled="disabled"` and `readonly="readonly"`. Non-XHTML–compliant sites might well use `disabled` and `readonly` instead.

Take a close look at Figure 10-7, and you can see how Internet Explorer renders these two special form elements.

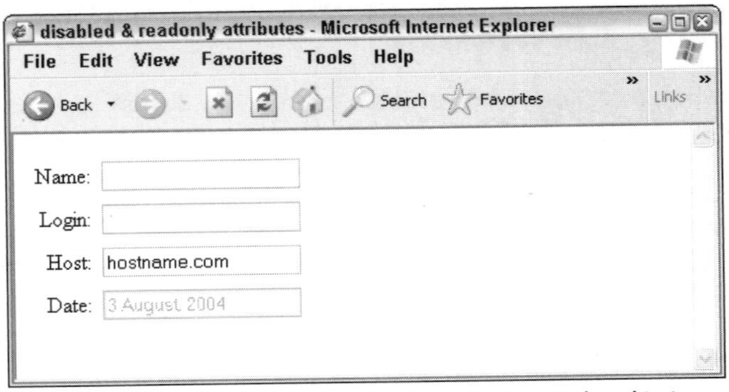

Figure 10-7: The disabled and readonly attributes rendered in Internet Explorer.

Table 10-2: HTML Tags Covered in This Chapter

HTML Tag	Close Tag	Meaning
`<input`		
`type="button"`		Specifies general purpose button type
`onClick="s"`		Specifies action to take when button is clicked (JavaScript)
`<label`	`</label>`	Indicates label associated with a specific element
`for="s"`		Specifies element associated with label (use `id="s"` in element)
`<fieldset>`	`</fieldset>`	Divides form into logical parts
`<legend`	`</legend>`	Specifies name associated with `fieldset`
`align="s"`		Specifies alignment of legend in display (top, bottom, left, right)
`tabindex="x"`		Specifies order of elements when user presses Tab key
`accesskey="c"`		Specifies key to allow keyboard shortcuts to specific elements
`disabled="disabled"`		Disables element but displays it onscreen
`readonly="readonly"`		Displays element onscreen but element not editable

Summary

In this chapter, you explored the button input type—particularly useful for scripting—and how to enable users to get the most out of your forms. You also learned how to fine-tune the interaction between form elements using a number of advanced HTML design elements, including the `label` and `fieldset` variables and the `tabindex`, `accesskey`, `disabled`, and `readonly` attributes. In the next chapter, you turn your attention to JavaScript, a simple scripting language that enables you to include Java-like programming instructions in the HTML text of your Web pages.

Activating Your Pages with JavaScript

In This Chapter

Understanding JavaScript basics

Testing browser compatibility

Employing graphical rollovers

Telling time

Testing form values

Scripting solutions other than
    JavaScript

After you have mastered HTML, XHTML, and CSS, you might think "Phew! Done. Now I'm ready to start building some cool Web sites!" So do give yourself a pat on the back. You have made great progress. But depending on how you want your site to evolve, you still have tons of additional things to learn. If you want to have beautiful graphics or designs, you should explore some wonderful development tools for artists, including Adobe Photoshop, Macromedia Dreamweaver, Flash, Fireworks, and many more. If you want to interface with backend database systems, powerful scripting languages like PHP, and query languages like SQL, you'll be delving more into the programming side of things.

But this chapter isn't about that. Indeed, any one of these topics is easily the subject of another book—or two—and quite a bit more complex than I can cover in this book. However, a critical additional level of sophistication for truly cool Web sites is within your reach: JavaScript.

Imagine a reasonably simple scripting language that's designed for Web page use, and you'd be talking about the JavaScript language.

In this chapter, I provide a brief overview of the language and then dig into five nifty and informative ways that JavaScript can really expand and improve the interactivity of a Web page. Finally, I wrap up with a brief look at some of the other major scripting and development languages in common use.

An Overview of JavaScript

In the beginning was HTML, and all was well. No one wanted to do anything particularly complex or sophisticated, and its capability to include text and graphics of different sizes within the same document was quite compelling. As time passed, however, pages became increasingly sophisticated, so the two major Web browser companies, Netscape and Microsoft, each began to develop a scripting language for use on Web pages, a language that would allow programs to be run on the visitors' systems as they viewed the pages.

For Microsoft, it was Visual Basic Script, the same scripting language found in the Microsoft Office Suite, among others. For Netscape, it was a scripting language that looked vaguely like the popular new Java object-oriented language. Sparing you the gory details, Netscape won, Microsoft lost, and JavaScript is the Web's de facto scripting language.

note

To clear up a common point of confusion, JavaScript and Java aren't the same thing. In fact, Java is what's known as an *object-oriented programming language*, and it's not for the faint of heart. JavaScript, however, which shares only some minimal syntax structure in common with Java, is a simple scripting language that you can add to your Web pages quickly and easily.

I'm going to discuss programming, but don't panic. JavaScript is *fun* and *easy*. You'll see.

Variables

The building blocks of all scripting are *variables*, the named containers that store specific information and enable you both to manipulate and display it whenever you want. If you remember your algebra, where x = y + 4, you're already familiar with variables because that's what the *x* and *y* are in that equation. If you imagine the two variables as boxes that can take on any value, the equation describes a relationship between them. If *y* is 10, *x* is 14.

JavaScript features three primary types of variables that you need to know: *numeric, string,* and *Boolean.* Numeric variables are just like the *x* and *y* of the preceding paragraph and can store either an integer value (123) or a floating-point value (4.4353). String variables store a sequence of letters, digits, or punctuation. By using a string variable, you can say name = "Dave Taylor" and it has the effect of putting the letters D, a, v, e, and so on, into the container name. By contrast, Booleans can have only one of two possible values: true or false.

To use a variable, you have to define it and assign it a value. Variables are defined in JavaScript with the var statement, and the = symbol assigns values. For example:

```
var doggie_in_window_cost = 200;
var favoriteDirector = "David Lean";
```

tip

Notice here that both lines end with a semicolon. In JavaScript, all properly formed lines must end with a semicolon.

Remember the mathematical expression above? Here's how it looks in JavaScript:

```
var x, y;
y = 3;
x = y + 4;
```

That's the JavaScript equivalent of x = y + 4. Not too hard, is it?

Where do you put JavaScript?

Before you delve any further into JavaScript, you're probably wondering where this stuff goes on your page. The answer is that JavaScript should always live within a `<script>` block, as shown here:

```
<script language="javascript">
var x, y;
y = 3;
x = y + 4;
</script>
```

This `<script>` block adds two variables within the JavaScript portion of your Web page, named x and y. The former has the value of 7, and the latter has a value of 3.

You can have more than one `<script>` block on your page, and later `<script>` can reference variables set and functions defined by earlier blocks.

Events

Most people find that tying JavaScript to specific Web page *events* (quite literally, something that happens), including onLoad and onUnload among others, gives them more than enough flexibility.

Table 11-1 shows a list of interesting JavaScript events.

Table 11-1: Interesting Scriptable Events in JavaScript

Event Name	Description
onblur	Input element loses focus (user moves cursor elsewhere)
onchange	Similar to oblur, but contents change
onclick	A mouseclick event occurs
ondblclick	A double-click occurs
onfocus	User clicks into, or tabs into, an input element

Continued

Table 11-1: *Continued*

Event Name	Description
onload	The page completes loading in the browser
onmousedown	The user clicks the mouse button
onmouseup	The user releases the mouse button
onmouseout	The cursor moves away from the element
onmouseover	The cursor moves over the element
onmove	The window moves
onresize	The window is resized
onselect	User selects text in an input or textarea element
onunload	Opposite of onload; user leaves the page

The four events most commonly used with JavaScript are onclick, onmouseover, onmouseout, and onload. I explore how to utilize these four events later in this chapter.

Expressions

Much more interesting than variable assignment statements (JavaScript instructions that assign a value to a specified variable) are *expressions*, which are the real building blocks of JavaScript. Expressions can evaluate to a Boolean (as in "if this condition is true, then . . .") or can evaluate to a string or numeric expression. Table 11-2 takes a look at each of these expressions.

Table 11-2: Three Types of Expressions in JavaScript

Expression	What It Evaluates To
x + y > z	Evaluates to a Boolean: either *true* or *false*
x + (2 x y)-3	Evaluates to a numeric value, the sum of these two variables
name + " (given name)"	Appends the specified string to the end of the value of the string name

JavaScript simplifies working with *strings*, sequences of characters such as names, addresses, product codes, and URLs. You can build up strings of other values by using the + symbol, as shown here:

```
var name = "Gareth", name2 = "Ashley";
names = name + " and " + name2;
```

The resultant variable names is set to Gareth and Ashley.

You can create mathematical expressions in lots of ways. Not only can you use +, -, *, and / for addition, subtraction, multiplication, and division, respectively, you can also use shortcuts, such as ++ to add one, − to subtract one, and even structures like x += y; to add y to the current value of x or salary /= 2; to divide the value of salary by two.

Looping mechanisms

Although writing programs without any sort of looping or conditional execution is theoretically possible, doing so is a complete nightmare, requiring you to type and type and type until the cows come home. Instead, JavaScript offers a typical lineup of looping and control structures, as shown in Table 11-3. By utilizing these structures, you can have sections of JavaScript that only run if certain conditions are true or if variables have specified values. You can also execute statements more than once, based on similar conditions.

Table 11-3: JavaScript Looping Mechanisms

Looping Mechanism	What It Does
if (expr) statement	Conditionally executes statement or statement block.
else statement	Executes statement if expr is false (must be associated with an if statement)
switch (expr)	Acts like a case statement, a series of if/else tests
while (expr) statement	Loops, continually executing a statement until expr is false
do statement while (expr)	Same as while, but guarantees one time through loop
for (expr1;expr2;expr3) statement	Loops, continually executing a statement until expr2 is false: expr1 is the initializing expression prior to looping, and expr3 is done after each loop but before expr2 evaluates

Don't let the complex appearance of a for loop turn you off; it's the most useful looping mechanism in JavaScript. A for loop consists of three components: an initializer, a conditional, and a loop increment, as you see in the following example:

```
for (var j = 0; j < 10; j++) {
  salary += salary;
}
```

The preceding setup is 100 percent identical to the following example:

```
var j = 0;
while (j < 10) {
  salary += salary;
  j++;
}
```

The for loop is a delightfully succinct way to express this sort of sequence, with the initializer as the first part of the for loop, the conditional statement as the second part, and the loop increment as the third, all separated by semicolons.

Subroutines, built-in and user-defined

Many programs have sequences of statements that appear over and over again. Smart programmers turn those into *subroutines*, named functions that you can invoke anywhere in your JavaScript. A simple user-defined function might look like the following example:

```
function swap(a, b) {
  var hold = b;
  a = b; b = hold;
}
```

This function enables you to easily swap the values of any two variables, for example, name and address, which you can reference in your JavaScript with swap(name, address);.

Subroutines can also return values by using the return statement. Here's a subroutine that returns the square of the given value:

```
function square(x) {
  return (x * x);
}
```

A statement such as y = square(20); results in y having the value of 400 (20 squared).

Built-in functions

The really good news is that hundreds of different functions are built into the JavaScript language. Consequently, most of your user-defined subroutines end up implementing your algorithms instead of doing the real dirty work of string or number manipulation.

Because JavaScript is an object-oriented programming language, you invoke many functions by essentially appending their names to a given variable. For example, you obtain the length of the string variable name by using name.length,

so you can use this attribute in a conditional as follows:

```
 if (name.length > 50)
```

JavaScript uses many more built-in functions than I can squeeze into this book, but Table 11-4 highlights several that are of particular value to site developers.

Table 11-4: A Few Great JavaScript Functions

Function	What It Does
`back()`	Returns to the previous URL
`close()`	Closes the specified window
`confirm()`	Confirms an action with an `OK`/`CANCEL` answer
`open()`	Creates and opens a new window
`submit()`	Submits the specified form, as if you'd clicked the Submit button

How can you use these functions? Here's an example:

```
if (confirm("You want to close this window?")) close();
```

This code pops up a dialog box that reads, `You want to close this window?` and has two buttons: OK and Cancel. If you choose OK the `confirm()` function returns *true* and the `close()` statement executes. (The window closes.) If you choose Cancel, `confirm()` returns *false* and JavaScript skips the `close()` statement.

note   There's a lot more to JavaScript than I can squeeze into these few pages. Many online sources give you additional information, including `http://www.Javascript.com/`.

Testing Browser Compatibility

JavaScript is commonly used to figure out what kind of Web browser you're running. You might not realize it, but every time you communicate with a Web server, you're sending along various (nonspecific) identifying information, including your unique computer (IP) address, and a browser identification string such as the following:

```
Mozilla/4.0 (compatible; MSIE 5.0; Windows 98; DigExt)
```

Although this browser says that this user is running Mozilla/4.0, it's really not. Mozilla is the code name for Netscape's Navigator Web browser, but this user is actually running MSIE—Microsoft Internet Explorer—5.0 masquerading as Mozilla (that's what the *compatible* means in parentheses). Notice it also indicates that the user is running Windows 98, of all things.

You can test all this information within JavaScript quite easily, making it possible for you to write Web pages that refuse to work for certain browsers or, in a more friendly vein, perhaps congratulate users on their choice of Web browsers or operating systems. Here's an example:

```
<body>

<script language="JavaScript">
function showInfo()
{
  document.writeln("<div style='font-size: 75%'>");
  document.writeln("Information about your browser:\n<ul>");
  for (propertyName in navigator) {
    document.writeln("<li>", propertyName, " = ",
      navigator[propertyName], "</li>");
  }
  document.writeln("</ul></div>");
}

document.writeln("<h1>Welcome, ", navigator.appName, " User</h1>");

document.write("<h3>You're running ");

if (navigator.appName.indexOf("Win") > -1) {
  document.writeln("Microsoft Windows</h3>");
} else if (navigator.appName.indexOf("Mac") > -1) {
  document.writeln("Apple MacOS</h3>");
} else {
  document.writeln(navigator.platform, "</h3>");
}

showInfo();

</script>
</body>
```

This code is fairly sophisticated. In the following paragraphs, I explain the main things you need to understand about this JavaScript example.

First, this code includes a function to output all the possible values in the `navigator` object. The line `for (propertyName in navigator)` steps through all the values. But focus on the middle line that says `Welcome`. Have a look at Figure 11-1 to see how it looks in a browser.

The `indexOf()` call is a built-in subroutine that returns either the location in the given string where the specified pattern appears or the value -1 if the pattern doesn't appear. So, the first conditional—`if (navigator.appName.indexOf("Win") > -1`—is testing to see if the sequence `"Win"` appears in the application name string. If it does, then the value returned is greater than -1 and the user is running Windows. If not, JavaScript goes to the next test, which looks for `"Mac"` and if that fails too, JavaScript just writes whatever platform-name value the user's browser returns.

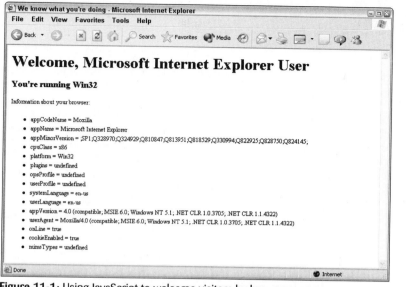

Figure 11-1: Using JavaScript to welcome visitors by browser name.

note When run on a Linux system, `navigator.platform` is `Linux i686`.

If this seems like vast overkill, here's how you can simply slip in an *optimized for* message on a Web page that actually lists *the user's specific browser* (the value contained in `navigator.appName`):

```
<script language="JavaScript">
document.writeln("<h4>This site optimized for ",
   navigator.appName, "</h4>");
</script>
```

That's it. Tricky, eh? If you're perverse, you could use a simple conditional to have your page always indicate that it's optimized for the browser the user *isn't* running, although, of course, the page itself would still render properly!

Graphical Rollovers

One of the most popular ways to use JavaScript is creating a *rollover*, a Web page element that changes its appearance or behavior when you hover the cursor over it. Before I show you how to create a rollover, don't forget that you can use CSS to accomplish a rollover text effect by using the hover attribute, as shown in the following code:

```
<style type="text/css">
a:hover { background-color: #ccffcc; text-decoration: none; }
</style>
```

This bit of code removes the underline from all hypertext links on the page while the cursor is over the link, but it also changes the background color of the link itself to a very light green.

But if you want to accomplish a similar effect with graphics, work with the *document object model* (DOM). This is the data structure that Web browsers use to understand and render every page of HTML you view. Recall that everything on a Web page is a container, so the `hover` style that I just showed you changes the background of the *link container* when a `mouseover` event takes place. The change doesn't affect the page or the paragraph, just the actual linked text itself.

Similarly, all graphical elements also live in containers within the document object model, even if they don't look like it when you're viewing a page.

What does this mean? It means that to have a graphic change after the page has loaded, you must figure out the appropriate way to reference the container that holds the image. In addition, you need to create a new image container so that the alternative image can also be loaded. The following sections guide you through creating a new image container.

Creating a new image container

The first step when creating a graphical rollover is to create an image container. Use the following code:

```
var myImageObject = new Image();
```

The `Image()` function is a built-in function in JavaScript that returns a complex object with a variety of attributes, notably `src`, the image's URL.

When you are trying to implement a rollover quickly, you see that two image objects are necessary: one for the default image and another for the new rollover image. So, in fact, the first couple of lines look like this:

```
var newImageObject = new Image();
var defaultImage = new Image();
```

These lines would appear within a JavaScript block, of course.

Assigning a URL to the new image container

The next step is to assign a URL, which is surprisingly easy to do:

```
newImageObject.src =
  'http://www.intuitive.com/coolsites/examples/Graphics/b-off.jpg'
defaultImage.src =
  'http://www.intuitive.com/coolsites/examples/Graphics/b-on.jpg;
```

Not only does this create two new image objects, one of which represents the rollover's button-off state (b-off.jpg) and one that represents the rollover's button-on state (b-on.jpg), but it also associates them with actual graphics by using the URL of two different images.

note Although these are fully qualified URLs, most rollovers use a lazier shorthand notation like defaultImage.src = 'b-on.jpg" or something similar.

Changing values on the fly

To make the rollover actually work, first, you write a function that changes the image from one value to another; and second, you hook the function into the Web page with the appropriate JavaScript events, as discussed earlier in this chapter.

Start by looking at the code that's needed in the img tag to make it a rollover:

```
<img src="http://www.crewtags.com/create/images/tags/front/
emoticonsmile.jpg"
  alt="fun keychains: happy or sad" id="changingface"
  onMouseOver="makeSad();" onMouseOut="makeHappy();" />
```

Most of this should look like a typical image inclusion, with the src attribute for the image's URL, and the alt tag for text to display in lieu of the graphic. What's new is that you give this particular image container a unique identifying name: id="changingface". That change becomes important when you want to refer to this specific container in the DOM.

In addition, this code ties the function makeSad() to a Mouseover event and the function makeHappy() to a Mouseout event. Any guesses about how this is going to work?

The other half of this dynamic duo consists of the functions themselves, which are almost completely identical except that one refers to *happy* and the other refers to *sad*:

```
function makeHappy()
{
  if (document.images) {
    imageObject = document.getElementById("changingface");
    imageObject.src = happy.src;
  }
}

function makeSad()
{
```

Continued

Continued

```
  if (document.images) {
    imageObject = document.getElementById("changingface");
    imageObject.src = sad.src;
  }
}
```

The first function, `makeHappy()`, is called when the cursor *leaves* the container—the `onMouseOut` event—so its purpose is to restore the image to its initial state. First, it checks to ensure that the Web browser has a reasonably modern DOM (the test is to see if `document.images` is nonzero), and if so, it gets the image container's specific address by searching for its unique ID in the DOM tree. Now you can see why the `img` tag had to include an `id` attribute!

After the image container is found by referencing its unique ID, the image object's source—the `src` property—is changed to match the happy image object's source, which is set to the smiley face icon.

Here's the entire HTML file, top to bottom:

```
<html>
<head><title>Don't tread on me</title>
<script language="JavaScript">

var happy = new Image();
var sad   = new Image();

happy.src=
"http://www.crewtags.com/create/images/tags/front/emoticonsmile.jpg";
sad.src=
"http://www.crewtags.com/create/images/tags/front/emoticonsad.jpg";

function makeHappy()
{
  if (document.images) {
    imageObject = document.getElementById("changingface");
    imageObject.src = happy.src;
  }
}

function makeSad()
{
  if (document.images) {
    imageObject = document.getElementById("changingface");
    imageObject.src = sad.src;
  }
}
</script>
</head>
```

```
<body style='text-align:center;'>
<h2>Rollover demonstration</h2>

<img src="http://www.crewtags.com/create/images/tags/front/
emoticonsmile.jpg"
 alt="fun keychains: happy or sad" id="changingface"
 onmouseover="makeSad();" on mouseout="makeHappy();" />
<br /><br /><hr /><br />
Images courtesy of <br />
<a href="http://www.crewtags.com/"><img
  src="http://www.crewtags.com/create/images/logo.jpg"
  alt="CrewTags" border="0" /></a>
</body>
</html>
```

You can try it for yourself. You'll find that the initial state of the page is shown in Figure 11-2. Move your cursor over the smiley tag and see what happens!

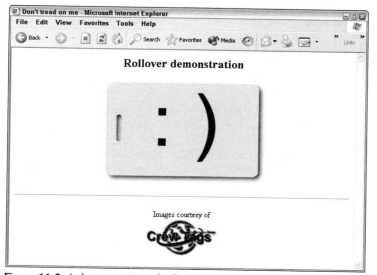

Figure 11-2: A demonstration of rollover graphics, courtesy of Crew Tags.

What might not be immediately obvious is that you can have JavaScript events tied to almost any element of a page, and that *they can change other containers, not just themselves.*

To change the page so that moving the cursor over the Crew Tags logo also changes the smiley to a sad face, use the following code:

```
<a href="http://www.crewtags.com/"><img
  src="http://www.crewtags.com/create/images/logo.jpg"
  onMouseOver="makeSad();" onMouseOut="makeHappy();"
  alt="CrewTags" border="0" /></a>
```

You only have to change one line—the line that is already in the img tag for the smiley tag. Simple enough!

With this sort of capability, you have many, many different ways to improve and add pizzazz to your Web sites.

Telling the time

JavaScript also enables your Web page to access the system clock and display the current date and time. The following code illustrates how to add this function:

```
<h2>The current date and time:
<script language="JavaScript">
var rightNow = new Date(); // create a new variable called 'rightNow'
document.writeln(rightNow); // assign in the date, then print it out
</script>
</h2>
```

This sequence of code works just fine, producing an HTML sequence like this:

```
<h2>The current date and time:
Wed Dec 17 20:01:54 MST 2003
</h2>
```

The problem is that the preceding method does not produce a very legible format for showing the time, compared to the friendlier formats you're used to seeing.

Fortunately, JavaScript has many different *methods* (a fancy object-oriented name for functions) available for working with the date and time information, as shown in Table 11-5.

Table 11-5: Time-Related JavaScript Methods

Method	Description
getDate	Day of month (range 1–31)
getDay	Day of week (range 0–6)
getFullYear	Returns four-digit year value
getHours	Hours unit (0–23)
getMinutes	Minutes unit (0–59)
getMonth	Month of year (range 0–11)
getSeconds	Seconds unit (0–59)
getTime	Number of milliseconds since reference date (1 January, 1970)
getYear	Years unit (may return year as 1900 on older systems)
setDate	Specifies new month in date object (range 0–11)

Method	Description
setFullYear	Specifies new year (4-digit) in date object
setHours	Specifies new hours value in date object (range 0–23)
setMinutes	Specifies new minutes value in date object (range 0–59)
setMonth	Specifies new month in date object (same as setDate)
setSeconds	Specifies new seconds in date object
setTime	Specifies time for date object in milliseconds (see getTime)
setYear	Specifies new year in date object (See note in getYear)
toLocaleString	Returns locale-based date/time string (most useful for switching date format strings to local conventions and languages, as the individual user specifies)

These methods make producing attractive output a breeze, because they do all the hard work of isolating individual date elements for you.

Time of day, the friendly version

Want to include the time of day? Use getTime():

```
At the tone, it's
<script language="JavaScript">
document.writeln(rightNow.getHours() +":"+ rightNow.getMinutes());
</script>
exactly.
```

Typical output for this code might look like the following:

```
At the tone, it's 20:12 exactly.
```

Locale-specific date and time

You might not think of *locale* as the collection of all standard information that defines how your part of the world specifies numeric values, dates, time, and many other things, but that's exactly how computers think of it. So the method toLocaleString() proves tremendously helpful. The following code produces a helpful (and amusing) result:

```
<div style='font-size:75%;color:#333'>
Page last modified
<script language="JavaScript">
document.writeln(rightNow.toLocaleString());
</script>
</div>
```

Here is the result:

```
Page last modified Wednesday, December 17, 2003 8:12:44 PM
```

This is amusing because the page always reports that it was last modified at exactly the moment the visitor is viewing the page!

A built-in clock

One additional neat thing you can do with the time methods is to output a clock container that stays up-to-the-second while someone is viewing the page. It's a bit more complex, because it uses a lot of JavaScript. Here's the code:

```
<html>
<head><title>Does anybody really know what time it is?</title>
<script language="JavaScript">
function clock() {
  var now = new Date();

  var hours = now.getHours();
  var amPm = (hours > 11) ? "pm" : "am";
  hours = (hours > 12) ? hours - 12 : hours;

  var minutes = now.getMinutes();
  minutes = (minutes < 10) ? "0" + minutes : minutes;

  var seconds = now.getSeconds();
  seconds = (seconds < 10) ? "0" + seconds : seconds;

  dispTime = hours + ":" + minutes + ":" + seconds + " " + amPm;

  if (document.getElementById) {
    document.getElementById("clockspace").innerHTML = dispTime;
  }
  setTimeout("clock()",1000);
}
</script>
</head>
<body onload="clock()">
The actual time right now is:
<span id="clockspace"></span>
</body>
</html>
```

Figure 11-3 shows a screenshot of the preceding code with all the additional snippets explored in this section thrown in for good measure. Notice that the page loaded at 16:23 (4:23 p.m.), but because the built-in clock keeps track of time, the actual time indicates 4:42 p.m. The difference between the two times can be a bit subtle: The first time indicates when the page was loaded into the Web browser, whereas the second time, like a clock on the wall, keeps incrementing each second. The longer you have the page sitting in your browser, the greater the difference between these two times. When the page first loads, of course, they are identical. Make sense? Also notice the locale-specific date and time at the bottom of the page.

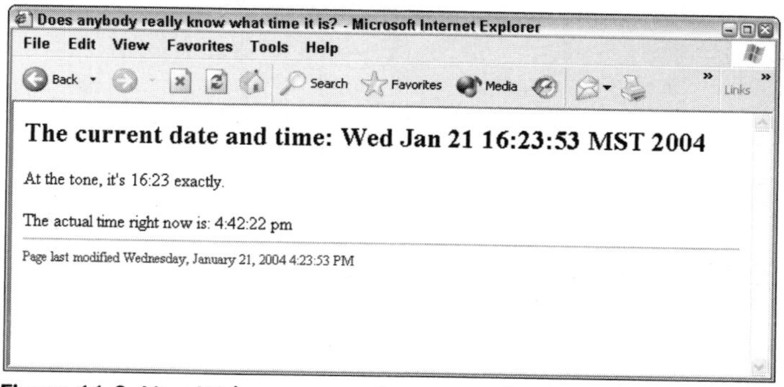

Figure 11-3: Your Web pages can show up-to-the-second time of day.

> **note** The setTimeout() method used here is particularly interesting: It tells the Web browser to call the clock() function again after 1000 milliseconds pass.

When looking at Figure 11-3, notice in particular the difference between the *at the tone* time (which is the current time when the page was loaded) and the *actual time* (which is incrementing, second by second).

There's a lot more you can do with the time and date methods, including a simple masthead for a publication. But since getMonth returns 0–11 as its value (as shown in Table 11-5), you want to map those numeric values to actual month names, probably with some sort of data structure, perhaps an array. You can also produce dynamic calendars with the current day highlighted, and much more.

Testing Form Values

Although the previous examples are fun for adding some excitement to your Web site, perhaps the most compelling use of JavaScript is to help with user-input forms. In Chapter 9, for example, you learn that by including the following code snippet, you can easily add a Google search box to your Web page:

```
<form method="get" action="http://www.google.com/search">
What you seek:
<input type="text" name="q">
<input type="submit" value="search google">
</form>
```

By default, if you submit the search without any query string, Google simply prompts for one. Instead, however, you can use JavaScript to refuse to send blank queries. To do this, you use an `onsubmit` event handler in the form tag that checks for the input. Use the `alert()` method to have the search query appear in a pop-up window:

```
<h2>Search Google for what you seek</h2>
<form method="get" action="http://www.google.com/search"
 name="google"
 onsubmit="alert(document.google.q.value);return false;">
What you seek:
<input type="text" name="q">
<input type="submit" value="search google">
</form>
```

This looks more complex than it is. Really. The form is called `google` and the variable you're interested in is called `q` (that's Google's name for it, not mine). So you can reference that object as `document.google.q`. The value attribute of this object contains whatever the user enters. Figure 11-4 shows what I'm talking about.

Figure 11-4: An alert box shows what's in the search box.

Did you notice the `return false` at the end of the `onSubmit` handler? That's a key idea for form validation: If an `onSubmit` event handler returns *false*, the form data isn't submitted to the action script. If it returns *true*, it is submitted. So any script that tests values prior to submission simply needs to return the appropriate value to control whether it is actually submitted or not.

Creating a test condition

To have this form actually test a value, you need a conditional expression. To improve the HTML's overall readability, move the conditional expression into a function at the top of the page:

```
<script language="JavaScript">
function validate()
{
  if (document.google.q.value.length == 0) {
    alert("Please enter a search pattern!");
    return false;
  }
  else
    return true;
}
</script>
```

Moving the conditional expression to the top of the page actually simplifies the form itself because the increasingly complex JavaScript is now elsewhere, not squished into the HTML:

```
<form method="get" action="http://www.google.com/search"
 name="google" onsubmit="return validate();">
What you seek:
<input type="text" name="q">
<input type="submit" value="search google">
</form>
```

Figure 11-5 shows what happens if a search is requested when there's no pattern.

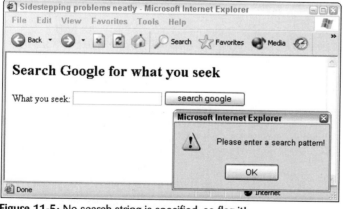

Figure 11-5: No search string is specified, so flag it!

If there is a search pattern, the function returns true, and the pattern is given to Google for a search.

A Temperature Converter

Another neat JavaScript example is a simple form that doesn't actually have a CGI script (a program that lives on the Web server) behind it; instead, it works completely through JavaScript.

 x-ref If you need a refresher on CGI scripts, turn to Chapter 9.

To enable this form's functionality, tie events to an `input type="button"` and avoid the `submit` element completely instead of embedding the script into the page by using JavaScript. This is an in-place Fahrenheit/Celsius `conversion` function:

```
function convertTemp(direction)
{
   // if you have a Fahrenheit temp, compute Celsius, or vice-versa
   var fObj = document.convert.ftemp, cObj = document.convert.ctemp;

   if (direction == "ftoc") {
     cObj.value = Math.round((fObj.value - 32) * (5/9));
   } else {
     fObj.value = Math.round((parseInt(cObj.value) * (9/5)) + 32);
   }
}
```

The conversion formulas here are `Celsius = Fahrenheit * (9/5) + 32` and `Fahrenheit = (Celsius + 32) * (5/9)`. The `direction` variable enables you to use the same function to calculate in either direction.

The associated HTML is as follows:

```
<form style="border: 1px double blue; background-color: #DDF;
 padding: 4px;text-align:center;" name="convert">
Fahrenheit:
<input type="text" name="ftemp" size="7"
 onchange="convertTemp('ftoc')"> is the
same as Celsius:
<input type="text" name="ctemp" size="7"
 onchange="convertTemp('ctof')">
<br />
<input type="button" value="clear" onclick="clearAll();">
</form>
```

It's pleasantly short and sweet. You can see in Figure 11-6 that I also added one more capability: The Clear button calls the following JavaScript function:

```
function clearAll()
{
  document.convert.ftemp.value="";
  document.convert.ctemp.value="";
}
```

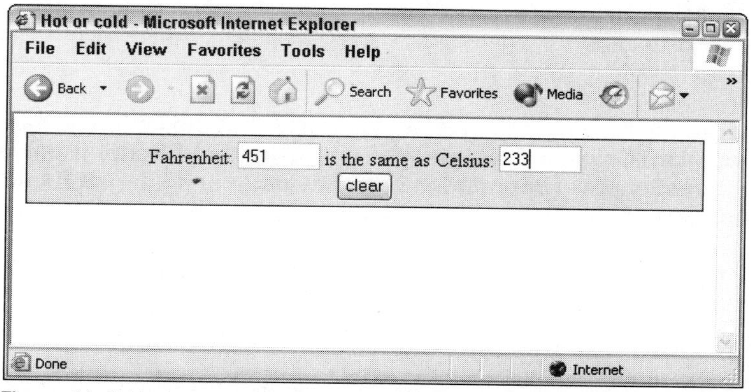

Figure 11-6: You can use JavaScript to add a temperature conversion calculator to your Web page.

Other Scripting Solutions

Although JavaScript is the most popular scripting solution for Web pages, a number of other scripting options deserve at least a brief mention. Some of these live within the HTML page, whereas others live on the server but still offer a remarkable amount of power over what you deliver to your visitor.

Visual Basic Script

JavaScript is powerful but unlike any language that most programmers and users have ever learned. Visual Basic, on the other hand, is a language based on the one that many folks learned when they were first starting out with computers or programming. Microsoft offers Visual Basic Script for Internet Explorer—VBScript—as an alternative to JavaScript.

Here's how a simple VBScript program might look:

```
<html>
<body bgcolor="white">
<script language="VBScript" event="OnClick" for="Button1">
  MsgBox "You clicked on the button and up popped me!"
</script>
```

Continued

```
Continued
<center>
<form>
<input name="Button1" type="button"
       value="Roses are red, beloved by the bee..."><br />
<i>click the button</i>
</form>
</center>
</html>
```

The script looks very similar to JavaScript in the HTML document, but the language itself is easier to work with, in my opinion. Unfortunately, you can do the math: VBScript is only supported in Internet Explorer; JavaScript is supported in both Navigator and Internet Explorer. As a result, JavaScript is unquestionably the scripting language of choice.

tip You can learn a lot more about Visual Basic Script by visiting Microsoft's reference site at `http://msdn.microsoft.com/vbasic/`.

Java

In terms of sheer enthusiasm in the press and incessant commentary from pundits everywhere, no new technology introduced on the Net has been as widely heralded as Java, from Sun Microsystems. Your favorite computer magazine probably told you that Java would save the world, cure world hunger, and, did I mention, lower the prime lending rate and wash your car?

The reality is somewhat different. Java is a complex, object-oriented programming language based on a powerful language called C++, which itself is a modified version of the C programming language so beloved by Unix folks. C was originally developed to write Unix device drivers, so it shares many characteristics with the most primitive of languages: Assembler. Add a layer of object-oriented capabilities, and you've got C++. Tweak it further for the Net, and you have Java.

The good news is that many different Java-development environments are available for Windows, Macintosh, and Unix/Linux systems, and they make things quite a bit easier. Even better, you can use Java *applets* (small programs providing a specific function), as they're called, without even having much of a clue about Java itself.

Start by having a look at a simple Java program:

```
class HelloWorld {
  public static void main (String args[]) {
    System.out.println("Hello World!");
  }
}
```

That is what's involved in getting the program to say "Hello World!" within a Web page. You can't send this script directly in your HTML page, though. You have to actually translate it into a Java applet binary by compiling it. To work with Java, you must have some sort of development environment.

Referencing Java applets

If you can't include the Java source or compiled binary in your HTML code, you might wonder just how you actually include Java applets on your page. The answer used to be the `applet` tag, but HTML 4 replaces that with the `object` tag. The `object` tag has a variety of parameters, the most important of which is the `classid` parameter, which specifies the exact name of the applet desired. Here is an example of the `object` tag at its simplest:

```
<object codetype="application/octet-stream"
   classid="java:DrawStringApplet.class"
   width="100" height="100"></object>
```

The `codetype` specified is actually what's called a MIME type. Originally, the MIME standard was intended for e-mail attachments—indeed, it stands for Multimedia Internet Mail Extensions—but it's now used as a general-purpose media attachment standard. In this case, you're informing the Web browser that the Java applet is a stream of program data.

The preceding HTML snippet defines a 100×100 box that shows the result of `DrawStringApplet` when loaded and run.

Online Java applets

You can add all sorts of Java applets to your own Web pages by simply adding the appropriate reference to your pages. There are dozens upon dozens of nifty applets online, many of which live at Sun's Java division Web site, Javasoft (go to `http://www.javasoft.com/applets/`), and many more that live at Gamelan's online Java library at `http://www.gamelan.com/`. Another great place is JARS.com, which is the Java Applet Resource Center. An online magazine called JavaWorld is just about Java. It is not only very good but it is also run by a bunch of friends of mine. You can visit it at `http://www.javaworld.com`. I encourage you to explore some of these resources online!

tip Elliotte Rusty Harold has written a fabulous Java programming tutorial at `http://sunsite.unc.edu/javafaq/javatutorial.html`. If books are your thing, check out Wiley's *Java 2 Bible* by Justin Couch and Daniel H. Steinberg, or *Java 2 For Dummies* by Barry Burd.

ActiveX

If Java is going to save the world, then ActiveX is going to save us from Java—or something like that. ActiveX is Microsoft's contribution to the programming-languages-on-the-Net debate and offers many of the same capabilities and complexities as Java. The big difference: Java works with both Navigator and Explorer, but ActiveX works only for the Microsoft browser.

tip NCompass Labs has a plug-in called Ncompass for Netscape Navigator that enables Navigator to use ActiveX Controls. Find out more at `http://www.ncompasslabs.com`.

ActiveX functions as a wrapper called an ActiveX *control*. The code being included interacts with the wrapper (ActiveX), and the wrapper interacts with the browser directly. Using this technique, just about any code can run within the browser space, from word processors and spreadsheets to simple games and animation.

Each ActiveX control has a unique class ID and is included as an `object` tag, with parameters specified in the `param` tag—remarkably similar to JavaScript. Here's an example of how you might include an ActiveX control in your page:

```
<object id="ClientLayout"
    classid="clsid:812ae312-8b8e-11cf-93c8-00aa00c08fdf">
    <param name="ALXPATH" ref_value="Client.alx">
</object>
```

note To learn more about ActiveX, visit Microsoft's Developer Network site at `http://msdn.microsoft.com/`. There's also a good ActiveX tutorial area, along with much more, at `http://www.webreference.com/`.

XSLT

Although it has a confusing acronym, XSLT, the Extensible Stylesheet Language Transformations, offers a very interesting approach to modifying XML-based pages within the Web browser. XSLT is an XML-based language, which means that it looks a lot like the document specification values you see in Chapter 16.

Take a quick look at this XSLT style sheet:

```
<?xml version='1.0'?>
<xsl:stylesheet xmlns:xsl="http://www.w3.org/1999/XSL/Transform"
version="1.0">
<xsl:template match="/">
<html>
<body bgcolor="#ccccff">
    <h2> <xsl:value-of select="Concert/Title" /></h2>
    <b>Performances:</b><ul>
        <xsl:for-each select="Concert/CourseDates/Date[Day!='']" >
            <li><xsl:value-of select="Month"/>/
            <xsl:value-of select="Day"/>/
            <xsl:value-of select="Year"/>
            at <xsl:value-of select="Time/Start"/>
            <xsl:value-of select="Mode" /></li>
        </xsl:for-each>
```

```
     </ul>
</body>
</html>
</xsl:template>
</xsl:stylesheet>
```

This is fairly complex stuff and not something you whip out in a few minutes. But if you think of a scripting language that's somewhere between the Structured Query Language (SQL) of database work and JavaScript, you can start to see some logic here. In this example, a header level 2 shows the name of the concert, and the performances are shown in an unordered list, by month/day/year, with starting times. The `xsl:for-each` is a `for` loop, just as JavaScript uses one, but this steps through possible matches in the input data stream (the XML document that references this XSLT style sheet).

Fortunately, if you're going to be working with XSLT, you're likely to have some tools available to help make it manageable!

note To learn more about XSLT and its associated technologies, start at O'Reilly's excellent `XML.com` Web site.

Flash

Another possibility for scripting your pages is to delve into a completely different environment that offers a high level of sophistication at the price of a plug-in. That environment is Macromedia Flash. First developed as an offshoot of Macromedia Director, Flash offers a complete time-based scripting environment with sophisticated transformations, so you can have elements zoom in, zoom out, spin, add music, and much, much more. Think of an animation toolbox, and you are on the right track. You'll know when you've hit a Flash-based site because it's much more like a multimedia experience than a regular non-Flash Web page.

For many applications, that's the problem with Flash; it's not a Web page at all. The content isn't indexed the same by search engines like Google, and users can't easily save the content. Also, it's almost always large and requires a great deal of bandwidth, it's more difficult to develop, and it requires expensive commercial software. However, comparing a typical HTML-only Web page to a well-designed professional Flash page is like comparing an oyster to a pearl. If you want the fancy jewelry, if you want the shine and the glitz, Flash might be well worth exploring.

note If you do want to learn more about Flash, there's no better place to go than Macromedia's Flash showcase Web site, with its list of Flash Site of the Day choices, at `http://www.macromedia.com/cfusion/showcase/`. You can also check out Wiley's *Macromedia Flash MX 2004 Bible* by Robert Reinhardt and Snow Dowd.

Summary

This chapter focused on using JavaScript to add pizzazz to your Web site. I started with a basic explanation of this simple programming language, and then I showed you how to test browser compatibility. I also demonstrated how to create fun graphical rollovers with just a few lines of JavaScript code, and even some ways that you can access and manipulate the system clock for different results. Finally, I explored a few calculators along with the interface between JavaScript and HTML forms. The next chapter switches gears and explores the nooks and crannies of Cascading Style Sheets—a must read!

Advanced Cascading Style Sheets

In This Chapter

Examining boxes and containers

Getting to know the CSS container parts

Assigning container dimensions

Putting containers where you want them

Using visibility to control the display

Designing three-dimensional pages with Z-indexes

By this point, I hope that you're comfortable with my convention of referring to the space that a Web-page element occupies as a *container*, because this session is going to focus on the concept of containers and how they affect your Web design in the CSS world. So jump right in!

Boxes and Containers

If you've been working with HTML for a while, you are already familiar with the containers that comprise a page. Whether a container is as overt as a data cell in a table, a paragraph, or a div, or as subtle as a hypertext reference or italicized passage, you construct all your Web pages from containers within containers within containers.

In regular HTML, this concept isn't really that important because, for the most part, you can't do anything with the containers or even really affect their layout, other than perhaps by using cellspacing and width on a table or margin attributes in a body tag.

Cascading Style Sheets are a different story, however; just about every HTML tag turns out to be a container—and you can modify them all to suit your needs!

As a simple example, consider the following HTML block:

```
<body>
<table>
<tr><td>
  <p>
  This is an <i>example</i> to explore.
  </p>
</td></tr>
</table>
</body>
```

How many different containers do you count in this example?

I count six. They're easier to see if I indent things to suggest the containers at work, as in the following version:

```
<body>
    <table>
        <tr>
            <td>
                <p>
                    This is an
                    <i>
                        example
                    </i>
                    to explore.
                </p>
            </td>
        </tr>
    </table>
</body>
```

If you imagine each level of container having its own attributes, you can see where the *cascading* part of Cascading Style Sheets can really force you to keep track of everything happening on your page and not just the closest enclosing tag values.

In the CSS world containers are said to *nest*, which means that the <i></i> container nests within the <p></p> container, the <td></td> container, and so on. Furthermore, the <i></i> container is the *child* of the <p></p> container. You also sometimes state this relationship by calling the <p></p> container the *parent* of the <i></i> container.

The Different Parts of a Container

Before I explore the elements of each container, take a look at Figure 12-1:

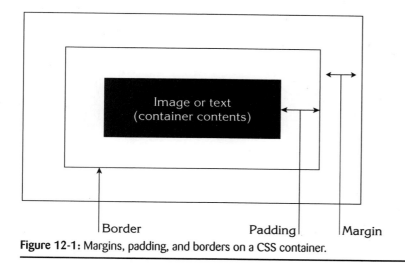

Figure 12-1: Margins, padding, and borders on a CSS container.

As you can see in Figure 12-1, an invisible buffer zone, or a *padding*, surrounds every element on a Web page. That buffer zone is identical in concept to the `cellpadding` attribute of a table data cell. On the very edge of the padding is a *border*, which is almost always invisible; and the space between the border and the rest of the contents of the page is the *margin* of the element.

Margins

The element of a container that people change most often is the margin. In a way, that process is analogous to setting the margin in your document before typing in a report, but it's considerably more powerful.

You set and alter margins in CSS by using the `margin` attribute, which is actually a shorthand way to access `margin-left`, `margin-right`, `margin-top`, and `margin-bottom`. You can give each of these attributes a different value—either a numeric measure (in, cm, em, and so on) or a percentage value. Because you almost always change all four margins at the same time, the `margin` attribute is often a convenient alternative.

The following example, from Arthur Conan Doyle's Sherlock Holmes story, *A Scandal in Bohemia*, shows how these values can affect layout:

```
<body style="margin: 1cm; ">
<p style="margin: 1cm;">
"I am about to be married."
</p><p style="margin: 1cm;">
<b>"So I have heard."</B>
</p>
<p style="margin-right: 3cm;">
"To Clotilde Lothman von Saxe-Meningen, second daughter
of the King of Scandinavia. You may know the strict
principles of her family. She is herself the very soul
of delicacy. A shadow of a doubt as to my conduct would
bring the matter to an end."
</p><p>
"And Irene Adler?"
</p><p style="margin-left: 25%">
"Threatens to send them the photograph. And she will
do it. I know that she will do it. You do not know her,
but she has a soul of steel. She has the face of the
most beautiful of women, and the mind of the most
resolute of men. Rather than I should marry another
woman, there are no lengths to which she would not
go—none."
</p>
</body>
```

Figure 12-2 shows how you can give the different paragraphs dramatically different spacing and layout simply by changing the margin settings. Notice that, by setting a default margin of 1cm in the <body> tag, I force more white space around the entire contents of the page, to which each paragraph container (other than "And Irene Adler?") adds its additional margin spacing. Most important, remember that margins affect top and bottom spacing in addition to left and right spacing.

The margin shorthand is the most complex shorthand attribute that you've seen so far: If you specify a single value, it applies to all four sides. Specify two values, and the first becomes the top and bottom whereas the second becomes the left and right. Specify three values, and you specify the top, left and right, and bottom margins, respectively. Specify four values, and you specify each of the four possible sides, proceeding clockwise from the top: top, right, bottom, and left.

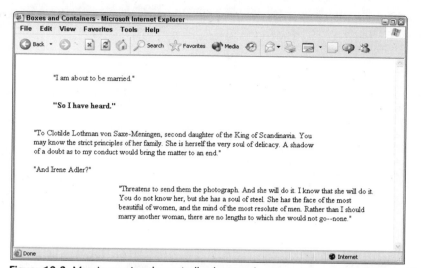

Figure 12-2: Margin spacing dramatically changes the appearance of text. Compare the margins surrounding each paragraph.

So that you don't think that margins only create mass confusion on your page, try to visualize the result of the following set of styles:

```
<STYLE TYPE="text/css">
BODY { margin: 1cm; }
P    { margin-left: 1cm; }
H1   { margin-left: -5mm; }
H2   { margin-left: -5mm; }
</STYLE>
```

If you're imagining an attractive indented paragraph format with headers that outdent, you're right!

note　Did you notice the `margin-left` attribute in the last example? If you don't want to use the `margin` shorthand, you can specify any (or all) of the four margin values for a container by using `margin-left`, `margin-right`, `margin-top`, and `margin-bottom`.

Borders

The best way to understand the different containers is to draw a box around them all—literally. As you saw in Figure 12-1, every container includes three elements: an external margin, a border, and an internal padding.

The border is the most obvious visual element, so I'm going to explore some of the CSS border capabilities, and then take a look at container padding. After you see the impact of borders, the effect of the padding becomes quite obvious.

A number of different CSS attributes enable you to define the characteristics of a container border: `border-width`, `border-style`, and `border-color`. To demonstrate, I add the following style to the very top of the HTML that I used for Figure 12-2:

```
<style type="text/css">
body { margin: 1cm;
       border-width: 4px; border-style: solid;
       border-color: #999; }
</style>
```

Figure 12-3 shows what this addition does: It draws an attractive four-pixel-wide gray box around the contents of this page of text.

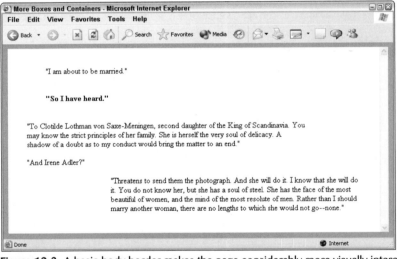

Figure 12-3: A basic body border makes the page considerably more visually interesting.

The `border-width` attribute can take a numerical measure, as you see here, or you can simply specify `thin`, `medium`, or `thick`. The `border-color` attribute can also take any of the usual color specifications, depending on your personal preference.

Multiple value options

Both `border-width` and `border-color` can take more than one value if you want finer control over your presentation, so you can achieve a left-margin-only border by using the following example:

```
border-width: 0 0 0 3px;
```

The code for a margin where the top and bottom borders are blue, the right is green, and the left is yellow, is written as follows:

```
border-color: blue green blue yellow;
```

Like the multiple-value margin attribute in the section "Margins," these two styles (border and padding) also interpret values as top, right, bottom, and left. If you specify only two values, the attribute interprets them as top/bottom and then left/right, and if you specify three values, it interprets them as top, left/right, bottom.

Just as you can sidestep the order of parameters to the margin style by using margin-left, margin-right, and so on, you can also specify sides by using border-width or border-color.

Here's another way to specify a three-pixel-wide left border:

```
border-left-width: 3px;
```

And here's another way to specify the rainbow border:

```
border-bottom-color: blue;
border-top-color: blue;
border-right-color: green;
border-left-color: yellow;
```

As a general rule, if you're going to specify different widths for different sides of a border element, it's good practice to use the explicit side name to avoid confusion.

tip To add to the potential confusion, a shorthand exists for each of the sides of the border, too. Use border-left: and you can specify width, color, and style all at once: border-left: 3px solid black.

One more element to consider before I get to the fun border-style values is border-collapse. The border-collapse CSS attribute takes two possible values: collapse or separate. This attribute comes into play only if two borders would otherwise touch each other on the page. If you specify collapse, the two borders merge and become one border (the size of the larger of the two, usually), whereas if you specify separate, they both show up, even if the result is essentially a double-wide border.

Border-style values

The most interesting of the border attributes is border-style, because it makes a number of way-cool values available to the page designer. See Table 12-1 for a list.

Table 12-1: The Many Values of border-style

Border Style Name	Explanation
none	No border (overrides parent border style).
hidden	Hidden border (again, overrides parent border style).
dotted	Dotted line.
dashed	Dashed line.
solid	Solid line, no shading.
double	Double solid line.
groove	Drawn as if it's carved into the screen.
ridge	Similar to groove but with an outward rather than inward cut appearance.
inset	Appears to indent the container's contents into the screen.
outset	Similar to inset but pushes contents outward.

These different values become quite apparent in the following example:

```
<style type="text/css">
body { margin: 1cm;
       border-width: 10px; border-style: groove;
       border-color: #999999; padding: 5px; }
</style>
<body>
<p style="border: 10px inset; ">
"I am about to be married."
</p><p style="border: 10px dashed;">
<b>"So I have heard."</b>
</p><p style="border: 10px outset;">
"To Clotilde Lothman von Saxe-Meningen, second daughter
of the King of Scandinavia. You may know the strict
principles of her family. She is herself the very soul
of delicacy. A shadow of a doubt as to my conduct would
bring the matter to an end."
</p><p style="border: 10px double;">
"And Irene Adler?"
</p><p style="border: 10px dotted;">
"Threatens to send them the photograph. And she will do
it. I know that she will do it. You do not know her, but
she has a soul of steel. She has the face of the most
beautiful of women, and the mind of the most resolute of
men. Rather than I should marry another woman, there are
no lengths to which she would not go—none."
</p>
</body>
```

Take a look at Figure 12-4 and you see how this example renders in Internet Explorer. Quite a busy page all of a sudden, isn't it?

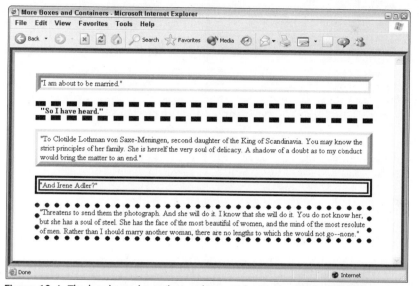

Figure 12-4: The border-style attribute values produce a drastically different page in Microsoft Internet Explorer.

In Figure 12-4, although Internet Explorer doesn't appear to implement the `inset` and `outset` border styles, it actually does, but it just doesn't know how to render them visible if they're black.

on the web — Since both Figure 12-4 and Figure 12-5 are in color, a quick visit to `http://www.intuitive.com/coolsites/` might help you visualize what each figure looks like on-screen. Reproducing colors in a black-and-white book is difficult!

Padding

The next topic to consider in dealing with container spacing is the padding, which affects the space between the border and the contents of the container. In the example in the preceding section, I added `padding: 5px;` to ensure that the outermost border and the borders of each paragraph container don't touch, but instead maintain a fixed pixel space from each other.

The following example gives you one more variation on the Holmes snippet, with padding added within the many different containers to help you clearly see the difference. Watch for the negative padding to see what happens!

```
<style type="text/css">
body { margin: 1cm;
       border-width: 10px; border-style: groove;
       border-color: #999999; padding: 5px; }
</style>
<body>
<p style="border: 10px inset blue; padding: 5px; ">
"I am about to be married."
</p><p style="border: 10px dashed green; padding: 1em;">
<b>"So I have heard."</b>
</p><p style="border: 10px outset yellow; padding: -10px;">
"To Clotilde Lothman von Saxe-Meningen, second daughter of
the King of Scandinavia. You may know the strict principles
of her family. She is herself the very soul of delicacy.
A shadow of a doubt as to my conduct would bring the matter
to an end."
</p><p style="border: 10px double red; padding: 2%;">
"And Irene Adler?"
</p><p style="border: 10px dotted; padding: 1mm;
 border-top-color: blue; border-left-color: red;
 border-bottom-color: yellow; border-right-color: cyan;
 border-top-width: 4px;">
"Threatens to send them the photograph. And she will do it.
I know that she will do it. You do not know her, but she
has a soul of steel. She has the face of the most beautiful
of women, and the mind of the most resolute of men. Rather
than I should marry another woman, there are no lengths
to which she would not go—none."
</p>
```

Figure 12-5 shows how padding affects container borders. Notice in particular that the spacing around each paragraph is different, and that the width of the paragraphs has changed.

Notice the complex border specification of the very last paragraph and its results on-screen. It's quite festive! And did you catch that the browser interprets a negative padding as a zero-padding request? That's quite fortunate, in my opinion; otherwise you might have some pretty peculiar and unreadable results.

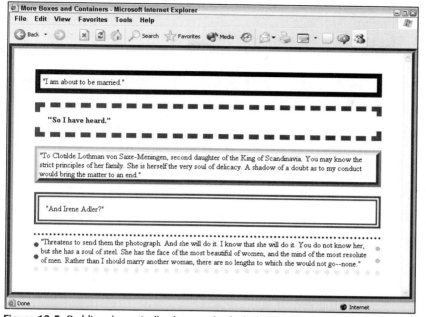

Figure 12-5: Padding dramatically changes the feel of container borders.

Container Dimensions

Two key CSS attributes enable you to control the dimensions of each container of information on your Web page: `width` and `height`. The following example shows how you can use them to specify the exact container size you want, regardless of current page layout:

```
<p style="width: 50%; margin-left: 25%;
    border: 1px solid; padding: 2px;">
The stout gentleman half rose from his chair and gave
a bob of greeting, with a quick little questioning
glance from his small fat-encircled eyes.
</p>
<p>
"Try the settee," said Holmes, relapsing into his
armchair and putting his fingertips together, as was
his custom when in judicial moods. "I know, my dear
Watson, that you share my love of all that is bizarre
and outside the conventions and humdrum routine of
everyday life. You have shown your relish for it by
the enthusiasm which has prompted you to chronicle,
and, if you will excuse my saying so, somewhat to
embellish so many of my own little adventures."
</p>
```

For the CSS attributes listed in the first paragraph that I explained earlier in this chapter, here's a review: I'm specifying here that the first container (paragraph) is 50 percent of the width of the parent container (the body), with a left margin that's 25 percent of the width of the parent container (effectively centering the material). A one-pixel, solid-black border is drawn around the contents of the container, with a two-pixel padding. The results are as shown in Figure 12-6.

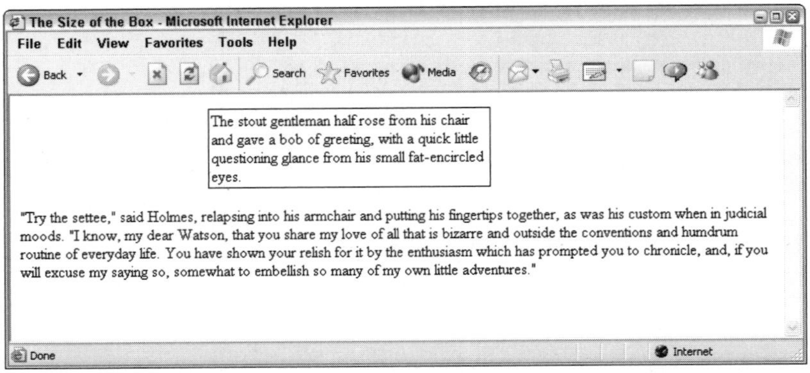

Figure 12-6: Width can profoundly affect the appearance of material on a Web page.

The value of the `width:` attribute is obvious, but the value of `height:` is a bit subtler.

Setting the container height

By default, containers are automatically created at the minimum height necessary to contain all their information. If you specify a `height` value, however, the container takes on a fixed size and no longer automatically expands to include all the information. If you have more material than fits in the specified container size, the material spills out of the container. You can use the `overflow` attribute (which I talk about in the section "Clipping Containers," later in this chapter) to duplicate some of the Internet Explorer-only `iframe` HTML tag characteristics, but I'm just going to let it spill over for this example.

The only change in HTML between what you see in Figures 12-6 and 12-7 is that I add `height: 1em;` to the `style` attribute of the first paragraph for the second figure, as shown in the following example:

```
<p style="width: 50%; margin-left: 25%; height: 1em;
    border: 1px solid; padding: 2px;">
```

As a result, specifying a height that's insufficient for the contents of a container can give you bizarre results, as Figure 12-7 demonstrates when you view this page in Netscape 7.1.

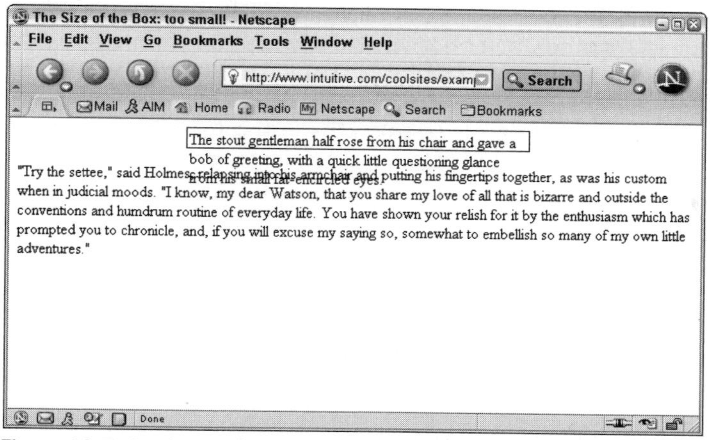

Figure 12-7: Don't specify a height that's too small to contain the text, or the text spills out of the container.

Text and container flow

To really understand why the `height:` attribute is useful, look at the `float:` attribute, which enables you to align a container relative to the rest of the content of the page.

The best way to understand how the `float:` attribute works is to recognize that it's exactly the same as the `align` attribute of the `<table>` tag. Within a `<table>` tag, you can specify `align=left` or `align=right`, and the subsequent material flows around the table on the side other than the one that you specify. To phrase it differently, left alignment causes the table to align against the left margin, with the subsequent text flowing to its right.

The `float:` attribute works in the same way, as the following example shows:

```
<p style="width: 50%; margin: 10px; background-color: #FDF;
    float: left; border: 1px solid; padding: 2px;">
The stout gentleman half rose from his chair and gave a bob
of greeting, with a quick little questioning glance from
his small fat-encircled eyes.
</p>
<p>
"Try the settee," said Holmes, relapsing into his armchair and
putting his fingertips together, as was his custom when in
judicial moods. "I know, my dear Watson, that you share my love
of all that is bizarre and outside the conventions and humdrum
routine of everyday life. You have shown your relish for it by
the enthusiasm which has prompted you to chronicle, and, if you
will excuse my saying so, somewhat to embellish so
many of my own little adventures."
</p>
```

Notice that, in addition to specifying `float: left;` in the `style` attribute, I also add a 10-pixel margin around all four sides of the container border and spruce things up with a light-red background (which appears gray in the black and white figure).

> **note** Technically, #FDF results in a light purple—red + blue = purple—but your color may vary, as mine does! If you really want purple, try #C9F instead.

Figure 12-8 shows the attractive results and should certainly inspire you regarding ways to improve long passages of text!

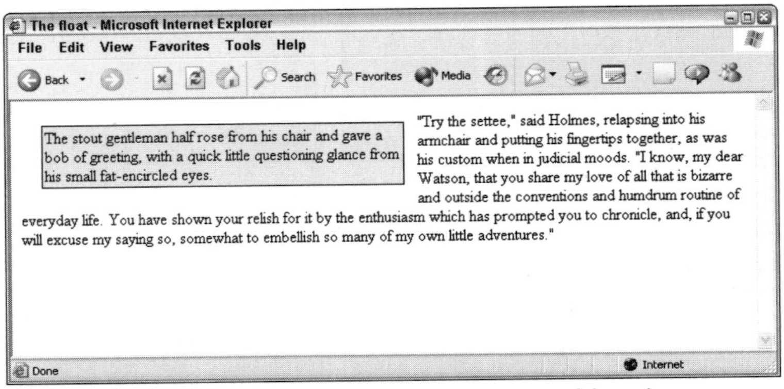

Figure 12-8: Float and container tweaks produce a delightful result.

The `float:` CSS attribute can take three possible values: `left`, `right`, or `none`; you use the last to override the parent `float:` value if you specify one.

Remember that this attribute affects *any container, even one that has child containers*, so you can use this layout technique with a parent container that includes multiple paragraphs of text, graphics, hyperlinks, or whatever. It still acts as a single unit for any CSS presentation specifications that you apply at the parent container level.

Container Positioning

The idea that containers can hold child containers and that you can alter the appearance of the parent through CSS is a cornerstone of advanced Dynamic HyperText Markup Language (DHTML) Web design. It's also why accurately and precisely positioning the container is so important. In the CSS world, you have four different container-positioning options: `absolute`, `relative`, `fixed`, and `static`.

The good news is that one of these—`static`—is the default, so you're already familiar with it. In `static` positioning, the container lays out as it would if you didn't specify any positioning, with preceding material appearing on-screen before the container and subsequent material appearing after the container.

Absolute positioning

Absolute positioning offers a way to specify, pixel by pixel, *exactly* where the container appears on-screen. You set this positioning through a combination of three CSS attributes. The most obvious is `position:` with the value `absolute`, but you also need to specify some combination of the `top:`, `left:`, `right:`, and `bottom:` values, all of which are relative to the edges of the parent container.

Those last few words are so critical, I want to repeat them again: *all of which are relative to the edges of the parent container—not* relative to the Web page itself. If you specify `top:` and `left:`, for example, they're relative to the top-left corner of the parent container.

Here's an example of how you can use absolute positioning to change the appearance of our working passage from Arthur Conan Doyle's novel, *The Red-Headed League*:

```
<p style="width: 50%; margin: 10px; color: red;
    position: absolute; top: -6px; left: -6px;
    border: 1px solid; padding: 2px;">
The stout gentleman half rose from his chair and gave a bob of
greeting, with a quick little questioning glance from his small
fat-encircled eyes.
</p>
<p>
"Try the settee," said Holmes, relapsing into his armchair and
putting his fingertips together, as was his custom when in
judicial moods. "I know, my dear Watson, that you share my love
of all that is bizarre and outside the conventions and humdrum
routine of everyday life. You have shown your relish for it by
the enthusiasm which has prompted you to chronicle, and, if you
will excuse my saying so, somewhat to embellish so many of my own
little adventures."
</p>
```

Figure 12-9 shows the results.

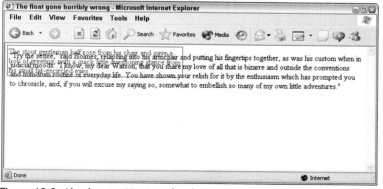

Figure 12-9: Absolute positioning often layers containers atop each other.

I don't know about you, but Figure 12-9 gives me a bit of a headache! The good news is that you have a couple of different ways to address the overlapping container problem. The fastest solution is to simply restore the background color so that you can't see the text of the second paragraph, which the following example accomplishes:

```
<p style="width: 50%; margin: 10px; background-color: #C9F;
    position: absolute; top: -6px; left: -6px;
    border: 1px solid; padding: 2px;">
```

When the preceding code replaces the previous `<p>` tag and `style` attributes, the result is as shown in Figure 12-10. You can see this is considerably easier on the eye.

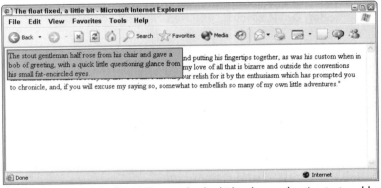

Figure 12-10: Specifying a background color hides the overlapping text problem.

It's not a completely satisfying solution, however, because you still face the issue of the missing text. In this particular example, the best solution is to use the `float: left` CSS attribute. Experiment with it yourself and find what works best for you.

Relative positioning

Absolute positioning is absolute only within the parent container, and most DHTML designers prefer *relative positioning*, which they consider part of the normal flow of the document for layout. In the example in the preceding section, switching from absolute to relative solves the overlap problem, but in a somewhat inelegant manner (leaving a big empty space to the right of the purple box), as follows:

```
<p style="width: 50%; margin: 10px; background-color: #C9F;
    position: relative; top: -6px; left: -6px;
    border: 1px solid; padding: 2px;">
```

Figure 12-11 shows the result of replacing the existing `<p>` tag `style` attribute with the values shown in the preceding code.

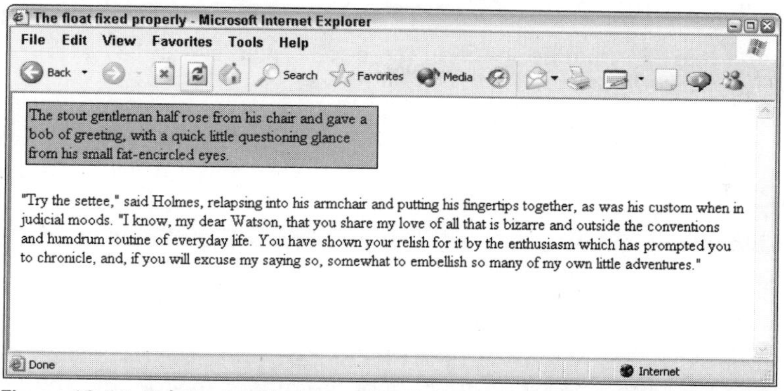

Figure 12-11: Relative positioning makes the container part of the regular document flow.

In this case, `float: left` produces a more attractive result.

So what's the point?

To see why the positioning of elements can prove so useful, I need to change the perspective a bit. Instead of merely providing you with a tool to create big containers of information, relative positioning can actually become your best friend when you want to exert fine control over the positioning of inline elements.

The `vertical-align` CSS attribute enables you to change the relative location of an element, such as the trademark symbol, in a line of text. Relative positioning offers far greater control over inline positioning, and that's its greatest value, as the following example shows:

```
<style type="text/css">
.tm { position: relative;  top: -2.2em; left: -2em;
     font: 8pt bold; border: 1px red groove; padding: 1px;
     background-color: #009; color: white; }
</style>
</head>
<body>

<p style="font: 36pt bold Courier;">
This book has been brought to you by
J. Wiley &amp; Sons, Inc.
<a href="trademark-info.html" target="new" class="tm">tm</A>—
formerly Hungry Minds, Inc., formerly IDG Books, Inc.
</p>
```

Here I create a new class, `.tm`, that creates a small blue box with white `tm` lettering inside that's actually a hyperlink to the trademark information on the site. By using the `top` and `left` attributes, I can carefully tune exactly where the box appears on the layout, pixel by pixel.

on the web A figure illustrating this example appears on the book's Web site at `http://www.intuitive.com/coolsites/`.

Fixed positioning

You have one more possible positioning value, *fixed*. This position is essentially the same as absolute positioning with one spiffy difference: *Fixed containers don't scroll as the rest of the page scrolls.*

Fixed positioning offers another way to get around the hidden text problem: Simply let the user scroll to reveal the otherwise hidden text. Probably not the most user-friendly solution, but it works!

Here's a nifty fixed header example that shows up on this book's Web site (at `http://www.intuitive.com/coolsites/`, in Chapter 12).

caution Before you jump up and try this fixed position example on your computer, I give you fair warning: Windows browsers don't support fixed positioning in my tests.

Clipping Containers

The capability to size and position containers with a high degree of precision is useful, but if the contents are larger than the container parameters, browsers ignore the specified dimensions. Two CSS attributes offer control over what happens if the contents of a container are larger than the size that you specify for the container itself.

The first is `overflow`, and it offers three possible values: `hidden`, `visible`, and `scroll`. For `hidden` or `scroll` to work, you must define a clipping region, using the `clip` CSS attribute. You define the clipping region as a rectangle. Think of it as a stencil cutout superimposed atop the region, with its top left and bottom right vertices defined. If the material can be seen through the cutout, it's displayed. If not, the material is hidden.

Now for the bad news:

Very few of the browsers available as of this writing support either `overflow` or `clip` as the CSS specification defines them. Worse, the Cascading Style Sheet 2.0 specification defines the rectangular region associated with the `clip` attribute as `rect(top, right, bottom, left)`, but Microsoft Internet Explorer, in its flaky implementation of `clip`, expects a rectangular definition of `rect(top, left, width, height)`.

I encourage you to experiment with a combination of `size`, `overflow`, and `clip` values to see whether you obtain results that are a reasonable solution for your specific design needs!

Here's how fixed positioning looks in HTML:

```
<p style="position: fixed; width: 75%;
    top: -25px; left: 12%; background-color: #CFC;
    font: 18pt bold Arial; padding: 8px;
    border: 3px dashed #090; text-align: center;">
ADVENTURE II. THE RED-HEADED LEAGUE
</p>
```

Hide Containers with the Visibility: Attribute

Examples in preceding sections demonstrate how you can assign containers a wide variety of layout attributes and can even make them float above other containers by setting position changes. Something that you may find remarkable is that every container also has a visibility: attribute—one that controls whether its contents appear on-screen or remain hidden to the viewer.

The following example shows how this visibility attribute works:

```
<p>
As he spoke there was the sharp sound of horses'
hoofs and grating wheels against the curb, followed
by a sharp pull at the bell. Holmes whistled.</p>

<p style="visibility: hidden;" ID="holmes1">

"A pair, by the sound," said he. "Yes," he continued,
glancing out of the window. "A nice little brougham
and a pair of beauties. A hundred and fifty guineas
apiece. There's money in
this case, Watson, if there is nothing else."
</p>
<p>
"I think that I had better go, Holmes."
</p><p>
"Not a bit, Doctor. Stay where you are. I am lost
without my Boswell. And this promises to be interesting.
It would be a pity to miss it."
</p>
```

Figure 12-12 shows the results.

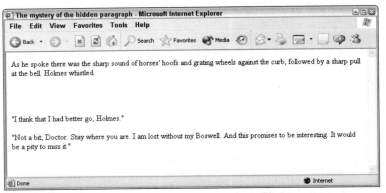

Figure 12-12: You still must allocate space even for hidden containers.

The most important thing to notice about Figure 12-12 is that the paragraph of information that's hidden still has its space allocated in the layout of the page. To work with the `visibility:` of a container, you specify a unique ID (in this case, `"holmes1"`).

To go further, you must jump into the world of JavaScript . . .

Controlling visibility with JavaScript

The `visibility:` attribute isn't of much use unless you can make it visible on demand. To accomplish any event-based scripting on a Web page requires JavaScript, the official scripting language of HTML 4.0 and CSS 2.0.

x-ref   For a refresher on JavaScript, flip back to Chapter 11.

The Web browser uses a *document object model* (*DOM*), and every container and element on the page is accessible through an appropriate reference to that element in the DOM.

on the web   To learn more about document object models, surf over to `http://www.w3.org/ DOM/`.

To switch the value of the `visibility:` attribute from `hidden` to `visible`, reference the paragraph by ID through the circuitous route of the DOM itself, as follows:

```
document.all.holmes1.style.visibility="visible";
```

I'd better explain.

You're already familiar with the idea that a series of nested containers surrounds a given element on your Web page, right? Simply imagine that you now want a method of referring uniquely to any of the elements in any of the containers, and you see that this *dot* notation (that is, separating elements with a period) makes sense. In fact, by using a unique ID value, all you really have in the preceding line is the following:

```
document.all.holmes1
```

This line refers uniquely to the container (paragraph) that you designate as `holmes1` on the Web page.

After you initially specify a unique element, you can access a wide variety of different attributes of that container by further utilizing the dot notation. To get to `visibility:`, you must use the `.style` element and then specify the exact name of the attribute that you want. Conceptually, it's as follows:

```
unique container descriptor.style.visibility
```

After you specify the `visibility:` attribute of the style of the `holmes1` paragraph, you can change its value by using a simple assignment statement in JavaScript, as follows:

```
document.all.holmes1.style.visibility = "visible";
```

I hope that makes a bit more sense.

tip　If you can't get the examples in this session to work, perhaps your Web browser is using an older document model. If that's the case, try using `document.holmes.visibility = "visible";` instead.

JavaScript is all eventbased, so to test this snippet of code, I'm going to associate the reassignment of `visible` to a simple event that occurs on all Web pages: `onload`. After you specify this event in the `<body>` tag of a page, `onload` enables you to easily specify JavaScript to execute as soon as the Web browser receives every element of the page from the network.

Inline JavaScript looks a little bit different from inline CSS because you don't have a single attribute that you always use, `style`. Instead, you list the desired event, with the associated JavaScript code on the right-hand side of the statement.

The `<body>` tag of your page may look like this:

```
<body onload="document.all.holmes1.style.visibility='visible';">
```

note　By convention, many people write JavaScript events in mixed upper- and lower-case letters, although to ensure that your page remains fully XHTML compliant, JavaScript events should be all lowercase.

Following is a complete listing of the source for Figure 12-13:

```
<body onload="document.all.holmes1.style.visibility='visible';">
As he spoke there was the sharp sound of horses'
hoofs and grating wheels against the curb, followed
by a sharp pull at the bell. Holmes whistled.
<p style="visibility: hidden;" id="holmes1">
"A pair, by the sound," said he. "Yes," he continued,
glancing out of the window. "A nice little brougham
and a pair of beauties. A hundred and fifty guineas
apiece. There's money in
this case, Watson, if there is nothing else."
</p>
<p>
"I think that I had better go, Holmes."
</p><p>
"Not a bit, Doctor. Stay where you are. I am lost
without my Boswell. And this promises to be interesting.
It would be a pity to miss it."</p>
```

If you view this example in a Web browser, you may expect the hidden paragraph to appear along with the other paragraphs of material.

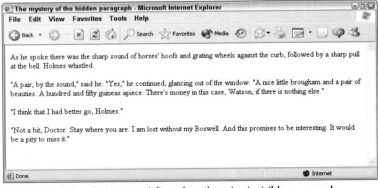

Figure 12-13: JavaScript materializes the otherwise invisible paragraph.

This example isn't too scintillating, but what if you add the following two hypertext reference links to this page? They both associate with the `onmouseover` event, which triggers whenever the user moves the cursor over the highlighted text.

```
<a href="#" onmouseover="document.all.holmes1.style.visibility='visible';">
make it visible</a> |
<a href="#" onmouseover="document.all.holmes1.style.visibility='hidden';">
hide it</a>
```

Now you can start to see where CSS plus JavaScript can really give you a tremendous amount of power! In this example, moving your cursor over the link `hide it` sets the `visibility:` of the `holmes1` element to `hidden`, hiding the paragraph of text. Move your cursor over `make it visible` and the `visibility:` of `holmes1` is set to `visible`, revealing the paragraph again.

 note The `href="#"` is a common trick for a null hypertext reference that you tie to a JavaScript event. If you click it, you go to the same Web page, effectively making it an empty reference.

You can also use `<span>` to tie a JavaScript event to a container, as in the following example:

```
"Not a bit, Doctor.
<span onmouseover="document.all.holmes1.style.visibility='visible';">Stay
where you are.</span>
I am lost without my
Boswell. And this promises to be interesting.
<span onmouseover ="document.all.holmes1.style.visibility='hidden';">
It would be a pity to miss it."</span>
```

The interesting thing about using `<span>` is that the enabled text appears completely identical to the surrounding text. Go back to Figure 12-13 and look closely at the two sentences shown in the preceding example: `Stay where you are.` and `It would be a pity to miss it.` You can see no visible indicator that they're turbocharged, capable of hiding or displaying a paragraph of the text on the user's whim!

The display: attribute controls visibility and flow

Although the `visibility:` attribute is definitely valuable, it has one characteristic that makes it less than the ideal layout element: The browser allocates space for the invisible element even if it never appears on-screen. You can see that in Figure 12-12.

CSS offers a second style attribute that enables you to simultaneously control the visibility and whether the space for the element is allocated: `display:`.

According to the CSS 2.0 specification, the `display:` attribute offers a whole group of possible values, as enumerated in Table 12-2.

Table 12-2: Possible Values for Display

Value	Explanation
inline	Container with no break before or after.
block	Container with a forced line break above and below.
list-item	Element that creates both a box and list-item box (indented).

Continued

Table 12-2: *Continued*

Value	Explanation
run-in	Element that you can insert into the subsequent container.
compact	Element that you can place adjacent to the subsequent container.
marker	Used for pseudocontainer references.
inline-table	Inline table container (not possible in regular HTML; regular tables are always block elements).
table	Table container.
table-cell	Table data-cell container.
table-row	Table data-row container.
table-row-group	Table data-row group container.
table-column	Table column container.
table-column-group	Table column group container.
table-header-group	Table header group container.
table-footer-group	Table footer group container.
table-caption	Table caption container.
none	Invisible container that gets no allocation for layout and flow.

The only values that need interest you are none, block, and inline. The attribute display: none sets the visibility: of the element to hidden and frees up any allocated space for the container in the page layout. The other two possibilities, block and inline, illustrate the same distinction that differentiates <div> and <span>: The former forces a blank line above and below, whereas the latter displays no break from the surrounding material.

Here's how you can use display: none with the <span> buttons of the last paragraph as your inspiration for this approach:

```
<body>
<p>
As he spoke there was the sharp sound of horses'
hoofs and grating wheels against the curb, followed
by a sharp pull at the bell. Holmes whistled.
</p>
<div id="holmes1"
  style="display: none; font-style: italic;">
"A pair, by the sound," said he. "Yes," he continued,
glancing out of the window. "A nice little brougham
and a pair of beauties. A hundred and fifty guineas
apiece. There's money in
this case, Watson, if there is nothing else."
</div>
```

```
<p>
"I think that I had better go, Holmes."
</p><p>
"Not a bit, Doctor.
<span onmouseover="document.all.holmes1.style.display='block';">
Stay where you are.</span>
I am lost without my
Boswell. And this promises to be interesting.
<span
onmouseover="document.all.holmes1.style.display='none';">
It would be a pity to miss it."</span>
</p>
</body>
```

This example is particularly interesting to experiment with on your own computer, but Figures 12-14 and 12-15 show how the page initially loads and how the page looks after I move my cursor over the sentence Stay where you are.

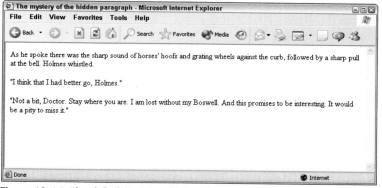

Figure 12-14: The default layout with the <div> block hidden from view.

Notice how no space or other indication in Figure 12-14 hints at anything lurking beneath the surface on this Web page; then take a look at Figure 12-15.

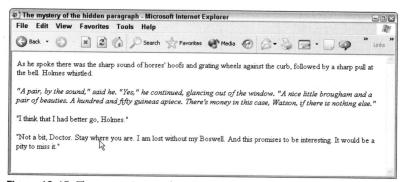

Figure 12-15: The mouse is over the magic phrase, so the hidden paragraph emerges.

In this case, the JavaScript is different because I'm working with a different CSS attribute. Instead of `visibility: hidden` and `visibility: visible`, the settings are `display: none` and `display: block`. Inline elements use `display: inline` instead.

Here's how you can use `display: inline` to make acronyms automatically spell themselves out if someone puts the cursor over the acronym:

```
<span
  onmouseover="document.all.css.style.display='inline';"
  onmouseout="document.all.css.style.display='none';">
  CSS</span>
<span id="css" style="display: none;">
(Cascading Style Sheets)</span>
```

Type this small code snippet in and try it yourself; you're sure to like the results!

Notice the addition of a second JavaScript event: `onmouseout` triggers after the cursor moves out of the container. In essence, I set `display` to `inline` if the cursor is over the abbreviation CSS and reset it to `none` after the cursor moves out.

Stacking: Using z-indexes for a 3D page

I know it may have been years ago, but do you remember your high school geometry class? In the class, you undoubtedly learned about the three primary *axes* or *dimensions* of our physical space. Other dimensions exist, notably time (duration), that also affect physical space, but fortunately, I'm going to just look at the three core dimensions: *height*, *width*, and *depth*.

Imagine that each container on a Web page has its own depth value and that, the deeper the element, the lower that depth value. A depth of zero is on the bottom, and a depth of 100 is on the topmost layer. If you have three layers, the depth values (which are known as *z-index values* in DHTML) may be z=0 for the bottom, z=1 for the middle, and z=2 for the topmost layer.

The attribute `z-index` easily translates this concept into CSS nomenclature. The `z-index` attribute accepts a single integer value from zero to 100, with higher values positioned above lower values on the Web page.

Here's an example:

```
<div style="position: absolute; z-index: 0;
  background-color: blue; width: 250; height: 100;
  top: 105px; left: 14px;"></div>

<div style="position: absolute; z-index: 1;
  background-color: red; width: 200; height: 150;
```

```
    top: 80px; left: 40px;"></div>

<div style="position: absolute; z-index: 2;
  background-color: green; width: 100; height: 325;
  top: 10px; left: 90px;"></div>
```

Figure 12-16 shows the result, which, on your computer screen, is quite attractive, particularly if you remember that each colored box is actually a full dynamic HTML container and can hold graphics, hypertext links, or whatever else you want.

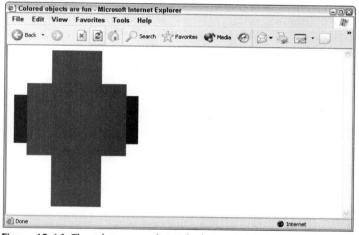

Figure 12-16: Three boxes, neatly stacked atop each other.

Using JavaScript to change z-index values

You can initially set z-index values within the CSS, but to dynamically change them, you must jump into JavaScript again. The `onclick` JavaScript event triggers the associated script after the cursor moves into the element and the user clicks the mouse button, as the following example demonstrates:

```
<div id="blue"
  style="position: absolute; z-index: 2;
         background-color: blue; width: 250;
         height: 100; top: 105px; left: 14px;"
  onclick="document.all.blue.style.zIndex=100;">
  </div>

<div id="red"
  style="position: absolute; z-index: 1;
         background-color: red; width: 200;
```

Continued

```
Continued
height: 150; top: 80px; left: 40px;"
 onclick="document.all.red.style.zIndex=100;"></div>

<div id="green"
 style="position: absolute; z-index: 0;
background-color: green; width: 100;
height: 325; top: 10px; left: 90px;"
 onclick="document.all.green.style.zIndex=100;"></div>
```

This change appears to achieve the result that you want. You create layers that you can click to bring to the foreground. If you try actually changing the z-index of the different layers in your browser, however, you quickly find that, after you move all three to the z-index of 100, they can't move farther towards the top—so nothing changes.

One solution to this problem is to make each layer move the other layers back to their original settings as it rises, so that each onclick looks more like the following example:

```
onclick="document.all.green.style.zIndex=100;
        document.all.blue.style.zIndex=2;
        document.all.red.style.zIndex=1;"
```

This solution works (sort of), but although each layer that you click does indeed jump to the front after you click it, your browser loses the relative z-index values of the other two layers after they automatically reset to their original values.

A more sophisticated approach to this situation makes the requested layer's z-index increment by one and the z-index of the other layers decrement by one, as follows:

```
onclick="document.all.green.style.zIndex += 1;
        document.all.blue.style.zIndex -= 1;
        document.all.red.style.zIndex -= 1;"
```

tip Here I'm using a convenient JavaScript shorthand: The += is an increment, so a+=1 is exactly the same as a = a + 1; it's just more succinct.

This solves the problem, but now a new problem appears. You don't want any layers to ever have a z-index of less than zero, because that's an illegal value. If you blindly subtract from a zIndex, you could easily end up with a negative number.

Another level of JavaScript sophistication can constrain the decrement statements so that the script checks for a zero value before deciding to subtract one, as in the following examples:

```
onclick="document.all.blue.style.zIndex += 1;
        if (document.all.green.style.zIndex > 0) {
        document.all.green.style.zIndex -= 1; }
        if (document.all.red.style.zIndex > 0) {
        document.all.red.style.zIndex -= 1; }"
```

In addition to ensuring that nothing is ever less than zero, you must also be sure that nothing is ever greater than 100, the maximum z-index value that you can have, as the following example shows:

```
onclick="if (document.all.blue.style.zIndex < 100 {
        document.all.blue.style.zIndex += 1;  }
    if (document.all.green.style.zIndex > 0) {
        document.all.green.style.zIndex -= 1; }
    if (document.all.red.style.zIndex > 0) {
        document.all.red.style.zIndex -= 1; }
```

To understand what's wrong with this seemingly reasonable solution, open this example from the book's Web site (http://www.intuitive.com/coolsites/) and click the red layer a half-dozen times, then click the blue layer.

The result that you want is for the blue layer to move to the front after you click, but it doesn't work. Clicking the red layer a half-dozen times increments its z-index each time, resulting in a red z-index of 7 (after starting out at z-index: 1, remember). Clicking blue then sets its z-index to 1 (after starting at 2 but decrementing to zero because of the clicks on red) and decrements the red layer from 7 to 6. Four more clicks on the blue region are necessary before the blue layer correctly moves to the top.

The complete solution is actually to write a sophisticated JavaScript function that checks the value of the other layers and ensures that the layer that you want increments sufficiently to move to the front. Subsequently clicking that layer doesn't result in any change in z-index values.

note Netscape Navigator includes a built-in *method* (a fancy name for a subroutine) to accomplish what you want: moveAbove(*id*). However, it requires that you use the Netscape <layer> approach to layers rather than the more standard CSS <div> tags, as shown here.

A JavaScript function implementing the moveAbove concept might look like this:

```
<script language="JavaScript">

function moveAboveIt(id1, id2) {
  id1o = eval("document.all."+id1+".style");
  id2o = eval("document.all."+id2+".style");

  if (id1o.zIndex > id2o.zIndex) {
    return 1; // already above, nothing to do
  }

  if (id2o.zIndex == 100) { id2o.zIndex -= 1; }

  id1o.zIndex = id2o.zIndex + 1;

  return 1;
}
</script>
```

This example represents quite a lot of JavaScript, but it's really rather straightforward: If `id1` already has a higher z-index value than `id2`, the function has nothing to do and exits directly. If `id2` is already at 100, `id1` can't be one higher, so `id2` must decrement by one, which you do by using the `-=1` shortcut. Finally, `id1`'s z-index is set so that it's one higher than `id2`'s z-index.

Table 12-3: CSS Styles Covered in This Chapter

Tag	Meaning
margin	Specifies spacing between container contents and surrounding material
margin-left	Specifies left margin setting only
margin-right	Specifies right margin setting only
margin-top	Specifies top margin setting only
margin-bottom	Specifies bottom margin setting only
padding	Specifies spacing between container contents and container edge
padding-left	Specifies left padding setting only
padding-right	Specifies right padding setting only
padding-top	Specifies top padding setting only
padding-bottom	Specifies bottom padding setting only
border	Specifies color, style, and size of container border element (other values include `border-left`, `border-right`, `border-top`, or `border-bottom`).
width	Specifies container width
height	Specifies container height
float	Specifies container's relationship container to surrounding material
position	Specifies container's position on page.
top	Specifies position of container's top relative to its parent container
left	Specifies position container left side relative to its parent container
overflow	Determines what Web browser does with content that doesn't fit in container (must define a clipping region with `clip`)
clip	Defines a clipping region to use with `overflow` attribute
visibility	Indicates whether container is visible or not
display	Controls container visibility and flow in page layout
zindex	Specifies container's relative z-index value

Summary

In this chapter, you learned how containers function within CSS and the myriad ways you can control and modify a container's presentation on your Web pages. Not only did you explore the difference between borders, margins, and padding as they relate to containers, you also examined how content flows both within and around containers. Finally, you delved into positioning containers on your pages, and how working with z-index values affects where a container's content appears on your Web pages. In Chapter 13, you will learn about weblog, a different and increasingly popular way to manage your Web site.

Site Development with Weblogs

In This Chapter

Understanding weblogs?

Creating a weblog

Getting a handle on RSS

Ensuring valid RSS feeds

Of the many trends to hit the Web in the last few years, few have had more impact on the daily experience of Web surfers than weblogs, or *blogs* as they're commonly known. Initially used as a system for creating online diaries, they've expanded to encompass business and other professional uses, and you can find weblogs at Yahoo!, the BBC World Service, Google, CNN, and many more sites.

But don't be intimidated! At its most fundamental, a weblog is a *content management system* that lets you design the site once and then focus on the content, on what you want to say, without worrying about CSS, HTML, and similar concerns.

To demonstrate, I will give you a guided tour of my own weblog, The Intuitive Life, and show you how it's built and how I can add new *weblog entries* with just a few clicks. I explore RSS feeds, a core underpinning of weblog popularity. The chapter wraps up with a quick examination of how to build your own RSS feed and validate it so that even if you don't want to use a blog, you can still reap the benefit of these new technologies on your own site.

What Is a Weblog?

Imagine a system that automatically does the following:

- Creates new Web pages that are visually consistent with the existing site
- Links all pages together
- Organizes content based on the entry date and user-defined categories
- Offers readers alternative methods of keeping track of what's new
- Works within a Web browser

Wouldn't that be a nice extension to your site?

These criteria are the fundamental elements of most weblog systems, and it should be immediately obvious why so many people are moving towards weblog as a content management system.

Before I proceed too much further, I want to highlight that two classes of weblog solutions are available. The first is *hosted solutions:* the weblog lives on a different server. The second is *software solutions,* which means a package is installed and configured on your own server (by you or your Internet Service Provider), and the weblog lives on your own server. Both have merit, but overall the tradeoff is that hosted solutions tend to be less flexible, whereas software solutions are more powerful, but more complex to install.

Two examples of hosted solutions are the very popular Blogger system, now owned by Google, and TypePad, from SixApart (the same company that produces Movable Type, a tremendously popular software solution). Figure 13-1 shows Tim Harrington's Blogger Web site, and Figure 13-2 shows David Lawrence's TypePad blog site. Both are attractive and quite easy to read.

Which of these solutions is better? It depends on whether you want to "serve your own" or depend on an outside server. If you're reading this book, I'm guessing that you're going to be more excited about having a software solution, a weblog system that lives on *your server* and lets you have complete and ultimate control over what appears, how it appears, and more.

For software solutions, the de facto standard seems to be Movable Type from SixApart. I use Movable Type to run four different weblogs: three public and one password-protected for a private community. Other software solutions exist, but I'm going to stick with Movable Type in this chapter to keep things simple. The alternative software programs have the same basic challenge of installation and configuration, followed by a typically similar interface for day-to-day use.

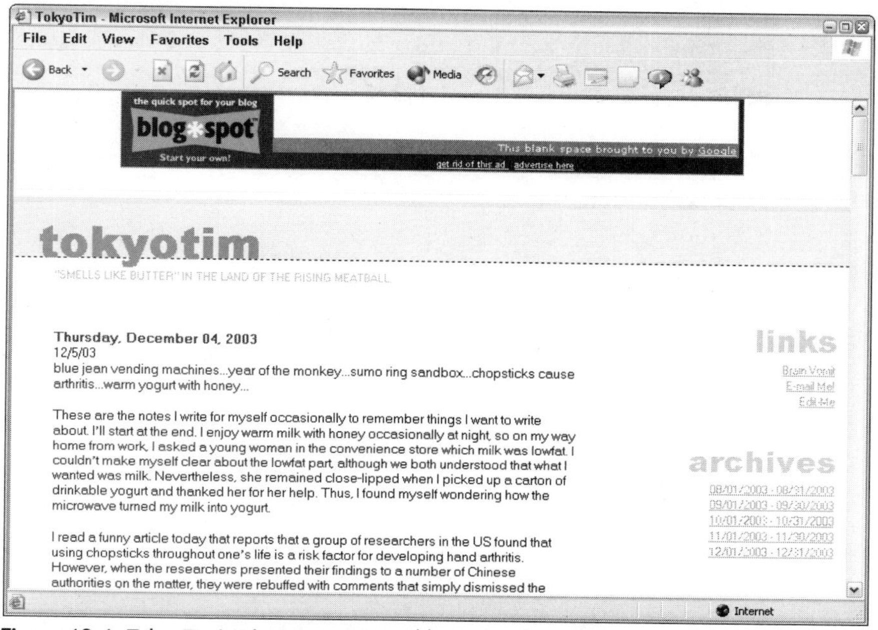

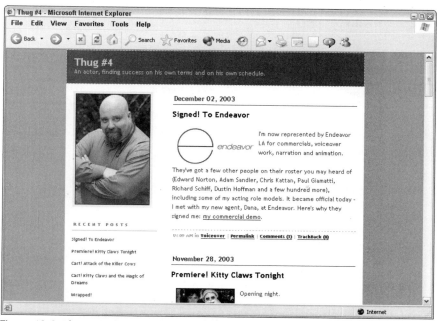

Figure 13-1: TokyoTim's Blogger site: http://tokyotim.blogspot.com/.

Figure 13-2: Thug #4's TypePad site: http://david.typepad.com/.

The key capability of weblogs is how much they let you customize the interface. Consider Figures 13-3 and 13-4; both are weblogs running under Movable Type, but they're quite different in appearance! This capability to customize the appearance is one of the great strengths of Movable Type.

Figure 13-3: The Intuitive Life, a weblog by this author that uses Movable Type.

The next section digs into how a weblog works, and you can begin to see how weblogs can improve your Web site design and deployment.

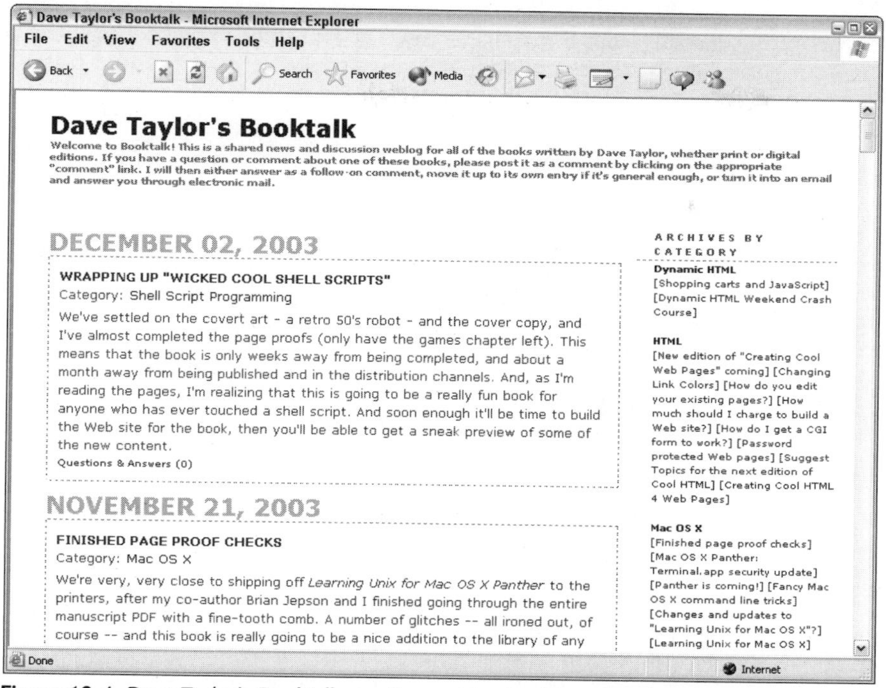

Figure 13-4: Dave Taylor's Booktalk, another weblog by this author that also uses Movable Type.

Working with a Weblog

Consider three areas when working with a weblog of your own: installation, configuration, and day-to-day entries and additions. This section looks at each in turn.

Installing a weblog

If you've opted for a hosted solution like TypePad or Blogger, you have no installation concerns. You can go straight to work on configuration.

If you're going to use Movable Type or a similar software solution, you must be fairly proficient at working in the depths of your Web server, or you need to contract with someone to install the application for you. When I installed Movable Type on my server, I followed the detailed installation instructions from SixApart, and it took me a few hours to get everything installed correctly.

tip

You can contract directly with SixApart to have one of their experts install the package on your server if you're so inclined. You have to share your account password with them, however, so be careful; that might violate the account usage policy of your ISP.

Configuring a weblog

Both hosted and software solutions use the same basic model for configuration: You pick a template for your site from a range of possibilities and then do either a small amount or a ton of fine-tuning to complete things to your liking.

Configuration is really where you'll spend lots of time. And I do mean *lots of time*. I probably spent upwards of 100 hours tweaking and fiddling with the various components of my weblog before I could finally move to another project. When I redesign my site, I'm sure I'll once more find the MTtemplates to be a veritable black hole.

The configuration time varies significantly based on how much you want to have your weblog look like your existing site (and/or want it to *not* look like everyone else's weblog). If you just use a predefined template, inevitably other sites on the Web may have the same column design, color scheme, type treatment, and so on. If that's okay with you, you can almost completely sidestep configuration and move onto the fun part of blogging: writing entries and beginning to share your ideas, thoughts, and vision with others.

If you are going to dig into the design, and you're running Movable Type, learn about the many templates the software uses. Figure 13-5 shows the basic administrative interface for my Intuitive Life weblog. Again, other systems have similar configuration menus.

From a configuration perspective, the buttons on the left are the most important. Start with WEBLOG CONFIG to ensure that the basics of your weblog name, archiving policy, whether you allow people to add comments to your blogs, and similar settings are all set to your liking. Then define your categories with CATEGORIES and finally move into the central design area, TEMPLATES.

caution

Think twice about allowing people to add comments to your weblog. In the last year or so *blogspam*, junk postings to weblogs that promote unrelated sites or businesses, has exploded. You can use some elegant solutions that you can learn more about from the blog vendors, but you should anticipate that this could be a problem as your site gets more popular.

Like many modern software systems, Movable Type is built atop a set of templates, essentially HTML pages with lots of CSS sprinkled in, and a special scripting language that says "insert new entry title here," "insert entry here," "link to archived articles here," and so on. These are a bit tricky to learn, but the good news is that many bloggers (as people who maintain weblogs are called) never touch any of the scripting code and just focus instead on fine-tuning the templates to get the look and feel they want.

Figure 13-6 shows the list of the main templates, including the two RSS feed templates, which I discuss a bit later in this chapter. For now, focus on the main templates. The RSS material isn't directly read by humans so you won't have to touch it.

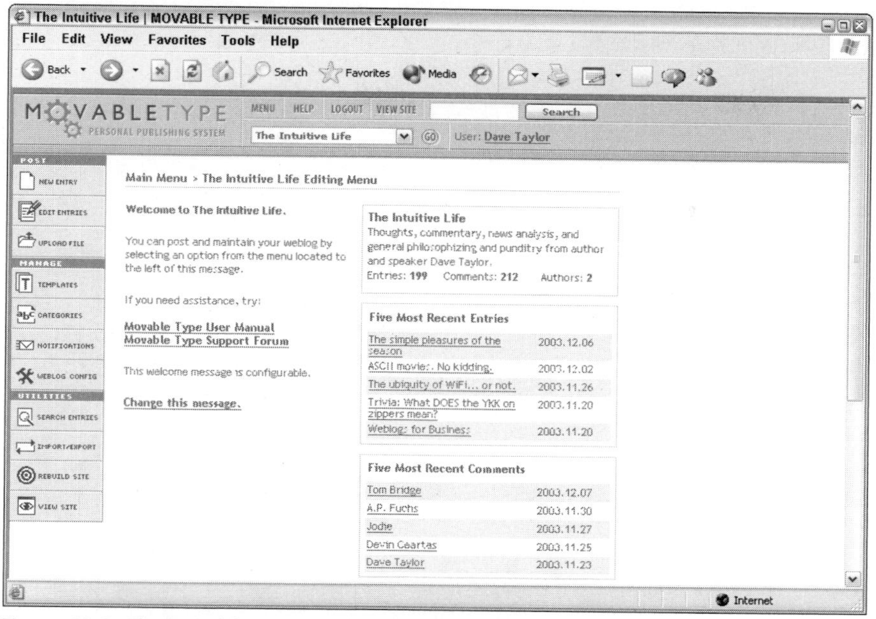

Figure 13-5: The Movable Type administrative interface.

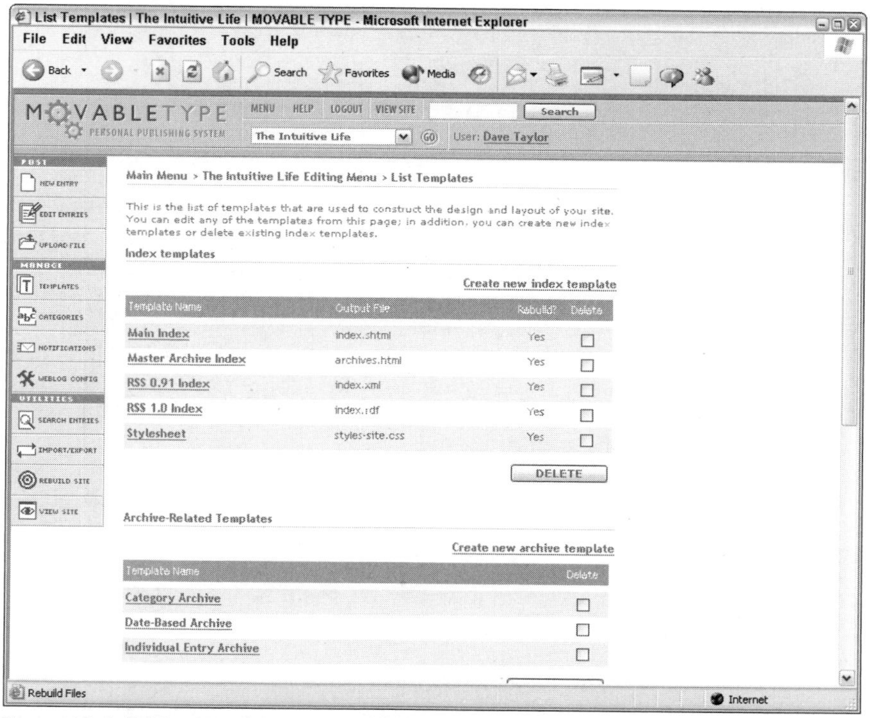

Figure 13-6: Editing templates in Movable Type.

To edit a specific template, click on its name and something similar to Figure 13-7 is displayed.

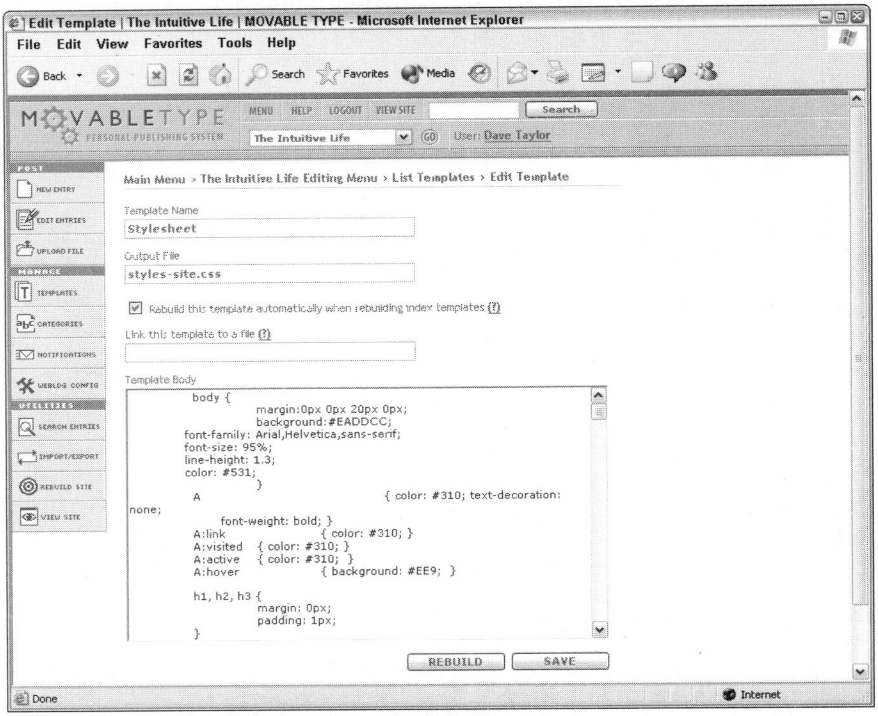

Figure 13-7: Viewing the CSS within Movable Type.

If you're looking at Figure 13-7 and thinking that it looks a bit tedious, well, it is. Bloggers who opt to really fine-tune their layout and site presentation end up spending a lot of time getting everything to be attractive. But in defense of that, I have to say that I found the process rather fun.

I have far too little space in this book to do justice to the complexity and capabilities of any blogging tool, whether it's a rudimentary hosting solution like Blogger or a sophisticated software package like Movable Type. Instead, let me just share how easy it is to add a new entry to the weblog after everything is configured properly!

Adding a weblog entry

The complexities of configuration are all worth it when you see how incredibly simple it is to add a new entry to a weblog. On my browser, I have a favorites link that takes me directly to the New Entry page. When I click that link (or click NEW ENTRY within any other area of Movable Type), I'm taken to a page that looks like Figure 13-8:

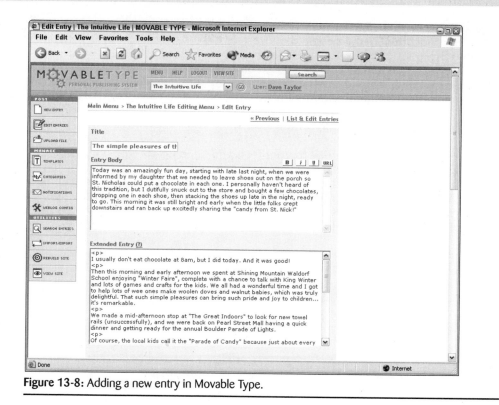

Figure 13-8: Adding a new entry in Movable Type.

That's about as complex as it gets. You can see in Figure 13-8 that I've already added a title and typed in a few paragraphs of text. When I'm ready, I just click on Publish (scrolled off the page in Figure 13-8), and I've added a new entry to my weblog, I've created a new archive page with the article contents, and made adding the new content to my site the work of a few minutes, not an hour or two.

Are weblogs for everyone? Probably not. Are they for you? Maybe. Spend some time exploring the many different weblogs on the net and see what you think. Then talk with some bloggers about what tools they use and how they like them. Finally, talk with your ISP to see if it has anything already installed, and then don't be afraid to take the plunge. It's fun!

The World of RSS

As I commented earlier, if you've been on the Web in the last year or two, it seems inevitable that you've stumbled across—or perhaps started your own—weblog. Although these online diaries and content management systems are cool and compelling, most of the weblog tools produce an incidental data stream that turns out to be the most valuable of all: RSS. Known as *really simple syndication*, RSS is a copy of the *content* of the weblog in a machine-parseable format based on XML, the eXtensible Markup Language.

When I'm asked to describe what RSS actually is, I explain it with a metaphor: When you update your Web page, how many people are aware of it? Those few who visit your site every few days, right? But what of the people who have stopped visiting your site because the content doesn't change frequently enough? If you go on holiday for a few weeks, do you lose your reader base? What if, instead, you had a system that was designed to track changes and notify people running special *aggregator* software when your site changes? That's what RSS is all about. With an RSS reader, you can keep track of the content of dozens—or hundreds— of different Web sites, and you see only what's new since your last visit.

With an RSS feed, people can *subscribe* to your feed and keep up-to-date on your Web site with a simple RSS reader or aggregator. A few great examples of aggregators are NewsGator (for Windows, it's at `http://www.newsgator.com/` and integrates with Microsoft Outlook), RssReader (for Windows, it's at `http://www.rssreader.com/` and is a separate application) and NetNewsWire (for Macintosh, at `http://www.ranchero.com/`). Figure 13-9 shows RssReader displaying the RSS feed from my Intuitive Life weblog.

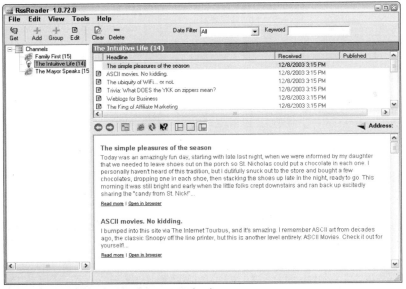

Figure 13-9: RssReader displaying RSS feeds.

RSS is a compelling solution for a lot of organizations. InfoWorld, for example, offers eight different RSS feeds for professionals in the information technology business. CNN, The New York Times, BBC World Service, and many other information sources also offer the capability to track their content via RSS.

Also, you can track hundreds, no, thousands, of personal weblogs just as easily—weblogs on topics as far-ranging as parenting, NASCAR drivers, acting, professional swimming, and many more topics. All these feeds can be neatly organized in an RSS aggregator program, whether you're on a Mac, Linux system, Unix box, Windows machine, or even PDA.

Creating Valid XML / RSS Feeds

Given this discussion of RSS, it might not be obvious that if you don't want to use a weblog at all, you can still build and maintain your own RSS feed! The format looks terrifyingly complex upon first glance, but in fact it's straightforward and even has an online validator that can help ensure that your nascent feed layout is valid and syntactically correct. Even better news: Most decent weblog tools, like Movable Type, already automatically generate RSS data, so you don't have to worry about doing it.

Start by having a peek at the RDF (also known as RSS 1.0) feed from my weblog. To see the contents of this particular file, I go to www.intuitive.com/blog/index.rdf, where the first few lines, the header of the file, are as follows:

```
<?xml version="1.0" encoding="iso-8859-1" ?>
<rdf:RDF xmlns:rdf="http://www.w3.org/1999/02/22-rdf-syntax-ns#"
xmlns:dc="http://purl.org/dc/elements/1.1/"
xmlns:sy="http://purl.org/rss/1.0/modules/syndication/"
xmlns:admin="http://webns.net/mvcb/"
xmlns="http://purl.org/rss/1.0/"
xmlns:content="http://purl.org/rss/1.0/modules/content/">
<channel rdf:about="http://www.intuitive.com/blog/">
<title>The Intuitive Life</title>
<link>http://www.intuitive.com/blog/</link>
<description>Thoughts, commentary, news analysis, and general
philosophizing
and punditry from author and speaker Dave Taylor.</description>
<dc:language>en-us</dc:language>
<dc:creator />
<dc:date>2003-12-02T23:15:59-07:00</dc:date>
<admin:generatorAgent rdf:resource="http://www.movabletype.org/?v=2.63" />
```

This looks overwhelming, but I've put in bold the entries that would have to change for a new custom RSS feed (the file itself is just plaintext, just as an HTML file doesn't have bold or italics, just markup tags).

XML is pretty similar to XHTML, but its use is context-dependent. In this case, the XML in use is specifically for an RSS feed, hence the information in this header. The good news is that all this information is completely identical for all similar types of RSS feeds; so as long as the first bunch of lines are correct, you can safely write this once and forget about it.

The next section is a block of links to the individual items in the feed (I've trimmed it a bit to make it easier to see what's going on):

```
<items>
<rdf:Seq>
<rdf:li rdf:resource="http://www.intuitive.com/blog/archives/000257.html"
/>
          There are fifteen lines like this because there are
```

Continued

```
Continued
        fifteen entries in the RSS feed. They're identically
        formatted.
<rdf:li rdf:resource="http://www.intuitive.com/blog/archives/000239.html"
/>
</rdf:Seq>
</items>
</channel>
```

And finally, each entry in the feed itself has its own item container, which has a link, title, description, and (HTML) encoded description:

```
<item rdf:about="http://www.intuitive.com/blog/archives/000257.html">
<title>ASCII movies. No kidding.</title>
<link>http://www.intuitive.com/blog/archives/000257.html</link>
<description>I bumped into this site via The Internet Tourbus,
and it's amazing.
I remember ASCII art from decades ago, the classic Snoopy
off the line printer,
but this is another level entirely: ASCII Movies. Check
it out for yourself!...</description>
<content:encoded>
<![CDATA[ I bumped into this site via <a href="http://www.tourbus.com/">The
Internet Tourbus</a>, and it's amazing. I remember ASCII
art from decades ago,
the classic Snoopy off the line printer, but this is
another level entirely:
<a href="http://www.romanm.ch/ascii-movies.htm">ASCII
Movies</a>. Check it out
for yourself!]]>
</content:encoded>
<dc:subject />
<dc:creator>Dave Taylor</dc:creator>
<dc:date>2003-12-02T23:15:59-07:00</dc:date>
</item>
```

That's all there is. Notice that the description and the content:encoded are the same material, but the description is just plaintext—no formatting tags—whereas the encoded content allows complex XHTML (and HTML, but make sure it's well-formed to avoid problems).

Duplicate this structure for each of the entries in your feed, add new ones at the top (as is typical), and you can even turn your guestbook into an RSS feed that people read via their news aggregators!

Validating an RSS feed

You opt to rough it and make your own RSS feed, which I hope you are thinking is kinda tricky, but not unimaginably hard, or use an RSS feed from another application like a weblog system. Either way, you can validate the RDF file just as you can validate an HTML, xhtml, or CSS file, with an online validator.

In Figure 13-10, I've entered my weblog site into a validator. This one is called Feed Validator, and it's found at `http://www.feedvalidator.org/`.

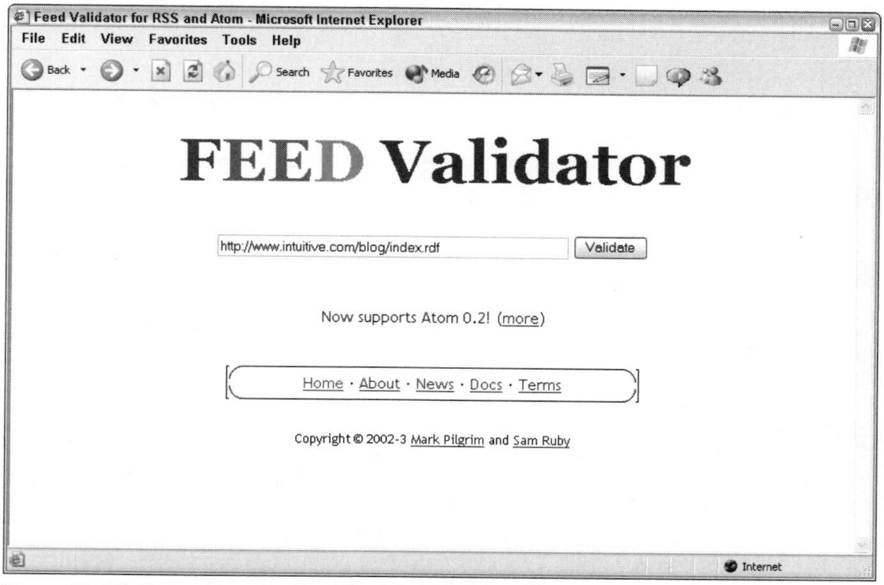

Figure 13-10: You can use Feed Validator to validate an RSS feed.

Feed Validator not only checks to ensure that all the RSS information is correct in the RDF file, but it's also smart enough to catch errors like the inclusion of a relative URL in an encoded content block. (A link like `<a href="/">web site home</a>` won't work in an RSS feed because it's interpreted as relative to the RSS aggregator, not relative to your Web site, by RSS readers.)

A quick check by the site and the RSS feed from my weblog receives the appropriate blessing, as shown in Figure 13-11.

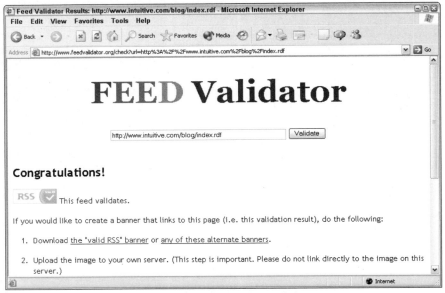

Figure 13-11: Feed Validator gives my RSS feed the green light.

Exploring further

If you want to learn more about building an RSS feed, you have a number of places to go. To learn more about the RSS specification, read the official document itself at http://web. resource.org/rss/1.0/. Then learn about some RSS readers by going to http://rss. intuitive.com/ for reference materials. The O'Reilly Network also has some very good RSS tutorial information at its RSS Devcenter, at www.oreillynet.com/rss/.

Summary

This chapter covered the new and exciting world of weblogs or blogs, starting with what they are and aren't and how to create a weblog. A tour of common weblog tools and utilities led to a behind-the-scenes tour of my own weblog, The Intuitive Life. This tour included a demonstration of how to add a new entry and how the software makes rebuilding the pages simple. Finally, I discussed RSS, starting with a description of what it is and how it works. I next showed you how you can create your own RSS feed of your content and validate it using common validation tools online. In the next chapter, I explore in depth the organization of your files on the server and different methods of streamlining site management.

Expanding Your Page into a Web Site

Part III

Web Sites versus Web Pages

In This Chapter

Using subdirectories intelligently

Protecting your Web sites and directories with passwords

Working with server-side includes

Now that you've learned the nuts and bolts of HTML and CSS Web page elements, it's time to expand your horizons and explore how to structure and organize a Web site comprised of many different Web pages. Web sites and Web pages are not the same thing, as you've probably noticed if you've built a site with more than a half-dozen pages.

No matter how you decide to organize your site, the fundamental goals are the same: to be able to edit pages, add new pages, and manage the content with a minimum of hassle.

Working with Subdirectories

It may seem a bit basic to step back and talk about how to lay out files and create subdirectories after all the code and layout discussed so far in this book. Trust me, it's really quite helpful to start out with a basic structure before your site grows into something unmanageable. More than once I have been asked to improve an existing Web site only to be horrified to find more than 300 files sitting in a single home directory, with no indication of what's new or what isn't in use any more. Often it has no separation of pages by functional category (such as *tour, catalog, biographies*), or no clear organization (such as having all the graphics neatly tucked into a directory different from the one that holds the content pages).

Besides enabling you to separate sets of files into more manageable chunks, subdirectories also make it easier to implement directory-specific security (which I discuss in the section "Protecting Web Sites and Directories") and create *beta* (test) sites. Subdirectories benefit even the smallest Web site. Consider a site I recently built for a regional bus transit pass (`http://www.OurEcoPass.org/`). The site has a total of seven pages, two PDFs, two graphics, and some CGI scripts. Originally, it was organized as shown in the following file listing. I've used the Unix list (`ls`) command to display the files residing in the directory:

```
$ ls
cgi-lib.pl            joinlist.cgi           nq-map.jpg
contact.html          lists.html             sponsors.html
flyer-back.pdf        mailform.cgi           thanks-join.html
flyer-front.pdf       new-contact-form.html  thanks.html
index.html            nq-map.gif
```

In this Unix file listing, you can see that everything lives in a single directory, with no use of subdirectories. The listing works reasonably well now, but it quickly becomes overwhelming if I decide to expand the Web site to include a directory of other regional EcoPass programs, offer a page or two for each of the other regional EcoPass groups, and include tips on which bus routes go to popular locations.

Fortunately, it's pretty easy to solve this problem! For this particular site, I created two subdirectories: `Graphics` and `collateral`. In the former, I dropped the JPEG and GIF images, and in the latter, the PDFs found a nice home.

note   If you're using an FTP program, it should be quite easy to create subdirectories on the remote system (the Web server). Some FTP programs allow you to move files around remotely without downloading them, but if your FTP client does not, simply download the file, move into the desired subdirectory on the remote system (that is, within the FTP program), and upload the file to its new home. Then delete the file from its former location to maximize the value of your organization and avoid later confusion about which is the *real* version of the file in question.

Utilizing the `-R` flag to the Unix `ls` command enables the program to show the contents of subdirectories, and the `-F` flag adds a / at the end of each directory name. Here's how `http://www.OurEcoPass.org/` looks now:

```
$ ls -RF
Graphics/            index.html             new-contact-form.html
cgi-lib.pl           joinlist.cgi           sponsors.html
collateral/          lists.html             thanks-join.html
contact.html         mailform.cgi           thanks.html

./Graphics:
nq-map.gif      nq-map.jpg

./collateral:
flyer-back.pdf   flyer-front.pdf
```

To help you see why it's helpful to use subdirectories for your Web site organization, in the next section you look at a site that's a bit more complex: AnswerSquad.

The subdirectory structure of AnswerSquad

The AnswerSquad site—`http://www.AnswerSquad.com/`—is more complex because it contains a lot more content. In fact, it has 24 different HTML pages, six CGI scripts or helpers, a couple of PDF files, and over 60 different graphics files. Instead of having all content in the same directory, I simplified management and maintenance of the site by splitting it up like this:

```
$ ls -F
Graphics/                insidepeek.html
answersquad.jpg          ip.shtml
answersquad.tgz          join-peek.cgi
archive/                 learnmore.shtml
bios.shtml               library.shtml
book.data                listrules.shtml
bookstore/               mailform.cgi
buildlibs                mailman-help.shtml
buildlibs.c              members.shtml
cgi-lib.pl               press/
check.cgi                pressroom.shtml
collateral/              privacy.shtml
contact-thanks.shtml     samples.shtml
contact.shtml            signup.shtml
covers/                  subscribe-cancel-thanks.shtml
faq.shtml                subscribe-thanks.shtml
foot.html                thanks-peek.shtml
head.html                thanks.cgi
index.shtml              thanks.shtml
```

In the previous listing, the `-F` flag to the `ls` command produces a trailing `/` on directory names, to make it easier to see what's what in the output. As you can tell, I have created six different subdirectories: `Graphics`, `archive`, `bookstore`, `collateral`, `covers`, and `press`.

An even bigger site: Intuitive.com

My main Web site, `http://www.intuitive.com`, contains over 600 different Web pages and hundreds of graphical elements, photographs, and more. Having all that content in a single directory can be completely overwhelming and unmanageable. As shown in the following code, I split the content into quite a few subdirectories, many of which have only one or two files, and others that are entire Web sites:

```
$ ls -F
Graphics/                library.shtml
apps/                    limpet/
```

Continued

```
Continued
articles/                     macosx/
bio.shtml                     origins/
blog/                         pearls/
cgi-lib.pl                    pilot/
cgi-local/                    popup/
clanpb.shtml                  portfolio/
consulting.shtml              robots.txt
contact.shtml                 send-query.cgi
coolsites/                    sites/
coolweb/                      social-faq.html
custer/                       solaris/
dhtml/                        spam/
directions/                   spam-assassin-rule-help.html
ebay/                         speaking-testimonials.shtml
errordoc-404.shtml            speaking.shtml
errordoc-500.shtml            stylesheet.css
favicon.ico                   taylor/
footer.html                   teaching.shtml
games.html                    thanks-author-news.shtml
globalsoftware/               thanks.shtml
header.html                   temp/
index.count                   tyu24/
index.shtml                   tyusa/
join-author-news.cgi          wicked/
kana.shtml                    writing.shtml
library/
```

To see what I mean, take a peek into a couple of the subdirectories. Some of these subdirectories are redirects for Web sites that now have their own URLs. An example is the custer subdirectory:

```
$ ls custer
index.html
```

In this case, the index.html file simply says "we've moved" and points to the new URL for the Custer Battlefield Museum and Historical Society.

A slightly more sophisticated example is the origins subdirectory, which is again a redirect to a new Web site address. This time, however, it includes a graphical element called bomb.gif:

```
$ ls origins
bomb.gif               index.html
```

Making custer and origins separate subdirectories helps keep their content out of the main page and lets me easily ignore them as I manage the day-to-day changes and updates for the main Intuitive System Web site.

Although some subdirectories contain very little information, others are quite full. Take, for example, the subdirectory `tyu24`, for my book *Teach Yourself Unix in 24 Hours*, at the URL `www.intuitive.com/tyu24/`:

```
$ ls -F tyu24
Graphics/              exchange/              links.shtml
Previous/              exchange-cgi.html      middleslice.html
author.shtml           exchange.html          netiq.html
bottomslice.html       exchange.zip           printers.html
browsex.html           exchange2.zip          reviews.shtml
buyit.shtml            fget.html              samples.shtml
chap19.shtml           fget.zip               template.html
coming-soon.shtml      fget2.zip              toc.shtml
dickens.html           hello.cgi              topslice.html
download.shtml         index.shtml
```

I basically duplicate the directory structure you've already seen, with a `Graphics` subdirectory, an archive of the previous version of the HTML files called `Previous`, and a mix of HTML and CGI. Just for fun, peek into the `Graphics` subdirectory to see how many graphics files are being neatly sequestered:

```
$ ls tyu24/Graphics
2nd-ed-cover.gif       floppydisk.gif         slice3.gif
3rd-ed-cover.jpg       intsys.gif             slice4.gif
action-icon.gif        menubar.gif            slice5.gif
amazon.gif             menubar.gif.old        stars-4-0.gif
author.gif             note-icon.gif          stars-5-0.gif
background.gif         quote.gif              summary-icon.gif
buy-it.gif             slice1.gif             tyu24-banner.gif
description-icon.gif   slice2.gif
```

Quite a few files, don't you think? You can see immediately why putting all these graphic files into their own subdirectory simplifies site management. It ensures that these graphics aren't mixed in with the top-level graphics of the main intuitive.com pages, which are in another directory also called Graphics. The difference is that the top-level graphics are in `/Graphics/`, and these are in `/tyu24/Graphics/`—a critical difference.

With a site that contains hundreds and hundreds of files of various types, it's critical to categorize and organize. Think of the chaos that would result at the public library if it didn't have a filing and organizational system, or how your local school district would grind to a halt with thousands of student files dumped into a single folder!

Protecting Web Sites and Directories

After you have your Web site organized and you are beginning to do ongoing maintenance and updates, it's time to think about another important topic: protecting specific areas of the site from unauthorized viewing.

If your Web hosting provider is running the Apache Web server (and most do), odds are excellent that you can create password-protected areas on your Web site—or even protect the entire site itself—without a single line of CGI code!

note   Other Web server software programs also include various levels of security; you certainly don't have to be running Apache to have a password-protected area on your site. Check with your Web hosting provider to find out exactly what it offers and how you can use those facilities for your site. The rest of this section, however, is written for the tremendously popular (and free!) Apache Web server.

The first step toward protecting your Apache-based Web site is to create a file called .htaccess and put it in the directory you want to protect. After you create .htaccess, create a separate file containing the login name and password pairs for people who are allowed access to this directory.

I have password-protected one of my subdirectories on the intuitive.com site, my *spam* area. This particular area of my site lets me easily check my incoming e-mail for spam or junk messages, and then delete them without actually having them download to my system. But don't worry about the e-mail, per se; this directory is just an interesting example of a directory that I've password protected. The .htaccess file in the spam subdirectory contains the following code:

```
AuthUserFile /web/home/passwords
AuthGroupFile /dev/null
AuthName "Spam Analysis Tools"
AuthType Basic

<Limit GET>
require user taylor
require user demo
</Limit>
```

The contents of this file are identical across all Apache installations: The passwords file is specified as the AuthUserFile; it's /web/home/passwords in this example. The AuthGroupFile enables you to specify a group-based access mechanism, although I've never seen it used in practice. In this instance, AuthGroupFile is set to /dev/null as a way of disabling this feature. The so-called *realm* or *security realm* identifier (which shows up when the user is prompted to enter his or her authorization credentials in the Web browser) is the AuthName, identified here as "Spam Analysis Tools". The AuthType specifies what kind of authorization you require from users. Basic is by far the most common choice.

Most important, as designated in the <Limit GET> block, only two user accounts can access this directory (given the correct password); taylor or demo. This is done because the actual passwords file can contain many more account/password pairs than just those of the people authorized to access this particular directory. The .htaccess file in different protected directories could have completely different accounts listed. This technique offers two levels of security and control instead of just the passwords file itself.

For an example of how this might be important, consider that I have subdirectories other than `spam` that are password protected, but I have one central passwords file for simplicity. People who are authorized to enter one area are not automatically allowed into all the others. This necessitates the use of the `<Limit GET>` block to specify exactly which accounts can access the specific directory area.

Before I show you the passwords file, Figure 14-1 shows what happens when you go to the password-protected `http://www.intuitive.com/spam/` URL.

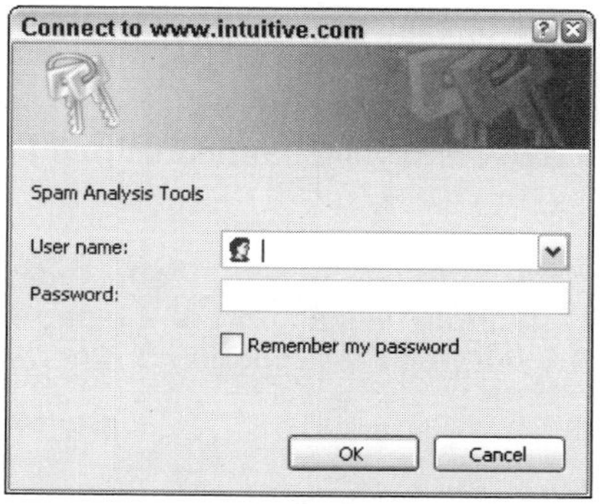

Figure 14-1: The .htaccess file forces visitors to log in before viewing the directory.

Notice in Figure 14-1 how the realm is shown as a reminder of what area on the site you're protecting ("Spam Analysis Tools"). This detail is quite helpful if you have a number of different directories protected with this mechanism.

note Why protect areas of your site? You have many possible reasons, ranging from privacy and confidentiality of information to commerce. On my server, I have areas for just my family members and friends, areas for partners in a specific business venture, and an area for people who pay to get access to the information therein.

You've looked at the `.htaccess` file, but now take a quick peek at the `/web/home/passwords` file so that you can see how it's organized:

```
hot:ycHlIQxpZ.Ck
taylor:YCE/5fFav6aQ
boulder:J8hgfSWw9Qsc
admin:VKJ994JdmHxA
demo:NweXYPIuKP2Y
board:XVHZLziAkrM2
```

Although I have placed my passwords file in the `/web/home` directory, you can give this file a different name or place it in a different directory location. Just make sure that the `AuthUserFile` entry in the `.htaccess` file points to the correct spot.

on the web You have more to learn about `.htaccess` and password files, including how to create an encrypted password entry and add it to the existing file. I have a helpful note addressing this topic on this book's companion Web site at `http://www.intuitive.com/coolsites/`.

Server-Side Includes

Step back from security issues for a moment and consider Web site organization again. Earlier you explored the value of having a smart subdirectory organization to ensure that you aren't overwhelmed with files as you maintain your site, but there's another side to this too. How do you manage dozens or hundreds of pages that all have remarkably similar header and footer content?

A smart way to create a site with lots of identical fragments is to use server-side includes (SSI). SSIs enable you to invisibly include the content of multiple files as part of the page sent to the user. Typically, you specify server-side includes by burying them within comments, like this:

```
<!--#include file="header.html" -->
```

A server often requires that files containing SSI instructions use a different suffix. The servers I use, for example, specify SSI material with `.shtml` instead of `.html`. This is quite common. If your Web server supports SSI, you can often specify a wide variety of SSI instructions that replace the SSI directive itself with the current time of day, a text-based counter, and more. It's not a universal solution, however, because many different types of Web servers either don't support SSI at all or support a different version, with different notation.

If you're not sure whether your server supports SSI, experiment by creating a simple page that has an `.shtml` suffix and contains the preceding SSI line. It might look like this:

```
<html><head><title>testing</title></head>
<body><h2>SSI test</h2>
<!--#include file="header.html"-->
</body></html>
```

When the page is viewed in your browser, if you get a `File not found` error after the `<h2>`, your server supports SSI. The file specified wasn't found because it doesn't exist. If you see nothing, and if choosing View ⇨ Source shows the SSI line, your server either doesn't support SSI or doesn't have it enabled.

You can access quite a bit with SSI on an Apache server—and Apache is the most popular Web server, so it's likely that your ISP is using an Apache server. I talk about some of the available SSI material in the following section.

Useful server-side include options

Some of the key SSI options you might want to experiment with are `config`, `include`, `echo`, `fsize`, `flastmod`, and `exec`. If you want to learn more about how SSI can simplify the process of creating cool Web pages, read on.

config

If you include SSI in your HTML document and include the `config` directive (that is, `<!-#config`), you gain control over various ways to display subsequent SSI options on your page. Here are the three valid `config` tags:

* `errmsg`: Lets you specify the message that's sent back to a client if a parse error occurs. Although most people leave the standard SSI error messages, you might find it helpful to suppress the message entirely or otherwise change what the Web server emits when it encounters a failure.

* `timefmt`: Gives the server a new format to use when providing dates with `flastmod` (see the "FLASTMOD" section a little later in the chapter). This is a string compatible with the `strftime` library call under most versions of Unix (that is, if you have a Unix system handy, you can type `man strftime` at the shell command line and find all the possible options for `timefmt`).

* `sizefmt`: Determines the formatting to use when displaying the size of a file. Valid choices are `bytes`, for a formatted byte count (1,234,567), or `abbrev`, for an abbreviated version displaying the number of kilobytes or megabytes the file occupies (1.2MB). The default value is `abbrev`.

include

The `include` directive inserts the content of a specified document into the parsed file as it's sent to the user. Any included file is subject to access control: If you're denied file permission, you can't sneak around the block with an SSI. The `include` directive accepts the following two attributes:

* `virtual`: Lets you specify a virtual path to a document on the server. You can access normal (`.txt` or `.html`) files this way, and you can also include another `.shtml` parsed document.

* `file`: Lets you specify a path name relative to the current directory. However, trying to sneak up the directory tree with a parent directory reference (`../`) is prohibited for security reasons.

echo

The `echo` directive outputs the value of specified variables and prints dates based on the currently configured `timefmt`. The only valid tag to this directive is `var`, whose value is the name of the variable you want.

fsize

The `fsize` directive shows the size of the specified file and employs the same tags as the `include` command (`virtual` or `file`). The resulting format of this directive is subject to the `sizefmt` parameter of the `config` directive.

flastmod

The `flastmod` directive shows the last modification date of the specified file. Valid tags are the same ones used with the `include` directive.

exec

The `exec` directive executes a given command or CGI script, including the output of the command in the HTML document. Very cool, and very helpful! Valid tags include the following:

- cmd: Executes the given string using the local command interpreter (`/bin/sh` on a Unix system, for example).
- cgi: executes the given virtual path to a CGI script and includes its output.

The following code snippet demonstrates some of the more interesting SSIs:

```
<table border="1" cellpadding="4" cellspacing="1">
<tr><td bgcolor="#DDDDDD">HTTP_USER_AGENT
<td>
<!--#echo var="HTTP_USER_AGENT"-->
<tr><td bgcolor="#DDDDDD">fsize ch14-2.shtml
<td>
<!--#fsize virtual="ch14-2.shtml"-->
<tr><td bgcolor="#DDDDDD">fsize again, but after setting<br>
the sizefmt to "bytes" with #config
<td>
<!--#config sizefmt="bytes"-->
<!--#fsize virtual="ch14-2.shtml"-->
bytes
<tr><td bgcolor="#DDDDDD">flastmod ch14-2.shtml
<td>
<!--#flastmod virtual="ch14-2.shtml"-->
</table>
```

Finally, here's an example of running a Unix command from within an HTML document. In this example, the `ls` command is run:

```
<pre>
$ <b>ls</b>
<!--#exec cmd="/bin/ls -Cl"-->
</pre>
```

Figure 14-2 shows the result of running the preceding two code snippets from a Web server. Note that the file requires an .shtml filename suffix to work correctly.

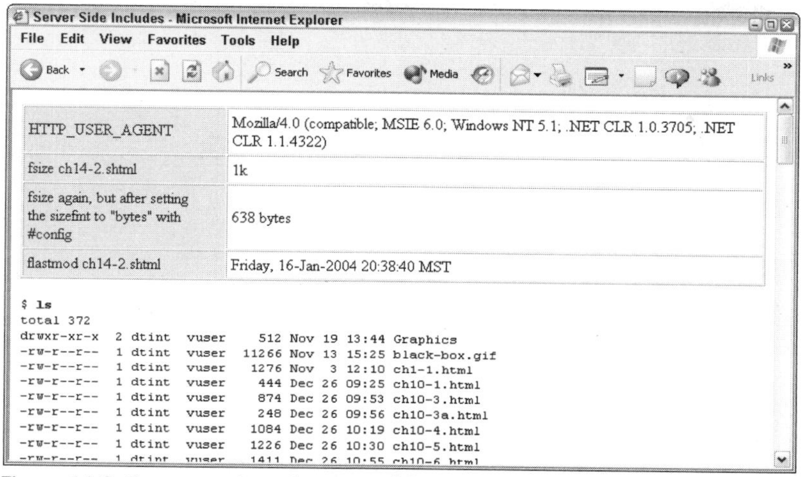

Figure 14-2: Demonstration of some useful server-side includes.

SSI environment variables

Many useful SSI environment variables are accessible to HTML documents through the <!-#echo server-side include. In addition to the CGI variable set shown in Chapter 9, the variables shown in Table 14-1 are also accessible.

Table 14-1: SSI Environment Variables

Variable	Function
DOCUMENT_NAME	Name of the current document
DOCUMENT_URI	Virtual path to current document (such as /home/taylor/ sample.shtml)
QUERY_STRING_UNESCAPED	Unescaped version of any search query sent by the client, with all shell-special characters escaped with \
DATE_LOCAL	Current date, local time zone. Subject to the timefmt parameter of the config directive
DATE_GMT	Identical to DATE_LOCAL, but in Greenwich mean time
LAST_MODIFIED	Current document's last modification date of; subject to timefmt like the other variables

Here's an example of how to write a small HTML snippet that includes almost all of these SSI variables:

```
<table border="1" cellpadding="4" cellspacing="1">
<tr><td bgcolor="#DDDDDD">DOCUMENT NAME</td>
<td>
<!--#echo var="DOCUMENT_NAME" - >
</td></tr>
<tr><td bgcolor="#DDDDDD">DOCUMENT URI</td>
<td>
<!--#echo var="DOCUMENT_URI" - >
</td></tr>
<tr><td bgcolor="#DDDDDD">DATE_LOCAL</td>
<td>
<!--#echo var="DATE_LOCAL" - >
</td></tr>
<tr><td bgcolor="#DDDDDD">DATE_GMT</td>
<td>
<!--#echo var="DATE_GMT" - >
</td></tr>
<tr><td bgcolor="#DDDDDD">LAST_MODIFIED</td>
<td>
<!--#echo var="LAST_MODIFIED" - >
</td></tr>
</table>
```

Figure 14-3 shows the results when you feed this code snippet through a Web browser by way of a Web server. Note that the file must have a `.shtml` suffix for your Web server to recognize that it contains SSI instructions.

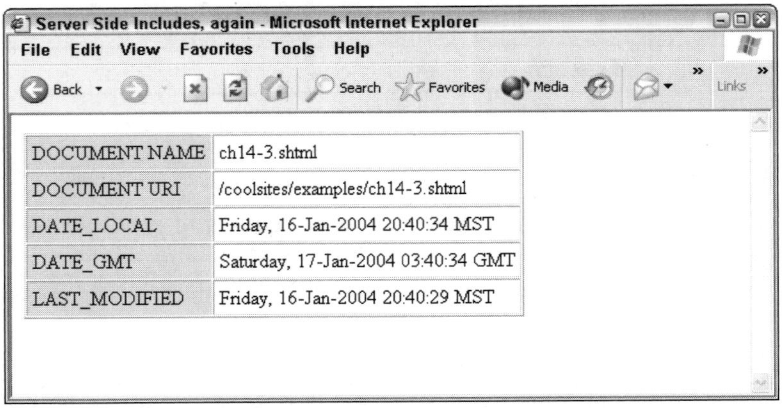

Figure 14-3: You can use SSI variables to display interesting information.

Building a Web site using SSI

The AnswerSquad site illustrates how liberal use of SSI enables you to easily expand a site while maintaining visual consistency. The trick to maintaining visual consistency is to pull the header and footer information into standard header and footer files, which you can simply include in your SSI.

If you sign up for the Inside Peek mailing list, the following HTML code is interpreted by the Web server and, post-SSI, served up to your Web browser:

```
<!-#include file="head.html"-->

<center>
<h2 style="margin-top: 5px">Thanks!</h2>
</center>

<p>
Thank you for signing up for the Inside Peek mailing list. You'll now
receive a confirmation email message from our system to confirm
that you really want to sign up. Simply reply to that message and
you'll be on the Inside Peek mailing list.
</p><p>
Thanks again.
</p>
<!-#include file="foot.html"-->
```

The page that's produced from this code is shown in Figure 14-4.

You can see this page on the Web. Just go to `http://www.AnswerSquad.com/` and sign up for the free InsidePeek mailing. To see just the `head.html` or `foot.html` file, simply open the respective URL, `http://www.AnswerSquad.com/head.html` or `http://www.AnswerSquad.com/foot.html`. Choose View ➪ Source to see the contents of these files because they're HTML fragments, not full pages.

By including headers and footers in your SSI, you can build remarkably flexible Web sites in very little time. I use them all the time. Believe me, it makes life so much easier when you can build one page and rip its header and footer HTML sections into separate files, `head. html` and `foot.html`, which you can easily include in all other pages on the site!

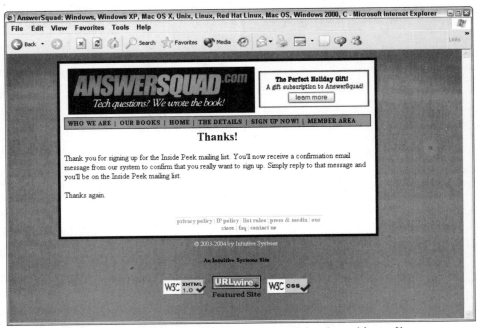

Figure 14-4: The Inside Peek mailing list's thank you page with header and footer files.

Table 14-2: HTML Tags Covered in This Chapter

Tag	Closing Tag	Meaning
<!--#	None	Begins an SSI directive; supports many possible values, depending on your Web server configuration

Summary

In this chapter, you learned how to use subdirectories and how to implement Web site and per-directory password security. You also saw the many advantages of using SSI to build your Web pages. In the next chapter, I step away from the nuts and bolts of individual HTML and CSS tags and, instead, consider usability and how to create a Web site that offers your visitors the best possible experience.

Thinking about Your Visitors and Your Site's Usability

You've built your site, added some helpful JavaScript to make it fun, tweaked things to ensure that your site is indexed well for search engines, and you've even validated your XHTML and CSS code (see Chapter 16), so you're finished, right?

Well, you *could* be done if all you want is a site that shows off your sense of cool.

But in this chapter, I spend some time talking about the user experience, about what your visitors may think about your design and how you can develop a Web site that's not only visually attractive and informative, but highly usable too. To do this, I have to delve into the world of human computer interaction, or HCI. But don't panic! I promise this'll be interesting and not overly academic.

Also, keep in mind that these rules are all in the "made to be broken" vein. You could theoretically build a site that is compliant with every nuance of every rule, but more likely you'll find that some help you produce cool sites, whereas other rules end up just being obstacles. That's okay.

What Makes a Site Usable?

I bet you've been to Web sites that cause you to say, "This is really clean." Other sites may make you say, "What the heck? How am I supposed to figure out what's what?" It turns out that much of this difference can be quantified, measured, and judged in a fairly impersonal way. Guidelines for usability can be a real help for site designers, so they can produce sites that are both cool and useful.

A key underlying question to determine usability revolves around the target audience for your site and the purpose of your site. If you're building a portal site to compete with Yahoo and MSN, you may want to include more information on the page than if you're translating a three-page brochure into a humble Web site for a small-business client.

note If you're building a Web site specifically to show off your coding skills, none of this may apply. But read through this chapter anyway. The sanity you save may be your own!

Amount of information presented

The first guideline for usability is to always *minimize the amount of information presented* by showing only what's necessary to the user.

This rule explains why the AOL and MSN home pages are baffling when first visited, why it's hard to figure out what's going on at Yahoo!, and why Google, by contrast, is relaxing and easy to use.

An example of a site with lots and lots of information that's still thoughtfully organized to ensure that it's not overloading the visitor is the U.S. Internal Revenue Service site. Figure 15-1 shows the current page.

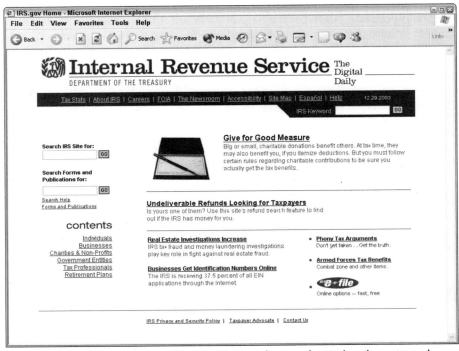

Figure 15-1: The Internal Revenue Service Web Site—clean, uncluttered, and easy to read.

The site is clean, open, inviting, and has a small number of links off this page so that the user isn't completely overwhelmed by the choices. Very nice!

Compare this with the U.S. Social Security Administration Web site, as shown in Figure 15-2. Here you can see many more choices. The designer seems unable to differentiate between what I call the *musts* and the *wants*. The musts are those links that must be on the home page or, for that matter, on the specific page in question, whatever it is. The wants, on the other hand, are those links that would be helpful to have up-front, but are not critical. Remember, the guideline here is to minimize the amount of information presented. Less is more.

Figure 15-2: The Social Security Administration Web Site—pretty overwhelming at first glance.

To help achieve this minimization, keep these points in mind:

- Use concise wording.
- Use tables with column headings where appropriate.
- Use familiar data formats.
- Avoid unnecessary detail.
- Use abbreviations appropriately.

note To find out more about enhancing the usability of your Web site, I recommend an excellent book on human-computer interaction: *A Guide to Usability,* edited by Jenny Preece (Addison-Wesley).

Organize information on the page

Another common mistake made on Web sites is the lack of any coherent organization. By organizing links and material, you significantly help the user find what he seeks. Although the Social Security page in Figure 15-2 has too much information, it is nonetheless a fine example of how grouping information can help make a Web page more usable. Notice the four key areas on the site entitled: *Retirement and Medicare, Disability and SSI, Widows, widowers and other survivors,* and *Get help with your situation.*

What I also really like about this page is that everything is written in an active manner; it's engaging, and it refers to me, the visitor. It doesn't say "get help with a life situation," it says "get help with *your* situation."

How can you ensure that your information is grouped appropriately? Here are some ideas:

- Use color coding (I get back to color usage shortly).
- Highlight elements using foreground or background colors.
- Add graphical borders or other dividers to visually cluster elements.
- Use different size text and different typefaces.

The last idea is very important for good Web page design, in my opinion. I'm always surprised how infrequently sites use different size type effectively.

Consider the IRS site back in Figure 15-1 for a moment. Notice how the word *contents,* is large and how the headlines are larger than the text underneath. Also notice the use of a graphical divider to organize information: the horizontal rule above and below the featured article titled, *Undeliverable Refunds Looking for Taxpayers.* By contrast, the Social Security site, by overloading its page with too much information, fails to take advantage of type sizes and ends up with links lost in a sea of words, almost all in blue.

note For reference purposes, the IRS Web page has 31 links on it, whereas the SSA Web page has 79 links.

Standardize the screen layout

Screen layout can really make or break a site design, whether it's complex or simple. The idea is that if you teach people to look in a certain place on your page for a specific type of information, make sure that it's always in that place on all pages on the site. Consider Figure 15-3, the Firstgov.gov home page.

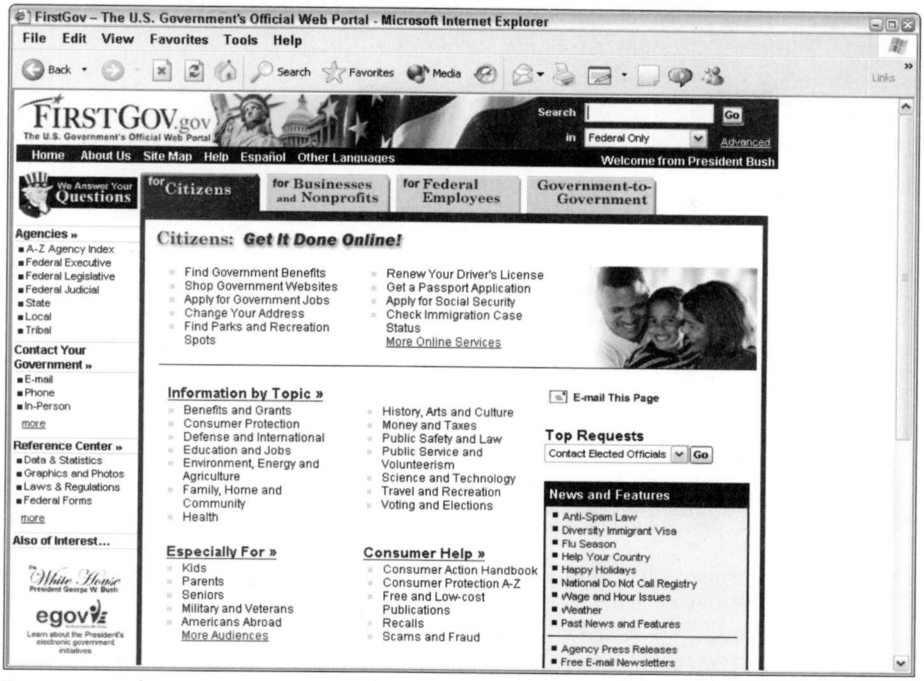

Figure 15-3: The Firstgov.gov home page—complex, but with a method to the layout madness.

This site is quite complex, but the content has a definite layout. There's a navigational bar along the top, a set of self-identifying categorization tabs, and a high-level categorization column along the left side. Just as important, a search box is placed on the top-right. All well and good!

The question is whether these basic organizational areas are carried through on other pages. To find out, I clicked *Welcome from President Bush* at the right end of the navigational bar. It revealed the page shown in Figure 15-4.

This is an example of how *not* to structure the layout for the pages on your site. Instead of having a standardized screen layout and sticking to it throughout all the major areas of the site, Firstgov has created an environment that's actively user unfriendly. As a user, you are forced to go back to the home page to get basic navigational elements (and notice that no Home link is visible in Figure 15-4 to take you back). You have to use the Back button on the browser.

note   To be completely fair about it, the President's welcome is actually part of the White House Web site, not part of Firstgov. Nonetheless, the problem remains: Visitors are taught to expect certain information in certain places on the Firstgov site, but after only one click they are facing a completely different layout. Instead, I'd like to see the letter of introduction duplicated on the Firstgov site so that the site is visually consistent.

Figure 15-4: One click in, and the Firstgov site has changed its screen layout completely.

Here are some ways that you can ensure standardization of information on your Web pages:

- Important information that needs to catch the attention of the visitor should always be displayed in a prominent place on the screen.
- Reports and reference information should be grouped together and shown on the less central areas of the screen.
- Redundant information should only be displayed if it truly helps the user navigate the site.
- Common elements, such as the site's privacy policy, contact information, and copyright, should be displayed on the bottom of the page.

If you opt to have a more complex site, it becomes critically important that you show information in a completely consistent manner. So pay extra attention to this facet of usability.

Presentation of text and graphics

Although graphics are an important part of the Web, it's still fundamentally a text-based medium. Consequently, think through very carefully how you want to present the text on your site. I talked about the importance of having larger and smaller text as a quick visual cue for visitors and about ensuring a consistent layout structure, but also consider some of the other important aspects of textual presentation:

- Conventional uppercase and lowercase text (like the sentence in this book) can be read significantly faster than all uppercase text.

- Right-justified text (also called `align="justify"`) is more difficult to read than text with a ragged right margin.

- Uppercase characters are most effective for drawing attention to items (and don't forget `small-caps` in this regard).

- Optimal spacing between lines is at least equal to the height of the characters themselves, and you can adjust this with line height in CSS. I almost always use at least a `line-height` of 1.25 to open up my design a little bit.

tip A liberal use of CSS styles on your Web sites ensures that all your text is displayed attractively and in a manner that is as user-friendly as possible.

In addition, the graphics you include on your Web site should not only convey useful information or design elements, they should be maximally effective. Here are some things to consider when you design graphics for your site:

- **Context of the graphical elements:** All visual metaphors and other graphical elements should be thematically consistent, including whether they are two- or three-dimensional and whether they are color or black and white. (A *visual metaphor* is a set of images or a picture that represents a certain function. The trashcan on your computer desktop, for example, is a visual metaphor for the file deletion function in the operating system.) To ensure a consistent graphical theme, a site that's built around a mockup of the Windows user interface shouldn't suddenly have buttons that look like they're pulled from an auto dashboard or a children's toy.

- **Task domain:** Not all applications that can have graphics should have graphics. Although graphical representations of data are often preferred, some types of data are best presented as a text table, such as a month-at-a-glance calendar format.

- **Graphic form of the element:** Choose either concrete representations of objects (photographs or finely detailed illustrations) or abstract representations (line art and symbols) to ensure consistency.

- **Extent to which elements can be discriminated in the overall design:** Having a series of icons or graphical elements with similar appearance just serves to confuse the visitor.

Another important issue is *consistency*, which I have woven through the different sections here. Whatever rules you choose to follow, do your best to ensure that your text, graphics, phrasing, and overall design are as logically consistent as possible.

Choice and uses of color

One final area to consider on page and site design is your use and application of color. Not only does color have significant cultural meaning that varies as you travel through the world, but you should also consider physiological issues. Bright red on bright blue and light grey on yellow, for example, are almost completely unreadable combinations on a computer screen.

Indeed, one aspect of color use to consider is whether your colors work for someone who is color blind: Most people with a color deficiency have a hard time differentiating between reds and greens. This may or may not influence your design depending on whether you anticipate that a significant percentage of your audience might have a color deficiency.

on the web   You can find lots of interesting information on color blindness online. One good place to start is the National Institutes of Health's usability.gov Web site. For specific information, jump straight to `http://usability.gov/web_508/tut-c.html`.

Nonetheless, color can and does convey meaning on a Web site, and it's hard to imagine a situation where you wouldn't use any sort of colors on your site, except perhaps if you are a photographer seeking a stark, black-and-white design. But that's another story!

In terms of good usage of color, I try to take to heart the usability.gov suggestion that color be used as a bonus for your design, rather than as a critical element of everything functioning well. Here are some guidelines for using color:

- Use color where it adds value or conveys information. Compare the usage of color at Yahoo! with the usage of color at MSN or AOL to see what I mean.

- Use logical colors for the meaning you seek: If you're creating a site about backpacking, for example, use outdoor colors, greens and browns. A techno or industrial site might have a lot of black, by contrast.

- Be sparing with inverse color choices: white on black is much more difficult to read than black on white, for example.

- Try to pick a color palette and stick with it.

- Be conscious of the cultural meaning of colors for your main audience. In Western culture, for example, black represents death, white represents purity and innocence, yellow represents warnings, and red represents danger. Given that, highlighting information in red *because it stands out,* is a usability error.

Having said all that, don't be afraid to experiment! Considering the color usage guidelines is important, but some sites look delightful with yellow text on dark blue, with green edges.

note   In addition to issues of color blindness, you may need to address other possible handicaps. These include screen readers for blind visitors (that is, how effective is your Web site if no graphics are loaded?), voice control or mouseless navigation (do you force users to navigate through pull-down menus exclusively?), and more. These are additional reasons to ensure that you always include alt tags with your images and offer non-graphical navigational alternatives.

Navigating Your Web Site

In addition to design and usability, it's worth thinking about how visitors navigate through your site. This area is one of the most difficult parts of site design, because you have to create an overarching hierarchy of information for your site when it might not have a coherent vision or organization in the first place!

For my personal site, I have over 900 pages online, and I've really tried to categorize them according to some basic concepts. Consequently, I have the four major sections of Teaching, Speaking, Writing, and Consulting. You can see them as the main navigational elements in Figure 15-5.

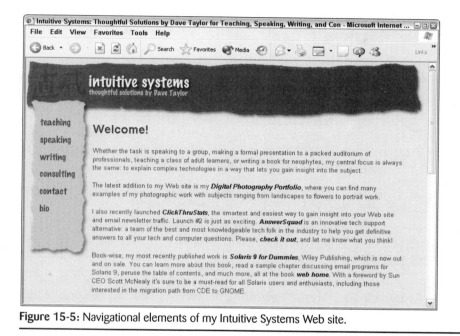

Figure 15-5: Navigational elements of my Intuitive Systems Web site.

Notice in Figure 15-5 that I'm also trying to stick with the usability guidelines discussed throughout. The site has an open design, subtle use of colors and graphical elements, fewer rather than more links, and the introduction of what proves to be a consistent information lay-out. Also notice that this first page has links to other areas (such as my digital photography portfolio) as part of the main prose, rather than as another navigational link. A downside is that no single place has all links to all areas immediately obvious; but the upside is that the site design is much less cluttered and less overwhelming than, say, the SSA site shown earlier.

Tracking navigation

One trick that many sites employ, and which can be particularly helpful for users, is to have a visual indication of where in the site hierarchy the particular page is located. Flip back to Figure 15-4 and notice how the White House site does a nice job of providing this site hierarchy information. If you look just under The White House logo, you can see that this page can be found in their hierarchy at Home ⇨ News & Policies ⇨ March 2002. Just as important, each of those phrases is clickable, so you can jump directly to the top-level News & Policies area, for example, by clicking the phrase on the page.

Sites such as Yahoo! and the Open Directory Project do a wonderful job of this type of hierarchical *cookie crumb trail* navigational element (see the following section for more information about cookies). It's well worth studying if you're building a site that's going to have any sort of deep organization.

You can also leave a relatively subtle hierarchical trail in the title of your pages, where each level is either appended or prepended to the standard title. It might look like this as you navigate through a site:

Norwood/Quince EcoPass Information

Region Map :: Norwood/Quince EcoPass Information

Norwood Ave :: Region Map :: Norwood/Quince EcoPass Information

This technique has the advantage that it helps create useful and informative bookmarks but still ensures that the key words are included in the title.

x-ref See Chapter 17 to find out more about bookmarks and how to ensure that potential visitors can find your site.

Site search engines

Another way to help people navigate your site is to include a search engine of some sort. This can be easier than you think. Many Web-hosting companies now include one or more common search engines that you can literally plug into your design and use after the engine has indexed your pages.

tip A popular search engine goes by the odd-looking name of ht://Dig. You can learn more about it at `http://www.htdig.org/`.

Another approach to having a search engine is to use an existing search engine and constrain its results to just your site. Chapter 12 has an extensive example of how you can use Google to add a search capability to your own site that lets visitors choose between searching just your site and searching the entire Web.

Site maps

A third option for helping people navigate the information on your site is to have a separate page called a *site map*. You've doubtless seen these on very large sites with hundreds of different areas. But site maps can be useful for smaller sites too, especially if you're worried that visitors won't necessarily figure out how you've organized your information, and you don't want to include a search engine.

Your site map can be as simple as a single-page indented list or as fancy as you desire, but the key idea is to include a Site Map link somewhere on every page on your site. Wherever people end up, they can always pop over to the map and figure out the path to what they're trying to reach.

As an added bonus, Google and other algorithmic search ranking systems tend to like sites with site maps, so it may also help with your site ranking.

x-ref For more information on improving your site ranking, flip to Chapter 17.

Using Cookies to Remember User Information

If your site offers user customization, user accounts, or other configuration elements that can change based on whether visitors have been there before or not, a very popular solution is to use cookies. *Cookies* are small packets of persistent data stored on the visitor's computer, not on the server. The word *persistent* is the key here. With cookies you can quit your browser, reboot your computer, and the data is still present and sent back to the site next time you visit. That's how sites like Yahoo! have *Welcome back* messages instead of a login area.

Your Web browser has a store of hundreds of cookies from different sites, I bet, and you might not even be aware of them. It's a rare site nowadays that doesn't feed some sort of persistent information to you when you're browsing: You'll find that some areas of my intuitive.com site do too.

Why use cookies? Because if you're asking visitors for information, the more your site can "remember" from the last visit, the easier and more usable your site becomes. In particular, with sites that require a log in, it's very nice to offer the option of staying logged in on a particular computer: That's all done with cookies.

If you're running MSIE6, it's not very easy to see your cookies. I recommend you download a simple little application called Karen's Cookie Viewer, written by expert Windows programmer Karen Kenworthy.

on the web Karen's Web site is at `http://www.karenware.com/`

Final Thoughts about Usability

In terms of usability, just remember one key point: Building a usable site is a *process* not a *goal*, per se. Listen to your visitors, invite input and feedback, and be focused on the goal of a site that's attractive and usable, not the goal of its being ultimately cool or a tour de force of graphical interactivity. Rebuild pages, reorganize information, and rethink presentation issues based on what your visitors tell you.

The application is free and makes it quite easy for you to browse all the cookies your Web browser has been dutifully saving for you. Figure 15-6 shows a list of my cookies and the specific details of one of the two cookies I am storing from Tim Carter's excellent Ask The Builder Web site.

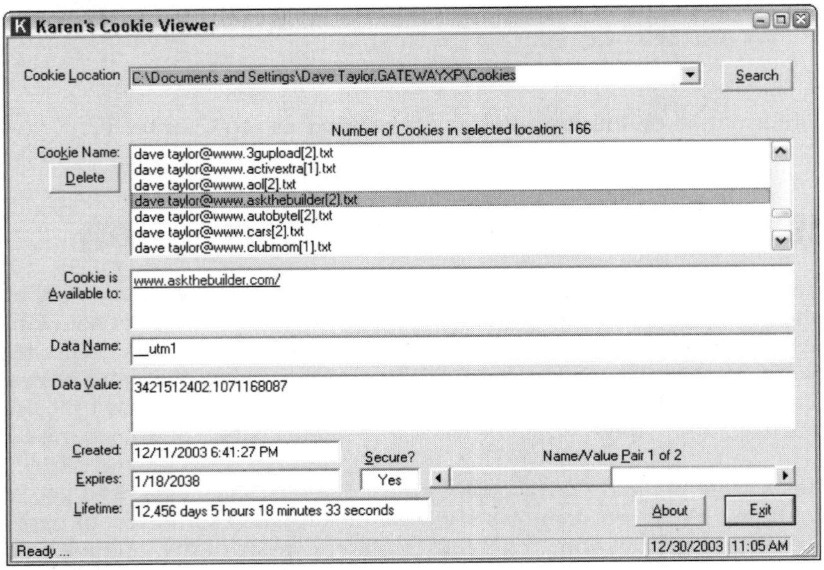

Figure 15-6: Displaying cookie information.

Summary

This chapter gave you a chance to step back from the nuts and bolts of Web page and Web site design and look at the user experience. You looked at how people are likely to perceive your Web site when they visit and what things you can do to make your site easier to understand and easier to navigate. Although the rules may seem obvious, many Web sites violate one or more of them regularly. These violations can make a site less enjoyable, less effective, and less useful than it might otherwise be. The next chapter looks at the other end of Web design: how to ensure that your CSS and HTML are perfectly written and valid.

Validating Your Pages and Style Sheets

chapter 16

In This Chapter

Validating HTML, XHTML, and CSS

Creating Web pages for wireless devices

Introducing WML and WAP

So far, you've learned how to work with various HTML tags, how to fine-tune presentation using CSS, and that Web browsers are quite forgiving about the occasional incorrect tag usage. If you add a wrong attribute, misspell a tag, or forget to close a list element, the browser does its best to fix your error without complaining. However, don't conclude that you can lapse into sloppy coding habits!

Validating HTML and XHTML Web Pages

Because modern Web browsers are so complex, it's important to ensure that your HTML is valid and correct. Fortunately, some terrific online tools help you produce clean, proper HTML. Notable among these is the World Wide Web Consortium's (W3C) HTML Validator Tool, which you can find at `http://validator.w3.org/`. I particularly like this validator because W3C is the group that manages and blesses the different HTML, XHTML, and CSS standards, so its validator should be the most accurate of the options available.

Unfortunately, using a validator isn't as easy as just pointing it to your Web page and clicking the Validate button. Try that and you promptly find the validation system complaining that it can't figure out what kind of HTML to check against, and what character set your page uses. (For more information about character sets, see the section "Specifying a character set" later in this chapter.)

To use the validator, you need to add a line called DOCTYPE to the beginning of your HTML files, as shown in the following example:

```
<!DOCTYPE HTML PUBLIC "-//W3C//DTD HTML 4.01 Transitional//EN"
"http://www.w3.org/TR/html4/loose.dtd">
```

This particular DOCTYPE declares the document to be HTML 4.01 transitional, which means that the validator requires that you have used the most recent HTML tags and format, but it also accepts older, correct, HTML. If you want to be forced to use only HTML 4.01 tags on your pages and not let any old or obsolete (referred to as *deprecated*) tags creep in, you should use Strict instead of Transitional.

note   What are the differences among all these versions of HTML? Really, they come down to nuances and the changes caused by evolution of the HTML language. If you want to learn about the specific differences among versions of HTML, your best bet is to read some of the excellent reference material on the W3C Web site, found at http://www.w3.org/. If you use HTML 4.01 (as I do in this book), additional formatting is necessary for your code to be valid XHTML.

Three other DOCTYPE options exist. The following example calls for HTML 3.2:

```
<!DOCTYPE HTML PUBLIC "-//W3C//DTD HTML 3.2 Final//EN">
```

When you use the HTML 3.2 Final designation, the validator flags any HTML 4.01 tags as errors in the source. If you've been working along with me and using the code I'm demonstrating, you're far beyond the HTML 3.2 specification, anyway.

The next example calls for strict HTML 4.01:

```
<!DOCTYPE HTML PUBLIC "-//W3C//DTD HTML 4.01 Strict//EN"
"http://www.w3.org/TR/html4/strict.dtd">
```

With the HTML 4.01 designation, earlier tags you may have used including <STRONG> and similar, are not acceptable and are flagged as errors. If you use this option, it's quite difficult, in my experience, to have your page reported as fully compliant.

This last example shows the DOCTYPE for XHTML 1.0 Transitional:

```
<!DOCTYPE html
    PUBLIC "-//W3C//DTD XHTML 1.0 Transitional//EN"
    "http://www.w3.org/TR/xhtml1/DTD/xhtml1-transitional.dtd">
```

I explore this designation later in this chapter. Notice that the DOCTYPE tag forces you to choose between HTML and XHTML.

Specifying a character set

In addition to the `DOCTYPE`, validators want to know what *character set* you're using. Because my page uses plain ASCII (alphanumeric characters, the set of characters you use for e-mail and other plain applications)—no special characters for foreign languages or special symbols—I simply add the following line to my HTML code:

```
<meta http-equiv="Content-Type" content="text/html;charset=us-ascii">
```

Character entities themselves are always plain ASCII, regardless of what symbol they produce when interpreted.

x-ref If you want your Web page to contain various Spanish or German characters, your best approach is to use the character entities explained in Chapter 5, and stick with plain ASCII. It's the most portable solution.

Validating an HTML page

You can feed your HTML to the W3C validator in two different ways. Open the Validation Service page at `http://validator.w3.org` and use one of these methods:

- In the Address box, specify the URI of the page you want to validate and click the Validate URI button.

- In the Local File box, type the path to your local file (or use the Browse button to find it on your system) and then click the Validate File button.

Now see what happens when you try validating this sample page:

```
<!DOCTYPE HTML PUBLIC "-//W3C//DTD HTML 4.01 Transitional//EN"
  "http://www.w3.org/TR/html4/loose.dtd">
<meta http-equiv="Content-Type" content="text/html;charset=us-ascii">
<html>
<head><title>Validation Test</title></head>
<h2>There are some errors in this file</h2>
<div color=blue>
Can you spot all the mistakes in this simple HTML file?
</body>
</html>
```

Figure 16-1 shows this page's URI—`http://www.intuitive.com/coolsites/examples/ch16-1.html`—entered into the Address box on the W3C validator page.

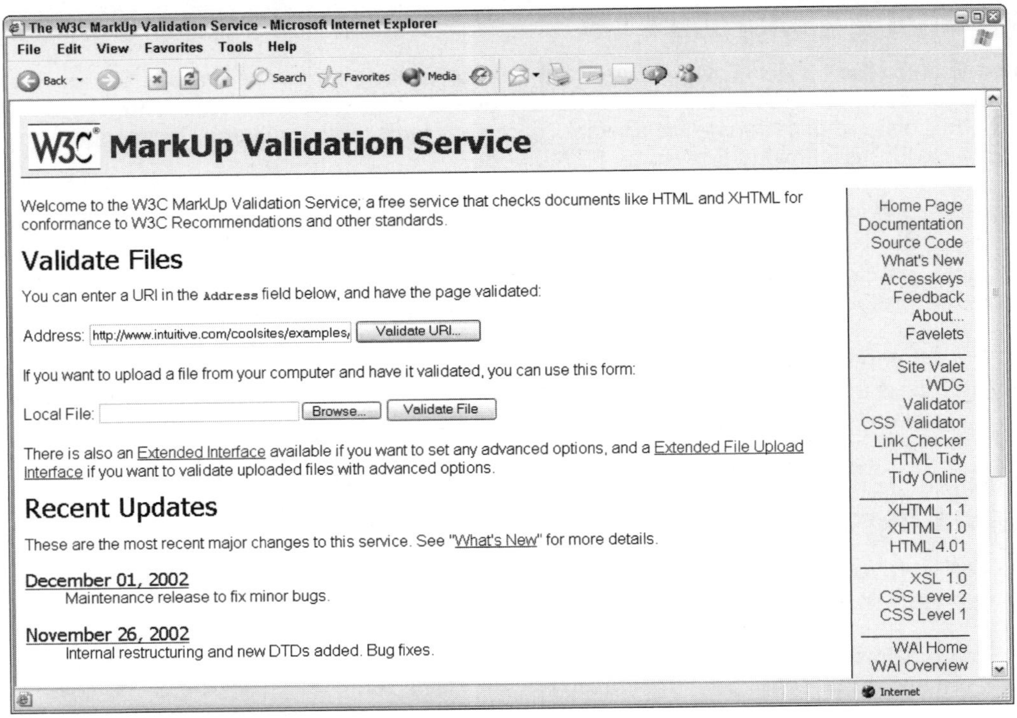

Copyright © 1994-2003, World Wide Web Consortium

Figure 16-1: Asking the W3C validator to check a test page for HTML compliance.

Figure 16-2 shows the result of the validation process on this test file after the Validate URI button is clicked.

The actual errors listed for this very short HTML page are as follows:

```
Line 4, column 5: document type does not allow element "HTML" here
  <html>
Line 7, column 11: there is no attribute "COLOR"
  <div color=blue>
Line 9, column 6: end tag for "DIV" omitted, but its declaration does not
permit this.
  </body>
Line 7, column 0: start tag was here.
  <div color=blue>
Line 10, column 8: "HEAD" not finished but document ended
  </ht...
Line 10, column 8: "HTML" not finished but document ended
  </ht...
```

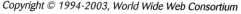

Copyright © 1994-2003, World Wide Web Consortium

Figure 16-2: The sample page is not valid HTML.

If you're like me, you look at all this and say, "Huh?" It's critical to remember that validators do the best job they can, but if something is not configured correctly, it can trigger an error that then messes up all the subsequent messages from the validators.

In this instance, a closer look at the HTML file reveals that the basic problem is that tags are out of order, and I left out an opening `<body>` tag and a closing `</div>` tag. If you make the necessary revisions (shown in bold in the following code), you get this new version of the HTML snippet:

```
<!DOCTYPE HTML PUBLIC "-//W3C//DTD HTML 4.01 Transitional//EN"
 "http://www.w3.org/TR/html4/loose.dtd">
<html>
<head>
  <meta http-equiv="Content-Type" content="text/html;charset=us-ascii">
  <title>Validation Test</title>
</head>
<body>
<h2>There are some errors in this file</h2>
<div style="color:blue">
```

Continued

```
Continued
Can you spot all the mistakes in this simple HTML file?
</div>
</body>
</html>
```

Does this validate as correct HTML 4.01 transitional? To find out, I applied these changes to the HTML file and created ch16-3.html, which I then specified as a URI to the validator. The result: yes! See Figure 16-3 for the good news.

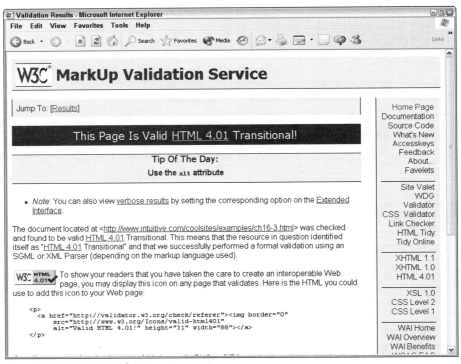

Copyright © 1994-2003, World Wide Web Consortium

Figure 16-3: HTML validates as correct HTML 4.01 transitional code.

Notice that after the page validates, the site offers you the capability to slap a happy "HTML 4.01" graphic (these are called *medallions* in the online marketing biz) on your page to show that it has been validated. W3C even offers this code to help you add this graphic:

```
<p>
    <a href="http://validator.w3.org/check/referer"><img border="0"
        src="http://www.w3.org/Icons/valid-html401"
        alt="Valid HTML 4.01!" height="31" width="88"></a>
</p>
```

Notice that although this snippet is valid HTML, it is *not* valid XHTML. Also, don't have a lapse in judgment: Include the medallion only on pages that *do* validate. You don't want to look foolish if a visitor decides to test your page and runs into errors.

note Would someone really test your page? Probably not, unless you proudly advertise that it's completely HTML compliant with the graphical icon. Then analyzing and revalidating the page is simply a matter of clicking on the medallion icon.

Validating XHTML Pages

Although HTML 4.01 is the latest version of HTML, the introduction and popularity of XML, the eXtensible Markup Language, has caused Web developers to move toward a hybrid markup language called XHTML. In a nutshell, XHTML offers all the capabilities and format of a regular HTML document, but forces a slightly more formal tag usage. The entire set of XHTML rules can be easily summarized, and I discussed them in Chapter 2. But here's the full set of XHTML rules to refresh your memory:

- Documents must be well-formed and exhibit proper nesting (all opened tags must be closed, and in the correct order).
- Elements and attributes must be in lowercase only.
- For non-empty elements, end tags are required (esp. the `<p>` tag).
- Attribute values must always be quoted.
- Attributes cannot be minimized (for example, `noshade` should be `noshade="noshade"`).
- Empty elements must otherwise end with a `/>` sequence.
- All `img` tags must have an `alt=""` attribute.

To explore the differences between HTML and XHTML validation, take the code snippet shown earlier and translate it into proper XHTML; then see if it validates. Here's my first attempt at this translation:

```
<!DOCTYPE html
    PUBLIC "-//W3C//DTD XHTML 1.0 Transitional//EN"
    "http://www.w3.org/TR/xhtml1/DTD/xhtml1-transitional.dtd">
<html>
<head>
  <meta http-equiv="Content-Type" content="text/html;charset=us-ascii">
  <title>Validation Test</title>
</head>
<body>
<h2>There are some errors in this file</h2>
<div style="color:blue">
Can you spot all the mistakes in this simple HTML file?
</div>
```

Continued

```
Continued
<center>

<p>
  <a href="http://validator.w3.org/check/referer"><img border="0"
    src="http://www.w3.org/Icons/valid-html401"
    alt="Valid HTML 4.01!" height="31" width="88"></a>
</p>

</center>
</body>
</html>
```

Did you notice that I'm using a different DOCTYPE, one that specifies transitional XHTML instead of HTML 4.01? To see if this code is valid and clean XHTML, simply ask the W3C validator to test it by going to the same page as before—http://validator.w3.org/—and feeding in the URL http://www.intuitive.com/coolsites/examples/ch16-04.html.

The results are not good. The validator reports that the page is not valid XHTML 1.0 transitional and lists the following errors:

```
Line 6, column 71: end tag for "meta" omitted, but OMITTAG NO was
specified
  ...nt-Type" content="text/html;charset=us-ascii">
Line 6, column 2: start tag was here
    <meta http-equiv="Content-Type" content="text/html;charset=us-ascii">
Line 19, column 54: end tag for "img" omitted, but OMITTAG NO was
specified
        alt="Valid HTML 4.01!" height="31" width="88"></a>
Line 17, column 50: start tag was here
    <a href="http://validator.w3.org/check/referer"><img border="0"
```

After a moment's thought, you know these errors all make sense. The meta tag doesn't have a paired </meta> tag; so even though it's part of what the validator wants (not necessarily part of your page), you need to slightly change the <meta> tag to have a /> ending. The <img> tag has exactly the same problem: Because it's not a paired tag, it must end with /> not just >. Here's the HTML source again, with two small tweaks to fix these problems:

```
<!DOCTYPE html
      PUBLIC "-//W3C//DTD XHTML 1.0 Transitional//EN"
      "http://www.w3.org/TR/xhtml1/DTD/xhtml1-transitional.dtd">
<html>
<head>
  <meta http-equiv="Content-Type" content="text/html;charset=us-ascii" />
  <title>Validation Test</title>
</head>
<body>
<h2>There are some errors in this file</h2>
```

```
<div style="color:blue">
Can you spot all the mistakes in this simple HTML file?
</div>
<center>

<p>
  <a href="http://validator.w3.org/check/referer"><img border="0"
    src="http://www.w3.org/Icons/valid-html401"
    alt="Valid HTML 4.01!" height="31" width="88" /></a>
</p>

</center>
</body>
</html>
```

note The URI for the corrected XHTML is `http://www.intuitive.com/coolsites/examples/ch16-4b.html`.

Figure 16-4 shows the valid result after I make these changes.

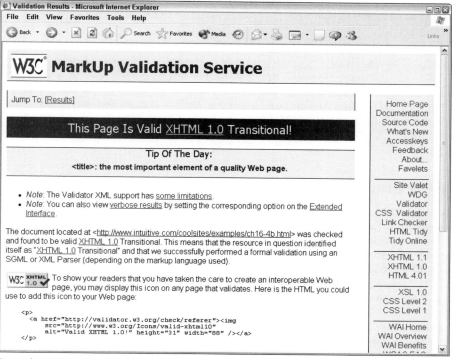

Figure 16-4: A few simple changes result in valid XHTML 1.0 transitional code.

Now that I've added the ending slash that somehow dropped out when I copied the snippet for the W3C medallion graphic, you can see that this is also valid XHTML:

```
<p>
    <a href="http://validator.w3.org/check/referer"><img
        src="http://www.w3.org/Icons/valid-xhtml10"
        alt="Valid XHTML 1.0!" height="31" width="88" /></a>
</p>
```

Validating CSS

If you can validate HTML and XHTML, is it any surprise that you can also feed your separate CSS pages to a CSS validator? Because some Web browsers automatically stop reading all CSS definitions after they encounter any error, and others silently skip errors without any feedback, it's smart to validate—perhaps even smarter than validating HTML.

To see what I mean, consider this snippet of CSS:

```
<style type="text/css">
body { background: #ccf font: 125%/200% Arial
    margin-left: 2in }
</style>
```

To someone who is familiar with CSS, the problem is probably obvious: I forgot a semicolon after the background color specification and before the font-size style. But to a Web browser, well, it sees the background color, but it doesn't know what to make of the subsequent material on that line, and so ignores it. This is an easy fix: Simply restore the semicolon after the #ccf. If you have a 50–200-line CSS file, however, finding these nitpicky problems can be much more difficult.

MIME types and brick walls

Frustratingly, the W3C CSS validator is very fussy about what it calls MIME types. *MIME* actually means *multimedia Internet mail extension*, but it's more generally used to define file and content types throughout the Internet, including the Web. Odds are good that if you give a CSS file to the validator at http://jigsaw.w3.org/css-validator/validator-upload.html, it'll complain with the following message:

```
I/O Error: Unknown mime type : text/plain
```

What this means is that your Web server isn't configured properly, so it's sending .css files as type text/plain rather than the more correct text/css. You can't override this behavior for the validator, unfortunately; so if you can't get your administrator to tweak the server configuration, you have to find a different method to validate your CSS.

Fortunately, that's not too hard to do.

Uploading CSS specifications by file

Instead of feeding the validator a URL, simply ensure that you have the file on your own computer—your PC or Mac—and upload the file to the validator directly. It's very simple: Go to `http://jigsaw.w3.org/css-validator/` and click on `Validate your cascading style sheet source file by upload`. This takes you to the file upload area, as shown in Figure 16-5.

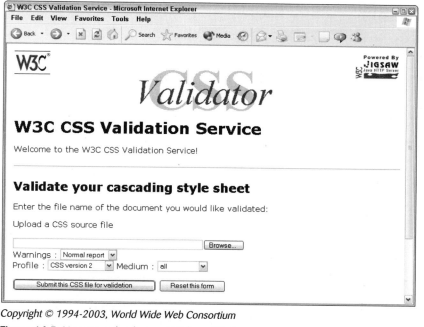

Copyright © 1994-2003, World Wide Web Consortium

Figure 16-5: You can upload your CSS for validation.

I have a style sheet that I've been building and would like to validate. It's on the Web at `http://www.intuitive.com/coolsites/sample.css`, and I've already saved it to disk with the same name. To validate it, I click the Browse button on the CSS Validation Service page and select the file; then I click the Submit This CSS File for Validation button.

W3C's validator shows that a small error is buried in the CSS, as shown in Figure 16-6.

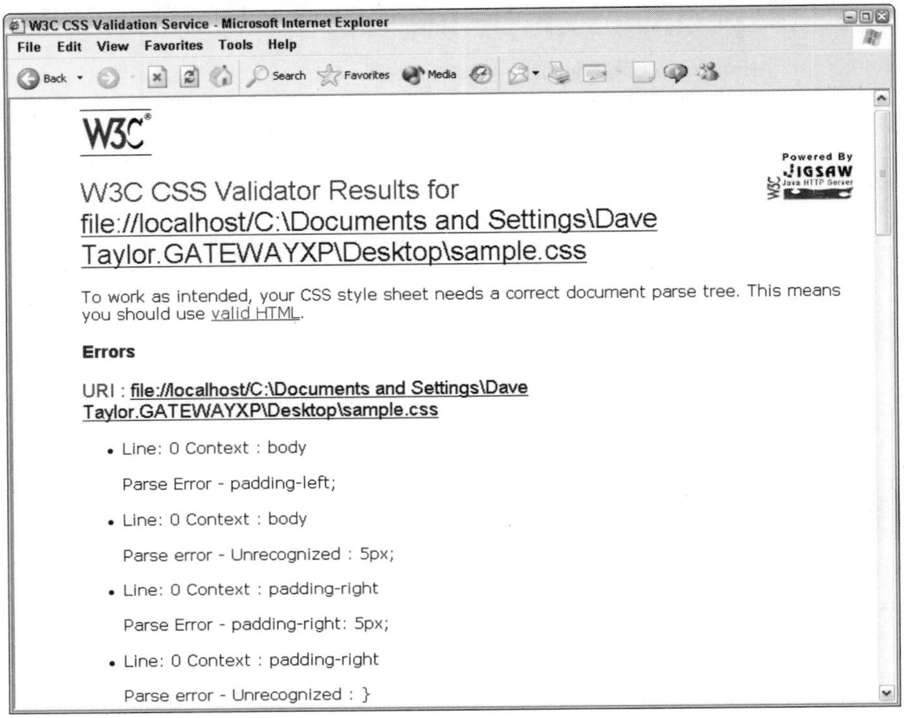

Copyright © 1994-2003, World Wide Web Consortium

Figure 16-6: The CSS Validator finds the error in my style sheet.

However, as is common with validators, the CSS validator has found an error, but it hasn't done much to help identify what the error is. To see what's wrong, look at the first section of the sample.css file, the section that has the error:

```
body { font: 11pt/14pt Times,serif;
       width: 600px; margin-left: 24px;
       border-left: 1px solid #666; border-right: 1px solid #666;
       padding-left; 5px; padding-right: 5px; }
```

Can *you* see what's wrong here?

The problem is that I accidentally typed a semicolon instead of a colon after padding-left. Not an error that's listed in the validator output, but if I make that one fix and resubmit the file, my CSS is validated, as shown in Figure 16-7. Finally.

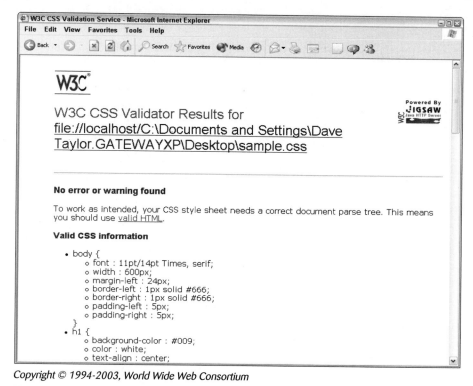

W3C CSS Validator Results for
file://localhost/C:\Documents and Settings\Dave
Taylor.GATEWAYXP\Desktop\sample.css

No error or warning found

To work as intended, your CSS style sheet needs a correct document parse tree. This means
you should use valid HTML.

Valid CSS information

- body {
    - font : 11pt/14pt Times, serif;
    - width : 600px;
    - margin-left : 24px;
    - border-left : 1px solid #666;
    - border-right : 1px solid #666;
    - padding-left : 5px;
    - padding-right : 5px;
    }
- h1 {
    - background-color : #009;
    - color : white;
    - text-align : center;

Copyright © 1994-2003, World Wide Web Consortium

Figure 16-7: CSS document validates!

Now that the code has been proven to be valid CSS, Web pages that use this style sheet can
include a spiffy Valid CSS medallion, like the medallion graphic for valid HTML or XHTML.

Creating Valid Mobile Web Page Layouts

If you're really building a site that has maximum flexibility, you might want to include support
for mobile devices. With screens the size of your thumb (well, a tiny bit bigger, but not much),
cell phones, PDAs and other devices have been gaining the capability to let users surf the
web, albeit with a very simplified browser application.

Pages for these devices are written in a crude subset of HTML called *Wireless Markup
Language* (WML). WML helps you write pages that work for wireless devices simply by
omitting most of the design elements. For example, WML supports only monochrome
bitmaps—no animated GIFs, no streaming media, nothing fancy, just crude graphics.

A deck of cards

WML pages are designed more like a deck of cards (lots of small data items) instead of the (longer, more complex) separate Web pages that you're used to working with. People accessing the Web with mobile devices don't want to scroll around a lot if they can help it. By keeping your pages very short, even if you produce lots more pages, downloads are faster and everything feels snappier. Interestingly, many WML developers actually design their sites to send all the common information for the "cards" at one time (a process called *in-device buffering*) to have nice displays with manageable download times.

To begin working with WML, you need a good emulator. A mobile device *emulator* lets you simulate a mobile device and see what your WML page looks like on it. By using an emulator, you don't have to download and test pages time and time again on your PDA or other mobile device as you learn WML. Fortunately there are two good choices in free emulators:

Nokia offers its emulator at `http://www.forum.nokia.com/main/1,6566,033,00.html`.

Phone.com, which produces many of the Web sites for current-generation mobile phones, offers its emulator (they call it a simulator) at `http://www.phone.com/products/upsdk.html`.

Both emulators are free, but you must register on each company's site to get them.

WAP versus WML

If you looked at the URLs above, you probably said "Um, WAP? What happened to WML?" In fact, it's critical to understand what differentiates the Wireless Application Protocol (WAP) and WML.

The basic difference is that WML is like HTML; it's a markup language optimized for wireless devices, and it looks a lot like HTML. WAP, on the other hand, is like HTTP, the hypertext transport protocol. Its role is to ensure that information is successfully transmitted between the wireless device and the server.

If you want to use the tired cliché of the Information Superhighway, think of WAP as the highway itself, whereas WML is the car on the highway. You can also look at the regular Web that way: little HTML (and XHTML) cars zooming along on the HTTP highway. But I'll drop this metaphor before I miss the exit ramp!

So what does WML look like?

Here is an example of a simple WML page:

```
<!DOCTYPE wml PUBLIC "-//WAPFORUM//DTD WML 1.1//EN"
"http://www.wapforum.org/DTD/wml_1.1.xml">
<wml>
<template>
</template>
 <card id="card1" title="Page 1">
   <p>
     <em>
        This is your cellphone on steroids.
        <br/>
        <i>Any questions?<br/></i>
     </em>
   </p>
 </card>
</wml>
```

The first line of a WML file is a DOCTYPE specifier, just like the HTML, XHTML, and CSS validators you've already seen. Because so many different variations of HTML are available now, it's critical for maximal flexibility that you properly identify what type of markup you're using.

The <template> block is where buttons that are common to all "cards in the deck" (remember the deck of cards metaphor) are specified. Liberal use of this section can significantly improve the performance of the resultant deck.

The <card> block is where you specify the information for this particular page. You can't do much sophisticated layout here, but you can include graphics using the *WBMP* (Wireless Bitmap) format:

```
<img src="sample.wbmp" alt="sample image" />
```

Did you notice the /> closing tag? That's because WML, like XHTML, is an XML-based markup language; so it requires proper formatting throughout.

tip   One of the best places to learn about WAP and WML is at http://www.wapforum. org/. The WAP Forum group is also the standards-setting body for this community (the wireless equivalent of the W3C, actually) so whatever it specifies is what phone manufacturers implement.

What I cover here only scratches the surface of what's required to produce Web pages and Web sites for the world of wireless connectivity, but hopefully it whets your appetite. If http:// www.wapforum.org/ isn't sufficient information to get you started, try visiting http://www. waptastic.com/ too. It's a very popular discussion forum and resource site for WAP/WML developers.

Summary

In this chapter, you learned how to validate HTML, XHTML, and CSS using W3C's online validators. You were also introduced to WML and WAP. WML is a markup language that enables you to build unencumbered Web pages for mobile devices. WAP is an application protocol, similar to HTTP, whose role is to ensure that information is successfully transmitted between the wireless device and the server.

The next chapter is sure to catch your attention now that your pages are all well-formed and valid HTML, XHTML, or CSS. In Chapter 17, I explore the world of search engines and how you can apply simple design rules to your Web sites to ensure that they are not just findable, but highly ranked for relevancy when people search for your content.

Building Traffic and Being Found

In this chapter, I discuss how Web search engines work and how to design your material so it will attract attention when it is indexed by Google, Lycos, MSN, Yahoo!, and the many other search systems available on the Web. I then talk about where you should announce your new Web site and other things you can do to build lots of traffic.

Having your own Web site is definitely worthwhile, but, like art exhibited in a gallery, the real fun begins when people come to visit. The fundamental puzzle of the World Wide Web—and the Internet as a whole—is how to find information. If you can't find other people's stuff, it stands to reason that others will have difficulty finding your stuff.

People have applied many different strategies for solving the indexing problem, which ranges from creating simple databases of Web sites that accept information about your site to unleashing powerful *crawler* programs that stealthily visit your site and add your information to their massive indexes.

Producing Crawler-Friendly Sites

Before you start to worry about which sites to visit when you're starting to build traffic, it's important to begin building the most search engine-friendly Web site possible. You have many ways to ensure that your site is understandable to the robots that roam the Net and index everything, but the two most important are unquestionably creating well-titled pages and using the `<meta>` HTML tag frequently. This tag offers information specifically intended for the robots to read.

Creating meaningful titles

When a visitor bookmarks your Web site, your site's exact title appears in that person's bookmark list. Furthermore, many search systems use the document title as the basis of their indexing. The more meaningful your title, the more likely your site will be found. To wit, if you're busy creating a site that explores the intricacies of coffee roasting, *Coffee Roasting: The Quest for the Perfect Cup* is much more explicit (and more interesting) than *The Coffee Home Page* or *Welcome!*

tip   I don't recommend including the words *home page* and *Web* in your page's title. Instead, add at least three or four descriptive words or keywords, such as *Satellite TV and DSS Central, including Dish Network and DirecTV.*

Titles are used not only by search tools; they are also what users see when they save your URL to their hotlists. A hotlist full of titles such as *The Intuitive Life, All About Starbucks, Digital Games Review,* and *Sony Consumer Electronics* offers a great deal more information with less clutter than *The Ray-O-Vac World Wide Web Site* or *Welcome to the New Stanford University Web Site Home Page.*

Some wit and verve can help, too. Which of these pages would you rather visit?

- Home Page for Tom Vilot
- Who Is This Tom Vilot Guy?
- Tom's Home Page
- Welcome to my Home Page

Needless to say, that last one offers no information about the Web page at all and should be avoided like the plague.

Using keywords in your title

Including keywords in your page's title is crucial. Keywords significantly improve your ranking on search engines (partially because so few people pay attention to titles as an index-generating entry). The principle is quite simple. The more keywords you have in your Web site's title, the higher your page ranks in a search engine. Thus, the more people who visit your site.

Go to a site like Google, MSN, or Yahoo!, and search for a common term such as *buy new computer* or *credit card*. You'll get thousands of results. But, what makes the first few show up as the most relevant of all those matches? The answer is their page rank, or the score that the search engine assigns their page when compared to your exact search pattern. Visit a page that's rated very highly. Then, go a few pages further into the results of the search, and visit a lower-ranked page. See if you can ascertain what is different in terms of title, headers, text prose, <meta> tags (choose View ➪ Source to see these), and similar elements. That's what I'm talking about here—how to design your pages and your site to maximize your page rank and improve your calculated relevance when people search for your service and products.

Take a peek at a few really good Web page titles to get your creative juices flowing. Notice how specific each title is to what each site contains:

- This is True by Randy Cassingham—Weird but True News from Around the World (http://www.thisistrue.com/)
- Ask The Builder—Home Building, Remodeling, and Improvement Information Page (http://www.askthebuilder.com/)
- Surfing the Net with Kids: Guide to the BEST KID SITES for kids of all ages (http://www.surfnetkids.com/)
- SafetySurf.com—Parental Control Software and Internet Monitoring Software. The parents' place to find software to protect their children on the Internet! Parents take control at SafetySurf.com, home of great Software for Parents! (http://www.safetysurf.com/)
- Intuitive Systems: Thoughtful Solutions by Dave Taylor for Teaching, Speaking, Writing, and Consulting (http://www.intuitive.com/)

What do these titles have in common? They describe the site's contents in an appealing, creative, and concise way. I particularly like what Tim Carter of Ask The Builder writes, Ask The Builder—Home Building, Remodeling, and Improvement Information Page. Notice the string of critical keywords—builder, building, remodeling, improvement, and information—all neatly tucked into a readable and human-friendly title. Smart!

Some search engine wizards tell me that the best possible titles actually have the keywords first and the company name or page title at the end, if at all. If you want to create a page devoted to the Nikon D100 digital camera, you might use something like *Nikon D100, Digital Photography, Digital Camera—All about the Nikon D100* as your page's title.

 note   I'm not convinced that changing the order of words in your title can meaningfully alter your page rank. But, naming your pages with keywords first is worth exploring if you don't mind a somewhat odd looking page title or two.

Using the <meta> tag

In addition to smart titles and thoughtful text layout, the <meta> tag can help ensure that crawler sites include meaningful information about your site. The <meta> tag doesn't display anything to the visitor. However, just about all the crawler sites highlighted in this chapter use the <meta> tag's contents as the abstract or summary description of your site and its contents instead of homing in on just the first few dozen words on your page.

> **tip**
>
> My search engine-optimizer friends (called SEOs in the biz) tell me that <meta> tags for keywords and description are passé and not worth including anymore. Titles and the first few sentences are much more important for page ranking on search engines. Personally, I still include the <meta> tags, but I strive to ensure that I'm doing everything else I can to maximize the findability of my sites.

Here's how you use the <meta> tag:

```
<meta name="keywords" content="technical support, Microsoft Windows, Mac,
Linux, Microsoft Office, Unix, Open Office, OpenOffice, X, GNOME, Novell,
NetWare, Help, Answers, AnswerSquad.com, MICROSOFT WINDOWS, MAC, LINUX,
ANSWERSQUAD.COM, Windows, Mac" />

<meta name="description" content="Got Technical Questions? You need
AnswerSquad! We offer a high-quality email discussion list staffed with
expert professionals - top-notch tech authors who can explain even the most
complex topics to normal human beings. Microsoft Windows, Mac, Linux,
Office? We Wrote the Book!" />
```

The search on a system such as AltaVista shows the title of the page and the description as the summary of the site rather than showing the first few dozen words found (which is the usual "description" used by search engines if they can't find something better to display). Here's how the result of the search might look:

```
AnswerSquad: Windows, Windows XP, Mac OS X, Unix, Linux, Red Hat Linux,
Mac OS, Windows 2000, C, C++, Java, HTML, Microsoft Office, Open Office,
X, GNOME and NetWare Support / Help / Questions Answered by Experts

Got Technical Questions? You need AnswerSquad! We offer a high-quality
email discussion list staffed with expert professionals—top-notch tech
authors who can explain even the most complex topics to normal human
beings. Microsoft Windows, Mac, Linux, Office? We Wrote the Book!
http://www.answersquad.com/ —size 14k—15 Jan 04
```

on the web Search Engine Watch is a great site for learning the latest scoop on how different search engines rate and index pages. Even better, it's run by a friend of mine, Danny Sullivan, so that's another good reason to visit! Check it out online at www.searchenginewatch.com.

Now that you know the value of meta keyword and meta description tags, poke around on some other sites, such as those suggested in the following sections, to see how they use the <meta> tag to improve their listings in search engines.

Microsoft (http://www.microsoft.com)

```
<META NAME="KEYWORDS" CONTENT="products; headlines; downloads; news; Web
site; what's new; solutions; services; software; contests; corporate
news;" />
<META NAME="DESCRIPTION" CONTENT="The entry page to Microsoft's Web site.
Find software, solutions, answers, support, and Microsoft news." />
```

Nostarch Press (http://www.nostarch.com)

```
<META NAME="description" CONTENT="catalog of computer books that make a
difference" />
<META NAME="keywords" CONTENT="computer books, linux books, linux,
javascript, mindstorms, LEGO, LEGO Mindstorms, robotics, web programming,
web scripting, bash shell, winzip, winzip help, .NET, zope, zclass,
zcatalog, livemotion, live motion, adobe, little red book, mao, chairman
mao, steal this book, steal this computer book, opera, opera web browser,
opera browser, needlecraft, computers, computer books that don't suck" />
```

Intuitive Systems (http://www.intuitive.com)

```
<META NAME="keywords"
    CONTENT="writing,teaching,speaking,keynote,lecture,seminar,workshop,
consulting,design,taylor,dave taylor,david taylor,author" />

<META NAME="description"
    CONTENT="Thoughtful Solutions by Dave Taylor for teaching, speaking,
writing, and consulting." />
```

The Internet Movie Database (http://www.imdb.com/)

```
<meta name="description" content="IMDb" />
<meta name="keywords" content="movies,films,movie
database,actors,actresses,directors,hollywood,stars,quotes" />
```

Contentious (http://www.contentious.com)

```
<META name="description" content="The Web-zine for writers, editors, and
others who create content for online media" />
<META name="keywords" content="writing, editing, writer, editor, write,
edit, journalism, journalist, journalists, news, content development,
content industry, online content, online media, media criticism" />
```

tip

If you aren't going to use the `<meta>` tag and still want the best possible design so your site can be easily found online, ensure that the first paragraph of text on your home page contains a meaningful description of its contents. Because some of the Web index systems only grab the first few sentences, you must carefully craft them so that people can find your information when they search with the various tools listed in this chapter. In particular, your first `<h1>` headline is important!

Other uses for the `<meta>` tag

The `<meta>` tag actually turns out to be a general purpose HTML tag that is used for a wide variety of things. Want your page to flip to another after a few seconds? The `<meta>` tag can do that, as this snippet from Paul Myers' TalkBiz site (`http://www.talkbiz.com/`) demonstrates:

```
<meta http-equiv="refresh"
    content="0;url=http://www.talkbiznews.com/" />
```

As quickly as possible (after zero seconds), the site's new home page replaces the current page on the screen. Another way to specify the same functionality is a bit easier to read. It looks like this:

```
<meta name="refresh" content="0"
  url="http://www.talkbiznews.com/" />
```

The new format of using three attributes—not two—is nicer in my view because it's more obvious which is a delay factor and which is the target URL.

Here is another example. Want to have your page automatically refresh every 30 seconds? Substitute 30 for 0, as shown in the following:

```
<meta http-equiv="refresh" content="30" />
```

For example, such frequent refreshes are perfect for Webcam sites!

News organizations also use this approach with slightly longer timeouts (that is, the amount of time between when you load the page and when it's refreshed). Here's how *The Wall Street Journal* (`http://www.wsj.com/`) does it:

```
<meta http-equiv="refresh" content="600" />
```

Every 600 seconds (five minutes), the page automatically reloads.

Content rating with PICS

Another `<meta>` value is used to detail the type of material included on a site using the convoluted PICS (Platform for Internet Content Selection) rating information. In late 1996, one of the most hotly argued topics was the quality and appropriateness of content on the Internet.

Congress passed the Communications Decency Act of 1996 (CDA), and Web developers added blue ribbon icons on their pages to protest the intrusion of government regulation onto the Net. One side of the debate chanted its mantra of "Free speech über alles" whereas the other side shouted "Protect our children!" Both sides raised valid and important issues, and the debate was very interesting. The CDA was later challenged in court and overturned. Publication of pornographic or offensive material on the Internet doesn't violate any specific electronic laws (although it might violate basic pornography and lewd conduct laws, but that's an entirely different debate).

The best news to come from this entire debate is that Paul Resnick of AT&T and James Miller of MIT's Computer Science Lab developed a content rating system. They distributed sample programs demonstrating that voluntary ratings for Web sites can be coupled with screening software, such as Net Nanny and SurfWatch, and even built into Microsoft's Internet Explorer program. These programs allow free discussion online while protecting children from stumbling into inappropriate material.

Resnick and Miller's system, PICS, enables you—as parent, teacher, or administrator—to block access to particular Internet resources without affecting what's distributed to other sites on the Internet. It's based on two ideas: instantaneous publishing of information on the Web (in this case, the ratings themselves) and access to Internet resources mediated by computers that can manage far more than any human being.

The two inventors of PICS state the following in their original paper, *PICS: Internet Access Controls without Censorship* (http://www.w3.org/PICS/iacwcv2.htm):

> Appropriateness, however, is neither an objective nor a universal measure. It depends on at least three factors.
>
> * **The supervisor:** Parenting styles differ, as do management styles.
> * **The recipient:** What's appropriate for one 15-year-old may not be appropriate for an 8-year-old, or even all 15-year-olds.
> * **The context:** A game or chat room that is appropriate to access at home may be inappropriate at work or school.

PICS allows complex site content ratings, which is both a strength and a weakness. If I want to create a movie stills archive but limit access to the archive to match the original ratings of the films, I can use a rating system for sites based on the movie ratings from the Motion Picture Association of America (MPAA). Here's how it would look:

```
((PICS-version 1.0)
  (rating-system "http://moviescale.org/Ratings/
Description/")
  (rating-service "http://moviescale.org/v1.0")
  (icon "icons/moviescale.gif")
  (name "The Movies Rating Service")
  (description "A rating service based on the MPAA's movie
rating scale")
```

Continued

```
Continued
  (category
   (transmit-as "r")
   (name "Rating")
   (label (name "G") (value 0) (icon "icons/G.gif"))
   (label (name "PG") (value 1) (icon "icons/PG.gif"))
   (label (name "PG-13") (value 2) (icon "icons/PG-13.gif"))
   (label (name "R") (value 3) (icon "icons/R.gif"))
   (label (name "NC-17") (value 4) (icon "icons/NC-17.gif"))))
```

Now it is time for a real example. Here's a PICS tag in use—this `<meta>` tag PICS rating is from the SurfNet Kids home page at `http://www.surfnetkids.com`:

```
<META
HTTP-EQUIV="PICS-Label" CONTENT='(PICS-1.1 "http://www.rsac.org/ratingsv01.
html" l gen true comment "RSACi North America Server" by "surfnetkids.com"
for "http://www.surfnetkids.com" on "1997.12.03T07:38-0800" r (n 0 s 0 v 0
l 0))' />
<META
HTTP-EQUIV="PICS-Label" CONTENT='(PICS-1.1 "http://www.classify.org/safesur
f/" l gen true for "http://www.surfnetkids.com" by "surfnetkids.com" r (SS~
~000 1))' />
<META
HTTP-EQUIV="PICS-Label" CONTENT='(PICS-1.1
"http://www.weburbia.com/safe/ratings.htm" 1 r (s 0))' />
```

Clearly, the PICS system is ugly and confusing. Is it going to change things? It seems unlikely, but, if the PICS system can become much easier to use and specify, people may start to voluntarily rate their Web sites. One way or the other, wrestling with the problem of inappropriate and obscene content on the Internet is unavoidable.

on the web Lots of information is available on this topic, including the original PICS design documents that is available at `http://www.bilkent.edu.tr/pub/WWW/PICS/` and the official home page of the PICS system at `http://www.w3.org/PICS/`.

Keeping crawlers away

If you're plugged into the Internet, your pages are eventually going to be indexed by one or more of the crawler programs, or *robots*, such as Google, WebCrawler, AltaVista, and various others. It's fun and very useful except when you prefer that portions of your Web site remain private or separate. To retain your privacy, you need a special file called `robots.txt`.

The `robots.txt` file—it must be called exactly that regardless of what kind of server you're working with, and it must be at the topmost level of your site organization—contains a set of commands that defines the level of access a robot program can have to your Web site. Unfortunately, it's a wee bit complex to write. But, once you've got it right, you never have to touch it again.

Two fields must be present in the `robots.txt` file: `User-agent` and `Disallow`. The first lets you specify either individual robots (maybe you intensely dislike public crawler programs but like one that's part of your own company), and the second is how you specify directories to omit your site from the automatic indexing. Take a look at a few examples of this to clarify:

```
User-agent: *
Disallow: /
```

This is the simplest method and says that everyone should simply leave this site unindexed. Here, the asterisk (*) for `User-agent` indicates that it applies to all crawler or robot programs. The slash (/) indicates everything from the very topmost directory down. Now look at another example:

```
User-agent: Scooter
Disallow: /cgi-bin/sources
Disallow: /access_stats
Disallow: /cafeteria/dinner_menus/
```

In this example, the Scooter robot isn't allowed to index any of the files in the `cgi-bin/sources` directory (a smart move), any of the access statistics (because they probably change quite frequently), or any of the cafeteria dinner menus (because they, one hopes, also change quite frequently). Any other indexing program that visits the site can index everything.

Here's an example section from the `robots.txt` file at ESPN's Web site (`http://msn.espn.go.com/robots.txt`):

```
# robots.txt for Disallow: /

User-agent: mozilla/4
Disallow: /

User-agent: Mozilla/4.0 (compatible; MSIE 4.0; Windows NT)
Disallow: /

User-agent: Mozilla/4.0 (compatible; MSIE 4.0; Windows 95)
Disallow: /
```

Here, you can see that the program tries to avoid user Web browsers that attempt to automatically crawl the site (Navigator 4 whose code name is Mozilla, and Internet Explorer whose code name is MSIE).

Another simple example is the `robots.txt` file from Nikon Corporation (`http://www.nikon.com/robots.txt`):

```
User-Agent: *
Disallow: /server_stats/
Disallow: /access_stats/
Disallow: /cgi-bin/
```

Continued

Continued
```
Disallow: /image/
Disallow: /test/
Disallow: /stylesheet/
```

Any robot can index anything on the (very nice) Nikon site with the exception of the directories `server_stats`, `access_stats`, `cgi-bin`, `image`, `test`, and `stylesheet`.

A handful of sites for you to explore on your own that have impressive and complex `robots.txt` files include CNN Online (`http://www.cnn.com`), Health and Human Services (`http://www.hhs.gov/`), the U.S. Army (`http://www.army.mil`), and Disney online (`http://www.disney.com/`).

One additional trick: There's a `meta` sequence you can add to your individual Web page (probably your home page would make the most sense) that tells crawlers to leave you alone:

```
<meta name="robots" content="noindex" />
```

on the web You can learn a lot more about Web robots and the `robots.txt` file at `http://www.robotstxt.org/`.

The Dark Side of Crawlers

Although most Web crawlers are benevolent, some people use them maliciously. *Spammers*, people who harvest and sell e-mail addresses, use their own sort of crawlers to find useful information on Web sites. But, these crawlers don't respect the `robots.txt` file. The story is quite the opposite. They add every directory listed on a Web page—even directories prohibited by the `robots.txt` file—to their search list. So, you have a decision to make. If you have content that you don't want indexed or searched by either good guys (Google) or bad guys (spammers), you might want to password protect that area rather than try to close it off with the `robots.txt` directives. That's my approach. I let crawlers index and search my entire site, and I then block more private areas with passwords.

tip See Chapter 14 for more information on protecting areas of your site with a password.

Registering with Web Index and Search Sites

Clearly, the search sites on the Net take different approaches to indexing the Web (that is, your Web site). So, where should you register? The answer is with all of them. Why not? All the sites are free, and lots of people use each service to find information, which may just be on your own home page. Two primary types of Web index sites are presented in this overview: directories of information submitted by users (such as Yahoo! and DMOZ) and crawler systems that find actual Web pages and index them automatically (such as Google, WebCrawler, and

Lycos). To join the former, you go to the sites and fill in a form with a brief description of your page or site. The latter services are easier. You simply pop over to these sites and add your URL to their databases.

Joining a directory site

In this section, I explore each type of registration more closely and then visit with Microsoft's Submit It! service. Submit It! announces your site to dozens of these search systems and directories for free.

Yahoo! (http://www.yahoo.com)

Of the many sites that offer a comprehensive database of other Web sites, my favorite is Yahoo!, which was created by then-Stanford graduate students David Filo and Jerry Yang. Filo and Yang developed Yahoo! as a mechanism for maintaining their own ever-growing list of cool Web sites, and the site grew so fast that their two UNIX servers couldn't keep up with the load. Today, Yahoo! is a media empire with a wide variety of businesses, partnerships, and plans.

That's the good news. The bad news is that, as the company has spun off into different businesses, it's become harder and harder to actually have your commercial site listed in the Yahoo directory without paying a substantial amount of money. Have a site that isn't commercial? Then, theoretically, it should be free and relatively speedy to add it to Yahoo!'s directory.

To join Yahoo!, find the appropriate category in the Yahoo! online directory and then click the small Suggest a Site link at the top right of the page. Yahoo! prompts you to choose one of these two options: Yahoo Express (a $299 fee whether your entry is chosen for inclusion in Yahoo! or not; seven-day turnaround) or Standard Consideration (free; no indication of how long it takes to evaluate your submission and include it in the directory). Pick the latter. Fill in all the blanks within the provided form. Your site will then be added after the administrative folks have a glance at your entry to ensure everything is accurate and the site is appropriate to the Yahoo! system.

The Open Directory Project (http://www.dmoz.org/)

Initially created as part of the Netscape open source browser project, the Open Directory Project (also known as DMOZ for its domain name) is a great alternative to Yahoo! with faster entry inclusion and administrators who actually maintain the links in a given category. To add your site, navigate to the appropriate spot in the directory, and click Suggest URL in the top-right. The form asks for a few key items of information, including URL, site title, and site description, and then submits the form to the appropriate category editor.

If that's not sufficient for your interests, don't forget that you can volunteer to become an editor at the Open Directory Project, which would then let you help manage a key online resource area dedicated to a specific topic that you're particularly interested in or knowledgeable about. Volunteering as a category editor is also a great way to join a thriving online community and help the Web grow. To start, click Become an Editor on the home page.

Signing up for a crawler or robot site

The alternative to a site where you describe your new Web page and how it should be organized and categorized are those sites where you provide your URL and their programs visit your page and read through your `meta` description and keyword information. (You didn't forget to include those, as detailed earlier in this chapter, right?) They then add your pages, one-by-one, to their massive databases.

As you learned earlier in this chapter, the programs that actually index the Web pages are called *robots*. There isn't much difference between the various robots. In fact, you don't really even need to register with these sites. If another page on the Web points to you, they'll eventually find the link and make it to your Web pages. Of course, it is worth visiting them because giving them your URL speeds up their finding and indexing your page.

caution I suggested earlier that you craft your pages to ensure that keywords and concepts appear in the first few sentences. Don't fall for the trick of setting your text to the same color as the background by thinking you can have search engine content that visitors won't see. Code like the following probably won't slip by the search engines:

```
<h1 style='font-size:5%;color:white'>list,of,various,key,words</h1>
```

The smartest of the search engines—notably Google—can catch this sort of trick and penalize you or perhaps not list your site at all. It's not worth the risk! In fact, the search engine sites are pretty darn smart. Any tricks you think will work probably won't. Just create good, informative pages with content, and you'll have the best results.

Google (http://www.google.com)

This is my favorite site on the entire Web when I'm searching for information. You can find almost anything by exploring Google, which has billions of documents indexed, and that makes it an important place for your Web site to be included. Fortunately, being included is easy.

To begin, click About on the stark home page and then click Add Your URL. Type the URL of your page, submit it, and you're done in just a few seconds.

tip You don't need to—and probably shouldn't—submit every page on your site. If all your pages are linked to each other, the Google crawler finds them all without any further assistance.

Lycos (http://www.lycos.com)

Taking a very different approach than Yahoo!, the Lycos site, which was first created at Carnegie-Mellon University and is now a part of the Spanish company Terra Lycos, indexes hundreds of millions of Web documents by building a database of URLs and the first few lines of description from each Web page. Lycos includes minimal textual information for the sites in its database, but the results are still surprisingly good.

To join the Lycos database, you click the Add Your Site to Lycos link almost hidden at the very bottom of the home page. Enter the information requested, and click Submit. It might take a week or two before the robot comes to your site and starts indexing your pages.

AltaVista (http://www.altavista.com)

AltaVista is a search system developed by Digital Equipment Corp. (DEC) that exploded onto the Web scene in late 1995 and is one of the busier search sites. A quick look shows that there's absolutely no way to browse any of the information; it's purely a search-and-see-results design. What's most impressive is the sheer volume of pages it has visited and indexed. Currently, the site has over 100 million Web pages indexed, that is, billions of words.

On the AltaVista site, you choose Submit a Site from the list of options on the bottom of the home page. Like Lycos, AltaVista only asks you for the actual URL of the base page, and it'll take a week or more before Scooter, its crawler program, actually reaches your site.

note Oh, did I mention that AltaVista is now owned by Overture, which was bought by Yahoo!? So, AltaVista might merge with the Yahoo! directory somewhere down the road...

Tying In with Related Sites Using a Web Ring

If you visit a site focused on the X-Files, Magic the Gathering, or even a site covering pregnancy and birth resources, you're likely to find that it points to other, similar Web sites by using what's called a *Web ring*—an informal group of similar Web sites that all point to each other. Although this sort of grassroots link-sharing is not at the forefront of Web design, it might be just what you need to help build some traffic if you're building an informational Web site. You can find an organization focused on these loose, cooperative groups of like-minded sites at http://www.webring.org. There are over 50,000 different Web rings hosted at that site.

The Web ring is a logical outgrowth of the ubiquitous Favorite Links area of a Web site with a bit of link exchange thrown in—a collection of a half-dozen or more sites that the creator of the site feels are related and of interest to the visitor. Instead of having them all listed on your own page, why not have a central collection of these related links and simply include a Next link on your site to take visitors to the next site on the list?

Now, you can imagine how these work. A central Web server maintains a list of sites tied to a specific theme or interest, and each site indicates its part of the ring and includes a pointer to the central ring server. Simple rings include a Next and Previous button allowing visitors to travel linearly through the list of links. More sophisticated ones offer subset list views—"show five ring sites"—and a random link that takes the visitor to one of the sites in the ring.

Interested in how Web rings work? Here's the code from the bottom of a page that's a part of a typical Web ring—in this case, Attached! Parenting, a parenting Web ring:

```
<TABLE BORDER="2" CELLSPACING="1">
<TR VALIGN="Middle">
<TD VALIGN="Top">
  <IMG SRC="art/ATTACH.JPG" WIDTH="130" HEIGHT="160" ALIGN="Left">
</TD>
<TD VALIGN="Top">
  <FONT SIZE="-1" FACE="Verdana,Helvetica,Arial"><BR>
  <BR></FONT>
  <CENTER><P>
  <FONT SIZE="-1" FACE="Verdana,Helvetica,Arial">
  <A href="http://members.aol.com/jedpblshg/book.html">
  <B>ATTACHED! Parenting Webring</B></A> <BR></FONT>
  <P>
  <FONT SIZE="-1" FACE="Verdana,Helvetica,Arial">
  <A href="http://www.webring.org/cgi-
bin/webring?ring=attached;id=6;prev">Previous</A><BR></FONT>
  <P>
  <FONT SIZE="-1" FACE="Verdana,Helvetica,Arial">
  <A href="http://www.webring.org/cgi-
bin/webring?ring=attached;id=6;next">Next</A><BR></FONT>
  <P>
  <FONT SIZE="-1" FACE="Verdana,Helvetica,Arial">
  <A href="http://www.webring.org/cgi-
bin/webring?ring=attached;id=6;next5">Next
  5 Sites</A><BR></FONT>
  <P>
  <FONT SIZE="-1" FACE="Verdana,Helvetica,Arial"><A
 href="http://www.webring.org/cgi-
bin/webring?ring=attached;random">Random
  Site</A></FONT></CENTER>
</TD>
</TR>
</TABLE>
```

You can join an existing Web ring to gain more exposure for your site, but I must admit I have somewhat mixed feelings about using Web rings for building traffic. If I can get someone to come to my site, why would I want to have him easily pop over to other, similar sites and possibly not come back? You have to make your own choice, but I encourage you to think this through carefully.

The Basics of Banner Advertising

Another way that you can build traffic to your Web site is to pay for banner advertisements and placements on other sites or search engines. These banners are typically 468 pixels wide and 60 pixels high, and a typical banner advertisement might look like Figure 17-1. Notice that a banner advertisement is small enough to be a minor part of an overall Web page, but it is large enough that it certainly attracts attention if well-designed.

Figure 17-1: AnswerSquad's banner advertisements are typical of what you might find on the Web.

The majority of sites that allow you to have your own banner also charge a fee for the advertisement, which is exactly akin to paying for an advertisement in a print publication. The costs for advertisements online are most often calculated in CPM, which is actually *cost per thousand impressions*.

> **note** The *M* in CPM is actually the Latin *mil,* which is *thousand*. Think of a millimeter being a thousandth of a meter to help you remember the acronym's meaning.

You're probably wondering what an *impression* is. This is one of those areas where you can see how the Web has grown far beyond just a hobbyist space. Madison Avenue has brought its jargon to the Internet, and you now have a whole language of banner ads to learn.

Some of the most important Web terms include *hit*, which represents a request received by the Web server; *page view*, which is the number of times an HTML document is requested; *impression* (or, sometimes, *eyeball*), which is the number of times that the banner advertisement is displayed onscreen; and *click-through*, which counts the number of times someone saw the banner advertisement and clicked it.

Now, you can look at a Web page with a more experienced eye. Each graphic on the page produces its own hit on the server so, even though a simple page such as Google only produces two hits for each visit to the home page, a complex page such as Compaq Computer's (http://www.compaq.com) actually has 91 separate, graphical elements that produce 92 hits for each viewing of the page. That's why you hear about Web sites that have millions of hits each month and why you shouldn't care. It's the number of visitors or the number of page views that tell you the real traffic story.

Banner ads are going to cost $2–$30 for each thousand impressions, and the number of people who click your banner ad is really more in your control than that of the site that shows your advertisement. To create effective banner advertisements, follow these three general rules:

1. Offer the viewer a special bargain or deal. An advertisement that just mentions your company isn't going to be very successful, particularly if no one knows who you are.

2. Keep the banner advertisement simple and uncluttered. It's competing for attention with the rest of the page so it must be elegant and effective.

3. Have a call to action. The best are as follows: Click Here or a mock button or search box as part of the banner.

Advertisements that offer a bargain and tell the viewer how to get that product (for example, a button labeled Buy Now!) are the most successful of all in the commercial space.

There is also a standard set of sizes for advertising banners on the Web, which is set by the Internet Advertising Bureau (IAB).

tip Visit the IAB online at `http://www.iab.net/`.

Table 17-1 enumerates the standard banner sizes.

Table 17-1: Standard Banner Advertising Sizes

Size	Typical Use
468×60	Produces a full banner.
392×72	Produces a full banner with vertical navigation bar.
234×60	Produces a half banner.
125×125	Produces a square button.
120×90	Produces a large button.
120×60	Produces a small button.
88×31	Produces a micro button.
120×240	Produces a vertical banner.

If you opt to try banner advertising, be skeptical of the claims of different Web sites, and test out your banner for click-through rates. A really successful banner might have a 2 or 3 percent click-through rate (which means that, if 1,000 people see the banner, only 20–30 click it to reach your site). Unless your ad is exceptionally interesting, you're just as likely to see fewer than 1 percent click-through as Web surfers become conditioned to skip the banner advertisement. If you do decide to use banner advertisements, one good strategy is to try a couple of different banner types and sizes (for example, some people report that 125×125 graphics do better) for a small number of impressions and try to identify which one is the most effective. Then, focus your campaign on that banner and its style.

Text Advertising Options and Pay Per Click

In the last year or two, another advertising option has cropped up—text-based ads placed automatically on relevant pages. A number of sites offer this capability—both search engines and advertising networks—but the premier choice is Google's AdWords program. You can learn more about AdWords at http://adwords.google.com/, or you can just look for the ads on a number of different Web sites, as demonstrated in Figure 17-2.

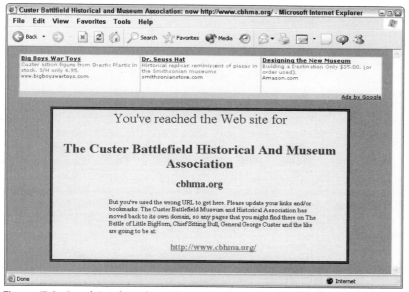

Figure 17-2: Google's AdWords produces simple, text-based advertisements, as illustrated in the three ads at the top of this Web page.

> **note** An interesting way to earn some pocket change (or more if you've a very busy site) is to allow Google to include AdWords advertisements on your Web site. You can learn more about that at http://www.google.com/adsense/. I allow this on some of my pages, and it more than pays for all my Web site hosting fees!

The basic idea behind AdWords is that you pay for each person who clicks your ad and jumps to your site, which is termed *pay per click* (PPC). This is a much better model for advertising in my opinion because you pay for performance and not for visibility. For example, if you run an ad at Google itself, you might be charged 5¢ per click for traffic. If your area isn't too busy, only a few dozen people might see your advertisement each day, and only one or two might click through.

Click-through is one area where it's critically important to ensure that the page that Web surfers come to on your site follows through with whatever you stated in the advertisement in the first place. Do *not* just drop people on your home page, for example, if you're trying to sell them a specific product.

A quick Google search reveals how other Web designers follow through on advertising claims.

Smart text advertisements

I searched on Google for *dish network* (a satellite TV provider) and *cover* (that is, I used a search pattern of `"dish network" cover`) and found quite a few sponsored links, as shown in Figure 17-3.

Heated 18" Satellite Dish	Dish Cover	Free Dish Network TV Deal	Dish covers Prices	Dish Network vs. DirecTV
Keep snow and ice from building up with a Hotshot heated **dish**	Huge selection, great discounts on everything. -aff	Get 3 Months Free. Installation & System is also included. affiliate	Compare Prices, Tax, & Shipping from online stores at NexTag	Free side by side comparison of **Dish Network** and DirecTV? USA only!
www.SolidSignal.com	eBay.com	www.satellitetvdeal.com	www.nextag.com	www.dishcomparison.com
Interest: ▬▬▬	Interest: ▬▬▬	Interest: ▬▬▬	Interest: ▬▬▬	Interest: ▬▬▬

Figure 17-3: Smart text advertisements can help you find what you're looking for.

Notice that some of these advertisements are exactly on-target for my search (*dish cover* and *dish covers prices*) whereas others just picked up on the key phrase *dish network* and present that less relevant match instead (*Free Dish Network TV Deal*, *3 Months Free Satellite*). On Google, the more an advertiser is willing to pay for the PPC functionality, the higher his ad appears on the page. In Figure 17-3, the more expensive ads appear on the left, and the less expensive ads appear farther to the right. (The figure shows just the ads themselves).

But, all is not necessarily as it appears here either. The second ad, *Dish Cover,* actually points to eBay, and the fourth ad, *Dish covers Prices*, points to a shopping comparison site called NexTag.com. So, if you subtract those two and subtract the *dish network* matches that aren't about covers, none of these ads are what I seek. But, a *Heated 18" Satellite Dish* at least sounds interesting. If you click-through to see what SolidSignal.com has to offer, you get to the page shown in Figure 17-4.

Figure 17-4: The Web Page shown when you click the Heated 18" Satellite Dish ad.

Very nicely done page. First off, it succeeds at the cardinal rule of online advertising. Always take people to a page specifically tied into the ad they clicked in the first place. But, notice also the title of the page (which might be a bit hard to read here in the book!) which is *Hotshot 18 Inch Heated Dish Antenna from Perfect Vision (HS18) | Perfect Vision HS18.* Nicely written!

If you want to run your own advertisements through Google, Overture, or a similar PPC network, think of an effective 5–10-word ad that points to a page that fulfills the ad's claim. If your ad reads *Nikon D100 Tips: How to get the most out of your camera,* you don't want it to lead to a page about making the perfect cup of coffee!

Publicizing Your Site

The best way to publicize your new Web site is to become active in the Internet community and to be sure to include your site URL in all your documents, advertisements, and other collateral materials you use to interact with your peers, friends, and customers. Find the cool Web sites in your area of interest, and ask them to include pointers to your information. Almost all sites do that for free, particularly if you agree to list them at your site, too.

on the web

Jill Whalen has a great newsletter at `http://www.highrankings.com/` with lots of wonderful tips about improving your findability. Check it out!

Table 17-2: HTML Tags Covered in This Chapter		
Tag	**Closing Tag**	**Meaning**
`<meta`	`</meta>`	Specifies additional information to assist search engines and crawlers in indexing and cataloging the Web page

Summary

After you learn how to build the best possible Web site, it's important to ensure that you've made specific decisions to maximize your *findability*. That's what this chapter has been about. Starting with a discussion of the importance of titles, it delved into `<meta>` tags and how to work with crawlers. It then explored various search engines, what they offer, and how to ensure that your site is in the search engine's directory. Finally, it presented advertising options, including Google's AdWords program.

Closing Thoughts

You've now completed *Creating Cool Web Sites* and should be an expert in the voodoo technologies of HTML, XHTML, and Cascading Style Sheets. You should now also have some significant knowledge of JavaScript, search engine optimization, and usability. You should have mastered how to efficiently build a Web *site* rather than just loosely stringing together a bunch of Web pages.

Building cool Web sites is as much an art as a science. Don't be afraid to break the rules, go against something suggested in this book, or even blaze a completely different trail for your development efforts. Lots and lots of terrific Web sites trade usability for searchability or visuals for speed. Some even have a completely different perspective on which colors are compatible with which other colors!

The most important thing to remember is that you should endeavor to make your Web sites fun and engaging. Although it's difficult enough getting people to your site in the first place, it's even harder to get them to stay on your site and explore what's there. Remember that all pages should work as a passable entry point into your site and any tricks you can use to help visitors find what they want quickly and painlessly more than repay any extra effort required in developing the site.

And, finally, thanks for sharing this journey with me. I've been building Web sites for many, many years, and most of the knowledge I have has come from the school of experience and not from a great reference book. Let me know how your own Web site creation projects are going and what you found most helpful in this book!

You can visit me at any time online at `http://www.intuitive.com/` and, of course, the Web site for this book is at `http://www.intuitive.com/coolsites/`.

Dave Taylor
Boulder, Colorado
`taylor@intuitive.com`

Step-by-Step Web Site Planning Guide

When you design a simple, one-page Web site for personal use, you might get away with just letting the page evolve as you experiment. However, when you design a complex set of interconnecting Web documents or a commercial site, you must go about the process more systematically. Here's a guide to planning the process, step-by-step.

Stage One: Conceptualization

A lot of your HTML choices and design decisions follow from overall decisions about the Web site's goal and the people you hope to reach. If you're working on a complex site design, thinking through those questions early in the process will save you a lot of time in the end.

Step 1: Establish the goal

As with any other project, you can expect the best results if you figure out up front exactly what you want the Web site to do for you, your company, or your client. It's sometimes a challenge to clearly articulate the purpose, but if you know what you're doing and why before you plunge into the design, you will avoid unnecessary revisions.

Part of setting the goal for your Web site is identifying as clearly as possible your intended audience. The tools for identifying who visits a Web page are limited, and, so far, there's no accepted standard for how to count the number of users to establish a return on investment or the number of people in the target audience who have received your message. However, if you spend some time thinking about what kind of people you want to reach, during the design process, you can focus on including things that will attract those people, judge which external links to incorporate, and zero in on the sites you most want to point to your site. In addition, you can do some contingency planning for what to do if your site turns out to be so intriguing that it's swamped by loads of visitors who aren't in the target audience.

Your target audience plays a big role in determining how you design your pages. For example, if you're preparing a site for Macintosh multimedia developers, you might assume that all targeted users will be able to play QuickTime movies. But, that might not be the case, however, for a site directed toward a more general audience. Or, if you're creating a site directed toward Netscape users, you could use Netscape-specific HTML extensions, but you might want to stick to the standard HTML and CSS for a broader audience.

Do you want a lot of repeat visitors? If so, plan to change elements of the site frequently to keep the site interesting to the real Web zealots. For example, some commercial sites are designed to change many times each day.

When considering the audience, think about which browser software you plan to support (and, therefore, test with). And remember, if you want to reach everyone, you'll need to include text alternatives to graphics for Lynx users and visitors with disabilities of one sort or another.

x-ref Usability issues are explored in Chapter 15.

Another factor that may control your design—especially in a corporate setting—is, "who's going to maintain the site, and how much time do they have to do it?"

Many companies find that managing and maintaining Web sites and responding to all the inquiries they generate take more time and money than originally anticipated. If a company goes on the Web but can't keep up with the visitors' demands for information or follow-up, the company seems unresponsive. So, make sure those issues are part of any discussion about a commercial Web site plan. (Interestingly enough, even if a commercial Web site doesn't include a company's Internet address, launching a Web site often leads to more e-mail from the outside world, sometimes radically more e-mail—something else to factor in.)

Remember that it's called the World Wide Web for a reason. Whether you mean to or not, you have a global audience. So, if your client or company or content has international aspects, be sure to include that in the Web site plan. For example, if you are planning to publish product information for a company that distributes its products worldwide, make sure to include international sales office contact information as well as U.S. contact information. If you don't distribute worldwide, say so. Some Web sites offer the users a choice of languages. Click your native language, and link to a set of pages that you can read without translating.

Step 2: Outline the content

When you have a goal in mind, it helps to outline what content you want to include in the Web site. As you outline, keep track of what content you merely collect, which you need to create, and which you retool for the online medium. Remember that some of the content may be links to information that's not part of your site—include that in your outline, too. The outline serves as a starting point for mapping out how the parts interact.

Which of the information is simply text? Which text should be scrollable? Which text should be in short chunks that easily fit within a window of the browser?

What kind of interactivity do you need to build in? Do you need to collect any information about the visitors to the page? Are you going to try to qualify visitors by having them register their addresses or other information in a form? That creates two tiers of visitors—browsers and users—whom you can attempt to contact in the future through the URLs they leave for you.

> **x-ref**   Forms are covered in depth, first in Chapter 9 and then again in Chapter 10.

Will the Web site link to any other pages on the same Web server or to external Web documents? Will you make internal links relative (all files in the same subdirectory or folder on the server so only the unique part of the path name appears in each link address) or absolute (with complete path and file name for each link)? (This topic is discussed in Chapter 6, *Putting the "Web" in World Wide Web: Pointers and Links.*)

Step 3: Choose a structure for the Web site

After you have the big picture of what the Web site covers and what external links you're likely to want, you can settle on a basic organization of the pages. Do you want a linear structure so users can switch from screen-to-screen like a slide show by using Next and Back navigation buttons? How about a branching structure with a choice of major topics on the home page that link to content or a choice of subtopics? If a branching hierarchy is too rigid, how about a more organic Web structure with many links that interconnect the parts of the content? What about a hybrid structure that combines a formal hierarchy with some linear slide shows and a complex Web (as appropriate) for the different parts of the site?

Whatever structure seems right for the purpose and content, in a complex site, it's a good idea to sketch out a map or storyboard for the pages by using lines to indicate links. You can make your map with pencil and paper, index cards and yarn on a bulletin board, a drawing program, or any other tool that works for you. Make sure the home page reflects the organization you choose. That really helps to orient users.

> **x-ref**   This and many other usability topics are discussed in Chapter 15.

Stage Two: Building Pages

After you have a plan for the pages, you can roll up your sleeves and get your hands into HTML. You can start with the home page, move on to the other pages, and then adjust the page design as necessary as you go along. You might feel more comfortable designing the linked pages first and finishing up with the home page. It doesn't really matter so choose which approach fits your style. Remember, it's a process.

Step 4: Code, preview, and revise

You might find that you work in cycles—coding, placing graphics and links, and then previewing what you've done, changing the code, and previewing again in the browser software (that is, unless you're working with one of those HTML editing tools that offers "what you see is what you get"). As you become accustomed to the effect of the HTML formatting tags and CSS styles, you have fewer cycles of coding, previewing, and revising the code, but even experienced site designers expect to go through many revisions.

Fortunately, finding mistakes in the code is relatively simple. Usually, the flaw in the page points you to the part of the HTML that's not quite right or the style specification that's not what you want.

Remember to format your pages so that it's easy to revise and debug and include comments about the code so that someone else can maintain the files later.

x-ref Check out Chapter 11 to find out more about JavaScript and other code additions to a Web page.

Step 5: Add internal and external links

After you have the basic framework for your pages, you can add the relevant links and check whether they make sense. Obviously, check and recheck links as you develop the material that links back and forth internally.

tip My book *Wicked Cool Shell Scripts* (NoStarch Press) includes some helpful scripts for automating the tests for bad internal and external links. Learn more at http://www.intuitive.com/wicked/.

If you plan carefully, you're better able to add links to external pages as you go along. Or, you can add external links later. Just leave placeholders if that's the route you choose. Some pages have sections set aside for a changing set of links to external pages. You can arrange to change the links every week, every day, or several times a day—depending on your target audience and the purpose of the page.

Step 6: Optimize for the slowest members of your target audience

After the pages have all the elements in place, make sure they work for the slowest connections you expect your target audience to use. Remember that a lot of people who use online systems such as CompuServe, America Online, and Prodigy still have 56 Kbps or even 28.8 Kbps modems. If you want to reach the lowest common denominator, you test your pages at that speed over the online systems and make design changes or offer low-speed alternatives to accommodate these slower connections.

Stage Three: Testing

Just in case you don't get the message yet, for a great Web site, plan to test and test and test your work.

Step 7: Test and revise the site yourself

Even when you think you've worked out all the kinks, it's not yet time to pat yourself on the back and celebrate. If you're serious about Web site design, test the pages with all the browsers you intend to support, at the slowest speeds you expect in your target audience, and on the different computer systems your target audience might use. For example, what happens to graphics when they're viewed on a monitor that shows fewer colors than yours?

x-ref   The nuances of graphics are discussed in Chapter 7.

Step 8: Have other testers check your work

You can only go so far in testing your own work. The same way you tend to overlook your own typos, someone else may find obvious flaws that you're blind to in your own Web site. As much as is practical, have people in-house test your Web site if you're creating a site at work or in an organization. Or, load it all on the Web server as a pilot project, and ask a few trusted testers to explore the site and report back any problems or suggestions for improvement.

Stage Four: Loading the Files onto the Web

When you have finished testing the files locally, you're ready to put them on the Web for a live test drive. You may need to do some preparation if you're sending the files to someone else's Web server for publishing.

Step 9: Prepare files for the server

Make sure your files are ready to go onto the server. Put all the files for your pages in one folder (or one directory) on the hard disk of the Web server for your own site. Within that folder (or directory), name the file you mean to be the home page `index.html`—that's the file most Web server software loads by default as the home page.

x-ref   See Chapter 14 to find out more about establishing directories and subdirectories.

If you're using someone else's server, find out if it uses any file naming conventions. For example, you may need to limit file names to eight characters plus a three-character extension, such as `webpp.htm`, for DOS-based servers. Do make sure that your filenames don't include spaces!

If you're using someone else's server, you probably have to send your Web page files there via FTP, Zmodem file transfer, or some other electronic file transfer. Be careful to transfer graphic files in binary format.

x-ref   Be sure to check out Appendix B, *Finding a Home for Your Web Site.*

Step 10: Double-check your URL

If you're not sure of your new site's URL, check with the Web site's administrator. Try out the URL to make sure it's correct before passing it around to testers or printing it on business cards.

Step 11: Test drive some more

This is the true test of your Web site. Can you find it on the Web? (This topic is analyzed in Chapter 17, "Building Traffic and Being Found"). What about the other testers you've lined up? Are your pages valid and correct HTML/XHTML/CSS? (Site validation is explored in Chapter 16, "Validating Your Pages and Style Sheets.") Test, revise, reload, and retest. It may take a while to iron out the wrinkles in a complex site, but hang in there.

If you transfer your files to a foreign operating system, you may see unexpected results such as line breaks in your Web page text where you don't intend them, particularly in text formatted with the `<pre>` tag. For example, perhaps the `<pre>` tag includes double-spaced text where you mean to show single-spaced text. If you can't easily solve the problem, you can use a UNIX filter to fix line break problems. Consult the Web site administrator if you're stuck.

Last Stage: Announcing Your Web Page

Finally, it's time to let the world know your Web page exists! Use the techniques in Chapter 17 to publicize your Web site, and take a moment to celebrate your World Wide Web publishing debut. Congratulations!

Finding a Home for Your Web Site

Now that you've built a cool Web site, the natural question is, "Now what? Where can I put my site so that everyone else on the Web can find and enjoy it?" That's an important question, but it's not as easy to answer as you might think. Why? Because a million different solutions present themselves ranging from sites that advertise their willingness to host your Web pages for free (if they're not too big) to sites that charge a very small amount annually. Some offer very fast connectivity but bill you based on megabytes transferred (which means you definitely don't want to have lots of huge graphics!). Finally, some sites host a reasonably big site for a small monthly fee.

The most important factor, in my opinion, is matching your expectations for your site with the capabilities of the *presence provider* (as they're called in the biz even though you may think of them as *ISP* or *Web host*). For example, if you want to create a site that will be viewed by thousands each day because you're going to include it in your print advertising or because your mom can plug it on her nationally syndicated radio show, you should certainly put your site on a fast machine with a fast, reliable network connection. If you're just having fun and want your friends to visit, a simpler setup with fewer capabilities at less cost should work just dandy.

Key Capabilities

Regardless of your performance demands, here are some questions to ask your presence provider to help you assess its key capabilities:

- **What speed is the connection between the system where your pages will reside and the Internet?** Good answers to this question are multiple T1 and T3. Bad answers are DSL, ISDN, or a fast dialup.

- **How many other sites are hosted on the same system?** The more Web sites on the system, the more likely you could be squeezed out in the crush of Web-related traffic. A few dozen are okay, but hundreds of sites on the same server could spell problems for you.

- **What guarantee of up-time and availability is offered?** A great server that's offline one day each week is worse than a slower system that guarantees 99 percent up-time.

- **Can you access your pages online to make changes or add something new?** Because you're now an expert at creating cool Web sites, you probably want easy access to your pages online rather than having to mail in your changes and updates. If you have something new to add to your Web site, you want to do it now!

Here's a run-down of some of the possibilities for free, inexpensive, and commercial Web page hosting. Of course, which kind you choose is up to you, and I don't necessarily vouch for the quality of any of these sites. They're just fast and seem to feature well-designed and—yes—cool Web sites. I tried to pick some of the more stable companies to list here, but this area of business has a lot of *churn.* Many small companies are acquired by larger ones, merge, or just go out of business. That's something to consider when you make the decision about where to host your site.

Free Sites

I wouldn't be surprised to find a lot more options than the few I list here, but these should get you started.

Freeservers

One option for hosting your free Web site is a freeserver. Like most free services, these offer many upgrade options which you can purchase, and their free hosting means that your site includes both banner ads and pop-ups, which can be pretty annoying to visitors. However, as a place to start, visit `http://www.freeservers.com`.

50Megs

This is another free Web site hosting choice (`http://www.50megs.com`). It offers—no surprise—an impressive 50MB of disk space for your new site, but it also includes pop-up ads and ad banners, among other things.

Tripod

Tripod (`http://www.tripod.com`) is a huge online community offering free Web space to anyone who would like to join the more than 750,000 members. The Tripod site is divided into 28 different pods, or areas, and lots of fun sites reside on this collection of high-speed server systems.

Yahoo! Geocities

The space isn't unlimited. It's also a bit tricky to get an account, but the Yahoo! Geocities concept is a brilliant one. It offers space for millions of different home pages that are divided into virtual cities. For example, if you pick Rodeo Drive, you can pick a "street address" to assign as your home page. It is a very fun concept, and some wild sites are hosted on this terrific system. Visit the home page at `http://geocities.yahoo.com`, and look for the "free GeoCities home page" link in the small print.

In addition, don't forget to check if your Internet access provider offers Web hosting space. For example, Comcast Networks includes 10MB of Web site storage space with a typical cable modem account. Southwestern Bell (in cooperation with Yahoo!) offers up to 760MB of space in its *briefcase* area (although I'm suspicious of any *up to* phrasing on a marketing page). America Online includes 20MB of space with an AOL dial-up account. Save yourself hours of searching, and go to `http://hometown.aol.com/` to find more information.

Inexpensive Presence Providers

The prices for Web presence can range all over the map, and it's astonishing how many different firms now offer some sort of Web site service. The majority of them though are clearly geared toward grabbing a slice of the business market as thousands of companies worldwide come onto the Internet each year. If you're looking for somewhere to keep your personal home page, you might want to carefully consider which of these spots has the aura you like. They definitely differ quite a bit!

The following listing doesn't even scratch the surface of all the available options. Hundreds—if not thousands—of firms offer relatively low-cost Web space. The following is a sampling of different-sized firms that gives you an idea of what's available.

Earthlink Communications

Earthlink is one of the largest Internet ISP and Web hosting companies and has a good track record of growing its business by offering national accessibility at low cost. Earthlink's basic offer is $21.95 per month for 10MB of disk space and the capability to have your own domain. Visit Earthlink's homepage at `http://www.earthlink.com` for more information.

Earthnet

It sounds like Earthlink Communications, but it's a completely different company. Based in my hometown of Boulder, Colorado, Earthnet offers great hosting choices, including a standard plan that includes 50MB of disk space, 5 mailboxes, PHP, CGI, Perl, and more for only $9.95 per month. Visit `http://www.earthnet.net` for more details and plan options.

Pair Networks

If you already have dial-up access or another way to get to the Internet, a very low-cost solution is Pair Networks (http://www.pair.com). For $9.95 per month, you get 200MB of disk space, 10 mailboxes, Telnet, SSH, FTP, and more. There is a one-time $25 setup fee, but it's a good deal.

SRLNet

A comprehensive hosting solution, SRLNet offers much more than just basic Web hosting. In particular, its online tutorials are worth visiting, and they support multiple domain names pointing to a single hosting account. The basic account, their Personal account, is $6.95 per month—with no setup fee—and includes 200MB of disk space, a private CGI directory for installing scripts, PHP, FTP, and more. Find this nice group online at http://wwwsrlnet.com!

Sonic.net

This company has a very good reputation for service, and its basic package includes dial-up, shell access (Linux), 80MB of storage space for your Web site, and access to CGI programs for custom and dynamic page generation (see Chapter 9 to learn more about CGI programming)—all for $18.95/month. For more information, check out http://www.sonic.net.

Verio/NTT

Based in Silicon Valley, Verio offers a wide variety of Web hosting packages, including one that would work just fine for your new site, I bet. For $25 per month, you get 250MB of disk space and 7.5GB per month of data transfer even though they do charge for excessive network traffic. The Web site for my firm, Intuitive Systems, is hosted on a Verio Virtual Private Server system, and I recommend Verio to all my clients. Tell 'em I sent you to http://hosting.verio.com!

The Well

If you're looking for a funky and fun online community with lots of writers, musicians, and even a few members of the Grateful Dead, the Well (http://www.well.com), which was created by the Whole Earth Access team, is the spot for you. Web page hosting is inexpensive here (starting at $15 per month for each 10MB of storage space) and includes a dial-up account on the system.

Not Enough Choices?

You can always dig around in the ever-fun Yahoo! online directory to find a wide variety of Web presence providers. And remember, if the provider can't publicize itself, it's not likely to help you publicize your site. Pop over to `http://www.yahoo.com`, and search for *Web presence* (or perhaps *Web*) and your city or state.

Nationally distributed Internet-related magazines can be a good place to find presence provider advertisements, too. A few magazines immediately come to mind—*PC World, MacWorld,* and *Smart Computing*. Finally, don't forget to check with your local computer magazines or news-papers. Most of the major cities in the United States now have one or more computer-related publications, and the advertisements in these are a terrific place to learn about local Internet companies and their capabilities. If you have access, I'd particularly recommend *Computer Currents*, which is available in at least eight U.S. cities.

Also remember that there's absolutely no reason why you have to work with a company in your own city. After you have some sort of access to the Internet (perhaps through school or work), you can easily work with a Web site hosting company located anywhere in the world. Indeed, I live in Colorado, but the Verio Web server that hosts my Web site is located at a facility in Washington, D.C.—almost 1700 miles away!

Index

Continued

Continued

Continued